Solutions Manual

Futures, Options, and Swaps

Third Edition

Robert W. Kolb

ISBN: 0-631-21619-7

Boston, MA & Oxford, UK

Printed in the United States of America

99 98 — 9 8 7 6 5 4

ISBN: 0-631-21619-7

Contents

1 | **Introduction**

Answers to Questions and Problems

1. If an arbitrage opportunity did exist in a market, how would traders react? Would the arbitrage opportunity persist? If not, what factors would cause the arbitrage opportunity to disappear?

   Traders are motivated by profit opportunities, and an arbitrage opportunity represents the chance for riskless profit without investment. Therefore, traders would react to an arbitrage opportunity by trading to exploit the opportunity. They would buy the relatively underpriced asset and sell the relatively overpriced asset. The arbitrage opportunity would disappear, because the presence of the arbitrage opportunity would create excess demand for the underpriced asset and excess supply of the overpriced asset. The arbitrageurs would continue their trading until the arbitrage opportunity disappeared.

2. Explain why it is reasonable to think that prices in a financial market will generally be free of arbitrage opportunities.

   Generally arbitrage opportunities will not be available in financial markets because well-informed and intelligent traders are constantly on the lookout for such chances. As soon as an arbitrage opportunity appears, traders trade to take advantage of the opportunity, causing the mispricing to be corrected.

3. Explain the difference between a derivative instrument and a financial derivative.

   A derivative is a financial instrument or security whose payoffs depend on any underlying asset. A financial derivative is a financial instrument or security whose payoffs depend on an underlying financial instrument or security.

4. What is the essential feature of a forward contract that makes a futures contract a type of forward contract?

   A forward contract always involves the contracting at one moment in time with the performance under the contract taking place at a later date. Thus, futures represent a kind of forward contract under this definition.

5. Explain why the purchaser of an option has rights and the seller of an option has obligations.

   The purchaser of an option makes a payment that is the consideration given to acquire certain rights. By contrast, the seller of an option receives payment at the time of sale and undertakes certain obligations in return for that payment.

6. In a futures contract, explain the rights and obligations of the buyer or seller. How does this compare with an option contract?

   In a futures contract, both the buyer and the seller have both obligations and rights. The buyer of a futures contract promises to make payment and take delivery at a future date, while the seller of a futures contract promises to make delivery and receive payment at a future date. This contrasts with the option market in which the buyer has only rights and the seller has only obligations following the original transaction.

7. Explain the difference between an option on a physical good and an option on a futures.

   An option on a physical good gives the owner the right to buy the physical good by paying the exercise price, and the seller of an option is obligated to deliver the good. When the owner of either a call or put futures option exercises, no delivery of any physical good occurs. Instead, both the buyer and seller of the futures option receive a position in a futures contract.

8. What is the essential feature of a swap agreement?

   Essentially, a swap agreement obligates the two counterparties to make payments to each other over time. These payment streams can be tied to the value of interest rate sensitive instruments, to foreign currency values, to the fluctuating value of physical commodities, or to any other item of value.

9. Distinguish between interest rate swaps and currency swaps.

   In an interest rate swap, one party pays to another a fixed rate of interest, while the second party pays a floating rate of interest. Generally, no principal changes hands, but the promised payments are tied to some measure of interest rates. In a currency swap, payments between the two counterparties are typically made in different currencies, and there is often an initial exchange of principal amounts in different currencies at the outset of the swap agreement.

10. What is a complete market? Can you give an example of a truly complete market? Explain.

    A **complete market** is a market in which any and all identifiable payoffs can be obtained by trading the securities available in the market. A complete market is essentially a theoretical ideal and is unlikely to be observed in practice.

11. Explain how the existence of financial derivatives enhances speculative opportunities for traders in our financial system.

    Speculators can use financial derivatives to profit from their correct anticipation of changes in interest rates, currency values, stock market levels, and so on. Financial derivatives are particularly powerful speculative instruments because they can be managed to give specific risk exposures while avoiding risks that are unwanted. In addition, financial derivatives markets are often more liquid than the underlying markets, and financial derivatives can be traded with lower transaction costs in many instances.

12. If financial derivatives are as risky as their reputation indicates, explain in general terms how they might be used to reduce a preexisting risk position for a firm.

    While an outright position in a financial derivative considered in isolation generally embodies considerable risk, these instruments can be used to offset other preexisting risks that a firm might face. For example, a savings and loan association might face potential losses due to rising interest rates, and this risk might arise from the normal conduct of its business. Such an association could use interest rate futures, options on interest rate futures, or swap agreements to offset that preexisting risk. Properly managed, financial derivatives can reduce a preexisting business risk through hedging.

13. Consider the following three securities. Let us assume that at one period in the future the market will move either up or down. This movement in the market produces the following payoffs for the three securities. (Note: This problem is a challenge problem and presumes some familiarity with arbitrage concepts. The issues raised by this problem are explored directly in Chapter 13.)

Security	Current Price	Payoff When the Market Moves Down	Payoff When the Market Moves Up
A	$35	$25	$50
B	$30	$15	$60
C	$40	$19	$56

A. Construct a portfolio consisting of securities A and B that replicates the payoffs on security C in both the up and down states subject to the constraint that the sum of the commitments to the two securities (A and B) is one. In other words, construct a synthetic share of security C. Assume that there are no restrictions associated with short selling any of the securities.

To create a synthetic share of security C, we must construct a portfolio of securities A and B that has the same payoffs as security C in both the up and down states of the market. That is, we must construct a portfolio with the following characteristics:

	Synthetic Security (Portfolio of Securities A and B)	Security C
Payoff when the market moves down	$25 \times W_A + \$15 \times W_B$	$19
Payoff when the market moves up	$50 \times W_A + \$60 \times W_B$	$56

subject to the constraint that $W_A + W_B = 1$. W_A and W_B are the proportions of the portfolio's value committed to instruments A and B. The two equations in the table constitute two equations in two unknowns. We solve them simultaneously, by multiplying the first equation times -2.0 and summing them to solve for W_B:

$$-2.0 \times (\$25 \times W_A + \$15 \times W_B) + \$50 \times W_A + \$60 \times W_B = -2.0 \times \$19 + \$56$$

$$W_A = \$18/\$30 = 0.6$$

Therefore, $W_A = 0.4$, because $W_A + W_B = 1$.

B. What are the commitments to securities A and B?

Forty percent of the investor's wealth is committed to security A, and 60 percent of the investors wealth is committed to security B, $W_A = .4$ and $W_A = .6$.

C. How much does it cost to construct a synthetic share of security C? Compare this cost with the market price of security C. Which security is cheaper?

The cost of constructing the synthetic security is:

$$.4 \times \$35 + .6 \times \$30 = \$32$$

Security C is trading at a price of $40. The synthetic security is cheaper.

D. Explain the transactions necessary to engage in riskless arbitrage. Explain why these transactions constitute a riskless arbitrage opportunity. How much profit can an investor make in this riskless arbitrage?

These prices present an opportunity for the investor to engage in riskless arbitrage. The synthetic security constructed to produce the same payoffs as security C in all states of nature is cheaper than security C itself. To take advantage of this situation, we must simultaneously sell the overpriced, expensive security and buy the underpriced, cheap security. That is, we must simultaneously sell security C and buy the synthetic security. Arbitrage is transacting to secure a riskless profit without investment. For this to be a riskless arbitrage opportunity, we must simultaneously enter into the purchase and sale transactions, and the transactions must be of the same scale. That is, we must buy and sell the same number of units of the securities. Note that the math of the problem requires one to sell fractions of a unit of a security. However, institutional constraints do not permit the sale or purchase of fractional units of a security. We can easily solve this problem by scaling up our purchase and sale transactions by 10. That is, we will sell 10 units of security C and buy 10 units of the synthetic security. Since we are assuming that the investor does not own security C, the investor will be engaging in short selling.

Riskless arbitrage transactions:

	Transactions	**Cash Flows**
Security C	Sell 10 units of C at $40.	+$400
Synthetic security	Buy 4 units of A at $35.	−$140
	Buy 6 units of B at $30.	−$180
Profit		+$80

The profit on the transactions is $80 on 10 units of the securities, or $8 profit per unit. The profit could be increased to infinity by scaling up the size of all of these transactions.

E. Explain why we do not have to worry about future obligations in a properly constructed riskless arbitrage transaction.

Consider the following:

	Obligation Associated with the Arbitrage Transactions	**Assets Held as a Result of the Arbitrage Transactions**	**Cash Flows**
Payoff when the market moves down	Short selling 10 units of security C obligates the trader to deliver 10 units of security C worth $19 per unit.	The investor holds 10 units of the synthetic security worth $19 per unit.	−$190 + $190 = $0
Payoff when the market moves up	Short selling 10 units of security C obligates the trader to deliver 10 units of security C worth $56 per unit.	The investor holds 10 units of the synthetic security worth $56 per unit.	−$560 + $560 = $0

The arbitrage transactions were structured such that the value of the investor's assets are equal to the value of the investor's obligations. In addition, the synthetic security was constructed such that the payoffs on the synthetic security were equal to the payoffs from investing in security C in both states of nature.

F. Explain why we would not expect such a structure of prices to exist in the marketplace.

If these prices were observed in the market, the investor could earn a certain profit with no commitment of her own resources. Persistence of such mispricing would permit all investors to become infinitely wealthy through riskless arbitrage.

G. Explain the purpose of short selling in riskless arbitrage. Discuss the impact on the investor's ability to engage in riskless arbitrage of regulations that limit an investor's access to the proceeds from a short sale transaction.

The purpose of short selling in arbitrage transactions is to finance the purchase of the "cheap" asset through the sale of the "expensive" asset. In arbitrage we sell high to finance the transaction. Any constraints that limit the investor's access to funds from short selling limit the investor's ability to engage in riskless arbitrage. For example, if margin requirements are such that the investor does not have access to any of the proceeds from short selling, then the investor will have to use her personal wealth to pay for the securities she has purchased "cheap." In this environment, the investor is no longer engaging in riskless arbitrage, because investment is now required and the arbitrage transactions are no long self-financing.

H. Construct a portfolio consisting of securities B and C that replicates the payoffs on security A in both the up and down states subject to the constraint that the sum of the commitments to the two securities (B and C) is one. In other words, construct a synthetic share of security A. Assume that there are no restrictions associated with short selling any of the securities.

To create a synthetic share of security A, we must construct a portfolio of securities B and C that has the same payoffs as security A in both the up and down states of the market. That is, we must construct a portfolio with the following characteristics:

	Synthetic Security (Portfolio of Securities B and C)	Security A
Payoff when the market moves down	$\$15 \times W_B + \$19 \times W_C$	$25
Payoff when the market moves up	$\$60 \times W_B + \$56 \times W_C$	$50

subject to the constraint that $W_B + W_C = 1$.

Multiplying the first equation in the table by –4 and adding the resulting equation to the second equation, we can solve the two equations in the table simultaneously for W_C.

$$-4 \times (\$15 \times W_B + \$19 \times W_C) + \$60 \times W_B + \$56 \times W_C = -4 \times \$25 + \$50$$

$W_C = 2.5$, and $W_B = -1.5$, where $W_B + W_C = 1$. That is, to construct synthetic security A, we must short sell security B and invest the proceeds from the short sale of security B in security C.

I. What are the commitments to securities B and C?

Construction of the synthetic security required the short sale of security B to finance the purchase of additional units of security C. Thus, the investor commits more than 100 percent of his wealth to security C. Specifically 250 percent of the investor's wealth is committed to security C financed by short sales of security B in an amount equal to 150 percent of the investor's wealth, $W_B = -1.5$ and $W_C = 2.5$.

J. How much does it cost to construct a synthetic share of security A? Compare this cost with the market price of security A. Which security is cheaper?

The cost of constructing the synthetic security is $55, –1.5 × $30 + 2.5 × $40 = $55. Security A is trading at a price of $35. Security A is cheaper than the synthetic security.

K. Explain the transactions necessary to engage in a riskless arbitrage. How much profit can an investor make in this riskless arbitrage? Assume that one trades 10 shares of security A in constructing the arbitrage transactions.

These prices present an opportunity for the investor to engage in riskless arbitrage. The synthetic security constructed to produce the same payoffs as security A in all states of nature is more expensive than security A itself. Therefore, we must sell the overpriced synthetic security and buy security A itself.

Riskless arbitrage transactions:

	Transactions	Cash Flows
Sell synthetic security	Buy 15 units of B at $30.	–$450
	Sell 25 units of C at $40.	+$1,000
Buy security A	Buy 10 units of A at $35.	–$350
Profit		+$200

Short selling the synthetic security requires the investor to purchase security B, and sell security C. The profit on the transactions is $200 on 10 units of security A, or $20 profit per unit.

L. Discuss the differences between the transactions necessary to capture the arbitrage profit when creating a synthetic share of security A and the arbitrage transactions undertaken to capture the arbitrage profit when creating a synthetic share of security C.

In the first problem, the construction of the synthetic security required positive commitments by the investor to each security, that is, the portfolio weights were positive. In addition, to capture the profit available from the mispricing of the securities, we sold the actual security short and bought the synthetic security. In the second problem, construction of the synthetic security required the investor to sell security B short to finance purchases of security C. We then short sold the synthetic security and bought the actual security to reap the arbitrage profits.

2 | Futures Markets

Answers to Questions and Problems

1. Explain the different roles of a floor broker and an account executive.

   A floor broker is located on the floor of the exchange and executes orders for traders off-the-floor of the exchange. Typically, the floor broker will either be an independent trader who executes orders on a contractual basis for a futures commission merchant (FCM), or the floor broker may be an employee of an FCM. An account executive is almost always employed by an FCM and is located off-the-floor of the exchange. The account executive is the person one typically thinks of as a broker. The account executive could be located in the local office of any major brokerage firm and has customers for whom he or she executes orders by communicating them to the exchange via the communication facilities of the FCM.

2. At a party, a man tells you that he is an introducing broker. He goes on to explain that his job is introducing prospective traders such as yourself to futures brokers. He also relates that he holds margin funds as a service to investors. What do you make of this explanation?

   The guy is a fraud. First, a defining characteristic of an introducing broker (IB) is that the IB does not hold customers' funds. Instead, the IB is associated with an FCM who holds the customers' funds. Second, the last person the IB wants his customer to meet is another broker. The IB's income depends on executing orders for his customers, so the IB wants to keep his flock of customers away from the wolves (other brokers) who are hungry for customers.

3. Assume that you are a floor broker and a friend of yours is a market maker who trades soybeans on the floor of the Chicago Board of Trade. Beans are trading at $6.53 per bushel. You receive an order to buy beans and you buy one contract from your friend at $6.54, one cent above the market. Who wins, who loses, and why? Explain the rationale for making such practice illegal.

   As described, this transaction costs your customer $.01 per bushel and transfers those funds to the friend from whom you purchase the contract at $6.54. On a 5,000-bushel contract, this amounts to $50. Thus, as described, the customer loses and the friend wins. It is important to see the motivation for the floor broker's engaging in this transaction. As described, the floor broker cheats her customer and helps the friend. Presumably, the motivation for such an action is the expectation that the friend will return the favor on another transaction. The rationale for making this transaction illegal is clear; it amounts to a direct theft from the customer.

4. You are back at the party, several hours later. Your buddy from question 2 buttonholes you again and starts to explain his great success as a dual trader, trading both beans and corn. What do you think?

   This guy is not bright. A dual trader is a person who trades for his or her own account and who executes orders for others at the same time.

5. You are having trouble escaping from your friend in question 4. He goes on to explain that liquidation-only trading involves trading soybean against soyoil to profit from the liquidation that occurs when beans are crushed. Explain how your understanding of *liquidation-only trading* differs from your friend's.

We hope that your understanding of liquidation-only trading runs as follows: Under liquidation-only trading, each trade must result in a reduction of a trader's open interest. Every trade must be an offsetting trade. Liquidation-only trading essentially amounts to the closing of a market, and this is done during serious market disturbances, such as a manipulation. Liquidation-only trading has nothing in particular to do with beans or any other commodities.

6. In purchasing a house, contracting to buy the house occurs at one time. Typically, closing occurs weeks later. At the closing, the buyer pays the seller for the house and the buyer takes possession. Explain how this transaction is like a futures or forward transaction.

   The purchase of a house has many features of a forward contract. Contracting occurs at one date, with performance on the contract occurring later at the closing. In buying a house, there is usually a good faith deposit or earnest money put up at the time of contracting. The contract is tailored to the individual circumstances, with the performance terms and the closing date being agreed on between the buyer and seller. The contract is not like a futures, because there is no organized exchange, the contract terms are not fixed, and settlement can occur at any time instead of at a fixed date.

7. In the futures market, a widget contract has a standard contract size of 5,000 widgets. What advantage does this have over the well-known forward market practice of negotiating the size of the transaction on a case-by-case basis? What disadvantages does the standardized contract size have?

   With standardized contract size and other terms, a futures contract avoids uncertainty about what is being traded. If these terms were not specified, traders would have to specify all of the features of the underlying good anew each time there is a contract. The futures style of trading has the disadvantage of losing flexibility due to the standardization. For example, the amount of the contract is fixed, as is the quality of the underlying good and the time the contract will be settled.

8. What factors need to be considered in purchasing a commodity futures exchange seat? What are all the possible advantages that could come from owning a seat?

   A seat on a commodity exchange is essentially a capital asset. The purchaser would want to consider the risk, including systematic risk, associated with such a purchase. The value of the seat depends mainly on the expected trading volume on the exchange, so we expect seat prices to be sensitive to the business cycle and to competition from foreign exchanges. Owning a seat allows one to trade on the exchange. Also, the seat holder can lease the seat for someone else to trade. Therefore, the seat offers the potential for cash inflows as well as capital appreciation.

9. Explain the difference between initial and maintenance margin.

   Initial margin is the amount a trader must deposit before trading is permitted. Maintenance margin is the minimum amount that must be held in the trader's account while a futures position is open. If the account value falls below the amount specified as the maintenance margin, the trader must deposit additional funds to bring the account value back to the level of the initial margin.

10. Explain the difference between maintenance and variation margin.

    Maintenance margin is the amount a trader must keep in the account to avoid a margin call. Variation margin is the payment a trader must make in a margin call. The margin call occurs when the account value drops below the level set for the maintenance margin. Upon receiving a margin call, the trader must make a cash payment of the variation margin. The maintenance margin is a stock variable, while the variation margin is a flow variable.

11. On February 1, a trader is long the JUN wheat contract. On February 10, she sells a SEP wheat futures, and sells a JUN wheat contract on February 20. On February 15, what is her position in wheat futures? On February 25, what is her position? How would you characterize her transaction on February 20?

On February 15, the trader holds an intracommodity spread, being long the JUN and short the SEP wheat. On February 25, the trader is short one SEP wheat contract. The transaction on February 20 was a transaction offsetting the original long position in SEP wheat.

12. Explain the difference between volume and open interest.

Open interest is the number of contracts currently obligated for delivery. The volume is the number of contracts traded during some period. For every purchase there is a sale, and the purchase and sale of one contract generates one contract of trading volume.

13. Define *tick* and *daily price limit.*

A tick is the minimum amount a futures contract can change. For example, in the T-bond contract, the tick size is 1/32 of one point of par. This gives a dollar tick value of $31.25 per T-bond futures contract. The daily price limit is the amount the contract can change in price in one day. It is usually expressed as some number of ticks, and it is measured from the previous day's settlement price. No trade can be executed at a price that differs from the previous day's settlement price by more than the daily price limit.

14. A trader is long one SEP crude oil contract. On May 15, he contracts with a business associate to receive 1,000 barrels of oil in the spot market. The business associate is short one SEP crude oil contract. How can the two traders close their futures positions without actually transacting in the futures market?

The traders close their futures positions through an exchange-for-physicals transaction (EFP). In an EFP, two traders with futures positions exchange the physical good for cash and report this transaction to the exchange, asking the exchange to offset their futures contracts against each other. This transaction is also called an ex-pit or against actuals transaction.

15. Explain how a trader closes a futures market position via cash settlement.

For a contract satisfied by cash settlement, there is no delivery. Instead, when the futures contract expires, the final settlement price on the futures is set equal to the cash price for that date. This practice ensures convergence of the futures price and the cash price. Traders then make or receive payments based on the difference between the previous day's settlement price and the final settlement price on the contract.

16. Explain *price discovery.*

In futures markets, price discovery refers to the revealing of information about future prices that the market facilitates. It is one of the two major social functions of the futures market. (The other is risk transference.) As an example, the futures price for wheat for delivery in nine months reveals information to the public about the expected future spot price of wheat at the time of delivery. While controversial, there is some reason to believe that the futures price (almost?) equals the spot price that is expected to hold at the futures expiration. This price discovery function helps economic agents plan their investment and consumption by providing information about future commodity prices.

17. Contrast anticipatory hedging with hedging in general.

In anticipatory hedging, a trader enters the futures market and transacts before (or in anticipation of) some cash market transaction. This differs from a hedge of an existing position. For example, a farmer might sell wheat futures in anticipation of the harvest. Alternatively, a merchant holding an inventory of wheat might hedge the inventory by selling wheat futures. The farmer is engaged in anticipatory hedging, because he or she is expecting to have the cash market position and hedges this anticipation. The wheat merchant already has the cash market position, in virtue of holding the wheat inventory, and therefore is not engaged in anticipatory hedging.

18. What is *front running?*

Front running is a market practice in which a broker holds a customer's order for execution and executes a similar order of his or her own before executing the customer's order. This practice can be particularly pernicious if the customer's order is large, because the order may itself move prices. By front running, the broker seeks to capitalize on the privileged information that the order is coming to market. This practice is unethical and against the rules of the futures exchange.

19. Explain the difference in the roles of the National Futures Association and the Commodity Futures Trading Commission.

The National Futures Association (NFA) is an industry self-regulatory body, while the Commodity Futures Trading Commission (CFTC) is an agency of the federal government. The same law that instituted the CFTC also provided for the futures industry to establish self-regulatory bodies. The NFA enforces ethical standards on most futures industry members and provides testing for licensing of brokers and other futures industry professionals. The NFA operates under the supervision of the CFTC.

3 Futures Prices

Answers to Questions and Problems

1. Explain the function of the settlement committee. Why is the settlement price important in futures markets in a way that the day's final price in the stock market is not so important?

   In futures markets, the settlement committee determines the settlement price for each contract each day. The settlement price estimates the true value of the contract at the end of the day's trading. In active markets, the settlement price will typically equal the last trade price. In inactive markets, the settlement price is the committee's estimate of the price at which the contract would have traded at the close, if it had traded. The settlement price is important, because it is used to calculate margin requirements and the cash flows associated with daily settlement. In the stock market, there is no practice comparable to daily settlement, so the closing price in the stock market lacks the special significance of the futures settlement price.

2. Open interest tends to be low when a new contract expiration is first listed for trading, and it tends to be small after the contract has traded for a long time. Explain.

   When the contract is first listed for trading, open interest is necessarily zero. As traders take positions, the open interest builds. At expiration, open interest must again be zero. Every contract will have been fulfilled by offset, delivery, or an EFP. Therefore, as the contract approaches the expiration month, many traders will offset their positions to avoid delivery. This reduces open interest. In the expiration month, deliveries that occur further reduce open interest. Also, EFPs typically reduce open interest. This creates a pattern of very low open interest in the contract's early days of trading, followed by increases, followed by diminution, followed by the contract's extinction.

3. Explain the distinction between a normal and an inverted market.

   In a normal market, prices for more distant expirations are higher than prices for earlier expirations. In an inverted market, prices for more distant expirations are lower than prices for earlier expirations.

4. Explain why the futures price converges to the spot price and discuss what would happen if this convergence failed.

   The explanation for convergence at expiration depends on whether the market features delivery or cash settlement, but in each case, convergence depends on similar arbitrage arguments. We consider each type of contract in turn. For a contract with actual delivery, failure of convergence gives rise to an arbitrage opportunity at delivery. The cash price can be either above or below the futures price, if the two are not equal. If the cash price exceeds the futures price, the trader buys the future, accepts delivery, and sells the good in the cash market for the higher price. If the futures price exceeds the cash price, the trader buys the good on the cash market, sells a futures, and delivers the cash good in fulfillment of the futures. To exclude both types of arbitrage simultaneously, the futures price must equal the cash price at expiration. Minor discrepancies can exist, however. These are due to transaction costs and the fact that the short trader owns the options associated with initiating the delivery sequence.

   For a contract with cash settlement, failure of convergence also implies arbitrage. Just before delivery, if the futures price exceeds the cash price, a trader can sell the futures, wait for expiration, and the futures price will be set equal to the cash price. This gives a profit equal to the difference between the cash and futures. Alternatively, if the cash price is above the futures price, and expiration is imminent, the trader can buy the futures and wait for its price to be marked up to equal the cash price. Thus, no matter whether the futures price is above or below the cash price, a profit opportunity will be available immediately.

In short, the futures and cash price converge at expiration to exclude arbitrage, and failure of convergence implies the existence of arbitrage opportunities.

5. Is delivery, or the prospect of delivery, necessary to guarantee that the futures price will converge to the spot price? Explain.

No, delivery is not necessary. As explained in the answer to question 4, cash settlement will also lead to convergence of the cash and the futures at expiration.

6. As we have defined the term, what are the two key elements of *academic arbitrage*?

The two elements are riskless profit and zero investment. Each condition is necessary for academic arbitrage, and the two conditions are jointly sufficient.

7. Assume that markets are perfect in the sense of being free from transaction costs and restrictions on short selling. The spot price of gold is $370. Current interest rates are 10 percent, compounded monthly. According to the cost-of-carry model, what should the price of a gold futures contract be if expiration is six months away?

In perfect markets, the cost-of-carry model gives the futures price as:

$$F_{0,t} = S_0(1 + C)$$

The cost of carrying gold for six months is $(1 + .10/12)^6 - 1 = .051053$. Therefore, the futures price should be:

$$F_{0,t} = \$370(1.051053) = \$388.89$$

8. Consider the information in question 7. Round-trip futures trading costs are $25 per 100-ounce gold contract, and buying or selling an ounce of gold incurs transaction costs of $1.25. Gold can be stored for $.15 per month per ounce. (Ignore interest on the storage fee and the transaction costs.) What futures prices are consistent with the cost-of-carry model?

Answering this question requires finding the bounds imposed by the cash-and-carry and reverse cash-and-carry strategies. For convenience, we assume a transaction size of one 100-ounce contract. For the cash-and-carry, the trader buys gold and sells the futures. This strategy requires the following cash outflows:

Buy gold	– $370(100)
Pay transaction costs on the spot	– $1.25(100)
Pay the storage cost	– $.15(100)(6)
Sell futures	0
Borrow to finance these outlays	+ $37,215

Six months later, the trader must:

Pay the transaction cost on one futures	– $25
Repay the borrowing	– $39,114.95
Deliver on futures	?

Net outlays at the outset were zero, and they were $39,139.95 at the horizon. Therefore, the futures price must exceed $391.40 an ounce for the cash-and-carry strategy to yield a profit.

The reverse cash-and-carry incurs the following cash flows. At the outset, the trader must:

Sell gold	+ $370(100)
Pay transaction costs on the spot	− $1.25(100)
Invest funds	− $36,875
Buy futures	0

These transactions provide a net zero initial cash flow. In six months, the trader has the following cash flows:

Collect on investment	+ $36,875$(1 + .10/12)^6$ = $38,757.59
Pay futures transaction costs	− $25
Receive delivery on futures	?

The breakeven futures price is therefore $387.33 per ounce. Any lower price will generate a profit. From the cash-and-carry strategy, the futures price must be less than $391.40 to prevent arbitrage. From the reverse cash-and-carry strategy, the price must be at least $387.33. (Note that we assume there are no expenses associated with making or taking delivery.)

9. Consider the information in questions 7 and 8. Restrictions on short selling effectively mean that the reverse cash-and-carry trader in the gold market receives the use of only 90 percent of the value of the gold that is sold short. Based on this new information, what is the permissible range of futures prices?

This new assumption does not affect the cash-and-carry strategy, but it does limit the profitability of the reverse cash-and-carry trade. Specifically, the trader sells 100 ounces short but realizes only .9($370)(100) = $33,300 of usable funds. After paying the $125 spot transaction cost, the trader has $33,175 to invest. Therefore, the investment proceeds at the horizon are: $33,175$(1 + .10/12)^6$ = $34,868.69. Thus, all of the cash flows are:

Sell gold	+ $370(100)
Pay transaction costs on the spot	− $1.25(100)
Broker retains 10 percent	− $3,700
Invest funds	− $33,175
Buy futures	0

These transactions provide a net zero initial cash flow. In six months, the trader has the following cash flows:

Collect on investment	$34,868.69
Receive return of deposit from broker	$3,700
Pay futures transaction costs	− $25
Receive delivery on futures	?

The breakeven futures price is therefore $385.44 per ounce. Any lower price will generate a profit. Thus, the no-arbitrage condition will be fulfilled if the futures price equals or exceeds $385.44 and equals or is less than $391.40.

10. Consider all of the information about gold in questions 7–9. The interest rate in question 7 is 10 percent per annum, with monthly compounding. This is the borrowing rate. Lending brings only 8 percent, compounded monthly. What is the permissible range of futures prices when we consider this imperfection as well?

The lower lending rate reduces the proceeds from the reverse cash-and-carry strategy. Now the trader has the following cash flows:

Sell gold	+ $370(100)
Pay transaction costs on the spot	− $1.25(100)
Broker retains 10 percent	− $3,700
Invest funds	− $33,175
Buy futures	0

These transactions provide a net zero initial cash flow. Now the investment will yield only $33,175(1 + .08/12)^6 = $34,524.31$. In six months, the trader has the following cash flows:

Collect on investment	$34,524.31
Pay futures transaction costs	− $25
Receive delivery on futures	?
Return gold to close short sale	0
Receive return of deposit from broker	$ 3,700

Total proceeds on the 100 ounces are $38,199.31. Therefore, the futures price per ounce must be less than $381.99 for the reverse cash-and-carry strategy to profit. Because the borrowing rate has not changed, the bound from the cash-and-carry strategy remains at $391.40. Therefore, the futures price must remain within the inclusive bounds of $381.99 to $391.40 to exclude arbitrage.

11. Consider all of the information about gold in questions 7–10. The gold futures expiring in six months trades for $375 per ounce. Explain how you would respond to this price, given all of the market imperfections we have considered. Show your transactions in a table similar to Table 3.8 or 3.9. Answer the same question, assuming that gold trades for $395.

If the futures price is $395, it exceeds the bound imposed by the cash-and-carry strategy, and it should be possible to trade as follows:

Cash-and-Carry Arbitrage

$t = 0$	Borrow $37,215 for 6 months at 10%.	+ $37,215.00
	Buy 100 ounces of spot gold.	− 37,000.00
	Pay storage costs for 6 months.	− 90.00
	Pay transaction costs on gold purchase.	− 125.00
	Sell futures for $395.	0.00
	Total Cash Flow	$0
$t = 6$	Remove gold from storage.	$0
	Deliver gold on futures.	+ 39,500.00
	Pay futures transaction cost.	− 25.00
	Repay debt.	− 39,114.95
	Total Cash Flow	+ $360.05

If the futures price is $375, the reverse cash-and-carry strategy should generate a profit as follows:

Reverse Cash-and-Carry Arbitrage

$t = 0$	Sell 100 ounces of gold short.	+ $37,000.00
	Pay transaction costs.	− 125.00
	Broker retains 10%.	− 3,700.00
	Buy futures.	0
	Invest remaining funds for 6 months at 8%.	− 33,175.00
	Total Cash Flow	$0

t = 6	Collect on investment.	+ $34,524.31
	Receive delivery on futures.	− 37,500.00
	Return gold to close short sale.	0
	Receive return of deposit from broker.	+ 3,700.00
	Pay futures transaction cost.	− 25.00
	Total Cash Flow	+ $699.31

12. Explain the difference between pure and quasi-arbitrage.

In a pure arbitrage transaction, the arbitrageur faces full transaction costs on each transaction comprising the arbitrage. For example, a retail customer with no initial position in the market, who attempts arbitrage, would be attempting pure arbitrage. By contrast, a quasi-arbitrage transaction occurs when a trader faces less than full transaction costs. The most common example arises in reverse cash-and-carry arbitrage, which requires short selling. For example, in stock index arbitrage, holding a large portfolio allows a trader to simulate a short sale by selling part of the portfolio from inventory. Therefore, this trader faces less than the full transaction costs due to the preexisting position in the market. By contrast, the pure arbitrage trade would require the actual short sale of the stocks, and short selling does not provide the full proceeds to earn interest in the reverse cash-and-carry transactions.

13. Assume that you are a gold merchant with an ample supply of deliverable gold. Explain how you can simulate short selling and compute the price of gold that will bring you into the market for reverse cash-and-carry arbitrage.

The breakeven price for reverse cash-and-carry arbitrage depends principally on the transaction costs the trader faces. With an existing inventory of gold, the trader can simulate short selling by selling a portion of the inventory. Further, because the trader already actually owns the gold, she can have full use of the proceeds of the sale. Therefore, the gold owner's reverse cash-and-carry transactions are similar to those in problem 10:

Reverse Cash-and-Carry Arbitrage

t = 0	Sell 100 ounces of gold short.	+ $37,000.00
	Pay transaction costs.	− 125.00
	Buy futures.	0
	Invest funds for 6 months at 8%.	− 36,875.00
	Total Cash Flow	$0

t = 6	Collect on investment.	+ $38,374.80
	Return gold to close short sale.	0
	Pay futures transaction cost.	− 25.00
	Receive delivery on futures. (Note: This is the futures price to give zero cash flow.)	− 38,349.80
	Total Cash Flow	+ $0

Therefore, if the futures price is $383.498 per ounce, the reverse cash-and-carry transactions give a zero cash flow. This is the breakeven price for reverse cash-and-carry. If the futures price is less that $383.498 per ounce, reverse cash-and-carry arbitrage will be possible for the trader who holds an initial inventory of gold. In problem 10, the price of gold has to be less than $381.99 for reverse cash-and-carry arbitrage to work. The trader there faced full transaction costs, due to the lack of a preexisting inventory.

14. Assume that silver trades in a full carry market. If the spot price is $5.90 per ounce and the futures that expires in one year trades for $6.55, what is the implied cost-of-carry? Under what conditions would it be appropriate to regard this implied cost-of-carry as an implied repo rate?

If the market is at full carry, then $F_{0,t} = S_0(1 + C)$ and $C = F_{0,t}/S_0 - 1$. With our values, $C = \$6.55/\$5.90 - 1 = .110169$. It would be appropriate to regard this implied cost-of-carry as an implied repo rate if the only carrying cost were the financing cost. This is approximately true for silver.

15. What is *normal backwardation?* What might give rise to normal backwardation?

Normal backwardation is the view that futures prices normally rise over their life. Thus, prices are expected to rise as expiration approaches. The classic argument for normal backwardation stems from Keynes. According to Keynes, hedgers are short in the aggregate, so speculators must be net long. Speculators provide their risk-bearing services for an expected profit. To have an expected profit, the futures price must be less than the expected future spot price at the time the speculators assume their long positions. Therefore, given unbiased expectations regarding future spot prices, we expect futures prices to rise over time to give the speculators their compensation. This leads directly to normal backwardation.

16. Assume that the CAPM beta of a futures contract is zero, but that the price of this commodity tends to rise over time very consistently. Interpret the implications of this evidence for normal backwardation and for the CAPM.

Because futures trading requires no investment, positive returns on long futures positions can be consistent with the CAPM only if futures have positive betas. With a zero beta (by our assumption) and a zero investment to acquire a long futures position (by the structure of the market), the CAPM implies zero expected returns. Therefore, a zero beta and positive returns is inconsistent with the CAPM. Even with zero beta, positive returns are consistent with normal backwardation resulting from speculators assuming long positions and being rewarded for their risk-bearing services.

17. Explain why futures and forward prices might differ. Assume that platinum prices are positively correlated with interest rates. What should be the relationship between platinum forward and futures prices? Explain.

Futures are subject to daily settlement cash flows, while forwards are not. If the price of the underlying good is not correlated with interest rates, futures and forward prices will be equal. If the price of the underlying good is positively correlated with interest rates, a long trader in futures will receive daily settlement cash inflows when interest rates are high and the trader can invest that cash flow at the higher rate from the time of receipt to the expiration of the futures. Because forwards have no daily settlement cash flows, they are unable to reap this benefit. Therefore, if a commodity's price is positively correlated with interest rates, there will be an advantage to a futures over a forward. Thus, for platinum in the question, the futures price of platinum should exceed the forward price. The opposite price relationship can occur if there is negative correlation. Generally, this price relationship is not sufficiently strong to be observed in the market.

18. Consider the life of a futures contract from inception to delivery. Explain two fundamental theories on why the futures prices might exhibit different volatility at different times over the life of the contract.

According to the Samuelson hypothesis, price volatility will be greater when more information about the price of the good is being revealed. According to this view, this tends to happen as the futures comes to expiration, particularly for agricultural goods. Therefore, the Samuelson hypothesis suggests that the volatility of futures prices should increase over the life of the contract.

There are several other theories that attempt to relate contract maturity and volatility. First, there seems to be some evidence for believing that volatility is higher for some commodities in certain seasons, particularly at times when information about the harvest of some good is reaching the market. With this view, volatility depends on the time of the year and not so much on the contract's expiration. Second, volatility also differs depending on the day of the week. Third, volatility is autocorrelated. High volatility in one month begets high volatility in the next month.

19. Consider the following information about the CMX gold futures contract:

Contract size: 100 troy ounce
Initial margin: $1,013 per contract

Maintenance margin: $750 per contract
Minimum tick size: 10 cents/troy ounce ($10/contract)

There are four traders, A, B, C, and D, in the market when next year's June contract commences trading.

A. Complete the following table showing the open interest for the contract.

Date	Buyer	Seller	Contracts	Price	Open Interest
July 6	A	B	5	$294.50	
July 6	C	B	10	$294.00	
July 6 Settlement Price				$294.00	
July 7	D	A	10	$293.50	
July 7	B	D	5	$293.80	
July 7 Settlement Price				$293.80	
July 8	B	A	7	$293.70	
July 8 Settlement Price				$299.50	

When trading commences, each trader has a zero net position. The open interest, which is the sum of the trader's net long positions, is also zero. Looking at each trade sequentially, we can track the traders' net positions and open interest as follows:

Net Position

Trade	Trader A	Trader B	Trader C	Trader D	Open Interest
1	+5	−5	0	0	5
2	+5	−15	+10	0	15
3	−5	−15	+10	+10	20
4	−5	−10	+10	+5	15
5	−12	−3	+10	+5	15

B. Calculate the gains and losses for Trader A. Assume that at the time of each change in position, Trader A must bring the margin back to the initial margin amount. Compute the amount in Trader A's margin account at the end of each trading day. Will Trader A get a margin call? If so, when and how much additional margin must be posted?

	Contracts						Margin	
Date	Buy	Sell	Net Position	Price	Gain (loss)	Position before Variation	Variation Margin	Position after Variation
July 6	5		+5	$294.50	–	$0	$5,065	$5,065
July 6 settlement			+5	$294.00	($250)	$4,815	$0	$4,815
July 7		10	−5	$293.50	($250)	$4,565	$500	$5,065
July 7 settlement			−5	$293.80	($150)	$4,915	$0	$4,915
July 8		7	−12	$293.70	$50	$4,965	$7,191	$12,156
July 8 settlement			−12	$299.50	($6,960)	$5,196	$6,960	$12,156

On July 6, Trader A goes long 5 contracts at a price of $294.50. At this time, she is required to post $1,013 margin per contract for a total of $5,065. The July 6 settlement price of $294.00 results in a $50 per contract loss (100 × −$0.50). Trader A's 5 contracts lose a total of $250 which is taken from the margin account. Trader A's margin account still has $963 per contract which is in excess of the minimum maintenance margin of $750 per contract. Therefore, no margin call occurs.

On July 7, Trader A reverses her long position and goes short 5 contracts. A $250 loss occurs on the reversed long position which is assessed against the margin account, bringing it down to $4,565. Since Trader A is now short 5 contracts, she adds $500 to her margin account to bring it back to the initial margin requirement of $5,065. At settlement on July 7, Trader A's position lost $150 which is taken from her margin account bringing it to $4,915. No margin call occurs.

On July 8, Trader A sells an additional 7 contracts, bringing her total to short 12 contracts. At the time of the transaction, her original position of 5 short contracts has gained $50 which is credited to her margin account, bringing it to $4,965. The required initial margin for 12 contracts is $12,156, so Trader A adds $7,191 to her margin account.

July 8 is not a good day for Trader A. The futures price of gold increases by $5.80 per ounce. Trader A's 12-contract short position loses $6,960, bringing her margin account to $5,196 or $433 per contract. Since this is below the maintenance level, Trader A gets a margin call. She must add $6,960 to bring her margin back to the initial margin level. Alternatively, she can close her position.

20. Today is June 30, 1998. You have an anticipated liability of $10 million due on December 31, 1998. To fund this liability, you plan to sell part of your store of gold. Looking in *The Wall Street Journal*, you note the following futures prices and bond equivalent yields for the T-bills maturing at or near the expiration of the futures contracts:

Delivery Month	Settle	R_f
Cash price	293.00	
AUG	297.40	4.86%
DEC	302.00	5.35%

A. What is the basis for the December futures contract?

The basis is computed as the cash price minus the futures price.

$$\text{Basis} = \$293.00 - \$302.00 = -\$9$$

B. Is the market normal or inverted? Explain.

In a normal market, the prices for the more distant contracts are higher than the prices for the nearby contracts. In an inverted market, futures prices decline as we go from the nearby contracts to the more distant contracts.

In this question, prices increase the more distant the delivery date, so the market is normal.

C. If you wanted to eliminate the risk of gold price variation, explain your alternatives.

There are several alternatives for eliminating price risk.

    Alternative 1: Sell gold via the December futures contract. This effectively locks in a
        December selling price of $302.
    Alternative 2: Sell gold today in the spot market and invest the proceeds in the 6-month
        T-bill.
    Alternative 3: Sell gold today in the spot market and invest the proceeds in the 2-month
        T-bill. At the same time, buy gold by using the August futures contract and sell gold
        using the December futures contract.

The most attractive alternative is the one which allows us to meet the $10 million liability while selling the least amount of gold.

D. Given the above prices, justify which of the alternatives you would prefer.

Alternative 1: Sell gold using the December futures contract.

$$\text{Ounces to Be Sold } = \frac{\$10\text{ million}}{\$302} = 33{,}113\text{ ounces}$$

Alternative 2: Sell gold today in the spot market and invest the proceeds in the 6-month T-bill.

$$\text{Cash Needed Today } = \frac{\$10\text{ million}}{\left(1 + \dfrac{0.0535}{2}\right)} = \$9.739\text{ million}$$

$$\text{Ounces to Be Sold Today } = \frac{\$9.739\text{ million}}{\$293} = 33{,}241\text{ ounces}$$

Alternative 3: Sell gold today in the spot market and invest the proceeds in the 2-month T-bill. At the same time, buy gold using the August futures contract and sell gold using the December futures contract.

We already know from alternative 1 that 33,113 ounces must be sold in December. Then 33,113 ounces must be bought in August.

$$\text{Cash Needed in August } = 33{,}113 \times \$297.40 = \$9.848\text{ million}$$

$$\text{Cash Needed Today } = \frac{\$9.848\text{ million}}{\left[1 + 0.0486\left(\dfrac{2}{12}\right)\right]} = \$9.769\text{ million}$$

$$\text{Ounces to Be Sold Today } = \frac{\$9.769\text{ million}}{\$293} = 33{,}340\text{ ounces}$$

Conclusion: Selling gold using the December futures contract requires the fewest ounces of gold to be sold.

E. At what August and December futures prices would you be indifferent between the alternatives?

Assuming negligible costs other than the time value of money, the following relationship must hold for you to be indifferent between alternatives:

$$F_{0,t} = S_0(1 + C)$$

In this relationship the cost of carry, C, is the borrowing and lending rate. For the December contract, the futures price at which you are indifferent between alternatives 1 and 2 is:

$$F_{0,\text{DEC}} = 293\left(1 + \frac{0.0535}{2}\right) = \$300.84$$

The August futures price at which you are indifferent between alternatives 1 and 3 is:

$$F_{0,\text{AUG}} = \$293\left[1 + 0.0486\left(\frac{2}{12}\right)\right] = \$295.37$$

21. It is now the beginning of July. In the cash market, No. 2 heating oil is selling for $0.3655 per gallon. The December futures contract for this commodity is selling at $0.4375. The cost of borrowing for these 6 months is 0.458 percent per month.

A. What is the lowest cost of storage and delivery that would prevent the opportunity for cash-and-carry arbitrage?

   If we borrowed for 6 months at 0.458 percent per month, we could buy heating oil today at $0.3655 per gallon and sell it in December for $0.4375 per gallon. Assuming no cost of storage or delivery, the cash-and-carry arbitrage profit would be:

$$\text{Arbitrage Profit} = F_{0,\text{DEC}} - S_0(1 + C)$$

$$= 0.4375 - 0.3655(1.00458)^6$$

$$= \$0.0618/\text{gallon}$$

   Any cost of storage and delivery (paid in December) exceeding 6.18 cents per gallon would prevent cash-and-carry arbitrage.

B. The August futures contract for the No. 2 heating oil is $0.3702. You can lock-in a 0.442 percent per month borrowing rate for the 4-month time period between delivery of the August contract and the delivery of the December contract. What is the lowest cost of storage and delivery that would prevent the opportunity for cash-and-carry arbitrage in this case?

   We could borrow 2 months forward, buy heating oil 2 months forward, and sell heating oil 6 months forward. This is a forward cash-and-carry arbitrage. Assuming no cost of storage or delivery, the arbitrage profit would be:

$$\text{Arbitrage Profit} = F_{0,\text{DEC}} - F_{0,\text{AUG}}(1 + C)$$

$$= 0.4375 - 0.3702(1.00442)^4$$

$$= \$0.0607/\text{gallon}$$

   Any cost of storage and delivery (paid in December) exceeding 6.07 cents per gallon would prevent cash-and-carry arbitrage.

22. Consider the following June spot and futures prices for the CBOT silver contract:

Delivery Month	Price
Spot	$5.32
August	$5.55
October	$5.80
December	$6.13

A. Assuming no storage costs, compute the implied spot repo rates.

The implied repo rate is equal to:

$$C = F_{0,\,t} / S_0 - 1$$

For August: $C = 5.55 / 5.32 - 1 = 4.32\%$
  Annualized $C = C\,(12\,/\,t) = 4.32\%\,(12\,/\,2) = 25.9\%$
For October: $C = 5.80 / 5.32 - 1 = 9.02\%$
  Annualized $C = C\,(12\,/\,t) = 9.02\%\,(12\,/\,4) = 27.1\%$
For December: $C = 6.13 / 5.32 - 1 = 15.23\%$
  Annualized $C = C\,(12\,/\,t) = 15.23\%\,(12\,/\,6) = 30.5\%$

B. Assuming no storage costs, compute the implied August forward repo rates.

The implied forward repo rates are given by:

$$\text{Forward } C = F_{0,\,t2} / F_{0,\,t1} - 1$$

For October: Forward $C = 5.80 / 5.55 - 1 = 4.5\%$
  Annualized Forward $C = C\,(12\,/t) = 4.5\%\,(12\,/\,2) = 27.1\%$
For December: Forward $C = 6.13 / 5.55 - 1 = 10.5\%$
  Annualized Forward $C = C\,(12\,/t) = 10.5\%\,(12\,/\,4) = 31.4\%$

Using Futures Markets   4

Answers to Questions and Problems

1. Explain how futures markets can benefit individuals in society who never trade futures.

   One of the main benefits that the futures market provides is price discovery; futures markets provide information about the likely future price of commodities. This information is available to anyone in the economy, because the prices are publicly available. It is not necessary to trade futures to reap this benefit.

2. A *futures price* is a market quoted price today of the best estimate of the value of a commodity at the expiration of the futures contract. What do you think of this definition?

   This claim is intriguing but controversial. If there is no risk premium embedded in the futures price, the statement is likely to be true. The definition implies that random holding of futures positions should earn a zero profit. This seems to be approximately true, but studies such as that by Bodie and Rosansky find positive returns to long futures positions. While the claim may not hold literally, it does seem to be close to correct. Further, those who reject the claim may have a difficult time in identifying futures prices that are above or below the future spot price.

3. Explain the concept of an unbiased predictor.

   A predictor is unbiased if the average prediction error equals zero. This implies that errors in the prediction are distributed around zero, and that the prediction is equally likely to be high as well as low.

4. How are errors possible if a predictor is unbiased?

   Saying that a predictor is unbiased merely claims that the predictions do not tend to be too high or too low. They can still be in error. For example, the futures price may provide an unbiased prediction of the future spot price of a commodity. Nonetheless, the errors in such a prediction are often large, because the futures price today can diverge radically from the spot price at the expiration of the futures.

5. Scalpers trade to capture profits from minute fluctuations in futures prices. Explain how this avaricious behavior benefits others.

   Scalpers trade frequently, attempting to profit by a tick here or there. In pursuing their profit, the scalpers provide the market with liquidity. Thus, a trader who wishes to take or offset a position benefits from the presence of scalpers ready to take the opposite side of the transaction. With many scalpers competing for business, position traders will be able to trade at prices that closely approximate the true value of the commodity. Expressed another way, as scalpers compete for profits, they force the bid-asked spread to narrow, therefore contributing to the liquidity of the market.

6. Assume that scalping is made illegal. What would the consequences of such an action be for hedging activity in futures markets?

Without scalpers, the liquidity of the futures market would be greatly impaired. This would imply a widening of bid-asked spreads. The potential hedger would face having to accept a price that was distant from the true price. Faced with the higher transaction costs represented by wider bid-asked spreads, some hedgers might find that hedging is too expensive and they might not hedge. Thus, without scalpers, hedging would be more expensive, and we would observe a lower volume of hedging activity.

7. A trader anticipates rising corn prices and wants to take advantage of this insight by trading an intracommodity spread. Would you advise that she trade long nearby/short distant or the other way around? Explain.

The answer depends on the relative responsiveness to nearby and distant futures prices to a generally rising price level for corn. If the nearby contract price rises more than the price of the distant contract, the trader should go long nearby/short distant, for example. For most agricultural commodities, there is no general rule to follow.

8. Assume that daily settlement prices in the futures market exhibit very strong first-order serial correlation. How would you trade to exploit this strategy? Explain how your answer would differ if the correlation is statistically significant but, nonetheless, small in magnitude.

With strong serial correlation, a price rise is likely to be followed by another price rise, and a price drop is likely to be followed by another price drop. Therefore, the trader should buy after a price rise and sell after a price fall. If the correlation is strong, the strategy should generate profits. However, the correlation must be very strong to generate profits sufficient to cover transaction costs. The correlation can be statistically significant, but still too small to be economically significant. To be economically significant, the correlation must be strong enough to generate trading profits that will cover the transaction costs. Studies typically find statistically significant first-order serial correlation in futures price changes, but they also find that these correlations are not economically significant.

9. Assume that you are a rabid efficient markets believer. A commodity fund uses 20 percent of its funds as margin payments. The remaining 80 percent are invested in risk-free securities. What investment performance would you expect from the fund?

For any efficient markets believer, rabid or calm, the expected return on the 80 percent of the funds is the risk-free rate. If there is no risk premium, the expected profit on the futures position is zero. Thus, we define a rabid efficient markets believer as one who denies the existence of a risk premium. Therefore, the rabid theorist expects returns from the funds that would be 80 percent of the risk-free rate.

10. Consider two traders. The first trader is an individual with his own seat who trades strictly for his own account. The other trader works for a brokerage firm actively engaged in retail futures brokerage. Which trader has a lower effective marginal trading cost? Relate this comparison in marginal trading costs to quasi-arbitrage.

This is a difficult question. The trader who owns a seat incurs the following costs to trade: the capital commitment to the seat, the opportunity cost of foregone alternative employment, and the exchange member's out-of-pocket transaction costs. These out-of-pocket costs are quite low. For the broker, the scale is much greater. Behind the broker in the pit stands the entire brokerage firm organization with the overhead it represents. Offsetting this overhead to some extent is the much greater scale associated with the brokerage firm. Also, for the trader associated with the brokerage firm, much of the overhead is associated with retail operations, and the marginal cost of trading an additional contract can be quite low. Thus, we judge that the brokerage firm has the lower marginal cost of trading. This difference in trading costs (whichever is really lower) can be important for quasi-arbitrage. Essentially, the fruits of quasi-arbitrage can be harvested by the trader with the lowest marginal transaction costs. If our assessment of these costs is correct, the brokerage firm should be able to squeeze out the market maker and capture these quasi-arbitrage profits.

11. Consider the classic hedging problems of the farmer who sells wheat in the futures market in anticipation of a harvest. Would the farmer be likely to deliver his harvested wheat against the futures? Explain. If he is unlikely to deliver, explain how he manages his futures position instead.

Most farmers who hedge would not deliver against the futures. Often the wheat would not be deliverable, due to differences in grade or type of wheat. Also, the wheat is probably distant from an approved delivery point, and trying to deliver the wheat would involve prohibitively high transportation costs. Instead of actually delivering, the farmer would be much more likely to sell the harvested wheat to the local grain elevator and offset the futures position.

12. A cocoa merchant holds a current inventory of cocoa worth $10 million at present prices of $1,250 per metric ton. The standard deviation of returns for the inventory is .27. She is considering a risk-minimization hedge of her inventory using the cocoa contract of the Coffee, Cocoa and Sugar Exchange. The contract size is 10 metric tons. The volatility of the futures is .33. For the particular grade of cocoa in her inventory, the correlation between the futures and spot cocoa is .85. Compute the risk-minimization hedge ratio and determine how many contracts she should trade.

We know that the hedge ratio is:

$$HR = \frac{\rho_{SF}\sigma_S\sigma_F}{\sigma_F^2}$$

where S and F indicate the spot and futures, respectively. Therefore, with our data, the hedge ratio is:

$$HR = \frac{\rho_{SF}\sigma_S\sigma_F}{\sigma_F^2} = \frac{.85(.27)(.33)}{(.33)(.33)} = .6955$$

Currently, the merchant holds $10,000,000/$1,250 = 8,000 metric tons. The hedge ratio indicates trading .6955 of the futures for each unit of the spot. This implies a futures position of 8,000(.6955) = 5,563.64 metric tons. With the futures consisting of 10 tons per contract, the correct futures quantity is 5,564/10 ≈ 56 contracts. Because she is long the physical cocoa, she should sell 56 futures contracts.

13. A service station operator read this book. He wants to hedge his risk exposure for gasoline. Every week, he pumps 50,000 gallons of gasoline, and he is confident that this pattern will hold through thick and Hussein. What advice would you offer?

The operator should probably not hedge. By construction, the operator faces a fairly small and recurring risk. If the futures price equals the expected future spot price, the expected gains from hedging are zero, ignoring transaction costs. If we consider transaction costs, the hedging program is almost certain to cost money over the long run. Futures hedging is better designed for large risks or special applications. Persistent hedging of repeated small and independent risks will lead to losses equal to the transaction costs the more often the hedge is attempted (assuming the futures price equals the expected future spot price).

14. The Mesa Rosa Tortilla Company is a large producer of tortilla chips whose main ingredient is corn. The demand for Mesa Rosa corn chips is seasonal with the largest demand occurring mid-November through the end of December. Production schedules require acquisition of 25 thousand bushels of corn in late September to meet the holiday season demand. Mesa Rosa management is concerned about the possibility that a rise in the price of corn between now and September could hurt profitability. Corn must be

acquired at a price of $2.25 per bushel or less to ensure profitability. The September corn futures contract (5,000-bushel quantity) is selling for $2.11 per bushel.

A. What can Mesa Rosa do to ensure its profitability?

Mesa can acquire corn today and store it until September, or Mesa can acquire corn using the September corn futures contract. Using the futures contract, it would buy 5 September contracts at $2.11 per bushel.

B. What risks does Mesa Rosa face in acquiring corn by its taking delivery of the futures contract? How should Mesa Rosa acquire the corn it needs?

When September arrives, Mesa can acquire the corn in one of two ways. First, it can take delivery of the corn via the futures contract. Unfortunately, the short side of the contract chooses the delivery location. This location may or may not be convenient for Mesa. The second alternative for acquiring corn eliminates this risk. In this method, Mesa acquires corn in the spot market and enters a reversing trade in the futures market. If the futures price has moved since the initiation of the hedge, any gains (losses) on the futures contract offset any losses (gains) in the cash market so that the effective price Mesa pays for corn is $2.11.

C. If the September spot price turns out to be $3.15 per bushel, show Mesa Rosa's transactions in the corn cash and futures markets and calculate its net wealth change.

Mesa's Long Hedge

Date	Cash Market	Futures Market
Today	Mesa anticipates need for 25,000 bushels of corn in September; wants to pay $2.11/bushel or $52,750 total.	Buy five 5,000-bushel SEP corn futures at $2.11/bushel.
September	Spot price of corn is $3.15/bushel. Mesa buys 25,000 bushels for $78,750.	At maturity, the futures price equals the spot price. Sell 5 futures contracts at $3.15/bushel.
	Opportunity Loss: $52,750 − $78,750 = − $26,000	Futures Profit: 25,000 ($3.15 − $2.11) = $26,000
	Net Wealth Change = 0	

15. It is August 10 and Farmer John is making final estimates of this year's wheat crop. His production is turning out to be much better than expected. This causes concern because if his production is better than expected, other farmers must be experiencing the same situation. The current spot price is $2.25 per bushel, and the September wheat futures (5,000 bushels per contract) price is $2.52 per bushel. At the current spot price, Farmer John would just break even with his anticipated 60 thousand bushels. His wheat will not be ready to harvest until September.

A. What can Farmer John do to ensure his profitability? Is this a long or a short hedge? Why?

Farmer John can sell his anticipated wheat production in the futures market. Any opportunity gains (losses) resulting from changing wheat prices will be offset by losses (gains) in the futures market. This is a short hedge because Farmer John is selling his production forward. The counterparty to his contract might be a producer acquiring wheat forward for whom the transaction would be a long hedge.

B. At harvest time in September, Farmer John's concerns are realized in that the cash price has dropped to $1.70 per bushel. Compute Farmer John's net wealth change due to the drop in corn prices, assuming he hedged his anticipated production and his final yield was 60,000 bushels.

Date	Cash Market	Futures Market
August 10	Farmer John anticipates the production of 60,000 bushels of wheat which he wishes to sell at $2.52/bushel for a total of $151,200.	Sell twelve 5,000-bushel SEP wheat futures contracts at $2.52/bushel.
September	Farmer John sells 60,000 bushels in the spot market at $1.70/bushel for a total of $102,000. Opportunity Loss: ($102,000 − $151,200) = − $49,200	At maturity, the futures price will equal the spot price. Farmer John buys 12 contracts at $1.70/bushel. Futures Profit: 60,000 ($2.52 − $1.70) = $49,200

Net Wealth Change = $0

C. Suppose Farmer John's production turned out to be only 50,000 bushels. Compute his net wealth change.

Date	Cash Market	Futures Market
August 10	Farmer John anticipates the production of 60,000 bushels of wheat which he wishes to sell at $2.52/bushel for a total of $151,200.	Sell twelve 5,000-bushel SEP wheat futures contracts at $2.52/bushel.
September	Farmer John sells 50,000 bushels in the spot market at $1.70/bushel for a total of $85,000. Opportunity Losses: Price Change = 60,000 ($1.70 − $2.52) = − $49,200 Production Variation = 10,000 × $1.70 = − $17,000 Total: − $66,200	At maturity, the futures price will equal the spot price. Farmer John buys 12 contracts at $1.70/bushel. Futures Profit: $49,200

Net Wealth Change = − $17,000

Farmer John's net wealth change is negative because he had anticipated 60,000 bushels of wheat production, but his final production was 10,000 bushels less. He could have sold those 10,000 bushels at $1.70 per bushel if he had them. This results in $17,000 opportunity loss attributable to production variation.

16. Ace Trucking Lines has a fleet of 10,000 trucks that carry a variety of commodities throughout North America. One of its major costs of operation is diesel fuel. There is no futures contract traded on diesel fuel, but there are futures contracts traded on No. 2 heating oil, closely related to diesel, and unleaded regular gasoline. Both of these contracts are traded in quantities of 42,000 gallons/contract. Identify three factors related to Ace Trucking Line's situation that would make any hedging activity be characterized as cross-hedging.

A cross-hedge is a hedge in which the commodity being hedged and the hedging instrument have dissimilar characteristics. These characteristics can relate to: the time span of the hedge and delivery data on the hedging instrument; the quantity hedged and the size of the underlying instrument; and the commodity being hedged and the commodity deliverable on the hedging instrument.

In Ace Trucking's case, most likely all three of these characteristics apply. First, Ace Trucking would not maintain much inventory of fuel. Most fuel would be purchased through retailers. This makes it difficult to identify a delivery date, as fuel is purchased on a continual basis. Second, Ace's demand for diesel fuel is likely to vary from exact multiples of 42,000 gallons. Hence, the quantity being hedged and the quantity deliverable on the underlying contracts are likely to vary. Finally, there is no diesel contract. The closest contract would be the No. 2 heating oil. Hence, the commodity being hedged is not the same as that deliverable on the hedging instrument.

Ace Trucking, if it would be interested in hedging its fuel price risk, might investigate risk-minimization hedging techniques. In this case, Ace would find the futures contract whose price is most highly correlated with the price of diesel fuel and use that contract for hedging.

17. QT has a network of 150 gasoline outlets throughout the central United States. At any one time, the company has 1.125 million gallons of gasoline inventory. Derek Larkin has suggested that QT hedge the risk of its gasoline inventories. He says that the appropriate hedging technique would be risk-minimization.

A. What is risk-minimization hedging?

In risk-minimization hedging, one trades futures contracts in the amount that will minimize the variation of the value of a portfolio composed of the cash position and the futures position. To determine the risk-minimizing hedge ratio, one regresses the price changes of the spot price against the hedging instrument's price changes over the same time period. The slope coefficient from the regression is the risk-minimizing hedge ratio. The regression result indicates the units of the hedging commodity to trade for each unit of the spot commodity.

B. Derek estimates the following relationship between spot, S_t, and futures, F_t, prices using the nearby 42,000-gallon unleaded regular gasoline contract:

$$\Delta S_t = \alpha + \beta \, \Delta F_t + \varepsilon_t$$

Derek's estimation gives the following results:

$$\hat{a} = 0.5231$$
$$\hat{\beta} = 0.9217$$
$$R^2 = 0.88$$

Based on these results, what should QT do to hedge its inventory price risk?

QT has 1.125 million gallons of gasoline in inventory. Derek's results suggest a hedge ratio of 0.9217 gallons of futures for each gallon of inventory. Computing the number of contracts:

Number of Contracts = 0.9217 (1,125,000 / 42,000) = 24.7

Derek's recommendation would be to sell 25 contracts to hedge QT's price risk.

C. Derek also estimated the same relationship using the nearby 42,000-gallon No. 2 heating oil futures contract with the following results:

$$\hat{a} = 0.7261$$
$$\hat{\beta} = 0.6378$$
$$R^2 = 0.55$$

Compare the results from the two regressions and comment on which contract would be most appropriate for hedging purposes.

Comparing the results of the two regressions, the most important consideration is the R^2. The R^2 tells the percentage of spot price change variation explained by changes in the futures price. A perfect hedging instrument would explain 100 percent of the price change variation. Failing that, Derek should recommend the hedging instrument with the highest R^2. In this case, the unleaded gasoline contract with its R^2 of 88 percent dominates the No. 2 heating oil contract with its R^2 of 55 percent.

Interest Rate Futures: Introduction | 5

Answers to Questions and Problems

1. A 90-day T-bill yields 8.75 percent. What is the price of a $1,000,000 face value bill?

   Applying the equation for the value of a T-bill, the price of a $1,000,000 face value T-bill is $1,000,000 − DY($1,000,000)(DTM)/360, where DY is the discount yield and DTM = days until maturity. Therefore, if DY = .0875, the bill price is:

   $$\text{Bill Price} = \$1,000,000 - \frac{0.0875\,(\$1,000,000)\,(90)}{360} = \$978,125$$

2. The IMM index stands as 88.70. What is the discount yield? If you buy a T-bill futures at that index value and the index becomes 88.90, what is your gain or loss?

   The discount yield = 100.00 − IMM index = 100.00 − 88.70 = 11.30 percent. If the IMM index moves to 88.90, it has gained 20 basis points, and each point is worth $25. Because the price has risen and the yield has fallen, the long position has a profit of $25(20) = $500.

3. What is the difference between position day and first position day?

   First position day is the first day on which a trader can initiate the delivery sequence on CBOT futures contracts. With the three-day delivery sequence characteristics of T-bond futures, for example, first position day is the second to last business day of the month preceding the contract's expiration month. For example, May 30 is the first position day for the JUN contract, assuming that May 30–June 1 are all business days. Position day is functionally the same, but it is not the first day on which a trader can initiate the sequence. For example, assuming June 10–12 are all business days, the position day could be June 10, with actual delivery occurring on June 12.

4. A $100,000 face value T-bond has an annual coupon rate of 9.5 percent and paid its last coupon 48 days ago. What is the accrued interest on the bond?

   $$\text{Accrued Interest} = \$100,000\,(.095/2)(48/182.5) = \$1,249.32.$$

   Note that we assume that the half-year has 182.5 days. There are specific rules for determining the number of days in a half-year.

5. What conditions are necessary for the conversion factors on the CBOT T-bond contract to create favorable conditions for delivering one bond instead of another?

   There is one market condition under which the conversion factor method creates no bias: the yield curve is flat and all rates are 8 percent. Under any other circumstance, the conversion factor method will give incentives to deliver some bonds in preference to others.

6. The Municipal Bond Index futures does not allow for delivery of bonds. Explain why the futures price must converge to the spot index value nonetheless.

The MBI uses cash settlement, so at expiration the final settlement price on the futures is set equal to the cash index value. This guarantees exact convergence at expiration. Prior to expiration, deviations between futures prices and the spot index will create arbitrage opportunities. If the futures price is too high relative to the spot index value, there will be cash-and-carry arbitrage opportunities. If the futures price is too low relative to the spot index, there will be reverse cash-and-carry arbitrage opportunities.

7. The JUN T-bill futures IMM index value is 92.80, while the SEP has a value of 93.00. What is the implied percentage cost-of-carry to cover the period from June to September?

For the JUN contract, the implied invoice amount is:

$$\text{Bill Price} = \$1,000,000 - .0720(\$1,000,000)(90)/360 = \$982,000$$

Paying this amount in June will yield $1,000,000 in September when the delivered T-bill matures. Therefore, the implied interest rate is:

$$\text{Implied Cost-of-Carry} = \frac{\$1,000,000}{\$982,000} - 1 = 0.018330$$

Therefore, the implied annual interest rate to cover the June–September period is 1.8330 percent. (The information about the SEP futures is just a distraction.)

8. A spot 180-day T-bill has a discount yield of 9.5 percent. If the bank discount rate for the next three months is 9.2 percent, what is the price of a futures that expires in three months?

To exclude arbitrage, the strategy of holding the 180-day T-bill must give the same return as investing for the first three-months at the repo rate and taking delivery on the futures to cover the second three-month period to make up the 180-day holding period.

Assuming $1,000,000 face values, the price of the 180-day bill must be:

$$\text{Bill Price} = \$1,000,000 - .095(\$1,000,000)(180)/360 = \$952,500$$

This is a ratio of face value to price of 1.049869. With a bank discount yield of 9.2 percent, a bill that pays $1,000,000 in 90 days must have a price of:

$$\text{Bill Price} = \$1,000,000 - 0.092\,(\$1,000,000)\,(90)/360 = \$977,000$$

giving a ratio of face value to price of 1.023541. Therefore, the ratio of the $1,000,000 face value to the price of the futures, X, must satisfy the following equation:

$$1.049869 = 1.023541\,X$$

$X = 1.025722$. Therefore, the futures price must be $1,000,000/1.025722 = $974,923, or $974,925 rounded to the nearest $25 tick.

9. For the next three futures expirations, you observe the following Eurodollar quotations:

MAR   92.00
JUN   91.80
SEP   91.65

What shape does the yield curve have? Explain.

These IMM index values imply Eurodollar add-on yields of 8 percent, 8.2 percent, and 8.35 percent, respectively. These rates apply to the following periods: March–June, June–September, and

September–December, respectively. Essentially, we may regard these futures rates as forward rates. If forward rates increase with futurity, the yield curve must be upward sloping.

10. Assume that the prices in the preceding problem pertain to T-bill futures and the MAR contract expires today. What should be the spot price of an 180-day T-bill?

To avoid arbitrage, the spot price of an 180-day T-bill must give the same return as taking delivery on the futures today and taking a long position in the JUN contract with the intention of taking delivery of it as well. For convenience, we assume a T-bill with a face value of $1,000,000.

With the strategy of two 90-day positions, a trader would need to take delivery of both one full JUN contract and enough bills on the MAR contract to pay the invoice amount on the JUN contract. For the JUN contract, the IMM index value implies a delivery price of $1,000,000 − .0820($1,000,000)(90)/360 = $979,500. For the MAR contract, the delivery price is $1,000,000 − .08($1,000,000)(90)/360 = $980,000. But the trader requires only $979,500 (or 97.95 percent) of the JUN contract. Therefore, for the short-term strategy, the current price of $1,000,000 in September is .9795($980,000) = $959,910. To avoid arbitrage, the 180-day bill must also cost $959,910, implying a discount yield of .08018.

11. The cheapest-to-deliver T-bond is a 12 percent bond that paid its coupon 87 days ago, and it is priced at 105-16. The conversion factor of the bond is 1.0900. The nearby T-bond futures expires in 50 days, and the current price is 98-00. If you could borrow or lend to finance a T-bond for a total outlay of 2 percent over this period, how would you transact? What if you could borrow or lend at 3 percent? What if you could borrow at 3 percent and lend at 2 percent? Explain.

To know how to respond to these quotations requires knowing the invoice amount that can be obtained for the bond and comparing this with the cost of carrying the bond to delivery on the futures. For convenience, we assume a face value that equals the contract size of $100,000. First, the accrued interest (assuming a 182.5-day half-year) is:

$$AI = (87/182.5)(.5)(.12)\$100,000 = \$2,860.27$$

At expiration, the accrued interest will be:

$$AI = (137/182.5)(.5)(.12)\$100,000 = \$4,504.11$$

For this bond and the futures price of 98-00, the invoice amount will be:

$$\text{Invoice Amount} = .9800(\$100,000)(1.09) + \$4,504.11 = \$111,324.11$$

Buying the bond and carrying it to delivery (at 2 percent interest for the period) costs:

$$(\$105,500 + \$2,860.27)(1.02) = \$110,527.48$$

Because the cost of acquiring and carrying the bond to delivery is less than the expected invoice amount, the trader could engage in a cash-and-carry arbitrage. Buying the bond and carrying it to delivery costs $110,527.48 and nets a cash inflow of $111,324.11. This gives an arbitrage profit. (Notice that the actual invoice amount is unknown, but transacting at the futures price of 98-00 guarantees the profit we have computed. This profit may be realized earlier depending upon the daily settlement cash flows.)
  If the cost of carrying the bond for these next 50 days is 3 percent instead of 2 percent, the total cost of acquiring and carrying the bond will not work. The total outlay will be:

$$(\$105,500 + \$2,860.27)(1.03) = \$111,611.08$$

Ignoring the short seller's options to choose the deliverable bond and the delivery date within the delivery month, the following reverse cash-and-carry strategy will be available with the 3 percent financing rate. The trader can buy the futures, borrow the bond and sell it short, and invest the proceeds to earn $111,611.08 by delivery. The short, we assume, obligingly delivers the same bond on the right day for the invoice amount of $111,324.11, and the profit is: $111,611.08 − $111,324.11 = $286.97.

If the trader can borrow at 3 percent and lend at 2 percent, these prices create no arbitrage opportunities. The cash-and-carry strategy is too expensive, because buying and carrying the bond costs $111,611.08, more than the invoice amount of $111,324.11. The reverse cash-and-carry strategy is also impractical, because it nets only $110,527.48, less than the invoice amount of $111,324.11.

12. You expect a steepening yield curve over the next few months, but you are not sure whether the level of rates will increase or decrease. Explain two different ways you can trade to profit if you are correct.

If the yield curve is to steepen, distant rates must rise relative to nearby rates. If this happens, we can exploit the event by trading just short-term instruments. The yield on distant expiration short-term instruments must rise relative to the yield on nearby expiration short-term instruments. Therefore, one should sell the distant expiration and buy the nearby expiration. This strategy could be implemented by trading Eurodollar or T-bill futures.

As a second basic technique, one could trade longer-term T-bonds against shorter maturity T-notes. Here the trader expects yields on T-bonds to rise relative to yields on T-notes. Therefore, the trader should sell T-bond futures and buy T-note futures. Here the two different contracts can have the same expiration month.

13. The Iraqi invasion of Alaska has financial markets in turmoil. You expect the crisis to worsen more than other traders suspect. How could you trade short-term interest rate futures to profit if you are correct? Explain.

Greater-than-expected turmoil might be expected to result in rising yields on interest rate futures. To exploit this event, a trader could sell futures outright. A second result might be an increasing risk premium on short-term instruments. In this case, the yield differential between Eurodollar and T-bill futures might increase. To exploit this event, the trader could sell Eurodollar futures and buy T-bill futures of the same maturity.

14. You believe that the yield curve is strongly upward sloping and that yields are at very high levels. How would you use interest rate futures to hedge a prospective investment of funds that you will receive in nine months? If you faced a major borrowing in nine months, how would you use futures?

If you think yields are near their peak, you will want to lock-in these favorable rates for the investment of funds that you will receive. Therefore, you should buy futures that will expire at about the time you will receive your funds. The question does not suggest whether you will be investing long-term or short-term. However, if the yield curve is strongly upward sloping, it might favor longer-term investment. Consequently, you might buy T-bond futures expiring in about nine months.

If you expect to borrow funds in nine months, you may not want to use the futures market at all. In the question, we assume that you believe rates are unsustainably high. Trading to lock-in these rates only ensures that your borrowing takes place at the currently very high effective rates. Given your beliefs, it might be better to speculate on falling rates.

15. The spot rate of interest on a corporate bond is 11 percent, and the yield curve is sharply upward sloping. The futures rate on the T-bond futures that is just about to expire is 8 percent, but the yield for the futures contract that expires in six months is 8.75 percent. (You are convinced that this difference is independent of any difference in the cheapest-to-deliver bonds for the two contracts.) In these circumstances, a corporate finance officer wants to lock-in the current spot rate of 11 percent on a corporate bond that her firm plans to offer in six months. What advice would you give her?

Reform your desires to conform to reality. The yield curve is upward sloping, and the spot corporate rate is 11 percent. Therefore, the forward corporate rate implied by the yield curve must exceed 11 percent. Trading futures now to lock-in a rate for the future locks in the rate implied by the yield curve, and that rate will exceed 11 percent. Consequently, she must expect to lock-in a rate above the current spot rate of 11 percent.

16. Helen Jaspers is sitting at her trading desk watching the T-bill spot and futures market prices. Her firm is very active in the T-bill market, and she is eager to make a trade. The quote on the T-bill having 120 days from settlement to maturity is 4.90 percent discount yield. This bill could be used for the September 20 delivery on the September T-bill futures contract that is trading at 95.15. The quote on the T-bill maturing September 20, having 29 days between settlement and maturity, is 4.70 percent discount yield.

A. Compute the T-bill and futures prices per dollar of face value.

T-bills are quoted in bank discount yield (DY), and T-bill futures are quoted in $100 - DY$. These must be converted to dollars using the following formula:

$$P = \left(1 - \frac{DY \times n}{360}\right) FV$$

where n is the number of days from settlement to maturity and FV is the face value.
Compute prices per dollar of face value:

120-day T-bill quoted at 4.90% DY: $P_{120} = \left(1 - \frac{.049 \times 120}{360}\right)\$1 = \$0.9837$

29-day T-bill quoted at 4.70% DY: $P_{29} = \left(1 - \frac{.047 \times 29}{360}\right)\$1 = \$0.9962$

The futures contract on its delivery date will call for a T-bill with 91 days from settlement to maturity. The discount yield on this T-bill is currently:

$$DY = 100 - 95.15 = 4.85\%$$

The dollar price of the T-bill is: $F_{0,t} = \left(1 - \frac{.0485 \times 91}{360}\right)\$1 = \$0.9877$

B. Compute the implied repo rate. Could the implied repo rate be used to tell Helen where arbitrage profits are possible? If so, how?

The implied repo rate, C, is: $C = (F_{0,t} / S_0) - 1$

In this case, C is: $C = (.9877 / .9837) - 1 = 0.4066\%$

What does this tell us? It tells us the return we get over the next 29 days if we buy the 120-day T-bill and deliver it against the September futures contract. This implied repo rate is compared to the 29-day borrowing/lending rate to point out opportunities for arbitrage. If C is greater than the 29-day financing rate, then the appropriate arbitrage is a cash-and-carry. If C is less than the 29-day financing rate, then a reverse cash-and-carry would be appropriate. The borrowing/lending rate over this 29-day time period is:

$$(FV / P_{29}) - 1 = (1 / .9962) - 1 = 0.3814\%$$

Since the implied repo rate is greater than the cost of financing, we have the possibility of cash-and-carry arbitrage.

C. What would be the arbitrage profit from a $1 million transaction?

A cash-and-carry arbitrage would call for borrowing for 29 days, buying the 120-day bill, and selling the 120-day bill forward using the futures contract. On the delivery date, the 120-day bill, then having 91 days to maturity, would be delivered against the futures contract. The proceeds would be used to pay off the 29-day borrowing.

Date	Cash Market	Futures Market
Today	Borrow $.9837 million for 29 days at 4.70% DY. Buy $1 million FV 120-day T-bill at a price of $.9837 million. Net investment = $0	Sell $1 million 91-day T-bills for September 10 delivery.
September 10	Pay off borrowing; amount due = .9837/.9962 = $.9874 million	Deliver 91-day T-bill against the futures contract; receive $.9877 million.

Net Profit = ($0.9877 − $0.9874) million = $300

17. Today is August 11. Matt Peterson, bond trader, is watching the Treasury bond spot and futures prices. He is particularly curious about the 8 percent of November 15, 2021, which is trading at 124-20. This bond would be deliverable against the September T-bond futures contract, which is trading at 124-15. The short-term interest rates between now and the delivery month of the futures contract are 4.70 percent to the beginning of September and 4.75 percent to the end of September. Assume simple interest for cash-and-carry financings.

A. Should Matt care about the interest rates to the beginning and the end of the delivery month?

Matt should care about the interest rates between now and various points in the delivery month. This is because the short side of the futures contract has a timing option for the delivery date. The bonds can be delivered against the futures contract, with proper notice, at anytime during the delivery month. The bondholder (short side) continues to accrue interest until delivery. This means that if the cost of financing is less than the rate of interest accrual on the bond, then the short side would prefer to delay delivery as long as possible. Conversely, if the interest accrual is less than the cost of financing, the short side would deliver as soon as possible.

B. Compute the cash-and-carry arbitrage profit opportunity for $100,000 of T-bond face value using the 8 percent bond of November 15, 2021, and assuming September 1 delivery. Note the following number of days between key dates: May 15 to August 11, 88 days; May 15 to September 1, 109 days; May 15 to September 30, 138 days; and May 15 to November 15, 184 days.

Assuming September 1 delivery, we first compute the invoice price that will be paid upon delivery of the November bond against the futures contract.

$$\text{Invoice} = \text{Quoted Price} + \text{Accrued Interest}$$

$$\text{Accrued Interest} = 109/184 \times .04 \times \$100,000 = \$2,370$$

$$\text{Futures Invoice Price} = (124 + 15/32)\% \times \$100,000 + \$2,370$$

$$\text{Futures Invoice Price} = \$126,839$$

The cost of the bond we will deliver is:

$$\text{Spot Invoice Price} = [(124 + 20/32)\% + (88/184)(.04)] \times \$100,000 = \$126,538$$

Cash-and-Carry Arbitrage

Date	Cash Market	Futures Market
Today	Borrow $126,538 at 4.70%. Buy November 15, 2021 bond for $126,538. Net cash flow = $0	Sell September T-bond futures at 124-15.
September 1	Repay financing: $126,538 [1 + .047(21/365)] = $126,880.	Deliver bond and receive $126,838.

Net Proceeds = $126,838 – $126,880 = – $42

C. Compute the cash-and-carry arbitrage profit opportunity for $100,000 of T-bond face value using the 8 percent bond of November 15, 2021, and assuming September 30 delivery.

Assuming September 30 delivery, the futures invoice price will be:

$$\text{Futures Invoice Price} = [124 + 15/32\% + (138/184)(.04)] \times \$100,000 = \$127,469$$

Date	Cash Market	Futures Market
Today	Borrow $126,538 at 4.75%. Buy November 15, 2021 bond for $126,538. Net cash flow = $0	Sell September T-bond futures at 124-15.
September 30	Repay financing: $126,538 [1 + .0475(50/365)] = $127,361.	Deliver bond and receive $127,469.

Net Proceeds = $127,469 – $127,361 = $108

D. Explain why Matt would not deliver the T-bond until the last possible moment.

Matt will wait until the last moment to deliver the bond because it is accruing interest at an 8 percent rate while his cost of financing over the month of September is less. Specifically, the accrual of 8 percent on $100,000 exceeds the accrual of 4.75 percent on $126,538. In general, upward sloping term structures make later delivery more desirable, and downward sloping term structures make earlier delivery more desirable.

18. Angela Vickers has the responsibility of managing Seminole Industries' short-term capital position. In three weeks, Seminole will have a cash inflow that will be rolled over into a $10,000,000 90-day T-bill. There is a T-bill futures contract that calls for delivery at the same time as the anticipated cash inflow. It is trading at 94.75. There have been signs that the financial markets are calming and that interest rates might be falling.

A. What type of hedge might Angela employ?

Angela might employ a long hedge of the anticipated $10 million cash inflow. This would be accomplished by buying 10 T-bill futures contracts with a delivery date matching the anticipated cash inflow. The rate she would be locking in is:

$$100 - 94.75 = 5.25\% \text{ discount yield}$$

B. Three weeks in the future, interest rates are actually higher. The 90-day T-bill discount yield is 6.00 percent. Calculate Seminole's net wealth change if the position is left unhedged.

Three weeks before the cash inflow, Vickers would have been able to lock-in a 5.25 percent discount yield using the futures contract. This would have allowed her to purchase $10 million of face value for:

$$\text{Anticipated Price} = \left(1 - \frac{.0525 \times 90}{360}\right)\$10,000,000 = \$9,868,750$$

When it comes time to actually invest, interest rates have risen to 6 percent discount yield. Then the price of $10 million of face value costs:

$$\text{Realized Price} = \left(1 - \frac{.06 \times 90}{360}\right) \$10,000,000 = \$9,850,000$$

Seminole had an opportunity gain of $18,750.

C. Calculate Seminole's net wealth change if the position is hedged.

If the position had been hedged, Seminole would have been long futures that were bought at 5.25 percent discount yield, or $9,868,750. This results in a loss of $18,750. The loss in the futures market is offset by the opportunity gain in the cash market so that the net wealth change is $0.

Date	Cash Market	Futures Market
Today	Anticipate the purchase of $10 million in T-bills for $9,868,750.	Buy $10 million of T-bill futures at $9,868,750.
3 weeks	Buy $10 million in T-bills for $9,850,000. Opportunity gain = $18,750	Sell $10 million T-bill futures contracts at $9,850,000. Futures loss = –$18,750
	Net wealth change = $0	

D. Would the hedge be a mistake?

In hindsight, Seminole would have been better off unhedged, but hindsight is 20/20. *Ex ante*, the concern was the risk of falling interest rates. Seminole viewed the 5.25 percent discount yield as acceptable for the investment and wanted to guarantee it. Therefore, *ex ante*, the hedge would not have been a mistake.

19. Fred Ferrell works for ABC Investments. As part of ABC's investment strategy, Fred is charged with liquidating $20 million of ABC's T-bill portfolio in two months. Fred has identified $20 million of T-bills that would be deliverable against the March T-bill futures contract at the time of liquidation. The price of the futures contract is 94.50. Fred is losing sleep at night over concerns about future economic uncertainty that could lead to a rise in interest rates.

A. What action can Fred take to reduce ABC's exposure to interest rate risk?

Fred could enter a short hedge using 20 March T-bill futures contracts. Since ABC anticipates liquidating $20 million in T-bills, ABC can lock in a liquidation price based on the $100 - 94.50 = 5.5$ percent discount yield.

B. At the time of liquidation, the price of the 90-day T-bill has risen to 5.25 percent discount yield. Compute the change in ABC's net wealth that has occurred if Fred failed to hedge the position.

If Fred does not hedge the position, ABC's net wealth change will be an opportunity gain or loss. ABC had the opportunity to lock-in a 5.5 percent discount yield but did not. The proceeds of $20 million face value at 5.5 percent are:

$$\text{Anticipated Proceeds} = \left(1 - \frac{.055 \times 90}{360}\right) \$20,000,000 = \$19,725,000$$

The realized price is calculated using 5.25 percent discount yield:

$$\text{Realized Proceeds} = \left(1 - \frac{.0525 \times 90}{360}\right) \$20,000,000 = \$19,737,500$$

The difference is the opportunity gain/loss:

$$\text{Realized Proceeds} - \text{Anticipated Proceeds} = (\$19,737,500 - \$19,725,000) = \$12,500 \text{ Gain}$$

C. Compute the change in ABC's net wealth that has occurred, assuming Fred hedged the position.

If Fred had hedged the position, he would have sold $20 million of face value using the futures contracts at a price of $19,725,000, and he would have closed that position at a price of $19,737,500. There would have been a $12,500 loss in the futures market. The net wealth change of ABC would then be zero, because the loss in the futures market would have exactly offset the opportunity gain in the cash market.

Date	Cash Market	Futures Market
Today	Anticipate selling $20 million of T-bills for $19,725,000.	Sell $20 million T-bill futures at $19,725,000.
March	Sell $20 million T-bills for $19,737,500.	Buy $20 million T-bill futures at $19,737,500.
	Opportunity gain = $12,500	Loss = –$12,500
	Net wealth change = $0	

20. Alex Brown is a financial analyst for B.I.G. Industries. He has been given responsibility for handling the details of refinancing a $500 million long-term debt issue that will be rolled over in May (five months from today). The new 8 percent, 30-year debt, with a face value of $500 million, is anticipated to have a 75-basis-point default risk premium over the yield on the 30-year T-bond. The 30-year T-bond is currently trading at 5.62 percent. Alex sees this risk premium as typical for corporate debt of a quality similar to B.I.G.'s debt. Alex looks at the June T-bond and notices that it is trading at 123-25. He is concerned that changing interest rates between now and May could have a negative impact on the refinancing cash flow.

A. Assuming no interest rate changes, what are B.I.G.'s anticipated proceeds from refinancing?

If interest rates do not change over the next five months, B.I.G. Industries can expect to price their bonds at:

$$\text{YTM}_{\text{B.I.G.}} = 5.62\% + .75\% = 6.37\%$$

The proceeds of $500 million face with an 8 percent coupon, thirty years to maturity, and a yield to maturity of 6.37%, would be:

$$\text{Anticipated Proceeds} = \sum_{t=1}^{60} \frac{.04(500,000,000)}{\left(1 + \frac{.0637}{2}\right)^t} + \frac{500,000,000}{\left(1 + \frac{.0637}{2}\right)^{60}} = \$608,443,959$$

B. What can Alex do to reduce the refinancing risks faced by B.I.G. Industries?

Alex could reduce the risk by selling T-bond futures. Alex's concern is rising interest rates. As interest rates rise, the proceeds from the debt issue are diminished. These diminished proceeds could be offset by profits made on the short position in the futures market because as rates rise, the futures prices fall and the short position makes money. Naively, Alex could sell $500 million in the T-bond futures contract to hedge the risk.

C. At the time of refinancing, the 30-year T-bond yield is 5.80 percent, the T-bond futures price is 121-09, and B.I.G.'s new debt issue is priced to yield 6.75 percent. Compute the realized proceeds from the refinancing.

When the debt is issued, it is issued with a yield to maturity of 6.75 percent. Interest rates have risen. The proceeds are given by:

$$\text{Realized Proceeds} = \sum_{t=1}^{60} \frac{.04(500,000,000)}{\left(1 + \frac{.0675}{2}\right)^t} + \frac{500,000,000}{\left(1 + \frac{.0675}{2}\right)^{60}} = \$579,955,566$$

This is an opportunity loss of $28,488,392.

D. Assuming Alex sold $500 million in T-bond futures at 123-25 to hedge the refinancing and liquidated the futures position when the refinancing took place, find the profit from the futures trade, and evaluate the net wealth change due to the change in the refinancing rate and the futures trade.

The futures profit is:

$$\text{Futures Profit} = \$500,000,000 \left[\left(123 + \frac{25}{32}\right)\% - \left(121 + \frac{9}{32}\right)\%\right] = \$12,500,000$$

This profit only partially offsets the opportunity loss in the cash market. The net wealth change is:

$$\text{Net Wealth Change} = -\$28,488,392 + \$12,500,000 = -\$15,988,392$$

Date	Cash Market	Futures Market
Today	Anticipate issuing debt at 6.37% for proceeds of $608,443,959.	Sell $500 million in T-bond futures at nominal price of $618,906,250.
May	Issue debt with yield of 6.75% for proceeds of $579,955,566.	Buy $500 million in T-bond futures at nominal price of $606,406,250.
	Opportunity loss = –$28,488,392	Gain = $12,500,000
	Net wealth change = –$15,988,392	

E. Discuss possible reasons why the net wealth change is not zero.

There are at least two reasons that the hedge did not do a better job of offsetting the cash market risk:

Cross-hedge: This was a cross-hedge for several reasons. First, Alex was hedging the interest rates of a corporate bond, but the hedging instrument was a T-bond. Second, the cheapest-to-deliver T-bond may not be a 30-year bond. It may have as little as 15 years to maturity. This will make the price sensitivity of the futures contract and the corporate bond differ. Third, the delivery date on the T-bond futures contract is June, but the refinancing is taking place in May.
Faulty expectations: First, Alex expected the default yield spread to stay fixed at 75 basis points, but it increased with the rise in interest rates to 6.75 percent, giving a rise of 95 basis points. Second, Alex expected the pricing of the T-bond futures contract to react to interest rates in the same manner as the 30-year T-bond, but in reality, the reaction of the T-bond futures price was not as strong as the reaction of the 30-year T-bond price.

While the hedge was not perfect, it did offset some of the refinancing price risk.

Interest Rate Futures: Refinements | 6

Answers to Questions and Problems

Assume today is January 30, 1992. You are considering two bonds as potential bonds for delivery against the JUN 92 T-bond futures contract, which settled at 102-08. First is the $7\frac{1}{4}$ bond that matures on May 15, 2016, with a conversion factor of 0.9205. Second, you might deliver the $13\frac{1}{4}$ bond that matures on May 15, 2014, but is callable on May 15, 2009, and has a conversion factor of 1.4833. Use this information for questions 1–7.

1. On January 30, 1992, what is the accrued interest on each bond?

   On January 30, both bonds are in the November–May half-year. For interest paid on the 15th in a leap year, the half-year has 182 days according to the table from the text. Since the last payment on November 15, 76 days have elapsed (15 in November, 31 in December, and 30 in January.) Assuming a $100,000 face value, we have the following accrued interest.

For the $7\frac{1}{4}$ bond:	AI = (76/182) $3,625 = $1,513.74
For the $13\frac{1}{4}$ bond:	AI = (76/182) $6,625 = $2,766.48

2. Consider a position day of June 15, 1992. What is the accrued interest on each bond?

   On June 15, 1992, we are in the May–November half-year. In a leap year for a bond paying on the 15th, the half-year is 184 days. Since the last payment on May 15, 31 days have elapsed.

For the $7\frac{1}{4}$ bond:	AI = (31/184) $3,625 = $610.73
For the $13\frac{1}{4}$ bond:	AI = (31/184) $6,625 = $1,116.17

3. Assuming the settlement price on position day (June 15, 1992) is 114-00, find the invoice amounts for both bonds.

   From the text, we know:

   $$\text{Invoice Amount} = \text{DSP} (\$100,000) (\text{CF}) + \text{AI}$$

   For the $7\frac{1}{4}$ bond:

   $$\text{Invoice Amount} = 1.14 (\$100,000)(.9205) + \$610.73 = \$105,547.73$$

   For the $13\frac{1}{4}$ bond:

   $$\text{Invoice Amount} = 1.14 (\$100,000)(1.4833) + \$1,116.17 = \$170,212.37$$

4. The $7\frac{1}{4}$ bond trades for 85-00 and the $13\frac{1}{4}$ is at 137-00. Which bond do you expect to be cheaper-to-deliver? (Assume a financing rate of 8 percent and a 360-day year for money market calculations.)

   From January 30 to delivery on June 15, 1992, there is an intervening coupon payment. The profit from delivery is:

   $$\pi = \text{DFP}_0(\text{CF}) + \text{AI}_2 - \{(P_0 + \text{AI}_0)(1 + C_{0,2}) - \text{COUP}_1(1 + C_{1,2})\}$$

The present is January 30, the coupon date is May 15, and the delivery date is June 15. These dates are $t = 0$, $t = 1$, and $t = 2$, respectively. From $t = 0$ to $t = 1$ is 106 days (January has 1, February has 29, March has 31, April has 30, and May has 15). From $t = 1$ to $t = 2$ is 31 days. Therefore, the interest factor from $t = 0$ to $t = 1$ is $1 + (106/360).08 = 1.0236$, and from $t = 1$ to $t = 2$ it is $1 + (31/360).08 = 1.0069$. From $t = 0$ to $t = 2$, there are 137 days and the interest factor is $1 + (137/360).08 = 1.0304$.

Applying the equation to the $7\frac{1}{4}$ bond we have:

$$\pi = DFP_0(CF) + AI_2 - \{(P_0 + AI_0)(1 + C_{0,2}) - COUP_1(1 + C_{1,2})\} = \$102{,}250(.9205) + \$610.73$$
$$- \{(\$85{,}000 + \$1513.74)(1.0304) - \$3{,}625(1.0069)\} = \$94{,}121.13 + \$610.73 - \{\$89{,}143.76 - \$3{,}650.01\}$$
$$= \$9{,}238.11$$

Applying the equation to the $13\frac{1}{4}$ bond we have:

$$\pi = DFP_0(CF) + AI_2 - \{(P_0 + AI_0)(1 + C_{0,2}) - COUP_1(1 + C_{1,2})\} = \$102{,}250(1.4833) + \$1{,}116.17$$
$$- \{(\$137{,}000 + \$2{,}766.48)(1.0304) - \$6{,}625(1.0069)\} = \$151{,}667.43 + \$1{,}116.17 - \{\$144{,}015.38$$
$$- \$6{,}670.71\} = \$15{,}438.93$$

The expected profit from delivering the $7\frac{1}{4}$ is \$9,238.11, but the expected profit from delivering the $13\frac{1}{4}$ is \$15,438.93. Therefore, we expect the $13\frac{1}{4}$ to be cheaper-to-deliver.

5. Assume that between now (January 30, 1992) and delivery on June 15, 1992, you can finance a cash-and-carry transaction at 8 percent. This is your borrowing and lending rate. Further assume that you have full use of all short sale proceeds. Find all possible arbitrage strategies.

From problem 5, both bonds would offer cash-and-carry arbitrage profits. For the $7\frac{1}{4}$ bond, the transactions are as follows:

For the $7\frac{1}{4}$ Bond

January 30, 1992

Sell the JUN 92 T-bond futures at 102-08.	\$0
Borrow \$86,513.74 for 137 days at 8%.	+ 86,513.74
Buy \$100,000 face value of the $7\frac{1}{4}$ bond paying \$85,000 plus accrued interest of \$1,513.74.	− 86,513.74
	Total Cash Flow \$0

May 15, 1992

Receive coupon.	+ \$3,625.00
Lend coupon amount for 31 days at 8%.	− 3,625.00
	Total Cash Flow \$0

June 15, 1992 (Assume futures is still at 102-08 for convenience only.)

Deliver bond and receive invoice amount of \$102,250(.9205) + \$610.73.	+ \$94,731.86
Collect on invested coupon: (\$3,625)(1.0069).	+ 3,650.01
Repay debt incurred on January 30: \$86,513.74(1.0304).	− 89,143.76
	Total Cash Flow \$9,238.11

For the $13\frac{1}{4}$ bond, the transactions are as follows:

For the $13\frac{1}{4}$ Bond

January 30, 1992

Sell the JUN 92 T-bond futures at 102-08.	\$0
Borrow \$139,766.48 for 137 days at 8%.	+ 139,766.48
Buy \$100,000 face value of the $13\frac{1}{4}$ bond paying \$137,000 plus accrued interest of \$2,766.48.	− 139,766.48
	Total Cash Flow \$0

May 15, 1992
Receive coupon.   + $6,625.00
Lend coupon amount for 31 days at 8%.   − 6,625.00
                                                                          Total Cash Flow $0

June 15, 1992 (Assume futures is still at 102-08 for convenience only.)
Deliver bond and receive invoice amount of $102,250(1.4833) + $1,116.17.   + $152,783.60
Collect on invested coupon: ($6,625)(1.0069).   + 6,670.71
Repay debt incurred on January 30: $139,766.48(1.0304).   − 144,015.38
                                                                          Total Cash Flow $15,438.93

We assume that the futures price on June 15 is 102-08, the same price as our original sale price. This simplification abstracts from daily settlement cash flows. For any ending futures price, the profit will be the same, assuming that we ignore the interest that might be earned or paid on the daily settlement cash flows.

6. Find the implied repo rates for both bonds.

   In terms of our notation:

$$\text{Implied Repo Rate} = \frac{\text{DFP}_0\,(100{,}000)\,(\text{CF}) + \text{AI}_2 + \text{COUP}_1\,(1 + C_{1,2}) - (P_0 + \text{AI}_0)}{(P_0 + \text{AI}_0)}$$

   Applying this equation to the $7\frac{1}{4}$ bond gives:

$$= \frac{\$94{,}121 + \$610.73 + \$3{,}625(1.0069) - (\$85{,}000 + \$1{,}513.74)}{\$85{,}000 + \$1{,}513.74}$$

$$= .1373$$

   For the $13\frac{1}{4}$ bond, the equation gives:

$$= \frac{\$151{,}667 + \$1{,}116.17 + \$6{,}625(1.0069) - (\$137{,}000 + \$2{,}766.48)}{\$137{,}000 + \$2{,}766.48}$$

$$= .1409$$

   The implied repo rates are 13.73 percent for the $7\frac{1}{4}$ bond and 14.09 percent for the $13\frac{1}{4}$ bonds. These are not annualized but are the rates for the period from January 30 to June 15.

7. Continue to assume that you can borrow and lend at 8 percent. However, now you can use only 90 percent of any short sale proceeds on a reverse cash-and-carry strategy. How does this change your trading strategy, if at all?

   This assumption has no effect, because both bonds offered a cash-and-carry opportunity, and there was no chance for a reverse cash-and-carry trade.

8. Explain the risks inherent in a reverse cash-and-carry strategy in the T-bond futures market.

   The reverse cash-and-carry strategy requires waiting to receive delivery. However, the delivery options all rest with the short trader. The short trader will initiate delivery at his or her convenience. In the T-bond market, this exposes the reverse cash-and-carry trader to receiving delivery at some time other than the date planned. Also, with so many different deliverable bonds, the reverse cash-and-carry trader is unlikely to receive the bond he or she desires. (These factors are fairly common for other commodities as well.) In the T-bond futures market, the short trader holds some special options such as the wildcard and end-of-month options. The reverse cash-and-carry trader suffers the risk that the short trader will find it advantageous to exploit the wildcard play or exercise the end-of-month option.

9. Explain how the concepts of quasi-arbitrage help to overcome the risks inherent in reverse cash-and-carry trading in T-bond futures.

In pure reverse cash-and-carry arbitrage, the trader sells the bond short and buys the future. The trader thereby suffers risk about which bond will be delivered and the time at which it will be delivered. If the trader holds a large portfolio of bonds and sells some bond from inventory to simulate the short sale, these risks are mitigated. Receiving a particular bond on delivery is no longer so crucial to the trader's cash flows; after all, whichever bond is delivered will merely supplement the trader's portfolio. Further, the timing of delivery presents fewer problems to the quasi-arbitrage trader. In selling a bond from inventory, as opposed to an actual short sale, the trader did not need to worry about financing the short sale for a particular time. Therefore, the selection of a particular delivery date by the short futures trader is less critical. While quasi-arbitrage helps to mitigate the risks associated with the reverse cash-and-carry trade, risks still remain, particularly the risks associated with the short trader's options.

10. Assume economic and political conditions are extremely turbulent. How would this affect the value of the seller's options on the T-bond futures contract? If they have any effect on price, would they cause the futures price to be higher or lower than it otherwise would be?

Generally, options are more valuable the greater the price risk inherent in the underlying good. This is certainly true for the seller's options on the T-bond futures contract. To see this most clearly, we focus on the wildcard option. Exploitation of the wildcard option depends on a favorable price development on any position day between the close of futures trading and the end of the period to announce delivery at 8 P.M., Chicago time. If markets are turbulent, there is a greater chance that something useful will occur in that time window on some day in the delivery month. The greater value of the seller's options in this circumstance would cause the futures price to be lower than it otherwise would be.

11. Explain the difference between the wildcard option and the end-of-the-month option.

The wildcard option is the seller's option to initiate the delivery sequence based on information generated between the close of futures trading and 8 P.M., Chicago time, the time by which the seller must initiate the delivery sequence for a given day. The settlement price determined at the close of trading is the price that will be used for computing the invoice amount. Trading of the T-bond futures contract ceases on the eighth to last business day of the expiration month, and the settlement price on that day is used to determine the invoice amount for all deliveries. Any contracts not closed by the end of the trading period must be fulfilled by delivery. Even though the short trader must make delivery in this circumstance, the short trader still possesses an end-of-the-month option. The short trader can choose which day to deliver and can choose which bond to deliver. The short trader will deliver late in the month if the rate of accrual on the bond planned for delivery exceeds the short-term financing rate at which the bond is carried. Also, changing market conditions can change which bond will be cheapest-to-deliver, and the right to wait and choose a later delivery date has value to the short trader.

12. Some studies find that interest rate futures markets were not very efficient when they first began but that they became efficient after a few years. How can you explain this transition?

The growing efficiency of these markets seems to be due to a market seasoning or maturation process. When these contracts were first initiated, it appears that some of their nuances were not fully appreciated. In particular, the complete understanding of the importance of the seller's options seems to have emerged only slowly.

13. Assume you hold a T-bill that matures in 90 days, when the T-bill futures expires. Explain how you could transact to effectively lengthen the maturity of the bill.

    Buy the T-bill futures that expires in 90 days. After this transaction, you will be long a spot 90-day bill, and you will hold (effectively) a spot position in a 90-day bill to begin in 90 days. The combination replicates a 180-day bill.

14. Assume that you will borrow on a short-term loan in six months, but you do not know whether you will be offered a fixed rate or a floating rate loan. Explain how you can use futures to convert a fixed rate to a floating rate loan and to convert a floating rate to a fixed rate loan.

    For convenience, we assume that the loan will be a 90-day loan. If the loan is to be structured as a floating rate loan, you can convert it to a fixed rate loan by selling a short-term interest rate futures contract (Eurodollar or T-bill) that expires at the time the loan is to begin. The rate you must pay will depend on rates prevailing at the time of the loan. If rates have risen, you must pay more than anticipated. However, if rates have risen, your short position in the futures will have generated a profit that will offset the higher interest you must pay on the loan.

    Now assume that you contract today for a fixed interest rate on the loan. If rates fall, you will be stuck paying a higher rate than the market rate that will prevail at the time the loan begins. To convert this fixed rate loan to a floating rate loan, buy an interest rate futures that expires at the time the loan is to begin. Then, if rates fall, you will profit on the futures position, and these profits will offset the higher than market rates you are forced to pay on your fixed rate loan.

15. You fear that the yield curve may change shape. Explain how this belief would affect your preference for a strip or a stack hedge.

    If the yield curve is to change shape, rates on different futures expirations for the same interest rate futures contract may change by different amounts. In this case, it is important to structure the futures hedge so that the futures cash flows match the exposure of the underlying risk more closely. Thus, if the cash market exposure involves the same amount at regular intervals over the future, a strip hedge will be more effective against changing yield curve shapes.

16. A futures guru says that tailing a hedge is extremely important because it can change the desired number of contracts by 30 percent. Explain why the guru is nuts. How much can the tailing factor reasonably change the hedge ratio?

    To tail a hedge, one simply reduces the computed hedge ratio by discounting it at the risk-free rate for the time of the hedge. For convenience, we assume that the untailed computed hedge ratio is 1.0. If the hedging period is one year, a 30 percent effect would require an interest rate of 43 percent, because $.7 = (1/1.43)$. If the hedging horizon is long, say a full two years, the interest rate would still have to be 19.52 percent to generate the 30 percent effect, because $(1.1952)^2 = 1/.7$. Thus, it seems extremely improbable that the tailing effect could be so large.

17. We have seen in Chapter 4 that regression-based hedging strategies are extremely popular. Explain their weaknesses for interest rate futures hedging.

    First, regression-based hedging (the RGR model) involves statistical estimation, so the technique requires a data set for both cash and futures prices. This data may sometimes be difficult to acquire, particularly for an attempt to hedge a new security. Second, the RGR model does not explicitly consider the differences in the sensitivity of different bond prices to changes in interest rates, and this can be a very important factor. The regression approach does include the different price sensitivities indirectly, however, since their differential sensitivities will be reflected in the estimation of the hedge ratio. Third, any cash bond will have a predictable price movement over time, and the RGR model does not consider this change in the cash bond's price explicitly. However, the sample data used to estimate the hedge ratio will reflect this feature to some extent. Fourth, the RGR hedge ratio is chosen to minimize the variability in the combined futures-cash position over the life of the hedge. Since the RGR hedge ratio depends crucially on the planned hedge length, one might reasonably prefer a hedging technique focusing on the wealth position of the hedge when the hedge ends. After all, the wealth change from the hedge depends on the gain or loss when the hedge is terminated, not on the variability of the cash-futures position over the life of the hedge.

18. You estimate that the cheapest-to-deliver bond on the T-bond futures contract has a duration of 6.5 years. You want to hedge your medium-term Treasury portfolio that has a duration of 4.0 years. Yields are 9.5 percent on the futures and on your portfolio. Your portfolio is worth $120,000,000, and the futures price is 98-04. Using the PS model, how would you hedge?

From the text, the PS hedge ratio is:

$$N = -\frac{P_i\, MD_i}{FP_F\, MD_F}\, RYC$$

For this problem, we are entitled to assume that RYC = 1.0, since no other value is specified. Applying this equation to our data gives:

$$N = -\frac{\$120,000,000 \times 3.652968}{\$98,125 \times 5.936073} = -752.5723$$

Therefore, the PS hedge would require selling about 753 T-bond futures.

19. Explain the relationship between the Bank Immunization Case and hedging with the PS model.

Both bank immunization and the PS model rely essentially on the concept of duration. A PS hedge finds the futures position to make the combined cash/futures position have a duration of zero. Similarly, in bank immunization with equal asset and liability amounts, the asset duration is set equal to the liability duration. For the combined balance sheet, the overall duration is effectively zero as well. Therefore, the two techniques are quite similar in approach, even if they use different instruments to achieve the risk reduction.

20. Compare and contrast the BP model and the RGR model for immunizing a bond portfolio.

The BP model essentially is an immunization model that is suitable for the bank immunization case. The BP hedge ratio is found empirically, but it is the hedge ratio that gives a price movement on the futures position that offsets the price movement on the cash position. As such, it is effectively reflecting the duration of the two instruments. (Notice that the BP model does not really help with the Planning Period Case, because it considers only the effect of a current change in rates, not a change over some hedging horizon.) The RGR model does not really take duration into account in any direct fashion, so it is not oriented toward immunizing at all.

21. It was a hot day in August, and William had just completed the purchase of $20 million of T-bills maturing next March and $10 million of T-bills maturing in one month. The phone rang, and William was informed that the firm had just made a commitment to provide $30 million in capital to a client in mid-December. If William had known this 20 minutes earlier, he would have invested differently.

A. What risks does William face by using his present investments to meet the December commitment?

William faces several interest rate risks using his present investments to fund the anticipated cash outflow. These risks stem from the fact that the maturity of his present investments do not match the timing of the cash outflow. The proceeds of the $10 million of September T-bills must be reinvested from September to December. William faces the risk that interest rates may fall between now and September, which would reduce the December proceeds from the reinvestment. The $20 million of March T-bills are subject to price risk. If interest rates rise between now and December, the proceeds from the sale of the March T-bills will be less than anticipated. Had he known about the firm's commitment earlier, he could have invested in $30 million of December maturity T-bills.

B. Using the futures markets, how can William reduce the risks of the December commitment? Show what transactions would be made.

William would like to lock-in a reinvestment rate for September and a selling price for December. He can accomplish this by buying $10 million September futures contracts and selling $20 million December futures contracts. He is in effect lengthening the maturity of his September bills and shortening the maturity of his March bills. His transactions would be:

Date	Cash Market	Futures Market
Today		Buy $10 million September T-bill futures; sell $20 million December T-bill futures.
September	Receive proceeds from $10 million September T-bills; reinvest $10 million into 90-day T-bills.	Reverse September T-bill futures position by selling $10 million September T-bill futures.
December	Receive proceeds from maturing December T-bills; Sell March T-bills in cash market.	Reverse December T-bill futures position by buying $20 million December T-bill futures.

Gains and losses in the futures market will offset losses and gains in the cash market so that the total proceeds available to meet the December commitment will be as anticipated.

22. Handcraft Ale, Ltd. has decided to build additional production capacity in the United States to meet increasing demand in North America. Uma Peele has been given the responsibility of obtaining financing for the project. Handcraft Ale will need $10 million to carry the firm through the construction phase. This phase will last two years, at which time the $10 million debt will be repaid using the proceeds of a long-term debt issue. Ms. Peele gets rate quotes from several different London banks. The best quote is:

Variable	Fixed
LIBOR + 150 bp	8.5%

Each of these loans would require quarterly interest payments on the outstanding loan amount. Peele looks up the current LIBOR rate and finds that it is 5.60 percent. The variable rate of 7.1 percent (5.60 + 1.5) looks very attractive, but Peele is concerned about interest rate risk over the next two years.

A. What could Peele do to take advantage of the lower variable rate while at the same time have the comfort of fixed rate financing?

Peele could hedge each of the anticipated interest rate adjustments using the Eurodollar futures contract. This would be a strip hedge. She would sell $10 million three-month Eurodollar futures contracts with expirations in the months when interest rates are adjusted. For longer-term loans, this can present a problem. Contracts may not be traded with the proper expiration date, or the market may be very thin making it difficult to find a counterparty. Alternatively, Peele could employ a stack hedge. In this case, she would stack the hedges for all interest rate adjustments on a single contract whose expiration is not so far into the future. For example, she could sell $70 million Eurodollars futures contracts with expiration in the month of the first interest rate adjustment.

B. Consider the following three-month Eurodollar quotes:

Delivery Month	Rate
AUGx0	94.32
SEP	94.34
OCT	94.31
NOV	94.33
DEC	94.35
JANx1	94.43
MAR	94.40
JUN	94.43
SEP	94.40
DEC	94.25
MARx2	94.30
JUN	94.27
SEP	94.23
DEC	94.15

Handcraft Ale takes out a floating rate note with the first interest rate adjustment coming in December. LIBOR at the time of loan initiation is 5.70 percent. Design a strip hedge to convert the Handcraft Ale floating rate note to a fixed rate note. What is the anticipated fixed rate?

Peele would hedge each of her interest rate adjustments by selling $10 million of three-month Eurodollars in the following months:

Expiration	Price	Anticipated Loan Rate
DEC	94.35	7.15
MARx1	94.40	7.10
JUN	94.43	7.07
SEP	94.40	7.10
DEC	94.25	7.25
MARx2	94.30	7.20
JUN	94.27	7.23

The anticipated loan rate for each adjustment date is computed as:

$$\text{Anticipated Rate} = 100 - \frac{\text{Price}}{100} + 1.5$$

While the hedge is not the same as pure fixed rate financing, there is very little variation anticipated. The range of anticipated rates is from 7.07 to 7.25 percent. The average rate over the life of the loan is 7.15 percent, including the initial period.

C. Suppose that Handcraft Ale's quarterly interest payments were in November, February, May, and August. Would a strip hedge be possible? Design a hedge that Peele could use in this case.

If Handcraft's interest payment cycle were November, February, May and August, Ms. Peele would have a problem. It would only be possible to match the timing of the nearest interest rate adjustment. This is a situation in which Ms. Peele could use a stack hedge. She would stack hedge all seven interest rate adjustments by selling $70 million in Eurodollar futures with November expiration. In November Handcraft would make its interest payment. At that time there will be a market for February Eurodollars, and Ms. Peele would stack the six remaining interest rate adjustments on the February contract. This process would continue until maturity with each interest rate adjustment reducing the size of the subsequent stack hedge by $10 million. Alternatively, Ms. Peele could hedge each rate adjustment using the Eurodollar futures contract that expires in the month just following the date the interest rate adjustment is made.

23. Jim Hunter is preparing to hedge his investment firm's decision to purchase $100 million of 90-day T-bills 60 days from now in June. The discount yield on the 60-day T-bill is 6.1 percent, and the June T-bill futures contract is trading at 94.80. Jim views these rates as very attractive relative to recent history, and he would like to lock them in. His first impulse is to buy 100 June T-bill futures contracts, but his recent experience leads him to believe that he should be buying something less.

A. Why is a one-to-one hedge ratio inappropriate in Jim's situation?

A one-to-one hedge ratio is not appropriate because the daily settlement gains and losses can be invested or must be financed. If no interest were earned on settlement cash flows, then a one-to-one hedge would be appropriate because the settlement cash flows would exactly offset the change in value of the underlying instrument. Because interest can be earned on the settlement cash flows, the delivery date value of the settlement cash flows will not exactly equal the change in value of the underlying instrument. The terminal value of the settlement cash flows will exceed, in magnitude, the change in value of the underlying instrument. The difference will be the interest earned and/or assessed between the settlement date and the delivery date.

B. Compute an appropriate hedge ratio given the market conditions faced by Jim.

The hedge ratio is slightly reduced to account for the interest that can be earned between daily settlement and the delivery date. This is called tailing the hedge. The amount by which the hedge is reduced is called the tailing factor. The tailing factor is the present value factor between the settlement date and the delivery date. When Jim initiates the hedge, the discount yield for the 60-day T-bill (his hedging time horizon) is 6.1 percent. Computing the tailing factor, which is the price per $1 of face value, we have:

$$\text{Tailing Factor} = 1 - \frac{.061 \times 60}{360} = 0.9898$$

The tailed hedge for the $100 million of 90-day T-bills to be purchased in two months is:

$$\text{Tailed Hedge} = \$100(0.9898) = \$98.98 \text{ million}$$

Jim would buy 99 June T-bill futures contracts.

C. Under what conditions might Jim need to adjust his hedge ratio between now and June?

The tailing factor is a function of the time to delivery and the level of interest rates. If interest rates change significantly, then Jim might need to adjust the hedge. The longer the time to settlement, the more influential interest rate movements will be. Even if interest rates do not move, the passage of time will call for adjustment, as the tailing factor will move toward the value of one on the delivery date.

24. Alex Brown has just returned from a seminar on using futures for hedging purposes. As a result of what he has learned, he reexamines his decision to hedge $500 million of long-term debt that his firm plans to issue in May. His current hedge is a short position of 5,000 T-bond futures contracts ($100,000 each). If the debt could be issued today, it would be priced at 119-22 to yield 6.5 percent. With its 8 percent coupon and 30 years to maturity, the duration of the debt would be 13.09 years. On the futures side, the futures prices are based on the cheapest-to-deliver bonds, which are trading at 124-14 to yield 5.6 percent. These bonds have a duration of 9.64 years.

A. List and briefly describe possible strategies Alex Brown could use to hedge his impending debt issue.

There are a number of different methods Alex could employ to hedge his impending debt issue:

Face Value Naive Model: In this method, Alex would trade one dollar of nominal futures contract per one dollar of debt face value. The major benefit of this method is the ease of implementation. Unfortunately, it ignores market values and the differential responses of the bond and futures contract prices to interest rates.

Market Value Naive Model: In this method, Alex would hedge one dollar of debt market value using one dollar of futures price value. That is, the hedge ratio is determined by the market prices instead of nominal and face values. Unfortunately, it does not consider the price sensitivities of the two instruments.

Conversion Factor Model: This model can be used when the hedging instrument is a T-note or T-bond futures contract. The conversion factor adjusts the prices of deliverable bonds and notes that do not have an 8 percent coupon to make them "equivalent" to the 8 percent coupon bond or note that is called for in the contract. The hedge ratio is determined by multiplying the face value naive hedge ratio by the conversion factor. The appropriate conversion factor to use is the conversion factor of the cheapest-to-deliver T-bond or T-note. This model still ignores price sensitivity differences between the hedging and hedged instruments.

Basis Point Model: This model uses the price changes of the futures and cash positions resulting from a one-basis-point change in yields to determine the hedge ratio. It is calculated as:

$$HR = -\frac{BPC_C}{BPC_F}$$

This model works well if the cash and futures instruments face the same rate volatility. If they face different volatilities and that relationship can be quantified, then the basis point model can be adjusted to account for the differing volatilities.

Regression Model: In the regression model, the historic relationship between cash market price changes and futures market price changes is estimated. This estimation is accomplished by regressing price changes in the cash market on futures price changes. The slope coefficient from this regression is then used as the hedge ratio. Alex may not find this model useful, as he is trying to hedge a new debt issue. Even if Alex had a historic price stream on 30-year corporate debt issues, the historic relationship with the futures price might prove to be an unreliable indicator of the present or future relationship. This stems from the fact that the price response of the futures contract is determined by the cheapest-to-deliver bond. The cheapest-to-deliver bond can vary in maturity from 15 years to 30 years. This means that the futures contract can have very different price responses to interest rates at different points in time.

Price Sensitivity Model: This may be a good model for Alex to use. It is designed for interest rate hedging, and it accounts for the differential price responses of the hedging and the hedged instruments. The model is duration-based so that it accounts for maturity and coupon rate differences of the cash and the futures positions. It is computed as:

$$N = -\frac{P_i MD_i}{FP_F MD_F} RYC$$

where:

FP_F and P_i are the respective futures contract and cash instrument prices;

MD_i and MD_F are the modified durations for the cash and futures instruments, respectively, and RYC is the change in the cash market yield relative to the change in the futures yield

B. What strategy is Alex Brown currently using? What are the strengths and weaknesses of this strategy?

Currently Alex has employed a face value naive hedge. For each dollar of debt principal he plans to issue, he is short $1 of nominal T-bond futures. The benefit of the strategy is its ease of implementation. The drawback is that the cash instrument and the T-bond futures may have differential price responses to interest rate changes.

C. Based on the knowledge Alex gained at the hedging seminar, he feels that a price sensitivity hedge would be most appropriate for his situation. Design a hedge using the price sensitivity method. Assume that the relative volatility between the corporate interest rate and the T-bond interest rate, RYC, is equal to one.

The price sensitivity hedge ratio is:

$$N = -\frac{P_i\, MD_i}{FP_F\, MD_F}\, RYC$$

$FP_F = 124.4375\% \times .1$ million $MD_F = 9.128788$
$P_i = 119.6875\% \times 500$ million $MD_i = 12.29108$

$$N = -\frac{\$598,437,500 \times 12.29108}{\$124,437.50 \times 9.128788} = -6,475 \text{ contracts}$$

To hedge the risk, 6,475 contracts should be sold.

D. At the time of refinancing, the T-bond futures price is 121-27 and B.I.G.'s new debt issue is priced at 116-08. Compute the net wealth change resulting from the naive hedge.

In the cash market, Alex suffers an opportunity loss because he anticipated issuing debt at 119-22, but he is only to get 116-08 for the debt. The opportunity loss is:

Opportunity Loss = $(1.1625 - 1.196875)$ \$500,000,000 = −\$17,187,500

In the futures market, Alex realizes a gain because he was short T-bond futures. His gain is:

Futures Gain = $(1.244375 - 1.2184375)$ \$500,000,000 = \$12,968,750

Net Wealth Change = −\$17,187,500 + \$12,968,750 = −\$4,218,750

E. Compute the net wealth change resulting from the price sensitivity hedge.

Examining the price sensitivity hedge, the cash market loss will still be \$17,187,500. The futures market gain will now be:

Futures Gain = $(1.244375 - 1.2184375)$ \$647,500,000 = \$16,794,531

Net Wealth Change = −\$17,187,500 + \$16,794,531 = −\$392,969

The price sensitivity hedge is much more effective than the face value naive hedge at reducing the risk.

7 Stock Index Futures: Introduction

Answers to Questions and Problems

1. Assume that the DJIA stands at 8340.00 and the current divisor is 0.25. One of the stocks in the index is priced at $100.00 and it splits 2:1. Based on this information, answer the following questions:

   a. What is the sum of the prices of all the shares in the index before the stock split?

   The equation for computing the index is:

   $$\text{Index} = \frac{\sum_{i=1}^{N} P_i}{\text{Divisor}}$$

   If the index value is 8340.00 and the divisor is 0.25, the sum of the prices must be 8340.00(0.25) = $2,085.00.

   b. What is the value of the index after the split? Explain.

   After the split, the index value is still 8340.00. The whole purpose of the divisor technique is to keep the index value unchanged for events such as stock splits.

   c. What is the sum of the prices of all the shares in the index after the split?

   The stock that was $100 is now $50, so the sum of the share prices is now $2,035.00.

   d. What is the divisor after the split?

   With the new sum of share prices at $2,035.00, the divisor must be 0.244005 to maintain the index value at 8340.00.

2. What is the main difference in the calculation of the DJIA and the S&P 500 index? Explain.

   The S&P 500 index gives a weight to each represented share that is proportional to the market value of the outstanding shares. The DJIA simply adds the prices of all of the individual shares, so the DJIA effectively weights each stock by its price level.

3. For the S&P 500 index, assume that the company with the highest market value has a 1 percent increase in stock prices. Also, assume that the company with the smallest market value has a 1 percent decrease in the price of its shares. Does the index change? If so, in what direction?

   The index value increases. The share with the higher market value has a greater weight in the index than the share with the smallest market value. Therefore, the 1 percent increase on the high market value share more than offsets the 1 percent decrease on the low market value share.

4. The S&P 500 futures is scheduled to expire in half a year, and the interest rate for carrying stocks over that period is 11 percent. The expected dividend rate on the underlying stocks for the same period is 2 percent of the value of the stocks. (The 2 percent is the half-year rate, not an annual rate.) Ignoring the interest that it might be possible to earn on the dividend payments, find the fair value for the futures if the current value of the index is 945.00.

   Assuming the half-year rate is .11/2, the fair value is:

   $$\text{Fair Value} = 945.00(1.055 - .02) = 978.075$$

   Assuming semiannual compounding, the interest factor would be 1.0536, and the fair value would be:

   $$\text{Fair Value} = 945.00(1.0536 - .02) = 976.752$$

5. Consider a very simple index like the DJIA, except assume that it has only two shares, A and B. The price of A is $100.00, and B trades for $75.00. The current index value is 175.00. The futures contract based on this index expires in three months, and the cost of carrying the stocks forward is .75 percent per month. This is also the interest rate that you can earn on invested funds. You expect Stock A to pay a $3 dividend in one month and Stock B to pay a $1 dividend in two months. Find the fair value of the futures. Assume monthly compounding.

   $$\text{Fair Value} = 175.00(1.0075)^3 - \$3(1.0075)^2 - \$1(1.0075) = 174.91$$

6. Using the same data as in problem 5, now assume that the futures trades at 176.00. Explain how you would trade with this set of information. Show your transactions.

   At 176.00, the futures is overpriced. Therefore, the trader should sell the futures, buy the stocks and carry them forward to expiration, investing the dividend payments as they are received. At expiration, the total cost incurred to carry the stocks forward is 174.91, and the trader receives 176.00 as cash settlement, for a profit of 1.09 index units. (This ignores interest on daily settlement flows.)

7. Using the same data as in problem 5, now assume that the futures trades at 174.00. Explain how you would trade with this set of information. Show your transactions.

   At 174.00 the futures is underpriced. Therefore, the trader should buy the futures and sell the stocks short, investing the proceeds. The trader will have to borrow to pay the dividends on the two shares. At expiration, the total outlays, counting interest, have been:

   $$\$175.00(1.0075)^3 - \$3(1.0075)^2 - \$1(1.0075) = 174.91$$

   With the convergence at expiration, the trader can buy the stocks for 174.00 and return them against the short sale. This gives a profit of $.91.

8. For a stock index and a stock index futures constructed like the DJIA, assume that the dividend rate expected to be earned on the stocks in the index is the same as the cost of carrying the stocks forward. What should be the relationship between the cash and futures market prices? Explain.

   The cash and futures prices should be the same. In essence, an investment in the index costs the interest rate to carry forward. This cost is offset by the proceeds from the dividends. If these are equal, the effective cost of carrying the stocks in the index forward is zero, and the cash and futures prices should then be the same.

9. Your portfolio is worth $100 million and has a beta of 1.08 measured against the S&P futures, which is priced at 350.00. Explain how you would hedge this portfolio, assuming that you wish to be fully hedged.

The hedge ratio is:

$$\left(\frac{V_P}{V_F}\right)\beta_P = \text{Number of Contracts}$$

With our data, we have:

$$\left(\frac{\$100,000,000}{(350.00)(500)}\right)1.08 = 617.14$$

The cash value of the futures contract is 500 times the index value of 350.00, or $175,000. Therefore, the complete hedge is to sell 617 contracts.

10. You have inherited $50 million, but the estate will not settle for six months and you will not actually receive the cash until that time. You find current stock values attractive and you plan to invest in the S&P 500 cash portfolio. Explain how you would hedge this anticipated investment using S&P 500 futures.

Buy S&P 500 index futures as a temporary substitute for actually investing the cash in the stock market. Probably the best strategy is to buy the contract that expires closest in time to the expected date for receiving the cash. If the S&P 500 index value is 300.00, then the dollar value of one contract will be $150,000 (300.00 × $500). Therefore, you should achieve a good hedge by purchasing about 333 ($50,000,000/$150,000) contracts.

11. William's new intern, Jessica, is just full of questions. She is particularly inquisitive about stock index futures. She notices that the futures price is consistently higher than the current index level and that the difference gets smaller as the contracts near their expiration dates.

A. Explain the relationship between the futures price, the spot price, interest rates, and dividends.

The futures contract effectively allows one to commit to the sale or the purchase of the Dow index stocks at a specific point in the future at a price agreed upon today. There are costs and benefits related to using the futures market as opposed to the cash market to buy the Dow index stocks. Take, for example, an individual who wishes to own the Dow stocks in three months. Her alternatives are to:

1. buy the stocks today and hold them, or
2. buy a futures contract with three months to delivery.

The benefit of using the futures contract is that there is no cash outlay today. The purchase price of the stocks can be invested for three months to earn interest. The downside of using the futures contract is that since the stocks are not held over the next three months, no dividends are received. This suggests the following relationship between the spot and the futures market prices:

$$F_{0,t} = S_0(1+C) - \sum_{i=1}^{N} D_i(1+r_i)$$

where:
$F_{0,t}$ is the futures price today for delivery at time t,
S_0 is the spot price for the index today,

C is the cost-of-carry,

D_i is the Ith dividend paid between now and time t, and

r_i is the rate of return received on the Ith dividend between the payment date and time t.

In general, the dividend yield is smaller than the cost-of-carry, so the index futures markets are generally normal (futures index above the spot index). As the delivery date approaches, the futures index converges to the spot index.

B. Jessica asks William to explain the Dow index to her. What type of index is the Dow? How is it constructed? How could she build a portfolio of stocks to replicate it?

The Dow is a price weighted index. The stocks are represented in the index in proportion to their price. The index is computed as:

$$\text{Dow Index} = \frac{\sum_{i=1}^{30} P_i}{\text{Divisor}}$$

where the P_i's are the prices of the stocks comprising the Dow, and the Divisor is a number used to compute the "average."

When the Dow first appeared with 30 stocks in 1928 (the Dow was first published in 1884 with 11 stocks), the divisor was 30. As stocks split or the components of the Dow changed, the divisor was adjusted to maintain continuity in the index. To form a portfolio that would replicate the Dow, Jessica should buy an equal number of shares of each stock in the Dow.

C. Jessica wants a numerical example of the relationship between a price weighted index and the futures contract based on that index. She supposes the following example. A futures contract is based on a price weighted index of three stocks, A, B, and C. The futures contract expires in three months. Stock A pays a dividend at the end of the first month, and Stock C pays a dividend at the end of month two. The term structure is flat over this time period with the monthly interest rate equal to 0.5 percent. The stock prices and dividends are summarized below.

Stock	Price	Dividend
A	$30	$0.11 in one month
B	$50	$0
C	$40	$0.15 in two months

Compute the index assuming a divisor of 3. How many shares of each stock should be bought to replicate the index?

The index is computed as:

$$\text{Index} = \frac{\sum_{i=1}^{3} P_i}{\text{Divisor}} = \frac{30 + 50 + 40}{3} = 40$$

To replicate the index, you would buy $\dfrac{1}{\text{Divisor}}$ shares of each stock. In our example, one-third share of each stock would replicate the index.

D. Suppose the divisor had been 0.5. Compute the index. How many shares of each stock must be bought to replicate the index?

With the divisor equal to 0.5, the index is:

$$\text{Index} = \frac{\sum\limits_{i=1}^{3} P_i}{\text{Divisor}} = \frac{30+50+40}{0.5} = 240$$

The number of shares of each stock to buy to replicate the index is $\frac{1}{0.5} = 2$. Two shares of each stock will replicate the index.

E. Assuming the divisor is 0.5, compute the fair value for the three-month futures contract.

The fair market value is computed using:

$$F_{0,t} = S_0(1+C) - \sum_{i=1}^{N} D_i(1+r_i)$$

$$F_{0,t} = 240(1+0.005)^3 - 2(0.11)(1.005)^2 - 2(0.15)(1.005)$$

$$F_{0,t} = 243.09$$

F. Right now the Dow Jones Industrial Average is at 8635. Its dividend yield is 1.76 percent. The 90-day T-bill rate is 5.6 percent bond equivalent yield. Compute a fair price today for the index futures contract expiring in 90 days.

For an index composed of a large number of securities, it is sometimes helpful to express the relationship between the futures and spot indexes as:

$$F_{0,t} = S_0(1 + C - \text{DIVYLD})$$

where DIVYLD is the dividend yield on the index stocks.

The fair price for the futures contract expiring in 90 days is:

$$F_{0,t} = S_0(1+C-\text{DIVYLD}) = 8,635\left(1 + \frac{0.056 \times 90}{365} - \frac{0.0176 \times 90}{365}\right)$$

$$F_{0,t} = 8,717$$

12. Casey Mathers manages the $60 million equity portion of Zeta Corporation's pension assets. This past Friday, August 7th, Zeta announced that it was downsizing its workforce and would be offering early retirement to many of its older employees. The impact on the portfolio Casey manages would be an anticipated $10 million withdrawal over the next four months. The stock market has been good for the past five years, but recently there have been signs of weakness. Casey is concerned about a drop in asset prices before the $10 million is withdrawn from the portfolio. Casey runs a fairly aggressive portfolio with a beta of 1.2, relative to the S&P 500 index. Casey sees the following S&P 500 index futures prices:

Expiration	Contract Value $250 × Index
SEP	1088.50
DEC	1100.00
MARx1	1110.50

A. How much of the portfolio should Casey hedge? Justify your answer.

Casey anticipates $10 million being withdrawn from the portfolio over the next four months. Casey is concerned about the risk that falling stock prices will result in more shares having to be sold to raise the $10 million. It is just the anticipated withdrawal that should be hedged.

B. Design a hedge based on your answer to part A above.

To hedge the risk, Casey should use the futures contract with expiration as soon after the anticipated withdrawal as possible. This would be the December futures contract. Since Casey's portfolio has a beta of 1.2 relative to the S&P 500, Casey should sell $1.2 of future contract value per $1 of portfolio hedged. Then the number of contracts to trade is computed by:

$$N = \frac{V_P}{V_F}(\beta_P) = \frac{\$10,000,000}{(1100)\$250}(1.2) = 43.6 \text{ contracts}$$

To hedge the risk of the $10 million withdrawal, Casey should sell 44 contracts. As the assets are withdrawn from the portfolio, the hedge should be gradually unwound. The transactions would be as follows:

Date	Cash Market	Futures Market
Today	Anticipate the withdrawal of $10 million from the portfolio over the next four months.	Sell 44 December S&P 500 futures contracts.
Between now and December	Sell securities to meet portfolio withdrawal demands.	Enter reverse trades to unwind the hedge as assets are withdrawn from portfolio.

13. Byron Hendrickson manages the $30 million equity portion of Fredrick and Sons' pension plan assets. Byron has been trying to get the management of Fredrick and Sons to move more of their assets from their fixed income portfolio (market value of $60 million) to the equity portfolio in order to achieve the objectives that management had set forth for growth of the plan. Management has decided to invest the proceeds of several bond issues that will be maturing over the next three months. The total proceeds from the bond issues will be $10 million. It is now December 15th. Byron believes that the January price runup will be particularly strong this year. Since his portfolio is not particularly aggressive, beta equal to 0.85, he would really like to have that $10 million working for him in January. Design a hedge that will prevent Byron from missing the January action, based on the following current market prices for the S&P 500 index futures:

Expiration	Contract Value $250 × Index
MAR	1157.00
JUN	1170.80

Byron wishes to commit $10 million to the stock market today, but the cash will not be available until March. Byron should make a long hedge using the March S&P 500 futures index. The number of contracts Byron should buy is computed as:

$$N = \frac{\$10,000,000}{(1157)\$250}(.85) = 29.4 \text{ contracts}$$

Byron should buy 29 March S&P futures contracts. This will generate gains to replace the opportunity loss from not having the $10 million invested between now and March. As the bonds mature and the proceeds are transferred to the equity side, the hedge should be unwound. Byron's transactions are summarized below.

Date	Cash Market	Futures Market
Today	Anticipate the investment of $10 million into the equity portfolio over the next three months.	Buy 29 March S&P 500 futures index contracts.
March	Buy stocks using $10 million plus any gains/losses from the futures position.	Unwind the futures position as the investments are made into the equity portfolio.

Stock Index Futures: Refinements

8

Answers to Questions and Problems

1. Explain the market conditions that cause deviations from a computed fair value price and that give rise to no-arbitrage bounds.

   The villains are market imperfections, principally transaction costs. When trading is sufficiently costly, the futures price can deviate somewhat from fair value, and no market forces will arise to drive the futures price back to its fair value. The greater the costs of trading, the farther the futures price can stray from its theoretical fair value without arbitrage coming into play to restore the relationship. These trading costs include: the bid-asked spread and direct transaction costs such as brokerage commissions and taxes. Also, restrictions on the use of the proceeds from short sales can be important.

2. The no-dividend index consists only of stocks that pay no dividends. Assume that the two stocks in the index are priced at $100 and $48, and assume that the corresponding cash index value is 74.00. The cost of carrying stocks is 1 percent per month. What is the fair value of a futures contract on the index that expires in one year?

$$\text{Fair Value} = 74.00(1.01)^{12} = 83.3851$$

3. Using the same facts as in problem 2, assume that the round-trip transaction cost on a futures is $30. The contract size, we now assume, is for 1,000 shares of each stock. Trading stocks costs $.05 per share to buy and the same amount to sell. Based on this additional information, compute the no-arbitrage bounds for the futures price.

   From the cash-and-carry transactions, we would buy the stocks, carry them to expiration, and sell the futures. This strategy would cost:

Purchase and carry stock:	$-\$148,000(1.01)^{12} = -\$166,770$
Stock transaction cost:	$+ 1,000(2)(\$.05) = -\$100$
Futures transaction cost:	$-\$30$
Total Outlay:	$-\$166,900$

   For this strategy to generate a profit, the futures must exceed 83.450 per contract. For the reverse cash-and-carry, we would sell the stocks, invest the proceeds, and buy the futures:

Sell stock; invest proceeds:	$\$148,000(1.01)^{12} = \$166,770$
Stock transaction cost:	$1,000(2)(\$.05) = -\$100$
Futures transaction cost:	$-\$30$
Total Inflow:	$-\$166,640$

   For this strategy to generate a profit, the futures must be less than 83.320 per contract. The no-arbitrage bounds on the futures range from 83.320 to 83.450.

4. Using the facts in problems 2 and 3, we now consider differential borrowing and lending costs. Assume that the 1 percent per month is the lending rate, and assume that the borrowing rate is 1.5 percent per month. What are the no-arbitrage bounds on the futures price now?

From the cash-and-carry transactions, we would buy the stocks, carry them to expiration, and sell the futures. Now the financing cost is 1.5 percent per month. This strategy would cost:

Purchase and carry stock:	$- \$148,000(1.015)^{12} = - \$176,951$
Stock transaction cost:	$+ 1,000(2)(\$.05) = - \$100$
Futures transaction cost:	$- \$30$
Total Outlay:	$- \$176,821$

For this strategy to generate a profit, the futures must exceed 88.411 per contract. The reverse cash-and-carry strategy is unaffected because the lending rate is still 1 percent. Therefore, the no-arbitrage bounds on the futures range from 83.320 to 88.411.

5. Using the facts in problems 2–4, assume now that the short seller receives the use of only half of the funds in the short sale. Find the no-arbitrage bounds.

The cash-and-carry transactions are the same as in problem 4 so they give an upper no-arbitrage bound of 88.411. For the reverse cash-and-carry, we would sell the stocks, invest the proceeds, and buy the futures:

Sell stock; invest 50% of proceeds:	$+ \$74,000(1.01)^{12} = \$83,385$
Stock transaction cost:	$- 1,000(2)(\$.05) = - \$100$
Futures transaction cost:	$-\$30$
Recoup 50% of unused funds:	$+ \$74,000$
Total Inflow:	$+ \$157,255$

For this strategy to generate a profit, the futures must be less than 78.628 per contract. The no-arbitrage bounds on the futures range from 78.628 to 88.411.

6. Consider the trading of stocks in an index and trading futures based on the index. Explain how different transaction costs in the two markets might cause one market to reflect information more rapidly than the other.

Let us assume that it is more costly to trade the individual stocks represented in the index than it is to trade the futures based on the index. (Once in a while we assume something consistent with reality.) Traders with information about the future direction of stock prices will want to exploit that information as cheaply as possible. Therefore, they will be likely to trade futures rather than the stocks in the index. Trading futures causes the futures price to adjust, and through arbitrage links, the stock price adjusts to the new futures price. In this scenario, the futures market reflects the new information before the stock market does.

7. For index arbitrage, explain how implementing the arbitrage through program trading helps to reduce execution risk.

Execution risk is the risk that the actual trade price will not equal the anticipated trade price. The discrepancy arises largely from the delay between order entry and order execution. By using program trading, orders are conveyed to the floor more quickly and receive more rapid execution. (At least this is true in the absence of exchange-imposed delays on program trades.) Therefore, the use of program trading techniques should help to reduce execution risk.

8. Index arbitragers must consider the dividends that will be paid between the present and the futures expiration. Explain how overestimating the dividends that will be received could affect a cash-and-carry arbitrage strategy.

Assume a trader estimates a dividend rate that is higher than the actual dividend rate that will be achieved. Further assume that the market as a whole correctly forecasts the dividend rate. For this investor, a strategy of cash-and-carry arbitrage will appear to be more attractive than it really is. This trader will be expecting to receive more dividends than will actually be forthcoming, so the trader will underestimate the net cost of carrying stocks forward. This overestimate of the dividend rate could lead the trader to expect a profit from the trade that will evaporate when adjusted for the actual dividends that will be received.

9. Explain the difference between the beta in the capital asset pricing model and the beta one finds by regressing stock returns against returns on a stock index.

The beta of the CAPM is a theoretical entity. The CAPM beta is a measure based on the relationship between a particular security and an unobserved and probably unobservable market portfolio. The beta estimated by regressing stock returns against the returns on an index is an estimate of that ideal CAPM beta. Because the index fails to capture the true market portfolio, the actually estimated beta must fail to capture the true CAPM beta. Nonetheless, the estimated beta may be a useful approximation of the true CAPM beta.

10. Explain the difference between an ex-ante and an ex-post minimum risk hedge ratio.

The ex-ante minimum risk hedge ratio is estimated using historical data. In hedging practice, this estimated hedge ratio is applied to a future time period. Almost certainly the hedge ratio that would have minimized risk in the future period (the ex-post hedge ratio) will not equal the estimated ex-ante hedge ratio. However, the ex-post minimum risk hedge ratio can only be known after the fact. Therefore, we must expect some inaccuracy in estimating a hedge ratio ex-ante and comparing it with the ideal ex-post hedge ratio.

11. Assume you hold a well-diversified portfolio with a beta of 0.85. How would you trade futures to raise the beta of the portfolio?

Buy a stock index futures. In effect, this action levers up the initial investment in stocks, effectively raising the beta of the stock investment. In principle, this levering up can continue to give any level of beta a trader desires.

12. An index fund is a mutual fund that attempts to replicate the returns on a stock index, such as the S&P 500. Assume you are the manager of such a fund and that you are fully invested in stocks. Measured against the S&P 500 index, your portfolio has a beta of 1.0. How could you transform this portfolio into one with a zero beta without trading stocks?

Sell S&P 500 index futures in an amount equal to the value of your stock portfolio. After this transaction, you are effectively long the index (your stock holdings) and short the index by the same amount (your short position in the futures). As a result, you are effectively out of the stock market, and the beta of such a position must be zero.

13. You hold a portfolio consisting of only T-bills. Explain how to trade futures to create a portfolio that behaves like the S&P 500 stock index.

Buy S&P 500 index futures. You should buy an amount of futures that equals the value of funds invested in T-bills. The resulting portfolio will replicate a portfolio that is fully invested in the S&P 500.

14. In portfolio insurance using stock index futures, we noted that a trader sells additional futures as the value of the stocks falls. Explain why traders follow this practice.

The goal of portfolio insurance is to keep the value of a portfolio from falling below a certain level or, alternatively expressed, to ensure that the return achieved on a portfolio over a given horizon achieves a certain minimum level. At the same time, portfolio insurance seeks to retain as much potential for beating that minimum return as is possible. The difference between the portfolio's current value and the value it must have to meet the minimum target we will call the *cushion*. If the portfolio has no cushion, the only way to ensure that the portfolio will achieve the target return, or the target value, is for the portfolio to be fully hedged.

We now consider the trader's response if the portfolio value is above the minimum level, that is, if there is some cushion and stock prices fall. The drop in stock prices reduces the cushion, so the trader must move to a somewhat more conservative position. This requires hedging a greater portion of the portfolio, which the trader does by selling futures. Therefore, an initial drop in prices requires the selling of futures, and each subsequent drop in prices requires the sale of more futures.

15. Casey Mathers, manager of the Zeta Corporation's equity portfolio, hires a new assistant, Alec. Alec is pretty sharp and immediately questions Casey's decision to hedge an anticipated $10 million withdrawal. Casey had hedged the portfolio using the S&P 500 index futures contract. In calculating the hedge, Casey used the portfolio beta of 1.2, which was computed using the S&P 500 index.

A. Explain to Casey why his hedge may not be a risk-minimization hedge.

Casey's hedge may not be a risk-minimization hedge because the beta used in calculating the hedge ratio was computed using the S&P 500 index. It is the index futures contract, though, that is used for hedging. So theoretically the portfolio's beta computed using the futures contract prices is what should be used in calculating the hedge. Additionally, the S&P 500 index futures contract is not the only possible hedging vehicle available. For example, there are the Dow Jones Industrial Average index futures and the NYSE Composite index futures. The portfolio's returns may be more highly correlated with one of these other contracts than with the S&P 500 index futures contract.

Alec calculates possible risk-minimizing betas for the Zeta portfolio using the S&P 500 index futures, the Dow Jones Industrial Average futures, and the NYSE Composite index futures, with the following results:

	S&P 500 Index Futures	DJIA Futures	NYSE Composite Index Futures
Contract size	$250 × index	$10 × index	$500 × index
Current quote (MAR) contract	1110.59	8715.00	559.30
Beta$_{RM}$	1.30	1.35	1.10
R^2	.83	.75	.90

B. Given Alec's results, is the S&P 500 futures index the most appropriate hedging vehicle? Be sure to justify your answer.

In risk-minimization hedging, the best vehicle to use is the instrument with the highest R^2. The R^2 tells the percentage of portfolio returns that is explained by the hedging instrument's price returns. Examining the R^2 figures from Alec's results, it can be seen that the NYSE Composite index contract has the highest R^2 of 90%. This is greater than the S&P 500 contract's R^2 of 83%. The NYSE Composite contract would be the better hedging instrument according to the risk-minimization technique.

C. Design a risk-minimization hedge using Alec's results.

Using Alec's results, the risk minimizing hedge would be accomplished by selling NYSE Composite index futures. The number of contracts to sell is computed as:

$$N = \frac{\$10,000,000}{559.30(\$500)}(1.10) = 39.3 \text{ contracts}$$

Alec would recommend selling 39 contracts.

D. Will Alec's hedging strategy turn out to be superior to Casey's hedging strategy? Justify your answer.

While Alec's hedging strategy will probably be superior to Casey's, this is not guaranteed, because the hedge calculation is based on historic relationships that are measured with error. This relationship will not hold exactly in the future.

16. Raymond J. Johnson, Jr. manages a $20 million equity portfolio. It has been designed to mimic the S&P 500 index. Ray has a hunch that the market is going south during the coming month. He has decided that he wants to eliminate his exposure for the next month and take off for Montana to go fishing. Ray has the following information at hand:

S&P 500 index futures with 1 month to delivery:	1084.50
Dividend yield on Ray's portfolio:	2.1%
S&P 500 index today:	1081.40

A. Design a hedge to eliminate Ray's market risk for the next month.

Ray, in effect, would like to sell his portfolio for a month and put the money into T-bills. The transactions costs make this strategy cost-prohibitive, though. Alternatively, Ray could sell futures contracts. Then, over the next month, any losses in the cash market will be offset by gains in the futures market. To eliminate his exposure to the market, Ray would calculate the number of S&P 500 futures contracts as:

$$N = \frac{20,000,000}{(1084.50)(\$250)}(1) = 73.8 \text{ contracts}$$

Ray should sell 74 S&P 500 futures contracts.

B. Compute the return he can expect to receive over the next month.

The futures index pricing relationship is:

$$F_{0,\,t} = S_0\,(1 + C - \text{DIVYLD})$$

where:
$F_{0,\,t}$ = index futures value
S_0 = spot price
C = cost-of-carry
DIVYLD = dividend yield

The cost-of-carry can also be viewed as an implied repo rate. This is the return Ray will receive over the next month:

$$C = \left(\frac{F_{0,t}}{S_0} + \text{DIV} - 1\right)12$$

$$C = \left(\frac{74(1084.50)(250)}{20,000,000} + \frac{.021}{12} - 1\right)12$$

$$C = 5.9\%$$

Ray can expect to earn a 5.9% annual return over the next month.

17. Remember Ray? He is the guy running the S&P 500 index fund who wanted to go fishing. Ray has changed his mind. The fishing reports from Montana were not favorable so he has decided not to go. Since he is not leaving, he decides to devise a portfolio insurance strategy for his $20 million portfolio. His objective is to not let his portfolio value fall below $18 million.

A. Design a portfolio insurance strategy that applies no hedges for portfolio values at or above $20 million and is fully hedged at or below $18 million.

Portfolio insurance is a dynamic hedging strategy that applies hedges as the hedged asset falls in value and removes hedges as the hedged asset increases in value. When the asset value is falling, hedges are applied until the assets are fully hedged. Theoretically a money manager could prevent the value of his positions from falling below some prespecified level because further decline in the assets' value is offset by futures gains. Ray wishes to apply hedges as the value of this portfolio falls from $20 million (no hedges) down to $18 million (fully hedged). Assume that Ray will apply the hedges in a linear fashion. That is, the percentage of assets hedged will be given by:

$$\% \text{ hedged} = \max\left(\left[\frac{20 - \max(V_P, 18)}{20 - 18}\right], 0\right)$$

When $V_P < 18$, the percentage of the portfolio hedged is 100 percent. When $V_P > 20$, the percentage of the portfolio hedged is 0 percent.

B. On day one, the stock portfolio value falls from $20 million to $19.4 million, and the S&P 500 futures price falls to 1052. What action should Ray take?

If the portfolio value falls from $20 million to 19.4 million on day one, the percentage of the assets that should be hedged is:

$$\% \text{ hedged} = \left(\left[\frac{20 - \max(19.4, 18)}{20 - 18}\right], 0\right)$$
$$\% \text{ hedged} = 30\%$$

Thirty percent of the assets should be hedged. This can be accomplished by selling contracts calculated as follows:

$$N = \frac{19,400,000}{(1052)\$250}(.30)(1) = 22.13$$

At the end of day one, Ray should sell 22 S&P 500 futures contracts.

C. On day two, the value of Ray's portfolio increases by 2 percent. The S&P 500 futures contract increases to 1073. What would be the change in value of Ray's portfolio (including any hedges that may be in place)? What action should Ray take?

Cash Market Gain:	Assets increase by 2% to $19,788,000
Future Market Loss:	22 (1052 − 1073) ($250) = − $115,500
End of Day Two Assets:	$19,788,000 − $115,500 = $19,672,500

The change in value of Ray's portfolio on day two is $272,500. Part of the portfolio must be liquidated to mark the futures contract to market. At the end of day two, Ray needs to adjust his hedge. The new percentage to hedge is:

$$\% \text{ hedged} = \frac{20 - 19.67}{20 - 18} = 16.4\%$$

The number of contracts to achieve this hedge is:

$$N = \frac{19,672,500}{1073(250)}(.164)(1) = 12.02$$

Ray is already short 22 contracts so he is overhedged. He should buy 10 S&P 500 futures contracts to bring his futures position to 12 short.

D. Is Ray really protected against his portfolio value falling below $18 million in value? Explain.

The protection Ray has depends upon several factors. First, the amount of protection depends on how closely Ray monitors his position. If Ray does not closely monitor his position, the portfolio value could fall below $18 million before Ray places a hedge. The more closely Ray monitors, and the more frequently he adjusts the hedge, the better the protection. Second, if market frictions prevent Ray from applying hedges in a timely fashion, the portfolio value could fall below $18 million. For many investors, this occurred during the stock market crash in 1987. The order flow overwhelmed the order handling and reporting systems of the stock market. Also, the price information coming from the stock markets was stale. This kind of event could mislead Ray in his hedging decision-making process. In this kind of extreme situation, Ray's assets could fall below $18 million before Ray knew it.

9 Foreign Currency Futures

Answers to Questions and Problems

1. The current spot exchange rate for the dollar against the Japanese yen is 146 yen per dollar. What is the corresponding U.S. dollar value of one yen?

   The dollar value per yen is simply the inverse of the yen per dollar rate:

   $$1/146 = \$.0068 \text{ per yen}$$

2. You hold the current editions of *The Wall Street Journal* and *The Financial Times*, the British answer to the WSJ. In the WSJ, you see that the dollar/pound 90-day forward exchange rate is $2.00 per pound. In *The Financial Times*, the pound 90-day dollar/pound rate is £.45 per U.S. dollar. Explain how you would trade to take advantage of these rates, assuming perfect markets.

   These rates are inconsistent because a rate of $2.00 per pound implies that the cost of one dollar should be £.50. Therefore, an arbitrage opportunity is available by trading as follows:

Geographical Arbitrage Transactions

***t* = 0**

In New York, using the WSJ rates, sell $2.00 for £1.00 90 days forward.	$0
In London, using *The Financial Times* rates, sell £1.00 for $2.22 90 days forward.	$0
	Total Cash Flow $0

***t* = 90**

In New York, fulfill the forward contract by delivering	– $2.00
$2.00 and collecting £1.00.	+ £1.00
In London, fulfill the forward contract by delivering £1.00	– £1.00
and collecting $2.22.	+ $2.22
	Total Cash Flow + $.22

3. In problem 2, we assumed that markets are perfect. What are some practical impediments that might frustrate your arbitrage transactions in problem 2?

   Transaction costs would be the major impediment. Every trade of foreign exchange faces a bid-asked spread. In addition, there is likely to be some commission to be paid, either in the form of an outright commission or in the form of an implicit commission for maintaining a trading function. In addition, forward contracts sometimes require margin, and this would be an additional cost that the potential arbitrageur must bear.

4. In the WSJ, you see that the spot value of the German mark is $.63 and the Swiss franc is worth $.72. What rate of exchange do these values imply for the Swiss franc and German mark? Express the value in terms of marks per franc.

   The rate of $.63 per mark implies a value of the mark equal to DM 1.5873 per $. The rate of $.72 per franc implies a value of the franc equal to SF 1.3889 per $. Therefore, DM 1.5873 and SF 1.3889 are equivalent amounts, both equal to $1. As a consequence, the value of the DM per SF must equal 1.5873/1.3889 = 1.1429.

5. Explain the difference between a pegged exchange rate system and a managed float.

In a pegged exchange rate system, the value of a pegged currency is fixed relative to another currency. For example, many Caribbean countries peg the value of their currency to the U.S. dollar. In a managed float, the value of the currency is allowed to fluctuate as market conditions require. This is the floating part of the policy. In a managed float, the central bank intervenes in the market to influence the value of the currency by buying or selling its own currency.

6. Explain why covered interest arbitrage is just like our familiar cash-and-carry transactions from Chapter 3.

In a cash-and-carry transaction, a trader sells the futures and buys the underlying good. The trader carries the underlying good to the expiration of the futures, paying the carrying cost along the way, and delivers the good against the futures. In covered interest arbitrage, the transaction has a similar structure. The trader sells the futures and buys the foreign currency. The trader carries the foreign currency to the expiration of the futures, paying the carrying cost along the way, and delivers the good against the futures. The carrying cost for the foreign currency consists of two components. First, there is the financing cost in the home currency for the funds borrowed to buy the foreign currency. Second, the foreign currency that is carried forward to delivery against the futures earns interest. This interest on the foreign currency offsets the first component of the carrying cost.

7. For covered interest arbitrage, what is the cost-of-carry? Explain carefully.

The cost-of-carry is the difference between the home currency interest rate and the foreign currency interest rate. For covered interest arbitrage, the trader borrows the home currency and pays the domestic interest rate for these funds. The trader uses these funds to buy the foreign currency in the spot market, and invests the foreign currency to earn the foreign interest rate. Therefore, the cost-of-carry is the domestic interest rate minus the foreign interest rate.

8. The spot value of the German mark is $.65, and the 90-day forward rate is $.64. If the U.S. dollar interest factor to cover this period is 2 percent, what is the German rate? What is the cost of carrying a German mark forward for this period?

From the interest rate parity theorem, we know that $1 invested in the United States must earn the same rate as the $1 converted into a foreign currency, investing at the foreign rate and converting the proceeds back into dollars via a forward contract initiated at the outset of the transactions. For our data:

$$\$1(1.02) = (\$1/\$.65)(1 + r_{DM})\$.64$$

where r_{DM} = the German interest rate for this 90-day period. Therefore, $r_{DM} = .0359$. This is also the cost to carry a German mark forward for the 90 days.

9. The French franc is worth $.21 in the spot market. The French franc futures that expires in one year trades for $.22. The U.S. dollar interest rate for this period is 10 percent. What should the French franc interest rate be?

$$1.10 = (1/.21)(1 + r_{FF}).22$$

where r_{FF} = the French franc interest rate for this period. Thus, $r_{FF} = .05$.

10. Using the data in problem 9, explain which country is expected to experience the higher inflation over the next year. If the expected inflation rate in the United States is 7 percent, what inflation rate for the French franc does this imply?

   The franc is expected to increase in value against the dollar from being worth $.21 now to $.22 in one year. Assuming PPP, this implies that the purchasing value of the dollar will decline relative to the franc.
   If the expected inflation rate in the United States is 7 percent, the real rate of interest is given by the equation:

$$1.10 = (1.07) \, (1 + r^*)$$

   where r^* is the real rate of interest in the United States, and $r^* = .028$. Assuming identical real rates in the United States and France, the expected French inflation rate is given by:

$$1.05 = [1 + E(I)](1.028)$$

   where $E(I)$ is the expected inflation rate in France, and it equals .0214.

11. Using the data of problem 9, assume that the French franc interest rate for the year is also 10 percent. Explain how you might transact faced with these values.

   Faced with the exchange rates of problem 9 and interest rates in both the United States and France of 10 percent, we could sell dollars for francs in the spot market, invest the franc proceeds at 10 percent, and arrange now to convert the franc funds in one year at the forward rate of $.22. Assuming an initial amount of $100, we would:

Dollar versus Franc Arbitrage

$t = 0$

Borrow $100 for one year at 10%.	+ $100.00
Sell $100 for FF 476.19 in the spot market.	+ FF 476.19
	– $100.00
Invest FF 476.19 at 10% in France.	– FF 476.19
Sell FF 523.81 one year forward for $115.24.	0
	Total Cash Flow $0

$t = 1$ year

Collect FF 523.81 on investment.	+ FF 523.81
Deliver FF 523.81 on forward contract; collect $115.24.	– FF 523.81
	+ $115.24
Repay debt from borrowing $100.00.	– $110.00
	Total Cash Flow + $5.24

12. Many travelers say that shoes in Italy are a big bargain. How can this be, given the purchasing power parity theorem?

   Travelers are wrong as a matter of fact, but we still must answer the question. If PPP held with perfection, shoes would have the same cost in any currency, and there would be no bargain shoes anywhere. Bargains can arise, however, due to market imperfections. First, transportation is costly. As a consequence, shoes in Italy could be cheaper than the same shoes in New York. The New York shoes must include the transportation cost. Second, even ignoring transportation costs, there are barriers to the free flow of shoes around the world. Governments impose tariffs and quotas, which can affect the price. Thus, if the United States protects its shoe industry by imposing tariffs or quotas on the Italian shoes, the shoes can cost more in the United States, thereby making shoes in Italy a bargain.

13. For the most part, the price of oil is denominated in dollars. Assume that you are a French firm that expects to import 420,000 barrels of crude oil in six months. What risks do you face in this transaction? Explain how you could transact to hedge the currency portion of those risks.

Here we assume that the price of oil is denominated in dollars. Further, contracts traded on the NYMEX in oil are also denominated in dollars. Therefore, hedging on the NYMEX will not deal with the currency risk the French firm faces. However, the French firm can hedge the currency risk it faces by trading forwards for the French franc. To see how the French firm can control both its risk with respect to oil prices and foreign exchange, consider the following data. We assume a futures delivery date in six months for the oil and for foreign exchange forward contracts. The futures price of oil is $30 barrel, and the six-month forward price of a French franc is $.20. With these prices, the French firm must expect a total outlay of $12.6 million for the oil, and a total franc outlay of FF 63 million. By trading oil futures and French franc forwards, it can lock-in this French franc cost. Because the crude oil contract is for 1,000 barrels, the French firm should buy 420 contracts. This commits it to a total outlay of $12.6 million. The French firm then sells FF 63 million in the forward market for $12.6 dollars. These two transactions lock-in a price of FF 63 million for the oil.

14. A financial comptroller for a U.S. firm is reviewing the earnings from a German subsidiary. This sub earns DM 1 million every year with exactitude, and it reinvests those earnings in its own German operations. This plan will continue. The earnings, however, are translated into U.S. dollars to prepare the U.S. parent's financial statements. Explain the nature of the foreign exchange risk from the point of view of the U.S. parent. Explain what steps you think the parent should take to hedge the risk that you have identified.

This risk is entirely translation risk, because we assume that the funds stay strictly in Germany. If the firm enters the futures or forward market to hedge the dollar value of the DM 1 million, it undertakes a transaction risk to hedge a translation risk. In other words, the firm increases its economic risk to hedge a purely accounting risk. From an economic point of view, this hedge would not make sense.

15. Joel Myers works for a large international bank. He has been watching the trading screen on this hot August morning and is disappointed in the lack trading activity. He is just about to take a break when a flurry of activity in the French bond and currency markets catches his attention. He quickly pulls up the following quotes:

Spot exchange rate:	$0.1656/FF
1-month forward:	$0.1659/FF
3-month forward:	$0.1665/FF
6-month forward:	$0.1673/FF

T-bill yields (bond equivalent)	
1-month:	4.95%
3-month:	5.01%
6-month:	5.11%

A. Compute the 1-month (30-day), 3-month (91-day), and 6-month (182-day) yields Joel should expect to see in the French money market.

For interest rate parity to hold, the French interest rates should be such that Joel would be indifferent between investing in the U.S. money market and the French money market. The interest rate parity relationship is:

$$1 + r_{DC} = \frac{1}{FC}(1 + r_{FC})F_{0,t}$$

where r_{DC} and r_{FC} are, respectively, the domestic and foreign interest rates, FC is the spot exchange rate expressed as the cost of one unit of foreign currency in terms of domestic currency, and $F_{0,t}$ is the forward exchange rate today for a transaction at time t expressed as the domestic currency cost of one foreign currency unit.

Solving for the foreign interest rate, r_{FC}, we have:

$$r_{FC} = \frac{FC}{F_{0,t}}\left(1 + r_{DC}\right) - 1$$

1-month rate: $\quad r_{FC} = \left[\frac{0.1656}{0.1659}\left(1 + \frac{.0495 \times 30}{365}\right) - 1\right]\frac{365}{30} = 2.74\%$

3-month rate: $\quad r_{FC} = \left[\frac{0.1656}{0.1665}\left(1 + \frac{.0501 \times 91}{365}\right) - 1\right]\frac{365}{91} = 2.81\%$

6-month rate: $\quad r_{FC} = \left[\frac{0.1656}{0.1673}\left(1 + \frac{.0511 \times 182}{365}\right) - 1\right]\frac{365}{182} = 3.02\%$

B. Suppose Joel sees that the 6-month yield in the French money market is 4 percent. Assuming there are no market frictions, is arbitrage possible? If so, show the arbitrage transactions and compute the profit for a $1 million arbitrage.

Joel has already determined that the no-arbitrage 6-month return in the French money market would be 3.02 percent. If the 6-month yield in the French market is 4 percent, then Joel could borrow domestically, exchange the dollars for French francs, and invest in the French money market. At the same time, he would lock in a 6-month forward exchange rate to convert the francs back to dollars so the borrowing can be repaid. The profit on a $1 million arbitrage would be computed as:

Date	Cash Market	Forward Market
Today	Borrow $1 million for 6 months at 5.11%.	Sell FF 6.1591 million 6 months forward at $0.1673/FF.
	Convert $1 million to FF at spot exchange rate of $0.1656/FF.	
	Invest FF 6.0386 million for 6 months at 4%.	
	Anticipated proceeds are FF 6.1591 million.	
	Net Investment = 0	
6 months	Receive anticipated FF 6.1591 million.	Deliver FF 6.1591 million and receive $1.0304 million.
	Repay borrowing; amount due is $1.0255 million.	
	Profit = ($1.0304 − $1.0255) million = $4,936	

16. As the fall semester starts, David McElroy is making arrangements for Oklahoma State University's Summer in London program for the next summer. This is a program in which OSU faculty teach courses to OSU students at Regents College in London, England. Room and board is £1,500 per participant to be paid May 15th. The enrollment is capped at 42 people, and OSU always operates at the cap. In the past, the Summer in London program has been burned by adverse movements in exchange rates. This happens because OSU has borne the exchange rate risk between the dollar denominated room and board rate quoted to the students and the British pound rate paid to Regents College. David wonders if there is some way that OSU could pass this risk off to someone else.

A. Does OSU face translation or transaction exposure?

A trader faces transaction exposure when one currency must be converted into another. This differs from translation exposure in which one currency is restated in but not converted to another currency. OSU faces transaction exposure because it will be converting dollars to pounds in May.

B. What could OSU do to reduce this exchange rate risk?

There are several ways OSU could reduce its exchange rate risk. First, OSU could negotiate a room and board contract denominated in dollars. This would transfer the risk to Regents College. This may be a viable alternative for future years, but it is too late for this year, as the contract has already been made. The second alternative is to buy British pounds forward using the futures market. This transfers the risk to a third party.

C. David asks a finance professor for advice. The professor pulls up the following $/£ quotes on the £62,500 futures contract:

Delivery	$/£
SEP (this year)	1.6152
DEC (this year)	1.6074
MAR (next year)	1.6002
JUN (next year)	1.5936

What strategy might the professor recommend to reduce OSU's exchange rate exposure? (Make a recommendation.)

The professor might suggest buying British pounds using the June futures contract. The amount of exposure OSU has is equal to the enrollment in the program multiplied by the pound-denominated room and board rate. The exposure will be:

$$\text{Exposure} = 42 \times £1500 = £63,000$$

To hedge this exposure, OSU should buy one June British pound futures contract at $1.5936 per £.

D. May 15th arrives, and the following situation is realized:

# of participants:	42
Dollar room and board rate:	$2,400
$/£ exchange rate:	$1.65
June futures contract:	$1.6451 per £

Compute OSU's gains and losses in the cash market and the futures market. Was the hedging strategy successful?

When May arrives, exchange rates have risen. That is, the British pound has become more expensive in dollar terms. Luckily, the June futures price has also increased, resulting in gains from OSU's futures position. The gains and losses are as follows:

Date	Cash Market	Futures Market
Today	Anticipate the need for $100,397 on May 15th to make £63,000 room and board payment.	Buy one June £62,500 futures contract at $1.5936 per £.
May 15th	Buy £63,000 in the spot market at $1.65 per £ for $103,950.	Sell one June futures contract at $1.6451 per £.
	Opportunity loss = – $3,553	Profit = $3,219
	Net Loss = –$334	

While the hedge did not totally eliminate OSU's transaction exposure, it did reduce it. Therefore, the hedge was a success.

17. Viva Soda is an up-and-comer in the highly competitive sports drink market. Viva owns three regional bottling facilities in the United States and one Canadian subsidiary that meets the demand for Viva in the

Canadian provinces. Great North Bottling, the Canadian subsidiary, accounts for 25 percent of Viva's total sales and net earnings at the present exchange rates. Dave Baker, CFO for Viva, is very concerned about Viva's translation exposure. Viva will be in the debt refinancing market in one year. Dave is acutely aware of the relationship between the cost of debt and earnings results. Dave's assistant has made the following forecasts of Great North's earnings before taxes for the next four quarters:

Quarter	Great North Earnings before Taxes
DEC	CAN$ 10 million
MAR99	CAN$ 7.5 million
JUN	CAN$ 8.5 million
SEP	CAN$ 12 million

A. What risks does Viva face with regard to its Canadian operations? What could Dave Baker do to hedge the risk?

The risk Viva faces with regard to its Canadian subsidiary is primarily translation exposure. Since Great North Bottling meets the demand of the Canadian provinces, Viva has a natural transaction hedge. This occurs when sales and expenses are denominated in the same local currency. The only risk then is the restatement (translation) of results in the home currency. Adverse movements in exchange rates could hurt Viva's reported results, which could, in turn, impact their cost of debt. Dave Baker could hedge the translation exposure by selling Canadian dollars forward. Any adverse impacts of exchange rates on Great North's contribution to Viva's bottom line will be offset by gains in the futures market.

B. Dave's assistant notes the following futures exchange rates for the Canadian dollar:

Delivery	U.S.$/CAN$
DEC	0.6603
MAR99	0.6609
JUN	0.6615
SEP	0.6621

Design a hedge that will solve Dave's problem. Assume one futures contract is for $100,000 Canadian dollars.

To hedge the translation exposure, Dave should sell each of Great North's anticipated pretax earnings in the futures market. To do this, Dave would sell 100 December contracts, 75 March contracts, 85 June contracts, and 120 September contracts.

C. Assuming the spot prices shown in the following table are realized, compute the translated earnings each quarter and the net impact on Viva's results considering the hedging activities.

Month	U.S.$/CAN$
DEC	0.6271
MAR99	0.6827
JUN	0.5961
SEP	0.7100

The anticipated contribution of Great North to pretax earnings each quarter is:

Quarter	Anticipated U.S.$/CAN$	Anticipated Pretax Earnings in U.S. $ (millions)
DEC	0.6603	6.603
MAR99	0.6609	4.957
JUN	0.6615	5.623
SEP	0.6621	7.945

The realized contribution of Great North to earnings before taxes each quarter is:

Quarter	Realized U.S.$/CAN$	Realized Earnings before Taxes in U.S. $ (millions)
DEC	0.6271	6.271
MAR99	0.6827	5.120
JUN	0.5961	5.067
SEP	0.7100	8.520

The impact of the exchange rate changes on the translated quarterly earnings is the anticipated earnings before taxes minus the realized earnings before taxes. These are:

Quarter	Realized EBT (U.S. $ millions)	Anticipated EBT (U.S. $ millions)	Gain (Loss) (U.S. $ millions)
DEC	6.271	6.603	(.332)
MAR99	5.120	4.957	.163
JUN	5.067	5.623	(.556)
SEP	8.520	7.945	.575

The gains and losses in the futures market are calculated as:

$$100,000(\text{Selling price} - \text{Buying price}) \times \text{\#contracts}$$

Quarter	Selling Price	Buying Price	# Contracts	Gain (Loss) (U.S. $ millions)
DEC	0.6603	0.6271	100	.332
MAR99	0.6609	0.6827	75	(.163)
JUN	0.6615	0.5961	85	.556
SEP	0.6621	0.7100	120	(.575)

The gains (losses) in the futures markets offset the translation losses (gains). One thing to keep in mind is that the translation gains and losses are accounting in nature. As long as Great North cash flows are not converted back into U.S. dollars, the gains and losses are only on paper. The futures trading gains and losses are cash gains and losses. Unless there is some cash benefit to reducing the translated earnings volatility, hedging the translation exposure might not be a good idea.

10 The Options Market

Answers to Questions and Problems

1. State the difference between a call and a put option.

   Call and put options are the two fundamental kinds of exchange traded options. They differ in the rights and privileges that ownership conveys. The owner of a call option has the right to buy the good that underlies the option at a specified price, with this right lasting until a stated expiration date. The put owner has the right to sell the good that underlies the option at a specified price with this right lasting until a stated expiration date. Thus, owning a call gives the right to buy and owning a put gives the right to sell. Correlatively, the seller of a call receives a payment and must sell the underlying good at the option of the call owner. The seller of a put receives a payment and must buy the underlying good at the option of the put owner.

2. How does a trader initiate a long call position, and what rights and obligations does such a position involve?

   To initiate a long call position, a trader buys a call option. At the time of purchase, the trader must pay the price of the option, which the seller of the call collects. Upon purchase, the owner of a call has the right to purchase the underlying good at the specified call price with that right lasting until the stated expiration date. The owner of a call has no obligations, once he or she pays the purchase price.

3. Can buying an option, whether a put or a call, result in any obligations for the option owner? Explain.

   The owner of a call or put has already paid the purchase price. After buying the option, the owner has only rights and no obligations. The option owner may exercise the option, sell it, or allow it to expire worthless, but the option owner is not compelled to do anything.

4. Describe all of the benefits that are associated with taking a short position in an option.

   Taking a short position in an option involves selling an option. Upon the sale, the seller receives a cash payment. This is the only benefit associated with selling an option. After receiving payment for the option, the seller has only potential obligations, because the seller may be required to perform at the discretion of the option owner.

5. What is the difference between a short call and a long put position? Which has rights associated with it, and which involves obligations? Explain.

   The short call position is obtained when a trader sells a call option. The seller of a call may be required to surrender the underlying good in exchange for the payment stated in the option contract. The short call position has a maximum benefit equal to the price that the seller received to enter the short call position. The short call position is most favorable when the price of the underlying good remains below the exercise price. Then the seller of the call retains the full price of the option as profit. The higher the stock price above the exercise price, the worse for the call seller.

In a long put position, the trader buys a put option. Owning the put gives the trader the right to sell the underlying good at the stated exercise price until the option expires. The put purchaser profits when the price of the underlying good falls below the exercise price. Then the owner of the put can require the put seller to buy the underlying good at the exercise price. When the underlying good has a price above the exercise price, the long put trader cannot exercise and loses the entire purchase price of the option.

In contrasting the short call and the long put positions, we note that the short call trader has a maximum profit equal to the original sales price, and the long put trader has a maximum loss equal to the original sales price. For the long put position, there is the chance of a virtually unlimited profit as the stock price falls to zero. For the short call position, there is the chance of a theoretically unlimited loss, as the stock price rises toward infinity.

6. Consider the following information. A trader buys a call option for $5 that gives the right to purchase a share of stock for $100. In this situation, identify: the exercise price, the premium, and the striking price.

The premium is the same as the option price and equals $5. The exercise price is the same as the striking price and equals $100.

7. Explain what happens to a short trader when the option he or she has sold expires worthless. What benefits and costs has the trader incurred?

At the time of trading, the short trader of a put or call receives a payment. This is the only benefit the short trader receives from trading. If the option expires worthless, then the option was not exercised and the short trader attains the maximum possible profit. In selling an option, the short trader exposes himself or herself to the risk that the purchaser will exercise. For accepting this risk, the seller has received the option premium. If the option expires worthless, the short trader has escaped that risk.

8. Explain why an organized options exchange needs a clearinghouse.

The clearinghouse guarantees the financial integrity of the market and oversees the performance of traders in the market. If there were no clearinghouse, each trader would have to be concerned with the financial integrity of his or her trading partner. Assuring that the opposite trading party will perform as promised is difficult and expensive. With a clearinghouse, each trader has an assurance that the opposite side of his or her transaction will be fulfilled. The clearinghouse guarantees it.

9. What is the difference between an American and a European option?

A European option can be exercised only at expiration, while an American option can be exercised at any time prior to expiration. This difference implies that the American option must be at least as valuable as the European option.

10. Assume a trader does not want to continue holding an option position. Explain how this trader can fulfill his or her obligations, yet close out the option position.

The trader will be either long or short. If the trader is long, he or she can close the position by selling the exact same option. The option that will be sold must be on the same underlying good, have the same expiration, and have the same striking price as the original option that is to be closed. If the trader were short initially, the trader would close the position by buying the identical option. In essence, the trader closes the position by trading to bring his or her net position back to zero. Again, making sure that all characteristics of the option match is an essential condition.

11. A developer has purchased 60 acres of rural property just north of Augusta, Georgia, to develop a golf course. The golf course development will also include a housing development. In order to generate operating capital, the developer is selling rights. The rights give the holder of the contract the right to purchase

lots in the housing development for a fixed price. Each lot in the housing development is half an acre. The agreements expire six months after they are signed. The developer is offering the following inducement. A potential homeowner can purchase a lot for $25,000 at the end of six months if the homeowner enters into the contract this week. The purchase price for a lot increases to $40,000 on all contracts signed after this week.

A. Describe the type of option being sold by the developer.

The developer is selling European call options.

B. Describe the position held by the potential homeowner as an option.

The potential homeowner has a long position in the European call option sold by the developer. The potential homeowner is the person who decides whether to exercise the right to purchase the property.

C. Discuss the risks associated with this transaction.

This is an over-the-counter transaction between the developer and the potential homeowner. The principal risk associated with this transaction is default (credit) risk. Both the developer and homeowner must be concerned with the possibility of the other party defaulting on the contract. However, the default risk is much lower for the developer. If the homeowner's check clears, then the developer has no default risk. However, the homeowner must be concerned with default by the developer at the end of six months.

D. Suppose we purchased the rights on a corner lot on the eighteenth hole during the inducement period, and we have just found out that legendary golfer Tiger Irons is building a house on the same block. Explain what you think will happen to the value of the right that you own. Is this contract in-the-money?

This news will in all likelihood dramatically increase the value of the property in the neighborhood and thus the contract you own. A contract that permitted you to purchase the land at a below market value would be in-the-money.

E. Suppose the developer was selling two contracts. One contract permits you to purchase a lot anytime during the six-month period, and the other allows you to purchase the lot only at the end of six months. Which of the two contracts is worth more? Explain why.

The developer is offering both American and European call options to potential homeowners. The American option must be at least as valuable as the European. It can be worth more if the underlying good has some payoff, analogous to a dividend on a stock, before the option expires. In this situation, it is not so clear that there is a "dividend" before expiration. With the revelation that a celebrity is moving into the neighborhood, the American option might be more valuable to the homeowner. The homeowner could exercise the option, acquire the property at below market value, and hold the property. The homeowner then has the option of selling the property immediately or at some date in the future, or the option to build on the property. The excess value of the American option over the European one depends on some incentive to early exercise. It is not obvious that there is such an incentive.

F. To reduce your cash outflows shortly before it became public knowledge that Tiger was going to build a house in the development, you signed a contract with a colleague. This contract gives you the right to sell the lot anytime in the next six months to your friend for $35,000. Describe your position and that of your friend.

You have a long position in an American put option that gives you the right to sell the property anytime in the next six months for $35,000. Your friend has a short position in an American put option.

G. Describe potential obligations associated with the options involving the developer and the two friends.

The original contract requires the developer to deliver the deed on the property for $25,000 if the potential homeowner chooses to exercise the contract. Exercising the contract requires the potential homeowner to deliver $25,000 in exchange for the deed to the property. The second contract gives the potential homeowner the opportunity to deliver the deed to the property to their colleague in exchange for $35,000. Your friend must take delivery of the deed and make a payment of $35,000 if you choose to exercise your right.

H. Suppose the contract that you signed required you to sell the property to your colleague at the end of six months for $35,000. What type of contract would this be?

This is a forward contract, since you must deliver the deed to the property at the end of six months to your colleague. You have a short position in a forward contract that requires you to deliver the deed to the property in exchange for $35,000.

I. Suppose that you signed the contract that required you to sell the property to your friend, but once you found out that Tiger was going to be your neighbor, you did not want to sell the property. What recourse is available to you?

One option would be to purchase the contract back from your colleague. However, your friend will have the power to capture all the gains associated with the increase in the value of the property. Thus, you will be negotiating from a position of weakness. Alternatively, you could repurchase the property from your friend at the current market price. If you were to default on the contract, your friend would take you to court and force you to live up to the terms of the contract. In addition, you would probably have to pay all the legal costs associated with your friend's court case, and any additional damages assigned by the court.

12. When you purchase or sell an option on the Chicago Board of Options Exchange you contract with the Options Clearing Corporation. Discuss the advantages of this type of trading arrangement.

The OCC acts as the buyer to every seller and the seller to every buyer. This arrangement increases the liquidity and marketability of exchange traded options contracts. If an investor wanted to reverse an options position, he or she could do so by submitting a reversing order to the options market. The investor is not forced to approach the original counterparty to negotiate a reversing transaction. In addition, every investor does not have to evaluate the credit (default) risk of other market participants. This reduces the cost of transacting in this marketplace, as each investor is concerned only with the credit risk of the OCC.

A. If all trades in a day match, describe the net position of the clearing corporation.

If all trades match, then the OCC has a net zero option position.

B. When a retail customer makes a margin payment, to which organization is the margin paid? Trace the flow of margin funds from the retail customer to the ultimate recipient.

A retail customer makes margin payments to his broker. If his broker is a clearing member firm, the broker will make margin payments to the OCC. If the broker is not a clearing member firm, then the broker will make margin payments to a clearing member firm and the clearing member firm will make the payments to the OCC. It is clearing member firms that make margin payments to the OCC.

13. Describe the services provided by a market maker, floor broker, and order book official. Discuss the differences between a market maker and an order book official.

A broker represents customer orders on the floor of the exchange. The broker is paid a commission for the provision of these services. The broker tries to fill orders as rapidly as possible at the best price available at the time of the transaction. The more orders the broker handles, the more commissions the broker earns. Order book officials represent public orders that are in the limit order book. They represent the exchange and have no equity positions in the market. They are responsible for maintaining an orderly and fair market in the handling of customer orders. A market maker holds a portfolio of options. A market maker manages her portfolio with the objective of maximizing her wealth. A market maker is required to trade a minimum number of options contracts at their quoted bid and ask price. Both market makers and order book officials maintain a portfolio of options. However, market makers trade to make a profit, and order book officials represent the orders of public customers (not professional traders).

14. During an extended period of financial difficulty, a firm's CFO offers the firm's treasurer the following contract in lieu of 25 percent of her salary. The contract permits the treasurer to "clip up to ten coupons" that entitle her to convert each coupon into 10,000 shares of stock at no cost anytime during a three-year period. Suppose the treasurer chooses to accept the contract. Explain what type of contract the treasurer holds.

Since the treasurer of the firm has the right to convert the coupons into a maximum of 100,000 shares of common stock anytime, the treasurer has a long position in an American call option written on the firm's shares. However, since the exercise price of the option is $0, the treasurer effectively owns 100,000 shares of the firm's stock.

15. Explain the "rights" attached to a stock option contract traded on the CBOE. Discuss the economic motivation for exercising a stock option at expiration.

A call option is a contract that extends to the holder of the contract the right to buy 100 shares of the underlying stock at the specified strike price anytime during the life of the contract. The stock options traded on the CBOE are American options. A put option is a contract that extends to the holder of the contract the right to sell 100 shares of the underlying stock at the specified strike price anytime during the life of the contract. When making the decision to exercise an option at expiration, the owner of a stock option is in effect asking himself the following questions.

Call option:
Is it cheaper to buy 100 shares of the stock underlying the option in the market at the market (spot) price or via the contract (call option) at the contracted buying price? The contracted buying price is the strike price of the option.

Put option:
Do I make more money by selling 100 shares of the stock underlying the option in the market at the market (spot) price or via the contract (put option) at the contracted selling price? The contracted selling price is the strike price of the option. If the owner of the option finds it more profitable to trade the underlying stock according to the terms of the contract, then he will exercise the option.

16. Explain the obligations associated with establishing a long position in an option contract.

The purchaser of an option (the long position) must pay for the option before the market opens for business on the trading day following the purchase of the option. If payment has not been received by the market's opening, the OCC closes the position.

17. Explain the obligations associated with a short position in call and put options.

The writer of an option (short position) does not have any obligations if the option is not exercised. If the person has written a call option and the option is exercised against her, the writer must deliver the quantity of the underlying commodity specified by the option's contract. Upon delivery, the writer of the option will receive payment in the amount specified in the contract. If the person has written a put option and the option is exercised against her, the writer must take delivery of the quantity of the underlying commodity specified by the option's contract. Upon delivery, the writer of the option must make payment in the amount specified in the contract to the owner of the option's contract. When an option is exercised, the OCC randomly selects individual(s) from the pool of individuals who have open short positions in the relevant options contract. Thus, it is possible that an individual may have a short position in an option and not have the option exercised against her.

18. A trader purchases an option for $6.50 that gives him the right to sell 100 shares of stock for $50 per share. Identify the type of option, the option's price, and the option's strike price.

    The investor is long a put option. The strike price is $50, and the price of the option is $6.50 on a per share basis. The total cost of the option is $650 ($6.50 × 100).

19. Consider the following "opportunities." Determine if the opportunity is an option, and if it is an option, explain what type of option the opportunity represents. Describe positions of the parties involved in the opportunity.

A. An old college classmate calls and offers you the opportunity to purchase automobile insurance. The insurance is renewable semiannually.

   Auto insurance is an American put option. If there is an accident involving an insured driver, then the insurance company makes a payment to the insured driver. The insurance company has written the put option. The insured is long the put option and "chooses" to exercise the option because of an accident.

B. You have just received your SAT scores from ETS. It turns out that you had a good day and scored a perfect 1600. One week later, you receive the following offer in a letter from Private School U. If you enroll in PSU in the fall, PSU will guarantee that your total annual cost of attending PSU will be $1. The offer applies only if you enroll at PSU for the upcoming fall semester.

   You hold a long position in a European call option. PSU has written a call to you. If you enroll in PSU in the fall, then you have the right to purchase your education for the fixed price of $1 per year.

C. The following day your parents, who attended the local state-supported university, receive a letter from their alma mater, Basketball Power U. The letter makes the following offer. If their child enrolls in BPU for the fall semester, BPU will guarantee that they can purchase 10 courtside basketball seats for the face value of the tickets as long as their child is enrolled in BPU.

   Your parents have nothing, but may come to have a long position in a portfolio of European call options. BPU has written the call options to the parents, contingent on the child's enrollment. If their child enrolls in BPU in the fall and remains enrolled at BPU, then they will have the right to purchase 10 valuable courtside basketball tickets at BPU each year their child is enrolled at BPU. The offer applies only if their child enrolls at BPU for the upcoming fall semester and only for each year their child maintains enrollment at BPU.

D. A high school classmate calls during dinner from his firm, High Pressure Telemarketing. He offers you the opportunity to enter into a long-term, fixed price, noncancellable lease on a condo in Miami Beach. This opportunity is not a time share, and you cannot sublet the condo.

   This is not an option. There is no right associated with the contract. The contract requires you to make the fixed payments over the life of the contract. Once you enter into the contract, you have an obligation to make the payments, and you cannot choose to avoid a payment.

E. You have just purchased 40 acres of heavily wooded land in the nearby hills. To minimize fire danger and relieve work-related stress, you plan to remove all the underbrush and dead trees from the property. The local hardware store is advertising a sale on chain saws. At the store, a sales consultant informs you that they are temporarily out of the saw that you are interested in. The salesperson offers you a rain check that gives the "opportunity" to purchase the saw at the sale price for two weeks.

You hold a long position in an American call option. You can return to the store anytime in the next two weeks and purchase the saw at the sales price if desired. The store has written the call giving you the right to purchase the saw at the sales price during the next two weeks.

F. As usual things are running late. After work you run home to get dinner. Arriving home, you frantically search for the telephone book. In the middle of the telephone book, you find a coupon from the local pizza parlor, My Pies, that gives you the opportunity to buy a large supreme pizza and two liters of pop for $15.99.

You are long an American call giving the right to purchase the pizza and pop for $15.99. My Pies has written the call option.

20. Compare the obligations associated with exercising stock index options and stock options.

The fundamental difference between the two contracts is that the index option is a cash settlement contract. An index option contract is settled at exercise by an exchange of cash, while an option on an individual stock is settled by the delivery of shares in exchange for cash.

21. An investor holds a long option position that she wishes to close. Explain the different means available to the investor to close this options position. Explain how your answer changes if the option position was entered on an exchange or over-the-counter.

There are three ways this long option position can be closed. The investor can exercise the option, the investor can allow the option to expire worthless, and, if the option was entered on an exchange, the investor can enter into a reversing (offsetting) trade. To reverse the position, the investor must sell the same quantity of the option she owns. The options that she sells must have the same strike price and the same expiration date. With OTC options, if the investor wishes to reverse her position, she must arrange a reversing trade with the same counterparty with whom she initially contracted. If the investor must sell the option, the counterparty will have market power when negotiating the terms of the reversing transaction.

22. Suppose that there are two call options written on the same share of stock, XYZ. Both options have the same expiration date and strike price. Explain why the American option is always worth at least as much as the European option.

The American option contract has an additional right attached to the contract. This contract gives the option's owner the right to exercise the option anytime prior to the option's expiration. If this right to exercise early is worthless, then the value of the American option is the same as the value of a comparable European option.

23. Explain why the bid-asked spread quoted by the market maker on the floor of the CBOE represents a real cost to an investor trading options. Explain why the investor is willing to trade at the quoted spread prices in a competitive market.

If a trader wishes to trade an option listed on the CBOE, the trader must trade that option through the floor of the CBOE. In addition, the trader must trade the listed option at the price (spread) quoted by the market makers. The trader purchases the option at the market maker's ask price and sells options at the market maker's bid price. If market makers are informed and are correctly valuing the traded option, their quoted ask price should be above the fair value of the option and the quoted bid price should be below the fair value of the option. If there were no market makers in the market and the market was competitive with fully informed investors who correctly valued the traded options, then investors would trade options at the fair value of the option. The bid-asked spread represents compensation paid by market participants to the market maker. In a competitive marketplace, the market maker earns a fair return for bearing the risk associated with holding an inventory of option contracts, and for providing liquidity to the market.

24. Mr. Smith holds a certificate of deposit (CD) from his local bank that matures in three months. Mr. Smith is well aware of the current bull market for stocks, and the opportunity cost of having his money tied up in a CD earning 4.5 percent. When the CD matures, Mr. Smith is planning to invest in the stock market. Mr. Smith feels that the market will continue its strong bull run for the next three months, and he does not want to wait three months to invest in the market. Discuss how Mr. Smith may use options to invest in the market today. Explain the type of contracts and the positions Mr. Smith could use to undertake this investment.

    Since Mr. Smith expects the value of the market to increase during the next three months, he should take a long position in a call option on the stock market. There are several different index options traded in the marketplace, including options written on the S&P 500, the S&P 100, the Russell 2000, and the Dow Jones Industrial Average. With a long position in an index call option, Mr. Smith can participate in the upward movements in the market with limited downside risk and a limited investment.

25. It is late in the afternoon of the third Friday of the expiration month, and an investor has an open long position in a deep in-the-money European call option. The investor must decide whether to sell the option in the market while the market is open or to exercise the option at the close of the market. For an option contract, the one-way transaction cost is $25. The exercise fee for an option is $25, and the commission for selling 100 shares of stock is $20. Discuss the impact of transactions costs on the investor's decision to either exercise the option or sell the option.

    Exercising the option requires two transactions by the investor, exercising the option followed by selling the stock. The cost of exercise is $25, and the cost of selling the shares acquired by the exercise is $20 for a total of $45. Simply selling the option to capture the same underlying value will cost only $25.

26. Consider the following option quotations.

Option	Strike	Exp.	Call Vol.	Call Last	Put Vol.	Put Last
IBM						
101 5/8	115	Sep	1632	3/16	10	13 1/4
101 5/8	115	Oct	861	1 1/4	10	14 1/4
101 5/8	115	Jan	225	4	3	14

A. What is the cost of 15 IBM Oct 115 call options?

$$15 \times \$1.25 \times 100 = \$1,875$$

B. Assume the clearing corporation is using the following schedule for the calculation of margin requirements: The maximum of:

> 100% of the proceeds from the sale of the options plus 20% of the value of the underlying stock position minus the dollar amount the option's contract is out-of-the-money, **or**
> 100% of the proceeds from the sale of the options plus 10% of the value of the underlying stock position.

What are the initial margin requirements for the buyer and seller of 3 IBM Jan 115 call options? Explain how the answer changes if the seller owns 300 shares of IBM.

If the investor owns 300 shares of IBM and chooses to lend them to his broker to collateralize his options position, then his margin requirement is $0. This investor will have written covered calls. If the investor has written naked calls, then his initial margin is the maximum of:

First Method		**Second Method**	
100% of the proceeds from the sale of the option	$3 \times \$4 \times 100 = \$1,200$	100% of the proceeds from the sale of the option	$3 \times \$4 \times 100 = \$1,200$
20% of the value of the underlying stock position	$3 \times (\$101.625 \times 100) \times 0.2 = \$6,097.50$	10% of the value of the underlying stock position	$3 \times (\$101.625 \times 100) \times 0.1 = \$3,048.75$
The dollar amount that the options contract is out-of-the-money	$(\$101.625 - \$115) \times 3 \times 100 = -\$4,012.5$		
Required margin	$3,285.00		$4,248.75

The margin requirement is the larger amount of $4,248.75.

C. Explain what happens to your option position if you are unable to meet a margin call.

A margin call requires the investor to recollateralize her margin position. If you do not have sufficient cash to recollateralize the position, the OCC reverses your position at the opening of the market on the next trading day. The existing balance in your margin account is used to cover your losses. The OCC also subtracts the relevant transactions costs from your margin account balances.

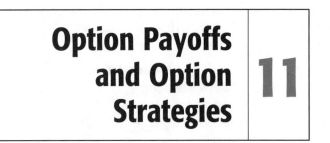

Option Payoffs and Option Strategies

11

Answers to Questions and Problems

1. Consider a call option with an exercise price of $80 and a cost of $5. Graph the profits and losses at expiration for various stock prices.

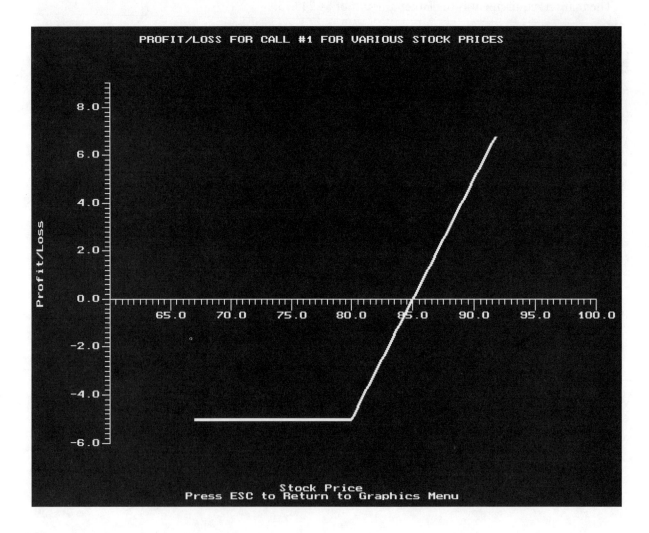

2. Consider a put option with an exercise price of $80 and a cost of $4. Graph the profits and losses at expiration for various stock prices.

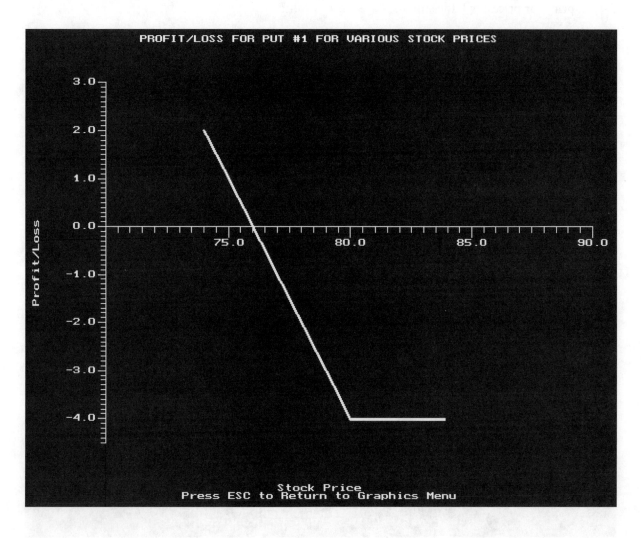

PROFIT/LOSS FOR PUT #1 FOR VARIOUS STOCK PRICES

3. For the call and put in questions 1 and 2, graph the profits and losses at expiration for a straddle comprising these two options. If the stock price is $80 at expiration, what will be the profit or loss? At what stock price (or prices) will the straddle have a zero profit?

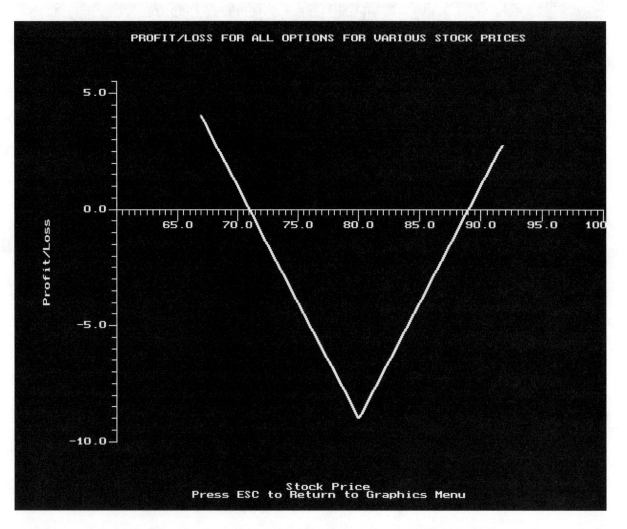

With a stock price at $80 at expiration, neither the call nor the put can be exercised. Both expire worthless, giving a total loss of $9. The straddle breaks even (has a zero profit) if the stock price is either $71 or $89.

4. A call option has an exercise price of $70 and is at expiration. The option costs $4, and the underlying stock trades for $75. Assuming a perfect market, how would you respond if the call is an American option? State exactly how you might transact. How does your answer differ if the option is European?

With these prices, an arbitrage opportunity exists because the call price does not equal the maximum of zero or the stock price minus the exercise price. To exploit this mispricing, a trader should buy the call and exercise it for a total out-of-pocket cost of $74. At the same time, the trader should sell the stock and deliver the stock just acquired through exercise for a $75 cash inflow. This produces a riskless profit without investment of $1. Because the option is at expiration, both the American and European options have the same right to exercise. Therefore, the American or European character of the option has no effect on the trading strategy.

5. A stock trades for $120. A put on this stock has an exercise price of $140 and is about to expire. The put trades for $22. How would you respond to this set of prices? Explain.

At expiration, the put price must equal the maximum of zero or the exercise price minus the stock price to avoid arbitrage. Therefore, the put price should be $20 in this situation, but it trades for $22. This difference gives rise to an arbitrage opportunity, because the put is priced too high relative to its theoretical value. To exploit this, the trader should simply sell the put and receive $22. Now the option can be exercised against the trader or not. If it is not exercised, the put expires worthless, the obligation is complete, and the trader retains the $22 as total profit. However, the purchaser of the option may choose to exercise immediately. In this case, the seller of the put must buy the stock for the exercise price of $140. The trader then sells the stock for $120 in the market, giving a $20 loss on the exercise. But the put seller already received $22, so he or she still has a $2 profit. In summary, selling the put leads to a $22 profit if the put buyer foolishly fails to exercise. Alternatively, if the put buyer exercises, the put seller still has a $2 profit. This is an arbitrage opportunity, because selling the overpriced put gives a profit without investment in all circumstances.

6. If the stock trades for $120 and the expiring put with an exercise price of $140 trades for $18, how would you trade?

As in the previous problem, these prices violate the no-arbitrage condition. Now, however, the put is underpriced relative to the other values. To conduct the arbitrage, the trader should buy the stock and buy and exercise the put. In this sequence of transactions, the trader pays $120 to acquire the stock, pays $18 to acquire the put, and receives $140 upon exercise of the put. These transactions yield a profit of $2 with no risk and no investment.

7. Consider a call and a put on the same underlying stock. The call has an exercise price of $100 and costs $20. The put has an exercise price of $90 and costs $12. Graph a short position in a strangle based on these two options. What is the worst outcome from selling the strangle? At what stock price or prices does the strangle have a zero profit?

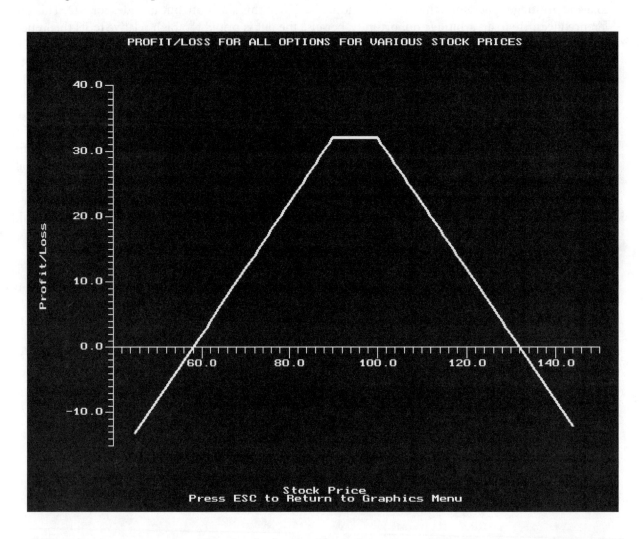

The worst outcomes occur when the stock price is very low or very high. First, the strangle loses $1 for each dollar the stock price falls below $58. With a zero stock price, the strangle loses $58. If the stock price is too high, the strangle also loses money. Because the stock could theoretically go to infinity, the potential loss on the strangle is unbounded. For stock prices of $58 or $132, the strangle gives exactly a zero profit.

8. Assume that you buy a call with an exercise price of $100 and a cost of $9. At the same time, you sell a call with an exercise price of $110 and a cost of $5. The two calls have the same underlying stock and the same expiration. What is this position called? Graph the profits and losses at expiration from this position. At what stock price or prices will the position show a zero profit? What is the worst loss that the position can incur? For what range of stock prices does this worst outcome occur? What is the best outcome and for what range of stock prices does it occur?

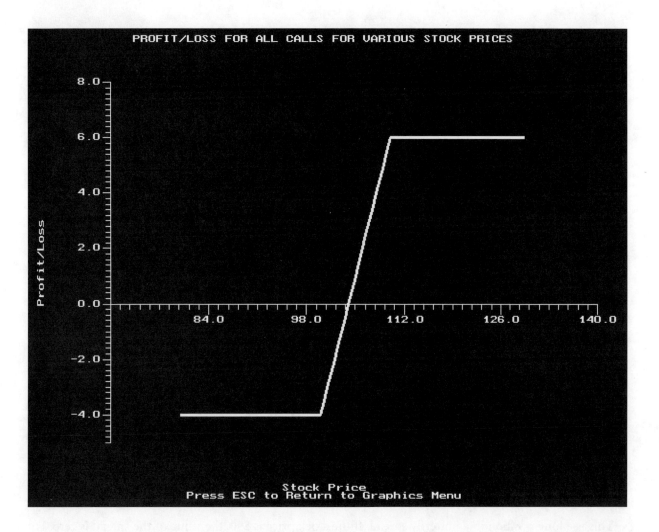

This position is a bull spread with calls, because it is designed to profit if the stock price rises. The entire position has a zero profit if the stock price is $104. At this point, the call with the $100 exercise price can be exercised for a $4 exercise profit. This $4 exercise value exactly offsets the price of the spread. The worst loss occurs when the stock price is $100 or below, because the option with the $100 exercise price cannot be exercised, and the entire position is worthless. This gives a $4 loss. The best outcome occurs for any stock price of $110 or above and the total profit is $6.

9. Consider three call options with the same underlying stock and the same expiration. Assume that you take a long position in a call with an exercise price of $40 and a long position in a call with an exercise price of $30. At the same time, you sell two calls with an exercise price of $35. What position have you created? Graph the value of this position at expiration. What is the value of this position at expiration if the stock price is $90? What is the position's value for a stock price of $15? What is the lowest value the position can have at expiration? For what range of stock prices does this worst value occur?

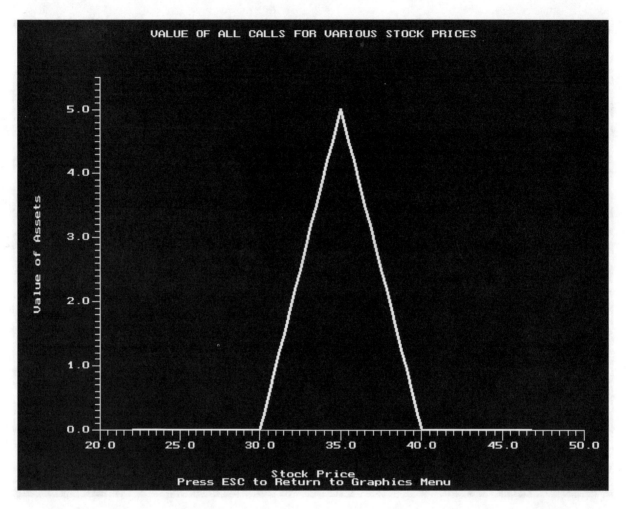

VALUE OF ALL CALLS FOR VARIOUS STOCK PRICES

Value of Assets

Stock Price
Press ESC to Return to Graphics Menu

This is a long position in a butterfly spread. If the stock price is $90, the value of the spread is zero. For a $15 stock price, the spread is worth zero. The entire spread can be worth zero at expiration. This zero value occurs for any stock price of $30 or below and $40 or above.

10. Assume that you buy a portfolio of stocks with a portfolio price of $100. A put option on this portfolio has a striking price of $95 and costs $3. Graph the combined portfolio of the stock plus a long position in the put. What is the worst outcome that can occur at expiration? For what range of portfolio prices will this worst outcome occur? What is this position called?

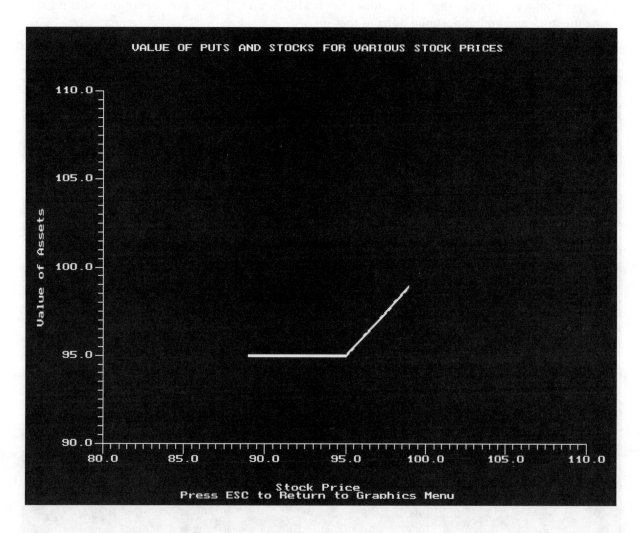

The worst result is a portfolio value of $95. The purchase of the put for $3 gives a loss of $8. This worst outcome occurs for a terminal stock portfolio value of $95 or less. This combined position is an insured portfolio. The position insures against any terminal portfolio value less than $95 or any loss greater than $8.

11. Consider a stock that sells for $95. A call on this stock has an exercise price of $95 and costs $5. A put on this stock also has an exercise price of $95 and costs $4. The call and the put have the same expiration. Graph the profit and losses at expiration from holding the long call and short put. How do these profits and losses compare with the value of the stock at expiration? If the stock price is $80 at expiration, what is the portfolio of options worth? If the stock price is $105, what is the portfolio of options worth? Explain why the stock and option portfolio differ as they do.

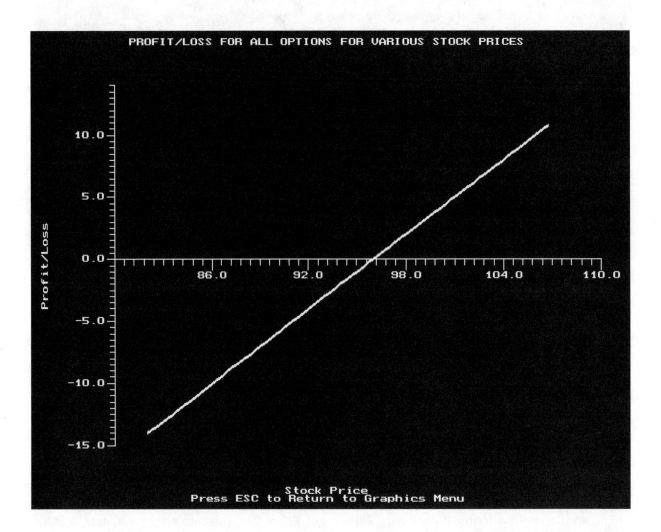

No matter what stock price results, the option portfolio will have $1 less profit than the stock itself. For example, the option portfolio costs $1, but both options are worthless at a stock price of $95. Therefore, at a stock price of $95, the stock has a zero profit, and the option portfolio has a $1 loss. Further, the option portfolio will be worth exactly $95 less than the stock at every price. With a stock price of $80, the call is worthless and the put will be exercised against the option holder for an exercise loss of $15. Therefore, the option portfolio is worth –$15 for an $80 stock price. If the stock trades for $105, the option portfolio will be worth $10.

12. Assume a stock trades for $120. A call on this stock has a striking price of $120 and costs $11. A put also has a striking price of $120 and costs $8. A risk-free bond promises to pay $120 at the expiration of the options in one year. What should the price of this bond be? Explain.

A portfolio consisting of one long call, one short put, and a riskless investment equal to the common exercise price of the two options gives exactly the same payoffs as a share of the underlying stock on the common expiration date. This put-call parity relationship requires that this portfolio of long call, short put, plus riskless investment should have the same price as the stock. With our data, the riskless bond must therefore cost $120 – $11 + $8 = $117. The riskless interest rate must be 2.53 percent.

13. In the preceding question, if we combine the two options and the bond, what will the value of this portfolio be relative to the stock price at expiration? Explain. What principle does this illustrate?

As the previous answer already indicated, the described portfolio (long call, short put, plus long bond) must have the same value as the stock itself. This illustrates the put-call parity relationship.

14. Consider a stock that is worth $50. A put and call on this stock have an exercise price of $50 and expire in one year. The call costs $5 and the put costs $4. A risk-free bond will pay $50 in one year and costs $45. How will you respond to these prices? State your transactions exactly. What principle do these prices violate?

These prices violate put-call parity. The long call, plus short put, plus riskless investment of the present value of the exercise price must together equal the stock price:

$$S = C - P + Xe^{-r\,(T-t)}$$

Instead, we have $50 ≥ $5 – $4 + $45 = $46. Therefore, the stock is overpriced relative to the duplicating right-hand side portfolio. Accordingly, we transact as follows, with the cash flows being indicated in parentheses: Sell stock (+$50), buy call (–$5), sell put ($4), and buy the riskless bond (–$45). This gives a positive cash flow of $4 at the time of trading. To close our position, we collect $50 on the maturing bond. If the stock price is above $50, we exercise our call and use our $50 bond proceeds to acquire the stock, which we can then repay to close our short position. The put cannot be exercised against us, so we conclude the transaction with our original $4 profit. If the stock price is below $50, the put will be exercised against us. If so, we lose $50 – S on the exercise, paying our $50 bond proceeds to acquire the stock. Now with the stock in hand, we close our short position and the call expires worthless. As a result, we still have our $4 original cash inflow as profit. No matter what the stock price may be at expiration, our profit will be $4.

15. A stock sells for $80 and the risk-free rate of interest is 11 percent. A call and a put on this stock expire in one year and both options have an exercise price of $75. How would you trade to create a synthetic call option? If the put sells for $2, how much is the call option worth? (Assume annual compounding.)

A synthetic call option consists of the following portfolio: long the stock, long the put, and short a risk-free bond paying the exercise price at the common maturity date of the call and put. Therefore, the following relationship must hold:

$$C = S + P - \frac{X}{\left(1 + r\right)^t}$$

Therefore, with the information given:

$$C = \$80 + \$2 - \$67.67 = \$14.43$$

16. A stock costs $100 and a risk-free bond paying $110 in one year costs $100 as well. What can you say about the cost of a put and a call on this stock that both expire in one year and that both have an exercise price of $110? Explain.

Put-call parity implies:

$$S - \frac{X}{\left(1+r\right)^{T-t}} = C - P$$

In this case, the stock and bond have the same price, so the left-hand side of the equation equals zero. For the right-hand side to equal zero, the call and put must have the same price as well. However, from the information given, we cannot determine what that price would be.

17. Assume that you buy a strangle with exercise prices on the constituent options of $75 and $80. You also sell a strangle with exercise prices of $70 and $85. Describe the payoffs on the position you have created. Does this portfolio of options have a payoff pattern similar to that of any of the combinations explored in this chapter?

This position will profit for very low (say below $70) or very high (say above $85) stock prices at expiration. For prices in the range of $75 to $85, the position will lose. The exact breakeven points cannot be determined from the information given, however. In effect, the pair of strangles described is a short condor position.

18. If a stock sells for $75 and a call and put together cost $9 and the two options expire in one year and have an exercise price of $70, what is the current rate of interest?

From the information given, and applying put-call parity, we know:

$$S - \frac{X}{1+r} = C - P = \$9$$

The stock price is $75 and must exceed the bond price by $9, so the price of the bond is $66. Thus, the present value of the $70 exercise price is $66, implying an interest rate of 6.06 percent.

19. Assume you buy a bull spread with puts that have exercise prices of $40 and $45. You also buy a bear spread with puts that have exercise prices of $45 and $50. What will this total position be worth if the stock price at expiration is $53? Does this position have any special name? Explain.

The bull spread with puts and these exercise prices implies buying the put with $X = \$40$ and selling the put with $X = \$45$. To buy the bear spread implies buying a put with $X = \$50$ and selling a put with $X = \$45$. If the stock price at expiration is $53, all of the puts expire worthless. In making this trade, one has bought puts with $X = \$40$ and $X = \$50$, and sold two puts with $X = \$45$. This is equivalent to a long butterfly spread with puts.

20. Explain the difference between a box spread and a synthetic risk-free bond.

The box spread gives a riskless payoff, so it is equivalent to a synthetic risk-free bond.

21. Within the context of the put-call parity relationship, consider the value of a call and a put option. What will the value of the put option be if the exercise price is zero? What will the value of the call option be in the same circumstance? What can you say about potential bounds on the value of the call and put option?

If the exercise price of a put is zero, there can be no payoff from the put so the price must be zero. In this circumstance, the call must be worth the stock price. With respect to bounds on the option prices, the call price can never exceed the stock price and the put price can never exceed the exercise price.

22. Using the put-call parity relationship, write the value of a call option as a function of the stock price, the risk-free bond, and the put option. Now consider a stock price that is dramatically in excess of the exercise price. What happens to the value of the put as the stock price becomes extremely large relative to the exercise price? What happens to the value of the call option?

$$C = S + P - \frac{X}{(1+r)^{T-t}}$$

The put price declines as the ratio S/X becomes large. The call option must increase in value. As we will see, the call must always be worth at least the stock price minus the present value of the exercise price.

23. The CBOE is thinking of opening a new market center in London that will trade only European options and has hired you as a consultant. The board of directors for the CBOE believes that there is demand in the market for options contracts that can be used by investors to insure their portfolios. A unique feature of this market is the fact that only put options will be traded.

A. Explain why it will not be necessary to trade call options in this market.

Because the options that will be traded in this market are European options. Arbitrage, in the form of put-call parity, guarantees that the call options will be priced fairly. Any investor can use put-call parity to construct the corresponding synthetic call option $c = p + S - Xe^{-r(T-t)}$ that will have the same value as an exchange traded call option.

B. Discuss the expected clientele in this market and explain why these traders might not desire to use American options traded in Chicago on the CBOE.

The target clientele for this market is hedgers. Hedgers desire to protect the value of an asset that they currently own for a specified time period. That is, the hedger has an investment horizon and desires to protect the value of her investment over that investment horizon. The price of the option contract traded in Chicago on the CBOE includes the value of the early exercise premium. Hedgers do not expect to exercise their options prior to expiration, and they are not interested in paying for the right to exercise the option prior to expiration. The value of this early exercise premium on an American option effectively increases the cost of the insurance available to hedgers.

C. The CBOE has asked you as a consultant to identify the important characteristics of the market and the option contracts that will ensure the success of this new market. Identify those characteristics that you feel will contribute to the success of the market.

For this marketplace to be successful, the contracts and services offered must be demanded by the market. The target clientele for these contracts is hedgers. Hedgers have an investment horizon and desire to protect the value of their investment over that investment horizon. To do an effective job, you must understand the demographics of the marketplace. The following questions might be relevant in determining the nature of the marketplace. What types of assets are owned by the investors who are likely candidates to be the clients of this market? Who are the likely users of the market, individuals or professional funds managers? Should the option contracts be written on individual shares of stock or should they be written on stock indices (portfolios)? Should the market include equities traded globally or should they focus on a specific geographic location (e.g., the United States)? Should the contracts be settled in cash or call for delivery of the underlying security? Should the market be open continuously? How frequently should the options expire—weekly, bimonthly, monthly, and so on? Should the options have expiration dates longer than one year? What is the optimal size of the contract (e.g., 100 shares)? What is the optimal differential between the strike prices of the traded options? Should there be any restriction on the size of the options position held by an investor? What is the optimal structure of transactions costs for the market?

24. Suppose an investor purchases a call option on XYZ with a $50 strike price and sells a put option on XYZ with the same strike price. Both options are European options that expire in one month. Describe the investor's position.

The investor has created a synthetic long position in a forward contract written on the underlying stock. The payoff on this position mimics the payoff on a long position in a share of the underlying stock ($S - X$, where X is the purchase price of the stock, and S is the spot price of the stock).

25. DRP is currently selling at $58 per share. An American call option written on DRP with six weeks until expiration has a strike price of $50.

A. If DRP does not pay a dividend, explain why it is not economically rational to exercise this American call option prior to expiration. Equivalently, explain why a call option is worth more alive than dead.

The price of an option consists of its intrinsic value $(S - X)$, and its time value (the option's price – the intrinsic value of the option). When you exercise the call option, you capture its intrinsic value $(S - X)$. (The option must be in-the-money for you to consider exercising it.) However, you lose the time value when you exercise. You can capture the time value by selling the option in the marketplace. For example, consider the following information: $S = \$50$, $X = \$40$, and $C = \$11.5$. If the call were exercised, the payoff to the investor would be $(\$50 - \$40) \times 100 = \$1,000$. If the call were sold, the payoff to the investor would be $\$11.50 \times 100 = \$1,150$.

B. If DRP pays a quarterly dividend, but the dividend will not be paid for eight weeks, explain why it is not economically rational to exercise this American call option prior to expiration.

In this problem, the dividend is irrelevant to the early exercise decision. The dividend is to be paid after the option's expiration and will not affect your decision regarding the early exercise of the option.

26. Call prices are directly related to the volatility of the underlying stock. That is, the more volatile the underlying stock, the more valuable the call option. However, higher volatility means that the stock price may decrease by a large amount. That is, the probability of a large decrease in the stock price has increased. Explain this apparent paradox.

Examination of the components of the price of an option reveals the answer to this apparent paradox. The price of an option consists of its intrinsic value, and its time value. A call option pays off when the market price of the stock exceeds the exercise price (contracted purchase price). That is, the call option pays off in only one direction, when the stock price rises (the up state). An option that is out-of-the-money at expiration is worthless. In other words, it does not matter how far out-of-the-money the option is at expiration. A call option that is deep-out-of-the-money is just as worthless as a call option that is barely out-of-the-money. Increases in the volatility of the stock underlying the option contract increase the expected payoff on the option in the up state, which increases the value of the option. Thus, although increases in the volatility of the underlying stock imply that the stock is more likely to experience a large decrease in price, it is the corresponding increase in the probability of a large increase in the stock price that increases the value of a call option.

27. An investor has just obtained the following quotes for European options on a stock worth $30 when the three-month risk-free interest rate is 10 percent per annum. Both options have a strike price of $30 and expire in three months.

    European call: $3
    European put: $1 3/4

A. Given the information above, determine whether the prices conform to the put-call parity rule.

Put-call parity states $p = c - S + Xe^{-r(T-t)}$; however,

$$\$1.75 \neq \$3 - \$30 + \$30e^{-0.1 \times 0.25}$$

$$p \neq c - S + Xe^{-r(T-t)}$$

$$\$1.75 \neq \$2.2593$$

B. If there is a violation, suggest a trading strategy that will generate riskless arbitrage profits.

The synthetic put costs $2.2593, and the exchange traded put is trading at $1.75. To capture the potential profits from this arbitrage opportunity, we must simultaneously sell the synthetic put and purchase the traded put. Selling the synthetic put requires one to sell the call for $3, purchase the stock for $30, and sell the present value of $30 of the risk-free bond, $29.2593, resulting in a cash inflow of $2.2593. Purchasing the put will cost $1.75.

C. Indicate how much profit you will make from the arbitrage transactions, if such an opportunity exists.

The profit from the arbitrage transactions will be the difference between the cash inflow from selling the synthetic put and the cash outflow from purchasing the traded put, $2.2593 − $1.75 = $.5093.

28. Suppose you are an information services professional with contracts throughout the industry. In conversations with colleagues, you get the feeling that Computer Associates International is likely to attempt to acquire Computer Sciences Corporation. You also remember from your finance courses in college that in the course of an acquisition, the share price of the target firm normally increases and the share price of the acquiring firm decreases. (You are confident that trading on the information gleaned in these conversations violates no law and is ethical.)

A. Discuss the advantages of using options to speculate on the expected stock price changes of the firms involved in an acquisition.

There are several factors favoring the use of options to speculate on expected changes in the prices of stocks involved in an acquisition. It is possible to replicate the payoffs to a particular stock position with the appropriate positions in option contracts. That is, one can replicate the payoffs to a long stock position by holding a call option and selling a put with the same strike price and expiration date. Additionally, you can replicate this payoff with options at a lower cost than purchasing the stock itself. However, options pay off in only one direction, calls in the up state, puts in the down state. Thus, if one expected the price of a particular stock to increase, one could hold a long call position and participate in the upside gains in the stock with a limited investment. A long call position offers the same action as a long stock position at a lower cost. Chapter 13 shows that a long call option is equivalent to a levered stock position. Since call options are cheaper than the stock underlying the option, an investor with a fixed amount to invest can increase his leverage by purchasing several call options. Consider an investor with $10,000 available to speculate in a $100 stock that has a call trading at $10. The investor could purchase 100 shares of stock, $100 \times $100 = $10,000$, or he could purchase 10 call options [(10 contracts × 100 shares per contract) × $10 = $10,000], significantly increasing his exposure to the market. The fact that an investor faces lower transactions costs in the options market is an important factor motivating investors to trade options. Additionally, there may be tax implications of trading options that induce particular investors to trade options rather than trading the underlying stock. The tax factor will be unique to the investor and will depend on the individual's tax obligations. Because it is possible to create synthetic securities with options, it may be possible to avoid stock market restrictions by trading options. In particular, there are specific regulations regarding the short selling of stock that may be avoided by creating a synthetic short position using the Treasury bill and traded options.

B. Based on your understanding of option payouts, discuss and explain the option positions that you would establish to speculate on these expected price changes. (Assume that traded options exist for both firms.)

Our expectations are the stock price of CSC will increase, and the stock price of CAI will decrease because of the expected acquisition. There are many strategies the investor could undertake to take advantage of the expected movements in the stock prices of CSC and CAI. One basic strategy would be to purchase call options written on CSC, and to purchase put options written on CAI. One could reduce the cost of this investment by writing puts on CSC, and writing calls on CAI. In addition, the investor must choose expiration dates and strike prices for the options. The decision regarding the maturity of the option contract will be influenced by expectations regarding the timing of the acquisition.

29. After watching a late night infomercial, a colleague comes to work professing the gospel of income enhancement via covered calls. The pitch man in the infomercial, Mr. Oracle, says that writing covered calls enhances the return on a stock investment with no cost. Discuss the sources of the apparent costless gains and the risks associated with writing covered calls.

When writing an out-of-the-money covered call, you contract to sell the stock you currently own at a price that is higher than the current stock price. As compensation for writing this contract, you receive premium income. The investor owns the underlying stock and is entitled to receive any distributions associated with owning the stock. These may include dividends, or additional shares of stock associated with a stock split or dividend. If the option is exercised against the investor, the investor sells the stock underlying the contract at the strike price. If the strike price is higher than the purchase price of the stock, then the investor will have earned a capital gain on the transaction. Thus, there are three potential sources of gains to the investor: premium income received from writing the call options, dividends, and capital gains from the sale of the stock. These potential returns do not, however, come without corresponding risk. By writing covered calls, the investor is exposed to an opportunity cost. If the option goes into-the-money, the potential gains associated with owning the stock will be offset by the obligations associated with the call option. Writing the covered call has reduced the upside potential of the long stock position. By writing the call option, the investor has given the owner of the call the right to purchase the underlying stock according to the terms of the option contract. It is the owner of the call who determines if and when an option is exercised. If the investor is holding the stock as a long-term investment, having a call exercised against him forces the investor to sell an asset that he wished to hold in his portfolio. If the investor desires to continue to hold the asset in his portfolio, he must return to the market to purchase the stock at the market price bearing all the transactions costs associated with reestablishing an existing position in the stock. Besides limiting the upside potential associated with owning a stock, a covered call position provides no protection against stock price decreases.

30. Late one Friday afternoon in March, an investor receives a call from her broker. Her broker tells her that the March options on Microsoft will expire in ten minutes, that Microsoft is currently trading at $94.50, and that the March 85 call is selling at $8. The investor tells her broker that he is mistaken and must have read his screen incorrectly. Explain which individual, the broker or the investor, is correct. Supposing that the broker is in fact correct, state the transactions that the investor would undertake to take advantage of this situation. Suppose the broker tells the investor that these options are European options. Discuss the impact of the fact that the options are European options on the actions of the investor.

Microsoft options are traded on the CBOE, and the stock options traded on the CBOE are American options. This means that the March 85 MSFT call option must trade at a price that is at least the intrinsic value of the option prior to the option's expiration. The intrinsic value of the call is $9.50 and the option is selling for $8.00, according to the broker. This mispricing represents a classic arbitrage opportunity. To capture the arbitrage profit of $1.50, the investor will simultaneously sell the appropriate number of Microsoft shares and purchase the appropriate amount of the March 85 MSFT call option. The investor will receive $94.50 from the sale of the stock and will pay $8.00 for the call (all on a per share basis). The investor will then exercise the call option paying $85 per share for MSFT. Exercising the option provides the investor with the shares necessary to cover her obligation from selling the stock (short position). The total cash outflows are $93 ($85 + $8), and the cash inflows are $94.5, resulting in $1.50 in riskless profit for the investor. While an investor cannot exercise a European call until the call option expires, the call options in question will expire in 10 minutes. The call should be trading at a price that is above the intrinsic value of the option, $9.50, at this point in the life of the European call option. That is, in ten minutes the call will be in-the-money and be worth $S - X$. The investor will undertake the same arbitrage transactions to profit from this mispricing.

31. As a finance major in college, you were taught the efficient market hypothesis. Because you believe that it is not possible for a mutual fund manager to consistently outperform the market, you hold a portfolio of the 30 stocks that make up the Dow Jones Industrial Average (DJIA). Your broker has just called you with the following offer. He can provide you with insurance that will guarantee that the value of your portfolio will not fall below an indexed level of 8,900. This insurance is evaluated at the end of each quarter and costs $500 per quarter. A quick search of the CBOE web site shows that the Dow is currently trading at an indexed level of 9,005, and that a three-month put option on the DJIA with a strike price of 89 is trading at 2 1/16. The DJIA options traded on the CBOE are quoted at strike prices that are 1/100 of the level of the DJIA. Each premium point is multiplied by $100 to determine the total cost of the option.

A. Should you accept the insurance contract offered by your broker? Explain.

It is possible to use the put option on the DJIA traded on the CBOE to create an insured portfolio. The cost of the traded put is less than the cost of the insurance offered by the broker. Therefore, a rational investor will use the option market to insure the value of his portfolio.

B. Explain how you can provide your own insurance for your portfolio. What is the cost of this insurance? What is the maximum loss on your insured portfolio?

The insured portfolio is constructed by combining your long position in the Dow with a long position in the DJIA put option with a strike price of 89 and an expiration in three months (the strike price of 89 translates to a Dow level of 8,900). The cost of this traded option is $206.25 (2.0625 × $100). If the Dow drops below 8,900 at the end of three months, then the three-month DJIA put option with a strike price of 89 will be in-the-money. The investor will exercise the option at expiration, and be paid cash equal to the difference between the strike price of 89 (DJIA level of 8,900) and the level of the market at the expiration of the option contract. This payoff will create a price floor for the portfolio at an index level of 8,900. The maximum loss on the portfolio would be 105 index points, 9,005 – 8,900.

32. You own shares of AGH that are currently trading at $100. A European put option written on AGH with a $100 strike price that expires in three months is priced at $4. The equivalent call option is priced at $5.

A. What is the price of a three-month T-bill that pays par ($100) implied by the prices given above?

$S = \$100$, $X = \$100$, $c = \$5$, $p = \$4$, $T - t = 0.25$ years

Given these prices, the put-call parity relationship implies that the price of the synthetic T-bill is $99.

$$c - p = S - Xe^{-r(T-t)}, \$5 - \$4 = 100 - Xe^{-r(T-t)}, Xe^{-r(T-t)} = \$99.$$

B. What is the continuously compounded three-month interest rate implied by these prices?

The continuously compounded three-month interest rate implied by these prices is .0402.

$$\$99 = \$100e^{-r(.25)}$$

$$\ln(99/100) = \ln(e^{-r(.25)})$$

$$-0.01005 = -r\,(0.25)$$

$$r = 0.0402$$

C. A quick check of the price of three-month T-bills on *The Wall Street Journal* web site reveals that this bill is trading at $98.50. Explain your actions upon finding this information.

The synthetic bill is overpriced according to the prices given above. Thus, there is an arbitrage opportunity for the investor. To capture the $.50 profit implied by these prices, the investor should simultaneously sell the synthetic Treasury bill and purchase the traded Treasury bill. The synthetic bill position is created by constructing a portfolio that consists of a long position in the stock, a short position in the call, and a long position in the put, $S - c + p = Xe^{-r(T-t)}$. To capture the profit opportunities, the investor must sell the stock short, buy the call, and sell the put resulting in a cash inflow of $99 (+$100 − $5 + $4 = $99). As a result of these transactions, the investor has effectively borrowed at a low interest rate, the short synthetic bond position, and lent at a higher rate, the long traded T-bill position.

33. A protective put position is created by combining a long stock position with a long position in a put option written on the stock $(S + P)$. Construct the equivalent position using call options, assuming all the options are European.

    An equivalent position can be created by combining a long position in a call option with an investment (long position) in the appropriate amount of a Treasury bill. The call and put option must be written on the same stock and have the same strike price and expiration date. The appropriate investment in the T-bill is determined by calculating the present value of the strike price of the put option used to create the protective put position, $Xe^{-r(T-t)}$.

34. TMS is currently trading at $40, which you think is above its true value. Given your knowledge of the firm, its products, and its markets, you believe that $35 per share is a more appropriate price for TMS. One means of purchasing TMS at $35 per share would be to write a limit order. A limit order is an order directed to a broker on the floor of the exchange that specifies, among other things, the purchase price of the stock. You also notice that TMS has traded options and that a $40 put option is selling for $5. An alternative investment strategy involves purchasing TMS for $40 and writing a TMS put option for $5.

A. If at the expiration of the option, TMS's stock is trading at a price above $40 per share, discuss the benefits of the buy stock/sell put investment strategy.

    When TMS is trading above $40 per share at the put's expiration, the put option that you have written is worthless. In this environment, you will have effectively purchased TMS for $35 per share, $40 to purchase TMS in the spot market less $5 received from writing the $40 put option.

B. If at the expiration of the option, TMS's stock is trading at a price below $40 per share, discuss the benefits of this alternative investment strategy.

    When TMS is trading below $40 per share at expiration, the short put option position is in-the-money and will be exercised against the investor. In this environment, the impact of the lower stock price on the cost of your position will vary linearly with the stock price. For prices between $35 and $40, the $5 premium income received from writing the put option will offset losses on the option position dollar for dollar. That is, at $39, the $1 loss on the option position will be offset by the $5 premium income resulting in an effective purchase price of $36 for a share of TMS. At stock prices lower than $35 per share, the losses from the option position will offset the gains from the premium income received resulting in an effective purchase price greater than $40 per share.

35. When you purchase property insurance, you must choose the dollar amount of the deductible on the policy. Similarly, when you construct a protective put position, you must choose the strike price on the put option. Discuss the similarities between the choice of the deductible on an insurance policy and the selection of a strike price for the protective put position.

    When selecting the deductible on the insurance policy, the investor is deciding the dollar amount of losses that she is willing to self-insure. That is, the choice of the deductible determines how much of a loss must be covered by the resources of the insured prior to any payment by the insurer. In general, the greater the risk that is self-insured, the lower the cost of the insurance. A protective put position is constructed to limit an investor's exposure to losses arising from decreases in the price of the stock held by the investor. The investor must choose the strike price on the put option when constructing the position. If the investor chooses a strike price that is well below the current stock price, the investor is bearing more risk from holding the stock, and the price of the insurance will be less. That is, the investor has self-insured more of the risk of a stock price decline. Therefore, the price of a deep-out-of-the-money put should be less than the price of a near-the-money put.

36. A client has recently sold a stock short for $100. The short sale agreement requires him to cover the short position in one month. The client wants to protect his position against stock price increases. You notice that the stock has puts and calls traded on the CBOE. Explain how your client can use either the put or call option to construct a portfolio that will limit his risk exposure to stock price increases. Compare the two alternative strategies.

In this situation, increases in the stock price represent a risk to the investor. If at the end of the month the stock is selling above $100, the investor will have to cover the position and will incur a loss. In this hedging problem, the investor needs to construct a portfolio such that increases in the stock price will result in an increase in the value of the hedging instrument that can offset the losses incurred on the short stock position. The first strategy would be to combine the short stock position with a long call position. Increases in the price of the stock will increase the value of the call option. The increases in the value of the call option position will offset losses in the short stock position. One decision the investor must make is the selection of the strike price of the option—that is, the selection of the amount of loss (risk) the investor is willing to bear. The price of a call option with a $110 strike price will be less than the price of a call with a $100 exercise price. The investor would choose to hold a call that expired in one month (the same time until the short position must be covered). For example, assume the investor held a $100 call that expired in one month. If the stock price at the end of the month was $105, then the investor would exercise the call and purchase the stock at $100 to cover the short position. The cost of the protection would be the price of the call option. The other strategy would combine a short put position with the short stock position. In this case, the investor would use the premium income received from writing the put to cover any losses associated with stock price increases. As happens with a covered call position, this premium income would provide limited protection against adverse stock price movements, and would limit potential gains associated with stock price decreases. For example, assume the investor wrote a $100 put that expired in one month. If the stock price at the end of the month was $95, then the owner of the put would exercise the put against your client, forcing your client to purchase the stock at $100. This loss of $5 on the option contract will offset the $5 gain in the value of the short stock position. At prices above $100, the put will expire worthless and the premium income will offset some of the losses in the short stock position.

Bounds on Option Prices | 12

Answers to Questions and Problems

1. What is the maximum theoretical value for a call? Under what conditions does a call reach this maximum value? Explain.

   The highest price theoretically possible for a call option is to equal the value of the underlying stock. This happens only for a call option that has a zero exercise price and an infinite time until expiration. With such a call, the option can be instantaneously and costlessly exchanged for the stock at any time. Therefore, the call must have at least the value of the stock itself. Yet it cannot be worth more than the stock, because the option merely gives access to the stock itself. As a consequence, the call must have the same price as the stock.

2. What is the maximum theoretical value for an American put? When does it reach this maximum? Explain.

   The maximum value of a put equals the potential inflow of the exercise price minus the associated outflow of the stock price. The maximum value for this quantity occurs when the stock price is zero. At that time, the value of the put will equal the exercise price. In this situation, the put gives immediate potential access to the exercise price because it is an American option.

3. Answer question 2 for a European put.

   As with the American put, the European put attains its maximum value when the stock price is zero. However, before expiration, the put cannot be exercised. Therefore, the maximum price for a European put is the present value of the exercise price, when the exercise price is discounted at the risk-free rate from expiration to the present. This discounting reflects the fact that the owner of a European put cannot exercise now and collect the exercise price. Instead, he or she must wait until the option expires.

4. Explain the difference in the theoretical maximum values for an American and a European put.

   The exercise value of a put option equals the exercise price (an inflow) minus the value of the stock at the time of exercise (an outflow). In our notation, this exercise value is $X - S$. For any put, the maximum value occurs when the stock is worthless, $S = 0$. The American and European puts have different maximum theoretical values because of the different rules governing early exercise. Because an American put can be exercised at any time, its maximum theoretical value equals the exercise price, X. If the stock price is zero at any time, an American put gives its owner immediate access to amount X through exercise. This is not true of a European put, which can be exercised only at expiration. If the option has time remaining until expiration and the stock is worthless, the European put holder must wait until expiration to exercise. With the stock worthless, the exercise will yield X to the European put holder. Because the exercise must wait until expiration, however, the put can be worth only the present value of the exercise price. Thus, the theoretical maximum value of a European put is $Xe^{-r(T - t)}$. In the special case of an option at expiration, $t = 0$, the maximum value for a European and an American put is X.

5. How does the exercise price affect the price of a call? Explain.

The call price varies inversely with the exercise price. The exercise price is a potential liability that the call owner faces, because the call owner must pay the exercise price in order to exercise. The smaller this potential liability, other factors held constant, the greater will be the value of a call option.

6. Consider two calls with the same time to expiration that are written on the same underlying stock. Call 1 trades for $7 and has an exercise price of $100. Call 2 has an exercise price of $95. What is the maximum price that Call 2 can have? Explain.

A no-arbitrage condition places an upper bound on the value of Call 2. The price of Call 2 cannot exceed the price of the option with the higher exercise price plus the $5 difference in the two exercise prices. Thus, the upper bound for the value of Call 2 is $12. If Call 2 is priced above $12, say, at $13, the following arbitrage becomes available.

Sell Call 2 for cash flow +$13 and buy Call 1 for cash flow –$7. This is a net cash inflow of +$6. If Call 2 is exercised against you, you can immediately exercise Call 1. This provides the stock to meet the exercise of Call 1 against you. On the double exercise, you receive $95 and pay $100, for a net cash flow of –$5. However, you received $6 at the time of trading for a net profit of $1. This is the worst case outcome.

If Call 1 cannot be exercised, the profit is the full $6 original cash flow from the two trades. Also, if the stock price lies between $95 and $100 when Call 1 is exercised against you, it may be optimal to purchase the stock in the market rather than exercise Call 2 to secure the stock. For example, assume the stock trades for $98 when Call 1 is exercised against you. In this case, you buy the stock for $98 instead of exercising Call 2 and paying $100. Then your total cash flows are +$6 from the two trades, +$95 when Call 1 is exercised against you, and –$98 from purchasing the stock to meet the exercise. Now your net arbitrage profit is $3. In summary, stock prices of $95 or below give a net profit of $6, because Call 1 cannot be exercised. Stock prices of $100 or above give a net profit of $1, because you will need to exercise Call 2 to meet the exercise of Call 1. Prices between $95 and $100 give a profit equal to +$6 +$95 – stock price at the time of exercise.

7. Six months remain until a call option expires. The stock price is $70 and the exercise price is $65. The option price is $5. What does this imply about the interest rate?

We know from the no-arbitrage arguments that: $C \geq S - Xe^{-r(T-t)}$. In this case, we have $C = S - X$ exactly. Therefore, the interest rate must be zero.

8. Assume the interest rate is 12 percent and four months remain until an option expires. The exercise price of the option is $70 and the stock that underlies the option is worth $80. What is the minimum value the option can have based on the no-arbitrage conditions studied in this chapter? Explain.

We know from the no-arbitrage arguments that: $C \geq S - Xe^{-r(T-t)}$. Substituting the specified values gives $C \geq \$80 - \$70e^{-0.12(0.33)} = \$80 - \$67.28 = \$12.72$. Therefore, the call price must equal or exceed $12.72 to avoid arbitrage.

9. Two call options are written on the same stock that trades for $70, and both calls have an exercise price of $85. Call 1 expires in six months, and Call 2 expires in three months. Assume that Call 1 trades for $6 and that Call 2 trades for $7. Do these prices allow arbitrage? Explain. If they do permit arbitrage, explain the arbitrage transactions.

Here we have two calls that are identical except for their time to expiration. In this situation, the call with the longer time until expiration must have a price equal to or exceeding the price of the shorter-lived option. These values violate this condition, so arbitrage is possible as follows:

Sell Call 2 and buy Call 1 for a net cash inflow of $1. If Call 2 is exercised at any time, the trader can exercise Call 1 and meet the exercise obligation for a net zero cash flow. This retains the $1 profit no matter what happens. It may also occur that the profit exceeds $1. For example, assume that Call 2 cannot be exercised in the first three months and expires worthless. This leaves the trader with the $1 initial cash inflow plus a call option with a three-month life, so the trader has an arbitrage profit of at least $1, and perhaps much more.

10. Explain the circumstances that make early exercise of a call rational. Under what circumstances is early exercise of a call irrational?

Exercising a call before expiration discards the time value of the option. If the underlying stock pays a dividend, it can be rational to discard the time value to capture the dividend. If there is no dividend, it will always be irrational to exercise a call, because the trader can always sell the call in the market instead. Exercising a call on a no-dividend stock discards the time value, while selling the option in the market retains it. Thus, only the presence of a dividend can justify early exercise. Even in this case, the dividend must be large enough to warrant the sacrifice of the time value.

11. Consider a European and an American call with the same expiration and the same exercise price that are written on the same stock. What relationship must hold between their prices? Explain.

Because the American option gives every benefit that the European option does, the price of the American option must be at least as great as that of the European option. The right of early exercise inherent in the American option can give extra value if a dividend payment is possible before the common expiration date. Thus, if there is no dividend to consider, the two prices will be the same. If a dividend is possible before expiration, the price of the American call may exceed that of the European call.

12. Before exercise, what is the minimum value of an American put?

The minimum value of an American put must equal its value for immediate exercise, which is $X - S$. A lower price results in arbitrage. For example, assume $X = \$100$, $S = \$90$, and $P = \$8$. To exploit the arbitrage inherent in these prices, buy the put and exercise for a net cash outflow of $-\$98$. Sell the stock for $+\$100$ for an arbitrage profit of $2.

13. Before exercise, what is the minimum value of a European put?

For a put, the exercise value is $X - S$. However, a European put can be exercised only at expiration. Therefore, the present value of the exercise value is $Xe^{-r(T-t)} - S$, and this is the minimum price of a European put. For example, consider $X = \$100$, $S = \$90$, $T - t = 0.5$ years, and $r = 0.10$. The no-arbitrage condition implies the put should be worth at least $5.13.

Assume that the put actually trades for $5. With these prices, an arbitrageur could trade as follows. Borrow $95 at 10 percent for six months and buy the stock and the put. This gives an initial net zero cash flow. At expiration, the profit depends upon the price of the stock. First, there will be a debt to pay of $99.87 in all cases. If the stock price is $100 or above, the put is worthless and the profit equals $S - \$99.87$. Thus, the profit will be at least $.13, and possibly much more. For stock prices below $100, exercise of the put yields $100, which is enough to pay the debt of $99.87 and keep $.13 profit.

14. Explain the differences in the minimum values of American and European puts before expiration.

The difference in minimum values for American and European puts stems from the restrictions on exercising a put. An American put offers the immediate access to the exercise value X if the put owner chooses to exercise. Because the European put cannot be exercised until expiration, the cash inflow associated with exercise must be discounted to $Xe^{-r(T-t)}$. The difference in minimum values equals the time value of the exercise price.

15. How does the price of an American put vary with time until expiration? Explain.

The value of an American put increases with the time until expiration. A longer-lived put offers every advantage that the shorter-lived put does. Therefore, a longer-lived put must be worth at least as much as the shorter-lived put. This implies that value increases with time until expiration. Violation of this condition leads to arbitrage.

16. What relationship holds between time until expiration and the price of a European put?

    For a European put, the value may or may not increase with time until expiration. Upon exercise, the put holder receives $X - S$. If the European put holder cannot exercise immediately, the inflow represented by the exercise price is deferred. For this reason, the value of a European put can be lower the longer the time until expiration. However, having a longer term until expiration also adds value to a put, because it allows more time for something beneficial to happen to the stock price. Thus, the net effect of time until expiration depends on these two opposing forces. Under some circumstances, the value of a European put will increase as time until expiration increases, but it will not always do so.

17. Consider two puts with the same term to expiration (six months). One put has an exercise price of $110, and the other has an exercise price of $100. Assume the interest rate is 12 percent. What is the maximum price difference between the two puts if they are European? If they are American? Explain the difference, if any.

    For two European puts, the price differential cannot exceed the difference in the present value of the exercise prices. With our data, the difference cannot exceed $($110 - $100)e^{-0.12(0.5)} = 9.42. If the price differential on the European puts exceeds $9.42, we have an arbitrage opportunity. To capture the arbitrage profit, we sell the relatively overpriced put with the exercise price of $110 and buy the put with the $100 exercise price. If the put we sold is exercised against us, we accept the stock and dispose of it by exercising the put we bought. This will always guarantee a profit. For example, assume that the put with $X = 100 trades for $5 and the put with $X = 110 sells for $15, giving a $10 differential. We sell the put with $X = $110 and buy the put with $X = $100, for a net inflow of $10. We invest this until expiration, at which time it will be worth $10e^{12(.5)} = 10.62. If the put we sold is exercised against us, we pay $110 and receive the stock. We can then exercise our put to dispose of the stock and receive $10. This gives a $10 loss on the double exercise. However, our maturing bond is worth $10.62, so we still have a profit of $.62.

    For two American puts, the price differential cannot exceed the difference in the exercise prices. If it does, we conduct the same arbitrage. However, we do not have to worry about the discounted value of the differential, because the American puts carry the opportunity to exercise immediately and to gain access to the value of the mispricing at any time, not just at expiration.

18. How does the price of a call vary with interest rates? Explain.

    For a call, the price increases with interest rates. The easiest way to see this is to consider the no-arbitrage condition: $C \geq S - Xe^{-r(T-t)}$. The higher the interest rate, the smaller will be the present value of the exercise price, a potential liability. With extremely high interest rates, the exercise price will have an insignificant present value and the call price will approach the stock price.

19. Explain how a put price varies with interest rates. Does the relationship vary for European and American puts? Explain.

    Put prices vary inversely with interest rates. This holds true for both American and European puts. For the put owner, the exercise price is a potential inflow. The present value of this inflow, and the market value of the put, increases as the interest rate falls. Therefore, put prices rise as interest rates fall.

20. What is the relationship between the risk of the underlying stock and the call price? Explain in intuitive terms.

Call prices rise as the riskiness of the underlying stock increases. A call option embodies insurance against extremely bad outcomes. Insurance is more valuable the greater the risk it insures against. Therefore, if the underlying stock is very risky, the insurance embedded in the call is more valuable. As a consequence, call prices vary directly with the risk of the underlying good.

21. A stock is priced at $50, and the risk-free rate of interest is 10 percent. A European call and a European put on this stock both have exercise prices of $40 and expire in six months. What is the difference between the call and put prices? (Assume continuous compounding.) From the information supplied in this question, can you say what the call and put prices must be? If not, explain what information is lacking.

From put-call parity, $S - Xe^{-r(T-t)} = C - P$. Therefore, the $C - P$ must equal:

$$\$50 - \$40e^{-0.5(0.1)} = \$11.95$$

We cannot determine the two option prices. Information about how the stock price might move is lacking.

22. A stock is priced at $50, and the risk-free rate of interest is 10 percent. A European call and a European put on this stock both have exercise prices of $40 and expire in six months. Assume that the call price exceeds the put price by $7. Does this represent an arbitrage opportunity? If so, explain why and state the transactions you would make to take advantage of the pricing discrepancy.

From question 21, we saw that the call price must exceed the put price by $11.95 according to put-call parity. Therefore, if the difference is only $7, there is an arbitrage opportunity, and the call price is cheap relative to the put. The long call/short put position is supposed to be worth the same as the long stock/short bond position. But the long call/short put portfolio costs only $7, not the theoretically required $11.95. To perform the arbitrage, we would buy the relatively underpriced portfolio and sell the relatively overpriced portfolio. Specifically, we would: buy the call, sell the put, sell the stock, and buy the risk-free bond that pays the exercise price in six months. From these transactions, we would have the following cash flows: from buying the call and selling the put –$7; from selling the stock +$50, and from buying the risk-free bond –$38.05, for a net cash flow of $4.95. This net cash flow exactly equals the pricing discrepancy.

At expiration, we can fulfill all of our obligations with no further cash flows. If the stock price is below the exercise price, the put we sold will be exercised against us and we must pay $40 and receive the stock. We will have the $40 from the maturing bond, and we use the stock that we receive to repay our short sale on the stock. If the stock price exceeds $40, we exercise our call and use the $40 proceeds to pay the exercise price. We then fulfill our short sale by returning the share.

23. Cursory examination of the table below shows a violation of a basic option pricing rule. Which pricing rule has been violated? Discuss the limitations of using a newspaper as the source of prices used to make inferences about pricing.

Option	Strike	Exp.	Call Vol.	Call Last	Put Vol.	Put Last
IBM						
$101\frac{5}{8}$	115	Sep	1632	$\frac{3}{16}$	10	$13\frac{1}{4}$
$101\frac{5}{8}$	115	Oct	861	$1\frac{1}{4}$	10	$14\frac{1}{4}$
$101\frac{5}{8}$	115	Jan	225	4	3	14

The pricing rule violated is the rule that the price of an American put option increases as the maturity of the option increases. That is, the longer the time until expiration, the more valuable a put option. The only characteristic that varies across the put options in the table is the time until expiration. This is a classic problem of stale prices. The information reported in the paper is historical information. Examining the reported trading volume reveals the likely source of this apparent problem. Very few put options were traded that day. In fact, only 3 Jan IBM 115 put options were traded on the day reported in the table. It is highly likely that the prices reported in the table represent prices recorded at different times during the day. To take advantage of mispricings, one needs to know the prices of all the relevant options at the same point in time.

24. Explain why an American call is always worth at least as much as its intrinsic value. Explain why this is not true for European calls.

The owner of an American call can exercise the option anytime over the life of the option and capture the option's intrinsic value $(S - X)$. Therefore, the price of the American call can never be less that the intrinsic value of the option. The owner of a European call cannot exercise the option until the option's expiration. If the option is in-the-money, the investor cannot capture this gain until the option's expiration; therefore, it is possible for the value of a European call to be less than the intrinsic value of the option. This is likely to happen if the option is deep-in-the-money and has a long time until expiration.

25. Give an intuitive explanation of why the early exercise of an in-the-money American put option becomes more attractive as the volatility of the underlying stock decreases, and the risk-free interest rate increases.

If the stock's volatility decreases, then the probability of a very large change in the stock price decreases. It is a large stock price move that will take the put deeper-into-the-money, making the put more valuable. If large price decreases are not very likely, then the probability of a large payoff from holding the put is very small and the value of the put will not increase. If at the same time that volatility is increasing the risk-free interest rate is increasing, then the opportunity cost of holding the put will increase. If the put were exercised, the exercise proceeds could be invested at the new higher risk-free rate.

26. Suppose that c_1, c_2, and c_3 are the prices of three European call options written on the same share of stock that are identical in all respects except their strike prices. The strike prices for the three call options are X_1, X_2, and X_3, respectively, where $X_3 > X_2 > X_1$ and $X_3 - X_2 = X_2 - X_1$. All options have the same maturity. Assume that all portfolios are held to expiration. Show that:

$$c_2 \leq 0.5 \times (c_1 + c_3)$$

Consider two portfolios. The first portfolio, A, consists of a long position in two call options with the strike price X_2. The second portfolio, B, contains a long position in one call option with a strike price X_1 and a long position in one call option with a strike price of X_3. Consider the payoffs that are possible at the option's expiration. Remember that there is a fixed dollar difference between the strike prices of the options, for example, $X_1 = 50$, $X_2 = 55$, and $X_3 = 60$.

		Stock Price at Expiration			
Portfolio	Current Value of Portfolio	$S \leq X_1$	$X_1 < S \leq X_2$	$X_2 < S \leq X_3$	$S > X_3$
A	$2c_2$	0	0	$2(S - X_2)$	$2(S - X_2)$
B	$c_1 + c_3$	0	$S - X_1$	$S - X_1$	$(S - X_1) +$ $(S - X_3)$
Relative value of the portfolio at expiration		$V_A = V_B$	$V_B \geq V_A$	$V_B \geq V_A$	$V_A = V_B$

Since the value of portfolio B is never less than the value of portfolio A at the expiration of the options, then the current value of portfolio B must be at least as large as the current value of portfolio A. If this were not the case, arbitrage would be possible. Thus, $c_1 + c_3 - 2c_2 \geq 0$ and $c_2 \leq 0.5 \times (c_1 + c_3)$.

27. Suppose that p_1, p_2, and p_3 are the prices of three European put options written on the same share of stock that are identical in all respects except their strike prices. The strike prices for the three put options are X_1, X_2, and X_3, respectively, where $X_3 > X_2 > X_1$ and $X_3 - X_2 = X_2 - X_1$. All options have the same maturity. Assume that all portfolios are held to expiration. Show that:

$$p_2 \leq 0.5 \times (p_1 + p_3)$$

Consider two portfolios, A and B. Portfolio A consists of a long position in two put options with a strike price of X_2. Portfolio B consists of a long position in one put option with a strike price X_1 plus a long position in one put option with a strike price of X_3. Consider the payoffs that are possible at the option's expiration. Remember that there is a fixed dollar difference between the strike prices of the options, for example, $X_1 = 50$, $X_2 = 55$, and $X_3 = 60$.

		Stock Price at Expiration			
Portfolio	**Current Value of Portfolio**	$S \leq X_1$	$X_1 < S \leq X_2$	$X_2 < S \leq X_3$	$S > X_3$
A	$2p_2$	$2(X_2 - S)$	$2(X_2 - S)$	0	0
B	$p_1 + p_3$	$(X_1 - S) +$ $(X_3 - S)$	$X_3 - S$	$X_3 - S$	0
Relative value of the portfolio at expiration		$V_A = V_B$	$V_B \geq V_A$	$V_B \geq V_A$	$V_A = V_B$

Because the value of portfolio B is never less than the value of portfolio A at the expiration of the options, the current value of portfolio B must be at least as large as the current value of portfolio A. If this were not the case, arbitrage would be possible. Thus, $p_1 + p_3 - 2p_2 \geq 0$ and $p_2 \leq 0.5 \times (p_1 + p_3)$.

13 | **European Option Pricing**

Answers to Questions and Problems

1. What is binomial about the binomial model? In other words, how does the model get its name?

   The binomial model is binomial because it allows for two possible stock price movements. The stock can either rise by a certain amount or fall by a certain amount. No other stock price movement is possible.

2. If a stock price moves in a manner consistent with the binomial model, what is the chance that the stock price will be the same for two periods in a row? Explain.

   There is no chance. In every period, the stock price will either rise or fall. Therefore, in two adjacent periods, the stock price cannot be the same. From this period to the next, the stock price must necessarily rise or fall. However, the stock price can later return to its present price. This depends on the up and down factors for the change in the stock price.

3. Assume a stock price is $120, and in the next year, it will either rise by 10 percent or fall by 20 percent. The risk-free interest rate is 6 percent. A call option on this stock has an exercise price of $130. What is the price of a call option that expires in one year? What is the chance that the stock price will rise?

   Our data are:

   $$C_u = \$2$$
   $$C_d = \$0$$
   $$US = \$132$$
   $$DS = \$96$$
   $$R = 1.06$$
   $$B^* = \frac{(C_u\, D - C_d\, U)}{[(U - D)\, R]} = \frac{2(0.8) - 0(1.1)}{(1.1 - 0.8)(1.06)} = \$5.03$$
   $$N^* = \frac{C_u - C_d}{(U - D)\, S} = \frac{2 - 0}{(1.1 - 0.8)\,120} = 0.0556$$

   Therefore, $C = 0.0556(\$120) - \$5.03 = \$1.64$. The probability of a stock price increase is:

   $$(R - D)/(U - D) = (1.06 - 0.8)/(1.1 - 0.8) = 0.8667$$

4. Based on the data in question 3, what would you hold to form a risk-free portfolio?

   Because $C = N^*S - B^*$, the portfolio of $C - N^*S + B^*$ should be a riskless portfolio.

5. Based on the data in question 3, what will the price of the call option be if the option expires in two years and the stock price can move up 10 percent or down 20 percent in each year?

Terminal stock prices in two periods are given as follows: $UUS = \$145.20$, $DDS = \$76.80$, and $UDS = DUS = \$105.60$. The probabilities of these different terminal stock prices are: $\pi_{uu} = (0.8667)(0.8667) = 0.7512$; $\pi_{ud} = (0.8667)(0.1333) = 0.1155$; $\pi_{du} = (0.1333)(0.8667) = 0.1155$; and $\pi_{dd} = (0.1333)(0.1333) = 0.0178$. The call price at expiration equals the terminal stock price minus the exercise price of $100, or zero, whichever is larger. Therefore, we have $C_{uu} = \$15.20$, $C_{dd} = 0$, $C_{du} = C_{ud} = 0$.

We have already found that the probability of an increase is 0.8667, so the probability of a down movement is 0.1333. Because the option pays off only with two increases, we need consider only that path. Thus, the value of the call is:

$$C = \pi_{uu} C_{uu}/R^2 = (0.7512)(\$15.20)/(1.06)^2 = \$10.16$$

6. Based on the data in question 3, what would the price of a call with one year to expiration be if the call has an exercise price of $135? Can you answer this question without making the full calculations? Explain.

   From question 3, we see that $US = \$132$. This is not enough to bring the call into-the-money. Therefore, we know that the call must expire worthless, so its current price is zero.

7. A stock is worth $60 dollars today. In a year, the stock price can rise or fall by 15 percent. If the interest rate is 6 percent, what is the price of a call option that expires in three years and has an exercise price of $70? What is the price of a put option that expires in three years and has an exercise price of $65? (Use **OPTION!** to solve this problem.)

   The call is worth $6.12 and the put is worth $3.04. The two trees from **OPTION!** are shown here:

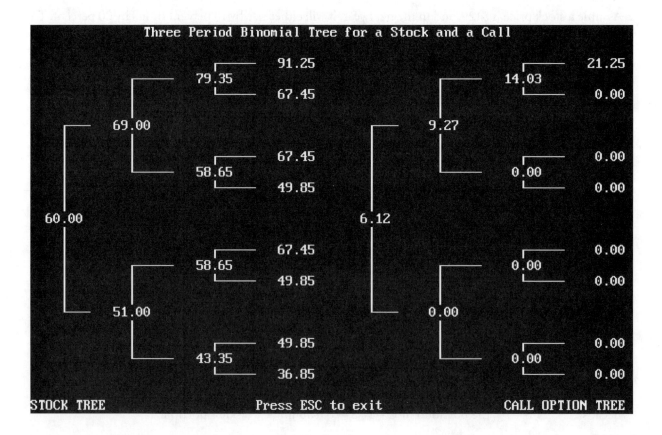

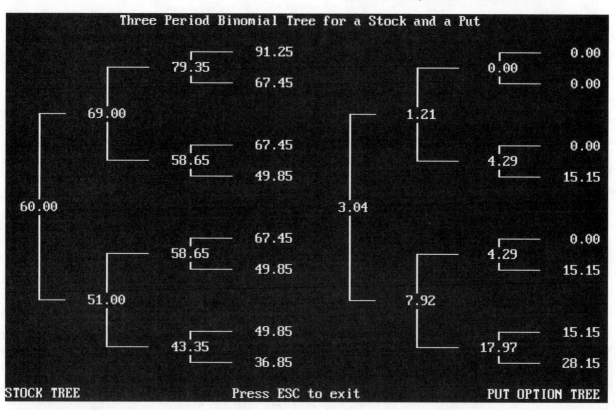

Three Period Binomial Tree for a Stock and a Put

STOCK TREE   Press ESC to exit   PUT OPTION TREE

8. Consider our model of stock price movements given in Equation 13.8. A stock has an initial price of $55 and an expected growth rate of 0.15 per year. The annualized standard deviation of the stock's return is 0.4. What is the expected stock price after 175 days?

Substituting values for our problem, and realizing that the expected value of a drawing for a $N(0,1)$ distribution is zero, gives:

$$S_{t+1} - S_t = \$55(0.15)(175/365) = \$3.96$$

Adding this amount to the initial stock price of $55 gives $58.96 as the expected stock price in 175 days.

9. A stock sells for $110. A call option on the stock has an exercise price of $105 and expires in 43 days. If the interest rate is 0.11 and the standard deviation of the stock's returns is 0.25, what is the price of the call according to the Black-Scholes model? What would be the price of a put with an exercise price of $140 and the same time until expiration?

$$d_1 = \frac{\ln\left[\dfrac{110}{105}\right] + \left[.11 + .5\left(.25\right)\left(.25\right)\right]\left[\dfrac{43}{365}\right]}{.25\sqrt{\dfrac{43}{365}}} = .7361$$

$$d_2 = d_1 - \sigma\sqrt{t} = .7361 - .25\sqrt{\frac{43}{365}} = .6503$$

From the **OPTION!** software, $N(0.7361) = 0.769165$ and $N(0.6503) = 0.742251$. Therefore,

$$c = \$110(0.769165) - \$105e^{-0.11(43/365)}(0.742251) = \$7.6752$$

For the put option with $X = \$140$:

$$d_1 = \frac{\ln\left[\dfrac{110}{140}\right] + \left[.11 + .5\,(.25)\,(.25)\right]\left[\dfrac{43}{365}\right]}{.25\sqrt{\dfrac{43}{365}}} = -2.6177$$

$$d_2 = d_1 - \sigma\sqrt{t} = -2.6177 - .25\sqrt{\frac{43}{365}} = -2.7035$$

The Black-Scholes put pricing model is:

$$p_t = Xe^{-r(T-t)}\,N(-d_2) - S_t\,N(-d_1)$$

$N(2.7035) = 0.996569$ and $N(2.6177) = 0.995574$. Therefore,

$$p_t = \$140e^{-0.11(43/365)}(0.996569) - \$110(0.995574) = \$28.21$$

10. Consider a stock that trades for $75. A put and a call on this stock both have an exercise price of $70 and they expire in 150 days. If the risk-free rate is 9 percent and the standard deviation for the stock is 0.35, compute the price of the options according to the Black-Scholes model.

$$d_1 = \frac{\ln\left[\dfrac{75}{70}\right] + \left[.09 + .5\,(.35)\,(.35)\right]\left[\dfrac{150}{365}\right]}{.35\sqrt{\dfrac{150}{365}}} = .5845$$

$$d_2 = d_1 - \sigma\sqrt{t} = .5845 - .35\sqrt{\frac{150}{365}} = .3601$$

$N(0.5845) = 0.720558$, $N(0.3601) = 0.640614$, $N(-0.5845) = 0.279442$, and $N(-0.3601) = 0.359386$.

$$c_t = \$75(0.720558) - \$70e^{-0.09(150/365)}\,(0.640614) = \$54.04 - \$43.21 = \$10.83$$

$$p_t = \$70e^{-0.09(150/365)}\,(0.359386) - \$75\,(0.279442) = \$24.24 - \$20.96 = \$3.29$$

11. For the options in question 10, now assume that the stock pays a continuous dividend of 4 percent. What are the options worth according to Merton's model?

$$d_1^M = \frac{\ln\left[\dfrac{75}{70}\right] + \left[.09 - .04 + .5\,(.35)\,(.35)\right]\left[\dfrac{150}{365}\right]}{.35\sqrt{\dfrac{150}{365}}} = .5113$$

$$d_2^M = d_1^M - \sigma\sqrt{t} = .5113 - .35\sqrt{\frac{150}{365}} = .2869$$

$N(0.5113) = 0.695430$, $N(0.2869) = 0.304570$, $N(-0.5113) = 0.612906$, and $N(-0.2869) = 0.387094$.

$$c_t^M = e^{-0.04(150/365)}\,\$75\,(0.695430) - \$70e^{-0.09(150/365)}\,(0.612906) = \$9.96$$

$$p_t^M = \$70e^{-0.09(150/365)}\,(0.387094) - \$75e^{-0.04(150/365)}\,(0.304570) = \$3.64$$

12. Consider a Treasury bill with 173 days until maturity. The bid and asked yields on the bill are 9.43 and 9.37. What is the price of the T-bill? What is the continuously compounded rate on the bill?

From the text, we have:

$$P_{TB} = 1 - .01 \left(\frac{B+A}{2} \right) \left(\frac{\text{Days until Maturity}}{360} \right)$$

$$= 1 - .01 \left(\frac{9.43 + 9.37}{2} \right) \left(\frac{173}{360} \right)$$

$$= .9548$$

Therefore, the price of the bill is 95.48 percent of par. To find the corresponding continuously compounded rate, we solve the following equation for r:

$$e^{r(T-t)} = 1/PTB$$

$$e^{r(173/365)} = 1/.9548$$

$$r = 0.0962$$

Thus, the continuously compounded rate on the bill is 9.62 percent.

13. Consider the following sequence of daily stock prices: $47, $49, $46, $45, $51. Compute the mean daily logarithmic return for this share. What is the daily standard deviation of returns? What is the annualized standard deviation?

Let P_t = the price on day t, $PR_t = P_t/P_{t-1}$, PR_μ = the mean daily logarithmic return, and σ = the standard deviation of the daily logarithmic return. Then,

PR_t	$\ln(PR_t)$	$[\ln PR_t - PR_\mu]^2$
1.0426	0.0417	.000454
0.9388	−0.0632	.006989
0.9783	−0.0219	.001789
1.1333	0.1251	.010962

$$PR_\mu = (0.0417 - 0.0632 - 0.0219 + 0.1251)/4 = 0.0204$$

$$\text{VAR}(PR) = (1/3)(0.000454 + .006989 + .001789 + .010962) = 0.006731$$

σ = the square root of 0.006731 = 0.082045.

The annualized $\sigma = \sigma$ times the square root of 250 = 1.2972.

14. A stock sells for $85. A call option with an exercise price of $80 expires in 53 days and sells for $8. The risk-free interest rate is 11 percent. What is the implied standard deviation for the stock? (Use **OPTION!** to solve this problem.)

$\sigma = 0.332383$. It is also possible to find this value by repeated application of the Black-Scholes formula. For example, with this option data, different trial values of σ give the following sequence of prices:

Call Price	Trial Value of σ	σ is:
$6.29	.1	too low
9.84	.5	too high
7.67	.3	too low
8.72	.4	too high
8.18	.35	too high
7.98	.33	too low
8.03	.335	too high
8.01	.333	too high
8.00	.332	very close

The OPTION! program follows a search like this to zero in on the correct value of σ so that the resulting option price matches the actual price.

15. For a particular application of the binomial model, assume that $U = 1.09$, $D = 0.91$, and that the two are equally probable. Do these assumptions lead to any particular difficulty? Explain. (Note: These are specified up and down movements and are not intended to be consistent with the Black-Scholes model.)

    Note that $0.5 (1.09) + 0.5 (0.91) = 1.0$, so the expected return on the stock is zero. The expected return on the stock must equal the risk-free rate in the risk-neutral setting of the binomial model. Therefore, these up and down factors imply a zero interest rate.

16. For a stock that trades at $120 and has a standard deviation of returns of 0.4, use the Black-Scholes model to price a call and a put that expire in 180 days and that have an exercise price of $100. The risk-free rate is 8 percent. Now assume that the stock will pay a dividend of $3 on day 75. Apply the known dividend adjustment to the Black-Scholes model and compute new call and put prices.

    With no dividends, the call price is $27.54, and the put price is $3.67. With the known dividend adjustment, the call price is $25.14, and the put price is $4.23.

17. A call and a put expire in 150 days and have an exercise price of $100. The underlying stock is worth $95 and has a standard deviation of 0.25. The risk-free rate is 11 percent. Use a three-period binomial model and stock price movements consistent with the Black-Scholes model to compute the value of these options. Specify U, D, and π_u, as well as the values for the call and put.

    The call price is $5.80, and the put price is $6.38. $U = 1.0969$, and $D = 0.9116$.

    $$\pi_U = \frac{e^{.11\left[\frac{50}{365}\right]} - .9116}{1.0969 - .9116} = .5590$$

18. For the situation in problem 17, assume that the stock will pay 2 percent of its value as a dividend on day 80. Compute the value of the call and the put under this circumstance.

    Recalling that these are European options, the call is worth $4.66, and the put is worth $7.14.

19. For the situation in problem 17, assume that the stock will pay a dividend of $2 on day 80. Compute the value of the call and the put under this circumstance.

    The call is worth $4.62, and the put is worth $7.16.

20. Consider the first tree in Figures 13.10 and 13.12. If the stock price falls in both of the first two periods, the price is $65.59. For the first tree in Figure 13.12, the put value is $8.84 in this case. Given that the exercise price on the put is $75, does this present a contradiction? Explain.

The apparent contradiction arises because the intrinsic value of the put is $75 - $65.59 = $9.41, which exceeds the put price of $8.84. However, because this is a European put, it cannot be exercised to capture the intrinsic value prior to expiration. Thus, the European put price can be less than the intrinsic value.

21. Consider the second tree in Figures 13.10 and 13.11. If the stock price increases in the first period, the price is $88.35. For the second tree in Figure 13.11, the call price is $12.94 in this case. Given that the exercise price on the put is $75, does this present a contradiction? Explain.

    One of the arbitrage conditions we have considered says that the call price must equal or exceed $S - X$. In this situation, $S - X = $88.35 - $75.00 = 13.35, which is greater than the call price of $12.94. Thus, it appears that an arbitrage opportunity exists. The apparent contradiction dissolves when we realize that the call price reflects the dividend that will occur before the option can be exercised.

22. As a cost-cutting measure, your CFO, an accountant, decides to cancel your division's subscription to Bloomberg. You rely on Bloomberg for real-time quotes on Treasury bill prices to value options using the Black-Scholes option pricing model. You discover that you can obtain real-time quotes on commercial paper rates from Reuters, to which you still have a subscription. Discuss the implications of using the yield on AAA rated commercial paper instead of Treasury bill yields to value options using the Black-Scholes model.

    It is assumed that the debt of the United States government is free of default risk. The yield on commercial paper, which is an unsecured debt obligation of a corporation, includes a default risk premium. Thus, the return on AAA rated commercial paper, r_{cp}, will be greater than the return on an equivalent Treasury bill, $r_{T\text{-bill}}$. The difference in the two returns, $r_{cp} - r_{T\text{-bill}}$, is equal to the default risk premium. Using the commercial paper rate instead of the Treasury bill rate will lead to the systematic overvaluation of call options, and the undervaluation of put options. The magnitude of the pricing error will be a function of the magnitude of the default risk premium. However, Chapter 14 shows that option prices are not very sensitive to changes in interest rates. Consequently using the commercial paper rate rather than the Treasury bill rate should not produce significant differences in the prices of options valued with the Black-Scholes model.

23. Assume that stock returns follow a random walk with a drift equal to the expected return on the stock. You are modeling stock returns using a binomial process for the purpose of valuing a European call option. Explain why creating an initial position in the stock and the call option that will remain riskless for the entire life of the option is not possible.

    Valuing options using the binomial model requires the construction of a synthetic option. The synthetic option is nothing more than a levered stock position. That is, a portfolio with an appropriate investment in the stock underlying the option, N^*, and Treasury bills, B^*. The synthetic option is combined with the traded option to create a riskless hedge portfolio. When the price of the underlying stock changes, the value of the traded option changes. Maintaining the riskless hedge requires periodic rebalancing of the synthetic option position as the value of the underlying stock changes. That is, one must alter one's position in the underlying stock and Treasury bill as the value of the traded option changes in concert with changes in the price of the stock.

24. WMM is currently priced at $117.50 per share. The 50-day options on WMM are currently being traded at three different strike prices, $110, $115, and $120. The 50-day Treasury bill is priced to yield an adjusted annual return of 6 percent compounded continuously. The prices and implied volatilities for the three different options are shown below.

Strike	Call	Implied Volatility
$110	$8.50	0.16
115	5.375	0.21
120	3.75	0.26

If the WMM options are priced by the Black-Scholes model, then the implied volatility of each of the 50-day option contracts would be the same.

A. Which of the three implied volatilities would you use as an estimate for the true volatility?

The recommended practice in the literature is to calculate a weighted average of several estimates of implied volatility. Many factors will influence the decision regarding the appropriate weighting scheme used in calculating a weighted implied volatility, including the trading volume for a particular option. Most weighting systems assign greater weights to options near-the-money.

B. If you knew that the true volatility of the stock was 0.20, what could you say about the value of the call options? What action would you take upon observing the implied volatilities shown in this table?

If the true volatility of the stock were 0.20, then the $110 call would be undervalued, the $120 call overvalued, and the $115 call would be near its true value. We would expect that the prices of the options would adjust to a level consistent with an implied volatility of 0.2. Thus, we would expect the price of the $110 call to rise and the price of the $120 call to fall. Our trading strategy would be to purchase the $110 call options and sell the $120 call options.

25. The dominant asset pricing models in finance maintain that the price of a share of stock depends on the amount of nondiversifiable covariation risk intrinsic in a stock. That is, the market only prices covariation risk that cannot be costlessly diversified away by shareholders. Only the nondiversifiable segment of total risk is priced by the market. The Black-Scholes model argues that the value of an option contract depends on the total variability of a stock's return. Reconcile these apparent inconsistencies in pricing theory. Should option prices depend only on the level of nondiversifiable risk? If not, explain.

When valuing the underlying asset, an investor has the opportunity to reduce risk exposure by constructing a diversified portfolio. This risk reduction by diversification can be achieved at no cost to the investor. Thus, no investor would pay to avoid the diversifiable risk. Consequently, diversifiable risk is not priced in a competitive market. An option is a derivative asset. The value of the option at any point in time depends on the value of the underlying asset at that time. However, the value of the option also varies with changes in the value of the underlying asset that may occur in the future. That is, the value of the option is equal to the present value of the expected payoffs on the option, and the expected payoffs on the option are determined by the volatility of the underlying asset.

26. Solving for the implied volatility of an option "by hand" is a laborious and time-consuming process of trial and error. The process requires you to choose a value for the option's implied volatility and calculate the value of the option using this guess. You compare the calculated value of the option with the value of the option observed in the market, and based on the direction and magnitude of the error, you develop another guess as to the value of the implied volatility. You repeat this process until the calculated value of the option is equal to the observed value of the option. Modern spreadsheets available on desktop computers have taken the labor out of the process of solving for implied volatility. Explain the process that would be used to solve for the implied volatility of an option using the Black-Scholes call option pricing model in a spreadsheet program.

If the Black-Scholes option pricing model is the true pricing model for European call options, then the observed price of traded call options should be determined according to the Black-Scholes model. Given the observed call price, the observed stock price, the observed risk-free interest rate, the strike price of the option, and the time until expiration of the option, one can solve for the volatility implied by these prices. This iterative process is laborious when performed by hand, but very simple when using a spreadsheet. In Excel, for example, one sets up a target cell that equates the value of the option calculated with the Black-Scholes model with the observed price of the option. The Solver function iterates the value of sigma, the firm's volatility, until the calculated value of the option is equal to the observed value of the option. The resulting value for sigma is the implied standard deviation.

27. We generally assume that the price of a share of stock decreases by the dollar amount of a dividend on the day when the stock goes ex-dividend, at least approximately. The ex-dividend date is the date on which the purchaser of a share of stock is not entitled to the next dividend paid by the firm. That is, the stock does not carry the right to the next dividend. Develop an arbitrage based argument why in a competitive market without frictions the price of a stock must fall by the dollar amount of the dividend on the day the stock goes ex-dividend.

    The price of a stock the instant before it goes ex-dividend, S_b, must be equal to the price of the stock the instant after it goes ex-dividend, S_a, plus the dollar value of the dividend, D. If the price of the stock before it goes ex-dividend, S_b, is greater than the sum of the price of the stock the instant after it goes ex-dividend, S_a, and the dollar value of the dividend, D, then it is possible to profit by selling the stock before it goes ex-dividend and purchasing the stock after it goes ex-dividend. Selling the stock obligates the seller to deliver a share of stock for which they are paid, $\$S_b$. The seller must deliver the stock and the dollar value of the dividend, D. However, the cost of the stock when purchased after the ex-dividend date, S_a, plus the dollar amount of the dividend, D, is less than the selling price, S_b, leaving the investor with a profit of $S_b - (S_a + D) > 0$. If the price of the stock before it goes ex-dividend, S_b, is less than the sum of the price of the stock the instant after it goes ex-dividend, S_a, and the dollar value of the dividend, D, then it is possible to profit by buying the stock before it goes ex-dividend and selling the stock after it goes ex-dividend. Purchasing the share of stock entitles the investor to the next dividend to be paid to shareholders. Selling the stock obligates the seller to deliver a share of stock for which they are paid S_a. The purchased stock will be used to deliver against the obligation created by selling the stock. The cost of the stock, S_b, is less than the sum of the cash received from selling the stock, S_a, and the dividend paid to the owners of the stock, $(S_a + D) - S_b > 0$. Thus, only stock prices that are consistent with $S_b - D = S_a$ will prevent arbitrage.

28. A quick check of the wire reveals that TMS is trading at $50 per share. Earlier in the day you were having lunch with a colleague and her husband Will, the CFO of TMS. During the lunch discussion, you talked about TMS's recently introduced new products. Will made it clear that if the products are well received by the market, TMS will be trading at $60 in six months, and if the market does not respond to the products, TMS will be trading at $42 in six months. The current six-month risk-free interest rate is 6 percent. Calculate the price of a six-month European call option written on TMS with a $50 strike price. Show that the price calculated using the one-period risk-neutral pricing model, $c = (c_U \pi_U + c_D \pi_D) / R$, is the same as the price calculated using the single-period no-arbitrage binomial pricing model, $c = N^*S - B^*$.

    The first step in determining the value of this call option is to examine what is expected to happen to the price of TMS's stock over the next six months. The value of the $50 call option will depend on the movements in the price of TMS's stock. At the end of six months, two outcomes are possible. TMS's stock price will either rise to $60 with the introduction of successful products or decrease to $42 if the new products are not successful.

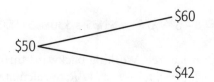

    Based on these stock prices, we can then calculate the value of the call option at expiration. The value of the call option at expiration is given by the intrinsic value function, MAX $[0, S - X]$. With successful products, the stock price will be $60, generating an intrinsic value of $10, $c_u = $ MAX $[0, \$60 - \$50]$. With unsuccessful products, the stock price will be $42, generating an intrinsic value of $0, $c_d = $ MAX $[0, \$42 - \$50]$.

Single-period binomial model

$$U = \$60/\$50 = 1.2 \quad D = \$42/\$50 = 0.84 \quad R = 1.06$$

$$B^* = \frac{c_U D - c_D U}{(U - D) R} = \frac{\$10(0.84) - \$0(1.2)}{(1.2 - 0.84)1.06} = \frac{\$8.4}{0.3816} = \$22.01$$

$$N^* = \frac{c_U - c_D}{(U - D) S} = \frac{\$10 - \$0}{(1.2 - 0.84)\$50} = \frac{10}{18} = 0.5556$$

$$c = N^* S - B^* = 0.5556(\$50) - \$22.01 = \$5.77$$

Single-period risk-neutral pricing model, $c = (c_U \pi_U + c_D \pi_D) / R$

$$\pi_U = \frac{R - D}{U - D} = \frac{1.06 - 0.84}{1.2 - 0.84} = 0.61 \quad \pi_D = \frac{U - R}{U - D} = \frac{1.2 - 1.06}{1.2 - 0.84} = 0.39, \ \pi_U + \pi_D = 1$$

$$c = \frac{(c_U \pi_U + c_D \pi_D)}{R} = \frac{\$10(0.61) + \$0(0.39)}{1.06} = \$5.76$$

The difference in the calculated values of the options is due to rounding error.

29. You are paired with the president of NYB to play golf in a tournament to raise money for the local children's hospital. After playing golf in the tournament, you learn that the president of NYB expects the price of his firm to increase by 6 percent per quarter if their new stores are successful in Seattle. If the stores are unsuccessful, he expects the stock price of NYB to decrease 5 percent per quarter. Checking Quote.com you find NYB trading at $30 per share. The current three-month risk-free interest rate is 3 percent, and you expect this rate to remain unchanged for the next six months.

A. Calculate the price of a six-month European call and put option written on NYB with $31 strike prices using the two-period risk-neutral pricing model.

$$U = 1.06 \quad D = 0.95 \quad R = 1.03$$

$$\pi_U = \frac{R - D}{U - D} = \frac{1.03 - 0.95}{1.06 - 0.95} = 0.7273 \quad \pi_D = 1 - 0.7273 = 0.2727$$

$$c = \frac{2.708 \times 0.7273^2 + 0.0 \times (0.7273 \times 0.2727) + 0.0 \times (0.2727 \times 0.7273) + 0.0 \times 0.2727^2}{1.03^2} = \$1.35$$

$$p = \frac{0.0 \times 0.7273^2 + .79 \times (0.7273 \times 0.2727) + .79 \times (0.2727 \times 0.7273) + 3.925 \times 0.2727^2}{1.03^2} = \$.57$$

B. Confirm that the put-call parity relationship generates the same price for the put option.

$$p = c - S + X/R^2 = \$1.35 - \$30 + 31/1.03^2 = \$.57$$

C. Construct the two-period stock price tree. Working backward through the stock price tree, use the one-period risk-neutral pricing model, $c = (c_U \pi_U + c_D \pi_D) / R$, to calculate the value of a one-period call option, given that the stock price has increased in period one, c_{up}. Calculate the value of a one-period call option, given that the stock price has decreased in period one, c_{down}. Calculate the current value of a one-period call option that has a value of c_{up} if the stock price increases or a value of c_{down} if the stock price decreases. (This process of valuing an option is known as the recursive valuation process.) Compare the price of the call option calculated using the recursive process with the price of the call option calculated using the two-period risk-neutral pricing model. Do the same for a put.

Stock price tree

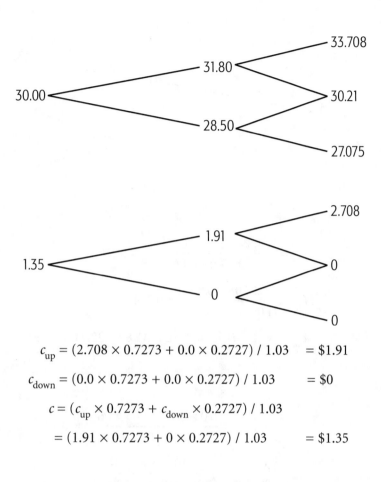

Call price tree

$$c_{up} = (2.708 \times 0.7273 + 0.0 \times 0.2727) / 1.03 \quad = \$1.91$$

$$c_{down} = (0.0 \times 0.7273 + 0.0 \times 0.2727) / 1.03 \quad = \$0$$

$$c = (c_{up} \times 0.7273 + c_{down} \times 0.2727) / 1.03$$

$$= (1.91 \times 0.7273 + 0 \times 0.2727) / 1.03 \quad = \$1.35$$

Put price tree

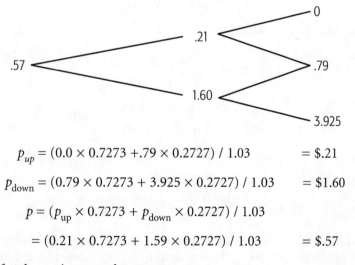

$$p_{up} = (0.0 \times 0.7273 + .79 \times 0.2727) / 1.03 \quad = \$.21$$

$$p_{down} = (0.79 \times 0.7273 + 3.925 \times 0.2727) / 1.03 \quad = \$1.60$$

$$p = (p_{up} \times 0.7273 + p_{down} \times 0.2727) / 1.03$$

$$= (0.21 \times 0.7273 + 1.59 \times 0.2727) / 1.03 \quad = \$.57$$

The calculated prices for the options are the same.

D. Repeat the process of part C for a call using the single-period no-arbitrage binomial pricing model, $c = N^*S - B^*$ to calculate the price of the single-period call option. Discuss what happens to N^* at each branch in the tree.

$$B^* = \frac{c_u D - c_d U}{(U - D) R}$$

$$N^* = \frac{c_u - c_d}{(U - D) S}$$

Stock price tree

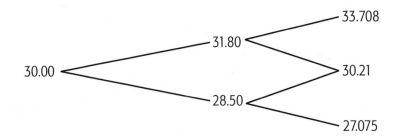

If $S = \$31.80$,

$$B_{up} = \frac{2.708 \times 0.95 - 0.0 \times 1.06}{(1.06 - 0.95)\,1.03} = 22.71$$

$$N_{up} = \frac{2.708 - 0.0}{(1.06 - 0.95)\,31.80} = 0.7742$$

$$c_{up} = N_{up}S - B_{up} = 0.7742 \times 31.80 - 22.71 = \$1.91$$

If $S = \$28.50$,

$$B_{down} = \frac{0.0 \times 0.95 - 0.0 \times 1.06}{(1.06 - 0.95)\,1.03} = 0$$

$$N_{down} = \frac{0.0 - 0.0}{(1.06 - 0.95)\,28.50} = 0$$

$$c_{up} = 0.0 \times 28.50 - 0 = \$0$$

If $S = \$30.00$,

$$B = \frac{1.91 \times 0.95 - 0.0 \times 1.06}{(1.06 - 0.95)\,1.03} = 16.02$$

$$N = \frac{1.91 - 0.0}{(1.06 - 0.95)\,30} = 0.5788$$

$$c = 0.5788 \times 30 - 16.02 = \$1.34$$

When the price of the underlying stock changes, the value of the traded option changes, and the appropriate investment in the stock underlying the option, N^*, changes. In the binomial model, we create a mimicking portfolio consisting of a stock position and a Treasury bill position. The outcome we are modeling changes as the underlying stock price changes. Thus, we must change our stock position in the mimicking portfolio. For example, when the stock price is $30.00, then $N^* = 0.5788$, and when the stock price is $31.80, then $N^* = 0.7742$. Thus, as the stock price increases, we increase our holdings of the underlying stock, and as the stock price decreases, we reduce our holdings of the underlying stock.

30. Both put and call options on HWP are traded. Put and call options with an exercise price of $100 expire in 90 days. HWP is trading at $95 and has an annualized standard deviation of 0.3. The three-month risk-free interest rate is 5.25 percent per annum.

A. Use a three-period binomial model to compute the value of the put and call options using the recursive procedure (single-period binomial option pricing model). Be sure to specify the values of U, D, and π_U.

$$U = e^{\sigma\sqrt{\Delta t}} = e^{0.3\sqrt{30/365}} = 1.0898$$

$$D = 1/U = 1/1.0898 = 0.9176$$

$$\pi_U = \frac{e^{r\Delta t} - D}{U - D} = \frac{e^{.0525 \times 30/365} - 0.9176}{1.0898 - 0.9176} = 05036 \quad \pi_D = 1 - 0.5036 = 0.4964$$

$$e^{-r\Delta t} = 0.9957$$

Stock price tree

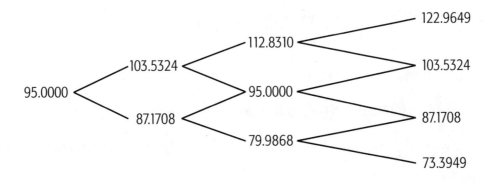

Call price tree

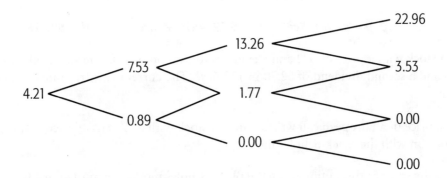

Call price, c = \$4.21

B. What is the risk-neutral probability of a stock price increase in period one, period two, and period three?

A characteristic of the multiplicative process used to model stock price movements in the binomial model is that the probability of a stock price increase in any period is independent of previous stock price changes. This process produces prices that follow a random walk. Thus, π_U does not change from period to period, and $\pi_U = 0.5036$.

31. Consider a stock, ABM, trading at a price of \$70. Analysis of ABM's recent returns reveals that ABM has an annualized standard deviation of return of 0.4. The current risk-free rate of interest is 10 percent per annum.

A. What is the price of a European call written on ABM with a \$75 strike price that expires in 180 days? Price the option according to the Black-Scholes model.

$$d_1 = \frac{\ln(70/75) + \left[0.10 + .5\left(0.4^2\right)\right](0.4932)}{.40\sqrt{(0.4932)}} = 0.0704$$

$$d_2 = 0.0704 - 0.40\sqrt{(0.4932)} = -0.2105$$

$$N(d_1) = 0.528061 \quad N(d_2) = 0.416638$$

$$c = 70 \times 0.528061 - 75e^{-0.1 \times 0.4932} \times 0.416638 = \$7.22$$

B. What is the price of a European put written on ABM with a $75 strike price that expires in 180 days? Price the option with the Black-Scholes model. Calculate the price of the put using put-call parity and compare it with the price calculated using the Black-Scholes model.

$$d_1 = \frac{\ln(70/75) + \left[0.10 + 0.5\left(0.4^2\right)\right](0.4932)}{0.40\sqrt{(0.4932)}} = 0.0704$$

$$d_2 = 0.0704 - 0.40\sqrt{(0.4932)} = -0.2105$$

$$N(-d_1) = 0.471939 \quad N(-d_2) = 0.583362$$

$$p = Xe^{-r(T-t)}N(-d_2) - S\,N(-d_1) = 75e^{-0.1 \times 0.4932} \times 0.583362 - 70 \times 0.471939 = \$8.61$$

Put-call parity

The price of the call calculated using the put-call parity equation, $p = c - S + Xe^{-r(T-t)}$, is the same as the put price calculated using the Black-Scholes put option pricing model.

$$p = c - S + Xe^{-r(T-t)} = \$7.22 - \$70 + \$75e^{-0.1 \times 0.4932} = \$8.61$$

32. Consider a stock with a price of $72 and a standard deviation of 0.4. The stock will pay a dividend of $2 in 40 days and a second dividend of $2.50 in 130 days. The current risk-free rate of interest is 10 percent per annum.

A. What is the price of a European call written on this stock with a $70 strike price that expires in 145 days? Price the option with the Black-Scholes model.

To calculate the value of this option using the Black-Scholes model, we must adjust the current stock price of $72 downward by the present value of the dividends to be received prior to the option's expiration. In this problem, both dividends are paid before the option's expiration. The first dividend will be received in 40 days, and the second will be received in 130 days.

$$D_1\,Xe^{-r(T-t)} = \$2 \times e^{-0.1 \times (40/365)} = \$1.98$$

$$D_2\,Xe^{-r(T-t)} = \$2.5 \times e^{-0.1 \times (130/365)} = \$2.41$$

$$S' = \$72 - \$1.98 - \$2.41 = \$67.61$$

$$d_1 = \frac{\ln(67.61/70) + \left(\left[.10 + .5\left(0.4^2\right)\right](0.3973)\right)}{.40\sqrt{(0.3973)}} = 0.1458$$

$$d_2 = 0.1458 - 0.40\sqrt{(0.3973)} = -0.1063$$

$$N(d_1) = 0.557958 \quad N(d_2) = 0.457664$$

$$c = 67.61 \times 0.557958 - 70e^{-0.1 \times -.3973} \times 0.457664 = \$6.93$$

B. What is the price of a European put written on this stock with a $70 strike price that expires in 145 days? Price the option with the Black-Scholes model.

$$d_1 = \frac{\ln(67.61/70) + \left(\left[.10 + .5\left(0.4^2\right)\right](0.3973)\right)}{.40\sqrt{(0.3973)}} = 0.1458$$

$$d_2 = 0.1458 - 0.40\sqrt{(0.3973)} = -0.1063$$

$$N(-d_1) = 0.442042 \quad N(-d_2) = 0.542336$$

$$p = Xe^{-r(T-t)}\, N(-d_2) - S\, N(-d_1) = 70e^{-0.1 \times 0.3973} \times 0.542336 - 67.61 \times 0.442042 = \$6.60$$

33. Consider a stock that trades for $75. A put and a call on this stock both have an exercise price of $70, and they expire in 145 days. The risk-free rate is 9 percent per annum, and the standard deviation of the stock is 0.35. Assume that the stock pays a continuous dividend of 4 percent.

A. What is the price of a European call written on this stock according to Merton's model?

$$d_1^M = \frac{\ln(S/X) + \left(\left[r - \delta + .5\left(\sigma^2\right)\right](T-t)\right)}{\sigma\sqrt{(T-t)}}$$

$$d_2^M = d_1^M - \sigma\sqrt{(T-t)}$$

$$d_1^M = \frac{\ln(75/70) + \left(\left[.09 - 0.04 + .5\left(0.35^2\right)\right](0.3973)\right)}{.35\sqrt{.3973}} = 0.5131$$

$$d_2^M = 0.5131 - 0.35\sqrt{.3973} = 0.2925$$

$$N\left(d_1^M\right) = .696056 \quad N\left(d_2^M\right) = 0.615045$$

$$c^M = e^{-\delta(T-t)}\, SN\left(d_1^M\right) - Xe^{-r(T-t)}\, N_2\left(d^M\right)$$

$$c^M = e^{-0.04(0.3973)}\, 75 \times 0.696056 - 70e^{-0.09(0.3973)} \times 0.615045 = \$9.84$$

B. What is the price of a European put written on this stock according to Merton's model?

$$d_1^M = \frac{\ln(75/70) + \left(\left[.09 - 0.04 + .5\left(0.35^2\right)\right](0.3973)\right)}{.35\sqrt{.3973}} = 0.5131$$

$$d_2^M\ 0.5131 - 0.35\sqrt{.3973} = 0.2925$$

$$N\left(-d_1^M\right) = .303944 \quad N\left(-d_2^M\right) = 0.384955$$

$$p^M = Xe^{-r(T-t)}\, N\left(-d_2^M\right) - e^{-\delta(T-t)}\, SN\left(-d_1^M\right)$$

$$p^M = 70e^{-0.09(0.3973)} \times 0.384955 - e^{-0.04(0.3973)}\, 75 \times 0.303944 = \$3.56$$

34. Your broker has just told you about TXF. He describes the firm as the real innovator in the entertainment industry. You search the web and discover that TXF has both put and call options trading on the exchange. Put and call options with an exercise price of $70 expire in 145 days. TXF is currently trading at $75, and has an annualized standard deviation of 0.35. The three-month risk-free interest rate is 9 percent per annum. A quick, back-of-the-envelope calculation reveals that TXF is paying dividends at a continuous rate of 4 percent.

A. Use a four-period binomial model to compute the value of both the put and call options using the recursive procedure (single-period binomial option pricing model).

$$U = e^{\sigma\sqrt{\Delta t}} = e^{.35\sqrt{(36.25/365)}} = 1.1166$$

$$D = 1/U = 1/1.1166 = 0.8956$$

$$\pi_U = \frac{e^{(r-\delta)\Delta t} - D}{U - D} = \frac{e^{(0.09-0.04)\times 0.0993} - 0.8956}{1.1166 - 0.8956} = 0.4950 \quad \pi_D = 1 - 0.4950 = 0.5050$$

$$e^{-r\Delta t} = 0.9911$$

Stock price tree

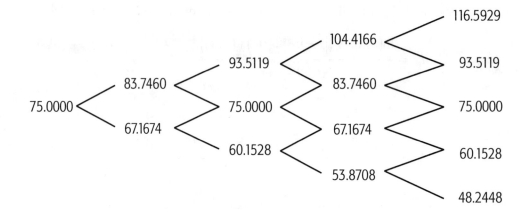

Call price tree

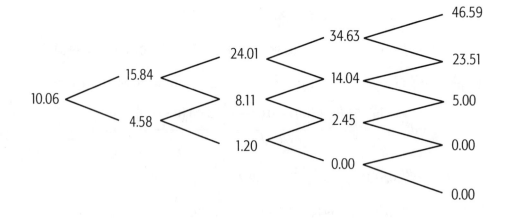

Put price tree

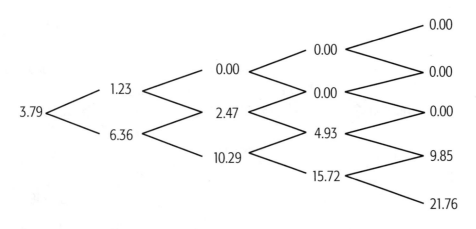

The call price is $10.06, and the put price is $3.79.

B. Compare the values of the put and call options calculated in this problem with the values of the put and call options calculated using Merton's model. Explain the source of the differences in the calculated values of the options.

In both cases, the prices for the options calculated using the binomial model are greater than the prices calculated using Merton's model. The prices calculated using the binomial model for the call and put options are $10.06 and $3.79, respectively, while the prices for the same options calculated with Merton's model are $9.84 and $3.56. This difference in valuation arises because we modeled a 145-day option using a four-period model. If we were to model the price movements in TXF using more periods in the binomial model, then the prices calculated using the binomial model would be very close to the prices calculated using the Merton model.

35. CSM is trading at $78 and has an annualized standard deviation of return of 30 percent. CSM is expected to pay a dividend equal to 3 percent of the value of its stock price in 70 days. The current risk-free rate of interest is 7 percent per annum. Options written on this stock have an exercise price of $80 and expire in 120 days.

A. Using a four-period binomial model, calculate the value of a European put option written on CSM using the recursive procedure (single-period binomial option pricing model).

$$U = e^{\sigma\sqrt{\Delta t}} = e^{0.3\sqrt{30/365}} = 1.0898$$

$$D = 1/U = 1/1.0898 = 0.9176$$

$$\pi_U = \frac{e^{r\Delta t} - D}{U - D} = \frac{e^{.07 \times 30/365} - 0.9176}{1.0898 - 0.9176} = 0.5120 \quad \pi_D = 1 - 0.5120 = 0.4880$$

$$e^{-r\Delta t} = 0.9943$$

Stock price tree

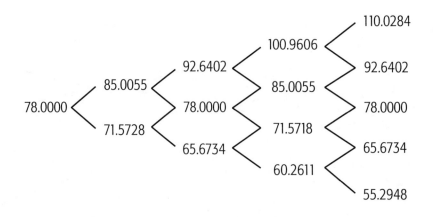

The stock prices in the tree must be adjusted for the dividend to be paid in 70 days before we can calculate the value of the options. Therefore, the stock prices in the tree in periods three and four must be adjusted downward by one minus the dividend yield paid by the firm $(1 - 3\%)$.

Dividend-adjusted stock price tree

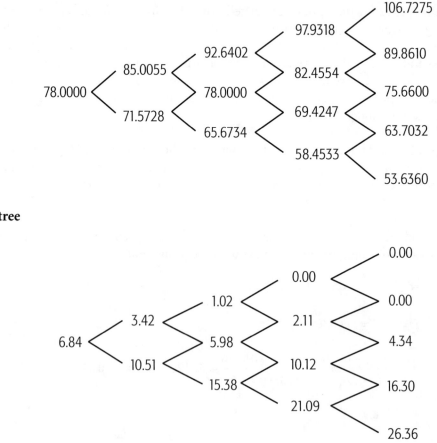

Put price tree

The price of the put option is $6.84.

B. Using a four-period binomial model, calculate the value of a European call option written on CSM using the recursive procedure (single-period binomial option pricing model).

Call price tree

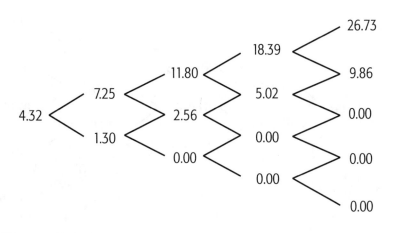

The price of the call option is $4.32.

36. One year later than the time of the previous question, the management of CSM announces that they are changing their dividend policy. CSM will now pay a fixed dollar dividend each quarter. CSM's management declares that the payout for the current year will be $6.00 to be paid equally each quarter. CSM now trades at $85. However, the firm's risk has increased. CSM's annualized standard deviation of return is now 40 percent. CSM will pay the first quarterly dividend in 10 days with the second quarterly dividend coming 90 days after the first dividend. The current risk-free rate of interest is 5.5 percent per annum. Options written on CSM have an exercise price of $80 and expire in 120 days.

A. Using a four-period binomial model, calculate the value of a European put option written on CSM using the recursive procedure (single-period binomial option pricing model).

$$U = e^{\sigma\sqrt{\Delta t}} = e^{.4\sqrt{30/365}} = 1.1215$$

$$D = 1/U = 1/1.1215 = 0.8917$$

$$\pi_U = \frac{e^{r\Delta t} - D}{U - D} = \frac{e^{.055 \times 30/365} - 0.8917}{1.1215 - 0.8917} = 0.4911 \quad \pi_D = 1 - 0.4911 = 0.5089$$

$$e^{-r\Delta t} = 0.9955$$

To construct the stock price tree necessary to calculate the value of this option, we must adjust the current stock price of $85 downward by the present value of the dividends to be received prior to the option's expiration. In this problem, both dividends of $1.50 will be paid prior to the option's expiration. The first dividend will be received in 10 days, and the second will be received in 100 days.

$$D_1 \, Xe^{-r(T-t)} = \$1.50 \times e^{-0.055 \times (10/365)} \qquad = \$1.4977$$

$$D_2 \, Xe^{-r(T-t)} = \$1.50 \times e^{-0.055 \times (100/365)} \qquad = \$1.4776$$

$$S' = \$85 - \$1.4977 - \$1.4776 \qquad = \$82.0247$$

Stock price tree

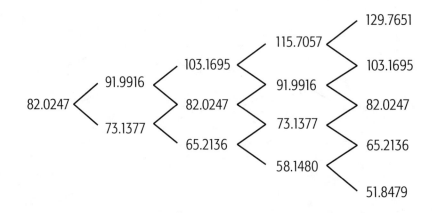

Put price tree

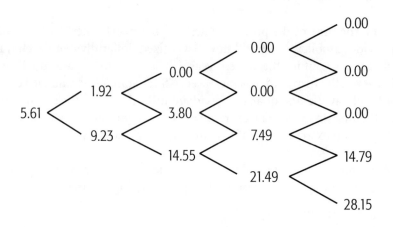

The price of the put option is $5.61.

B. Using a four-period binomial model, calculate the value of a European call option written on CSM using the recursive procedure (single-period binomial option pricing model).

Call price tree

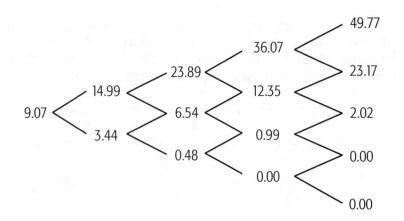

The price of the call option is $9.07.

37. Consider the following data used in all the various parts of this problem. The calculations required to solve these problems can be done in a spreadsheet, or by hand, for the masochist.

Today's date:	Friday, December 5, 1997		
Option's expiration date:	January 16, 1998		
Treasury bill yields:	Bid: 5.09%	Ask: 5.05%	

Date	HCJ Closing Price
October 22, 1997	135.6875
October 23, 1997	135.6250
October 24, 1997	135.3750
October 27, 1997	128.7500
October 28, 1997	133.3750
October 29, 1997	131.1250
October 30, 1997	128.6250
October 31, 1997	130.0000
November 3, 1997	134.1250
November 4, 1997	134.2500
November 5, 1997	133.5625
November 6, 1997	132.0625
November 7, 1997	131.5625
November 10, 1997	130.1875
November 11, 1997	130.6250
November 12, 1997	129.1875
November 13, 1997	131.5625
November 14, 1997	133.3125
November 17, 1997	134.8750
November 18, 1997	134.0000
November 19, 1997	135.0625
November 20, 1997	136.8750
November 21, 1997	137.8750
November 24, 1997	135.5000
November 25, 1997	139.0000
November 26, 1997	141.5625
November 28, 1997	141.5000
December 1, 1997	143.8125
December 2, 1997	142.2500
December 3, 1997	144.6875
December 4, 1997	142.5625

A. Determine the number of days until the January HCJ options expire.

Determining the number of days until an option expires requires one to count both the weekdays and weekends between the current date and the option's expiration date in January. The options expire in 42 days.

B. Determine the continuously compounded interest rate on the Treasury bill.

When calculating the continuously compounded interest rate on the Treasury bill, it is important to remember that the Treasury bill matures one day prior to the expiration of the option. That is, the

Treasury bill matures on the third Thursday of the month. In this calculation, we must adjust quoted yields on the discount instrument. The price of the Treasury bill is

$$P = 1 - 0.01((5.09 + 5.05)/2) \times (41/360) = 0.994226$$

The continuously compounded interest rate on the Treasury bill is:

$$r = \frac{365}{41} \ln\left(\frac{1}{0.994226}\right) = 0.051553$$

C. Calculate the annualized standard deviation of return on HCJ's stock using the time series of HCJ stock returns. Assume that there are 252 trading days in a typical year.

To calculate the historical volatility of HCJ, we must convert the price series into a return series. To do this, we construct a price relative series, $PR_t = P_t / P_{t-1}$, for using the data for days 1 through 31. The returns series is created by taking the natural logarithm of the 30 price relatives. The daily standard deviation of returns, σ_d, is 0.01762. The annualized standard deviation of returns, $\sigma_a = \sigma_d \sqrt{252}$, is 0.27967.

D. Using the Black-Scholes option pricing model, calculate the current price of the January 140 call and put options written on HCJ. The stock price is 143.125.

Days until expiration	42
Risk-free rate	5.1553%
Historical volatility	0.27967

$$c = S\,N(d_1) - Xe^{-r(T-t)}\,N(d_2)$$

$$d_1 = \frac{\ln(S/X) + \left(\left[r + .5(\sigma^2)\right](T-t)\right)}{\sigma\sqrt{(T-t)}}$$

$$d_2 = d_1 - \sigma\sqrt{(T-t)}$$

$$d_1 = \frac{\ln(143.125/140) + \left(\left[.051553 + .5(0.27967^2)\right](0.1151)\right)}{.27967\sqrt{(0.1151)}} = 0.3427$$

$$d_2 = 0.3427 - 0.27967\sqrt{(0.1151)} = 0.2478$$

$N(d_1)$	.634074
$N(d_2)$	.597853
Call price	$7.55
Put price	$3.59

E. Use the following information, as of December 4, to calculate the implied standard deviations for the January 135 and 145 HCJ call options.

Stock price	142.5625	142.5625
Exercise price	135	145
Days until expiration	43	43
Risk-free rate	5.15%	5.15%
Call price	$12.00	$4.75

	January 135 call	**January 145 call**
Implied volatility	0.371367	0.280073
Weighted average (equal weighting)		0.32572

F. Use the equally weighted average of the implied standard deviation on the January 135 and 145 call options in the Black-Scholes option pricing model to calculate the current price on the January 140 call and put options. Compare the option prices calculated using the historical volatility and the implied volatility.

Stock price	143.125
Exercise price	140
Days until expiration	42
Risk-free rate	5.1553%
Historical volatility	0.32572

$$d_1 = \frac{\ln(143.125/140) + \left(\left[.051553 + .5\left(0.32572^2\right)\right](0.1151)\right)}{.32572\sqrt{0.1151}} = 0.3087$$

$$d_2 = 0.3087 - 0.32572\sqrt{(0.1151)} = 0.1982$$

$N(d_1)$	0.621238
$N(d_2)$	0.578573
Call price	$8.39
Put price	$4.44

The option prices calculated using the implied volatility are higher than the prices calculated using the historical volatility, because the implied volatility is higher than the historical volatility.

G. Assume that stock prices follow a random walk with a drift. Use the weighted average of the implied volatilities on the January 135 and 145 call options and the continuously compounded return on the Treasury bill calculated in part B above to calculate the parameters in a binomial process, $U = e^{\sigma\sqrt{\Delta t}}$, $D = 1 / U$, and $\pi_u = e^{r\,\Delta t} - D / U - D$. Use a four-period binomial model to calculate the value of the January 140 call and put options written on HCJ. Compare the option prices calculated using the binomial model with option prices calculated using the Black-Scholes model. Explain the source of the differences in the option prices.

$$U = e^{\sigma\sqrt{\Delta t}} = e^{.32572\sqrt{(10.50/365)}} = 1.0568$$

$$D = 1/U = 1/1.0568 = 0.9463$$

$$\pi_U = \frac{e^{r\Delta t} - D}{U - D} = \frac{e^{.051553 \times 10.50/365} - 0.9463}{1.0568 - 0.9463} = 0.4996 \quad \pi_D = 1 - 0.4995 = 0.5004$$

$$e^{-r\Delta t} = 0.9985$$

Stock price tree

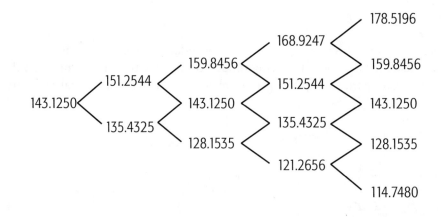

Call price tree

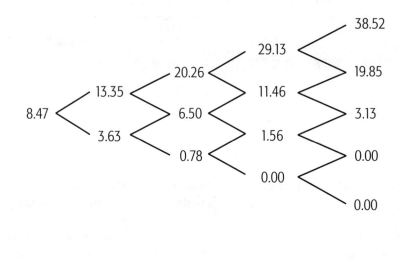

Put price tree

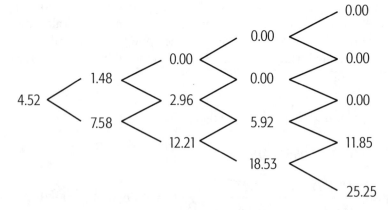

The call price is $8.47, and the put price is $4.52. These prices are higher than the comparable option prices calculated using the Black-Scholes model. The differences in the prices are due to the fact that we modeled the movement in HCJ stock over a 42-day period using only four periods. Adding more periods to our binomial model produces prices that are very similar to the prices calculated using the Black-Scholes model.

14 Option Sensitivities and Option Hedging

Answers to Questions and Problems

1. Consider Call A, with: $X = \$70$; $r = 0.06$; $T - t = 90$ days; $\sigma = 0.4$; and $S = \$60$. Compute the price, DELTA, GAMMA, THETA, VEGA, and RHO for this call.

$$c = \$1.82$$
$$\text{DELTA} = .2735$$
$$\text{GAMMA} = .0279$$
$$\text{THETA} = -8.9173$$
$$\text{VEGA} = 9.9144$$
$$\text{RHO} = 3.5985$$

2. Consider Put A, with: $X = \$70$; $r = 0.06$; $T - t = 90$ days; $\sigma = 0.4$; and $S = \$60$. Compute the price, DELTA, GAMMA, THETA, VEGA, and RHO for this put.

$$p = \$10.79$$
$$\text{DELTA} = -.7265$$
$$\text{GAMMA} = .0279$$
$$\text{THETA} = -4.7790$$
$$\text{VEGA} = 9.9144$$
$$\text{RHO} = -13.4083$$

3. Consider a straddle comprised of Call A and Put A. Compute the price, DELTA, GAMMA, THETA, VEGA, and RHO for this straddle.

$$\text{price} = c + p = \$12.61$$
$$\text{DELTA} = 0.2735 - 0.7265 = -0.4530$$
$$\text{GAMMA} = 0.0279 + 0 .0279 = 0.0558$$
$$\text{THETA} = -8.9173 - 4.47790 = -13.6963$$
$$\text{VEGA} = 9.9144 + 9.9144 = 19.8288$$
$$\text{RHO} = 3.5985 - 13.4083 = -9.8098$$

4. Consider Call A. Assuming the current stock price is $60, create a DELTA-neutral portfolio consisting of a short position of one call and the necessary number of shares. What is the value of this portfolio for a sudden change in the stock price to $55 or $65?

As we saw for this call, DELTA = 0.2735. The DELTA-neutral portfolio, given a short call component, is 0.2735 shares –1 call, costs:

$$.2735\ (\$60) - \$1.82 = \$14.59$$

If the stock price goes to $55, the call price is $.77, and the portfolio will be worth:

$$.2735\ (\$55) - \$.77 = \$14.27$$

With a stock price of $65, the call is worth $3.55, and the portfolio value is:

$$.2735\ (\$65) - \$3.55 = \$14.23$$

Notice that the portfolio values are lower for both stock prices of $55 and $65, reflecting the negative GAMMA of the portfolio.

5. Consider Call A and Put A from above. Assume that you create a portfolio that is short one call and long one put. What is the DELTA of this portfolio? Can you find the DELTA without computing? Explain. Assume that a share of stock is added to the short call/long put portfolio. What is the DELTA of the entire position?

   The DELTA of the portfolio is $-1.0 = -0.2735 - 0.7265$. This is necessarily true, because the DELTA of the call is $N(d_1)$, the DELTA of the put is $N(-d_2)$, and $N(d_1) + N(d_2) = 1.0$. If a long share of stock is added to the portfolio, the DELTA will be zero, because the DELTA of a share is always 1.0.

6. What is the GAMMA of a share of stock if the stock price is $55 and a call on the stock with $X = \$50$ has a price $c = \$7$ while a put with $X = \$50$ has a price $p = \$4$? Explain.

   The GAMMA of a share of stock is always zero. All other information in the question is irrelevant. The GAMMA of a share is always zero because the DELTA of a share is always 1.0. As GAMMA measures how DELTA changes, there is nothing to measure for a stock, since the DELTA is always 1.0.

7. Consider Call B written on the same stock as Call A with: $X = \$50$; $r = 0.06$; $T - t = 90$ days; $\sigma = 0.4$; and $S = \$60$. Form a bull spread with calls from these two instruments. What is the price of the spread? What is its DELTA? What will the price of the spread be at expiration if the terminal stock price is $60? From this information, can you tell whether THETA is positive or negative for the spread? Explain.

   As observed in problem 1, for Call A, $c = \$1.82$, DELTA $= 0.2735$, and THETA $= -8.9173$. For Call B, $c = \$11.64$, DELTA $= 0.8625$, and THETA $= -7.7191$. The long bull spread with calls consists of buying the call with the lower exercise price (Call B) and selling the call with the higher exercise price (Call A). The spread costs $11.64 - \$1.82 = \$9.82$. The DELTA of the spread equals DELTA$_B$ – DELTA$_A$ = $0.8625 - 0.2735 = 0.5890$. If the stock price is $60 at expiration, Call B will be worth $10, and Call A will expire worthless. If the stock price remains at $60, the value of the spread will have to move from $9.82 now to $10.00 at expiration, so the THETA for the spread must be positive. This can be confirmed by computing the two THETAs and noting: THETA$_A$ = -8.9173 and THETA$_B$ = -7.7191. For the spread, we buy Call B and sell Call A, giving a THETA for the spread of $-7.7191 - (-8.9173) = 1.1982$.

8. Consider again the sample options, C2 and P2, of the chapter discussion as given in Table 14.7. Assume now that the stock pays a continuous dividend of 3 percent per annum. See if you can tell how the sensitivities will differ for the call and a put without computing. Now compute the DELTA, GAMMA, VEGA, THETA, and RHO of the two options if the stock has a dividend.

   The presence of a continuous dividend makes d_1 smaller than it otherwise would be, because the continuous dividend rate, σ, is subtracted in the numerator of d_1. With a smaller d_1, $N(d_1)$ is also smaller. But, $N(d_1)$ = DELTA for a call, so the DELTA of a call will be smaller with a dividend present. By the same reasoning, the DELTA of the put must increase.

Sensitivity	C2	P2
DELTA	0.5794	−0.4060
GAMMA	0.0182	0.0182
THETA	−10.3343	−5.5997
VEGA	26.93	26.93
RHO	23.9250	−23.4823

9. Consider three calls, Call C, Call D, and Call E, all written on the same underlying stock; $S = \$80$; $r = 0.07$; $\sigma = 0.2$. For Call C, $X = \$70$, and $T - t = 90$ days. For Call D, $X = \$75$, and $T - t = 90$ days. For Call E, $X = \$80$, and $T - t = 120$ days. Compute the price, DELTA, and GAMMA for each of these calls. Using Calls C and D, create a DELTA-neutral portfolio assuming that the position is long one Call C. Now use calls C, D, and E to form a portfolio that is DELTA-neutral and GAMMA-neutral, again assuming that the portfolio is long one Call C.

Measure	Call C	Call D	Call E
Price	$11.40	$7.16	$4.60
DELTA	.9416	.8088	.6018
GAMMA	.0147	.0343	.0421

For a DELTA-neutral portfolio comprised of Calls C and D that is long one Call C, we must choose a position of Z shares of Call D to satisfy the following equation:

$$0.9416 + 0.8088 \, Z = 0$$

Therefore, $Z = -1.1642$, and the portfolio consists of purchasing one Call C and selling 1.1642 units of Call D.

To form a portfolio of Calls C, D, and E that is long one Call C and that is also DELTA-neutral and GAMMA-neutral, the portfolio must meet both of the following conditions, where Y and Z are the number of Call Cs and Call Ds, respectively.

DELTA-neutrality: $0.9416 + 0.8088 \, Y + 0.6018 \, Z = 0$
GAMMA-neutrality: $0.0147 + 0.0343 \, Y + 0.0421 \, Z = 0$

Multiplying the second equation by (0.8088/.0343) gives:

$$0.3466 + 0.8088 \, Y + 0.9927 \, Z = 0$$

Subtracting this equation from the DELTA-neutrality equation gives:

$$0.5950 - 0.3909 \, Z = 0$$

Therefore, $Z = 1.5221$. Substituting this value of Z into the DELTA-neutrality equation gives:

$$0.8088 \, Y + 0.9416 + 0.6018 \,(1.5221) = 0$$

$Y = -2.2968$. Therefore, the DELTA-neutral and GAMMA-neutral portfolio consists of buying one unit of Call C, selling 2.2968 units of Call D, and buying 1.5221 units of Call E.

10. Your largest and most important client's portfolio includes option positions. After several conversations it becomes clear that your client is willing to accept the risk associated with exposure to changes in volatility and stock price. However, your client is not willing to accept a change in the value of her portfolio resulting from the passage of time. Explain how the investor can protect her portfolio against changes in value due to the passage of time.

Your client wants to avoid changes in the value of her portfolio due to the passage of time. THETA measures the impact of changes in the time until expiration on the value of an option. Your client should create a THETA-neutral portfolio to protect the value of her option positions against changes in the time until expiration. To protect her portfolio against the wasting away effect associated with option contracts, she must first determine the THETA for her current portfolio. Given the THETA value of her portfolio, she should construct a position in option contracts that has a THETA value that is of an equal magnitude and opposite sign of the THETA of her portfolio. Thus, the THETA for the hedge portfolio, the original portfolio plus the additional options contracts used to create the hedge, is zero. The value of this portfolio should not change with the passage of time. However, the portfolio will have exposure to changes in other market variables, that is, interest rates, volatility, and stock price changes.

11. Your newest client believes that the Asian currency crisis is going to increase the volatility of earnings for firms involved in exporting, and that this earnings volatility will be translated into large stock price changes for the affected firms. Your client wants to create speculative positions using options to increase his exposure to the expected changes in the riskiness of exporting firms. That is, your client wants to prosper from changes in the volatility of the firm's stock returns. Discuss which "Greek" your client should focus on when developing his options positions.

Your client wants to create exposure to changes in the volatility of stock returns. VEGA measures the change in the value of an option contract resulting from changes in the volatility of the underlying stock. Once you have identified stocks with traded options that have significant Asian exposures, you want to construct positions based on the VEGA of the option. Because your client wants exposures to volatility risk, you would construct a portfolio with a large VEGA.

12. A long-time client, an insurance salesperson, has noticed the increased acquisition activity involving commercial banks. Your client wishes to capitalize on the potential gains associated with this increased acquisition activity in the banking industry by creating speculative positions using options. Your client realizes that bank cash flows are sensitive to changes in interest rates, and she believes that the Federal Reserve is about to increase short-term interest rates. Realizing that an increase in the short-term interest rates will lead to a decrease in the stock prices of commercial banks, your client wants the value of her portfolio of options to be unaffected by changes in short-term interest rates. Explain how the investor can use option contracts to protect her portfolio against changes in value due to changes in the risk-free rate, and to capitalize on the expected price changes in bank stocks.

Your client wants to create exposure to changes in bank stock prices. DELTA measures the change in the value of an option contract resulting from changes in the underlying stock price. Additionally, your client has a preference to construct a portfolio such that the value of the portfolio will not change as interest rates change. RHO measures the change in the value of an option contract resulting from changes in the risk-free rate of interest. Because your client wants exposure to stock price changes, you would construct a portfolio with a large DELTA. However, the RHO for the portfolio should be constrained to equal zero. Thus, the resulting portfolio would be RHO-neutral hedge with a large DELTA.

13. Your brother-in-law has invested heavily in stocks with a strong Asian exposure, and he tells you that his portfolio has a positive DELTA. Give an intuitive explanation of what this means. Suppose the value of the stocks that your brother-in-law holds increases significantly. Explain what will happen to the value of your brother-in-law's portfolio.

DELTA measures the change in the value of an option due to a change in the price of the underlying asset, which is usually a stock. If an investor holds a portfolio consisting of a single stock, the DELTA of the portfolio is one, because a one dollar increase in the stock price will produce a one dollar per share increase in the value of the portfolio. If the asset in question is an option, then the DELTA of the option measures the change in the value of the option contract because of a change in the underlying stock price. If your brother-in-law's portfolio has a positive DELTA, the value of his portfolio will move in the same direction as the value of the underlying asset. If the value of the stocks he holds increases, then the value of his portfolio will increase at a rate of DELTA times the dollar change in the asset price.

14. Your mother-in-law has invested heavily in the stocks of financial firms, and she tells you that her portfolio has a negative RHO. Give an intuitive explanation of what this means. Suppose the Federal Reserve increases short-term interest rates. Explain what will happen to the value of your mother-in-law's portfolio.

RHO measures the change in the value of an asset due to changes in interest rates. If the investor holds an option, then the RHO of the option measures the change in the value of the option contract because of a change in the risk-free interest rate. If your mother-in-law's portfolio has a negative RHO, that implies that the value of the portfolio moves in the opposite direction as changes in the interest rate. If the short-term interest rate is increased by the Federal Reserve, then the value of her portfolio will decrease.

15. Your brother, Daryl, has retired. With the free time necessary to follow the market closely, Daryl has established large option positions as a stock investor. He tells you that his portfolio has a positive THETA. Give an intuitive explanation of what this means. Daryl is also a big soccer fan, and is heading to France to watch the World Cup for a month. He believes that there is not sufficient liquidity in the market to close out his open option positions, and he is going to leave the positions open while he is in France. Explain what will happen to the value of your brother's portfolio while he is in France.

THETA measures the change in the value of an option because of changes in the time until expiration for the option contract. That is, with the passage of time, the value of an option contract will change. In most cases, the option will experience a decrease in value with the passage of time. This is known as time decay. Formally, THETA is the negative of the first derivative of the option pricing model with respect to changes in the time until expiration. Since your brother has constructed a portfolio with a positive THETA, the passage of time should increase the value of his portfolio. Thus, he should, all things being equal, return from his vacation to find that the value of his portfolio has increased.

16. Consider the following information for a call option written on Microsoft's stock.

$S = \$96$	DELTA = 0.2063
$X = \$100$	GAMMA = 0.0635
$T - t = 5$ days	THETA = −48.7155
$\sigma = 0.4$	VEGA = 3.2045
$r = 0.1$	RHO = 0.2643
	Price = $.5

If in two days Microsoft's stock price has increased by $1 to $97, explain what you would expect to happen to the price of the call option.

Two variables are changing in this problem, the underlying stock price, S, and the time until expiration, $T - t$. Thus, one needs to assess the impact of both DELTA and THETA on the value of the Microsoft option. DELTA is 0.2063, and THETA is −48.7155. A one dollar increase in the price of Microsoft would be expected to increase the price of the call option by $.2063 = $1 × 0.2063. However, as an option contract approaches expiration, the passage of time has a significant adverse effect on the value of the option. Here two days represent 40 percent of the life of the option. The THETA effect is equal to −$.2669 = (2/365) × −48.7155, which is a larger negative effect than the positive impact of a stock price increase on the value of the option. The combined DELTA and THETA effects are −$.0606 = $.2063 − $.2669. Thus, the expected price of the call option is $.4394. The price of the call option according to the Black-Scholes model is $.4162.

17. Consider a stock, CVN, with a price of $50 and a standard deviation of 0.3. The current risk-free rate of interest is 10 percent. A European call and put on this stock have an exercise price of $55 and expire in three months (0.25 years).

A. If $c = \$1.61057$ and $N(d_1) = 0.3469$, then calculate the put option price.

$$p = c - S + Xe^{-r(T-t)} = \$1.61057 - \$50 + \$55e^{-0.1 \times 0.25} = \$5.25262$$

B. Suppose that you own 3,000 shares of CBC, a subsidiary of CVN Corporation, and that you plan to go Christmas shopping in New York City the day after Thanksgiving. To finance your shopping trip, you wish to sell your 3,000 shares of CBC in one week. However, you do not want the value of your investment in CBC to fall below its current level. Construct a DELTA-neutral hedge using the put option written on CVN. Be sure to describe the composition of your hedged portfolio.

Construction of a DELTA-neutral hedge using the put option requires the investor to hold $-1 / \text{DELTA}_{\text{put}}$ put options per 100 shares of stock held by the investor. The put option extends the right to sell 100 shares of stock. The DELTA for the put option is $-0.6531 = 0.3469 - 1$. Thus, the hedge ratio is $1.5312 = -1/-0.6531$, put options per 100 shares of stock. Because you hold 3,000 shares of CBC, you must purchase $45.9348 = (3,000 / 100) \times 1.5312$, put options written on CVN that expire in three months with a strike price of \$55. Since purchasing a fraction of an option's contract is not possible, you would round this up to 46 options contracts purchased.

18. An investor holds a portfolio consisting of three options, two call options and a put option, written on the stock of QDS Corporation with the following characteristics.

	C_1	C_2	P_1
DELTA	0.8922	0.2678	−0.6187
GAMMA	0.0169	0.0299	0.0245
THETA	−5.55	−3.89	−3.72

The investor is long 100 contracts of option C_1, short 200 contracts of option C_2, and long 100 contracts of option P_1. The investor's options portfolio has the following characteristics.

DELTA $= 0.8922\,(100) - 0.2678\,(200) - 0.6187\,(100)$ $= -26.21$
GAMMA $= 0.0169\,(100) - 0.0299\,(200) + 0.0245\,(100)$ $= -1.84$
THETA $= -5.55\,(100) + 3.89\,(200) - 3.72\,(100)$ $= -149$

The investor wishes to hedge this portfolio of options with two call options written on the stock of QDS Corporation with the following characteristics.

	C_a	C_b
DELTA	0.5761	0.6070
GAMMA	0.0356	0.0247
THETA	−9.72	−7.04

A. How many contracts of the two options, C_a and C_b, must the investor hold to create a portfolio that is DELTA-neutral and has a THETA of 100?

The investor must determine how many of the call options a and b to hold to create a portfolio that has a DELTA of 26.21 and a THETA of 249. That is, the DELTA of the combined portfolio of options should be zero, and the THETA of the combined portfolio should be 100. We must solve this for N_a and N_b subject to the constraint that the DELTA of the portfolio is 26.21 and the THETA is 249.

$$0.5671\,N_a + 0.607\,N_b = 26.21$$
$$-9.72\,N_a - 7.04\,N_b = 249$$

$$N_a = -175.955$$
$$N_b = 207.568$$

To create a portfolio with a DELTA of 26.21 and a THETA of 249, the investor must sell 176 contracts of option C_a and purchase 208 contracts of option C_b.

B. If QDS's stock price remains relatively constant over the next month, explain what will happen to the value of the portfolio created in part A of this question.

If QDS's stock price remains relatively constant, then the passage of time should increase the value of the portfolio. The DELTA of the portfolio is zero and the THETA is positive. Thus, small changes in the stock price will have little impact on the value of the portfolio of options, and the passage of time should increase the value of the option portfolio.

C. How many of the two options, C_a and C_b, must the investor hold to create a portfolio that is both DELTA- and GAMMA-neutral?

The investor must determine how many of the call options C_a and C_b to hold to create a portfolio that has a DELTA of 26.21 and a GAMMA of 1.84. That is, the DELTA and GAMMA of the combined portfolio of options are zero. We must solve the equation for N_a and N_b subject to the constraint that the DELTA of the portfolio is 26.21 and the GAMMA is 1.84.

$$0.5671\ N_a + 0.607\ N_b = 26.21$$
$$0.0356\ N_a + 0.0247\ N_b = 1.84$$

$$N_a = 61.7573$$
$$N_b = -14.5166$$

To create a portfolio with a DELTA of 26.21 and a GAMMA of 1.84, the investor must purchase 62 contracts of option C_a and sell 15 contracts of option C_b.

D. Suppose the investor wants to create a portfolio that is DELTA-, GAMMA-, and THETA-neutral. Could the investor accomplish this objective using the two options, C_a and C_b, which have been used in the previous problems? Explain.

No. Creating neutrality in three dimensions requires at least three different option contracts. We need at least as many option contracts as parameters we are trying to hedge. To create a DELTA-, GAMMA-, and THETA-neutral portfolio would require an additional new option contract.

19. Both put and call options trade on HWP. Put and call options with an exercise price of $100 expire in 90 days. HWP is trading at $95, and has an annualized standard deviation of return of 0.3. The three-month risk-free interest rate is 5.25 percent per annum.

A. Use a four-period binomial model to compute the value of the put and call options using the recursive procedure (single-period binomial option pricing model).

$$U = e^{\sigma\sqrt{\Delta t}} = e^{0.3\sqrt{22.5/365}} = 1.0773$$

$$D = 1/U = 1/1.0773 = 0.9282$$

$$\pi_U = \frac{e^{r\Delta t} - D}{U - D} = \frac{e^{.0525 \times 22.5/365} - 0.9282}{1.0773 - 0.9282} = 0.5031 \quad \pi_D = 1 - 0.5031 = 0.4969$$

$$e^{-r\Delta t} = 0.9968$$

Stock price tree

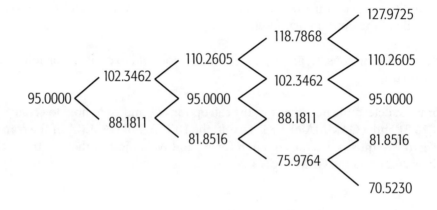

Call price tree

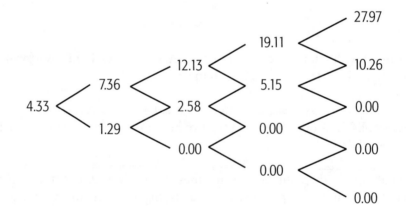

Put price tree

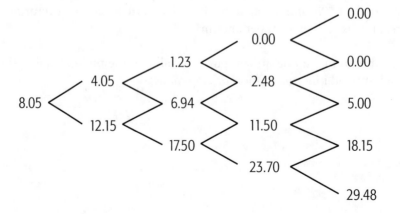

The call price is $4.33, and the put price is $8.05.

B. Increase the stock price by $.25 to $95.25 and recalculate the value of the put and call options using the recursive procedure (single-period binomial option pricing model).

If the stock price is increased by $.25, then the call price is $4.43 and the put price is $7.89.

C. For both the call and put options, calculate DELTA as the change in the value of the option divided by the change in the value of the stock.

Call DELTA
(4.43 – 4.33) /0.25 = 0.40

Put DELTA
(7.89 – 8.05) /0.25 = –0.64

D. Decrease the stock price by $.25 to $94.75 and recalculate the value of the put and call options using the recursive procedure (single-period binomial option pricing model).

When the stock price is decreased by $.25, then the call price is $4.24 and the put price is $8.20.

E. For both the call and put options, calculate DELTA as the change in the value of the option divided by the change in the value of the stock.

Call DELTA
(4.33 – 4.24) /0.25 = 0.36

Put DELTA
(8.05 – 8.20) /0.25 = –0.60

F. For both the call and put options, calculate GAMMA as the difference between the DELTA associated with a stock price increase and the DELTA associated with a stock price decrease, divided by the change in the value of the stock.

Call GAMMA
(0.40 – 0.36) /0.5 = 0.08

Put GAMMA
(–0.60 – (–0.64)) /0.50 = 0.08

G. Increase the risk-free interest rate by 20 basis points to 5.45 percent per annum and recalculate the value of the put and call options using the recursive procedure (single-period binomial option pricing model).

If the interest rate is increased by 20 basis points to 5.45 percent, then the call price is $4.35 and the put price is $8.02.

H. For both the call and put options, calculate RHO as the change in the value of the option divided by the change in the risk-free interest rate.

Call RHO
(4.35 – 4.33) /0.002 = 10

Put RHO
(8.02 – 8.05) /0.002 = –15

I. Increase the volatility of the underlying stock to 33 percent and recalculate the value of the put and call options using the recursive procedure (single-period binomial option pricing model).

If the volatility is increased to 33%, then the call price is $4.89 and the put price is $8.60.

J. For both the call and put options, calculate VEGA as the change in the value of the option divided by the change in the volatility of the stock.

Call VEGA

$(4.89 - 4.33)/0.03 = 18.6667$

Put VEGA

$(8.60 - 8.05)/0.03 = 18.3333$

K. Notice that each branch in the binomial tree represents the passage of time. That is, as one moves forward through the branches in a binomial tree, the life of the option wastes away. Also notice that the initial stock price of \$95 reappears in the middle of the second branch of the tree. Using the parameter values for U, D, π_U, π_D, Δt, and $e^{-r\Delta t}$ calculated using the initial information given, recalculate the value of the call and put options using a **two-period** model. That is, calculate the option prices after 45 days, assuming the stock price is unchanged.

$$U \quad = \quad e^{\sigma\sqrt{\Delta t}} = e^{0.3\sqrt{22.5/365}} = 1.0773$$

$$D \quad = \quad 1/U = 1/1.0773 = 0.9282$$

$$\pi_U \quad = \quad \frac{e^{r\Delta t} - D}{U - D} = \frac{e^{.0525 \times 22.5/365} - 0.9282}{1.0773 - 0.9282} = 0.5031 \quad \pi_D = 1 - 0.5031 = 0.4969$$

$$e^{-r\Delta t} \quad = \quad 0.9968$$

Stock price tree

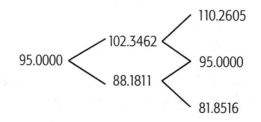

Call price tree

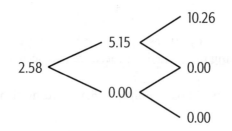

Put price tree

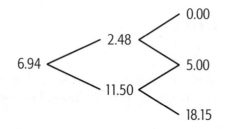

The call price is \$2.58, and the put price is \$6.94.

L. For both the call and put options, calculate THETA as the difference in the value of the option with two periods to expiration less the value of the option with four periods to expiration, divided by twice the passage of time associated with each branch in the tree, that is, $2 \times \Delta t$.

Call THETA

$(2.58 - 4.33) / [2 \times (22.5/365)] = -14.1944$

Put THETA

$(6.94 - 8.05) / [2 \times (22.5/365)] = -9.0033$

20. Consider a stock, ABM, trading at a price of $70. Analysis of ABM's recent returns reveals that ABM has an annualized standard deviation of return of 0.4. The current risk-free rate of interest is 10 percent per annum.

A. What is the price of a European call and put written on ABM with a $75 strike price that expires in 180 days? Price the options using the Black-Scholes model.

$$d_1 = \frac{\ln(70/75) + \left(\left[0.10 + 0.5\left(0.4^2\right)\right](0.4932)\right)}{0.40\sqrt{(0.4932)}} = 0.0704$$

$$d_2 = 0.0704 - 0.40\sqrt{(0.4932)} = -0.2105$$

$$N(d_1) = 0.528061 \quad N(d_2) = 0.416638$$

$$c = 70 \times 0.528061 - 75e^{-0.1 \times 0.4932} \times 0.416638 = \$7.2201$$

$$p = c - S + Xe^{-r(T-t)} = \$7.22 - \$70 + \$75e^{-0.1 \times 0.4932} = \$8.6111$$

The call price is $7.2201, and the put price is $8.6111.

B. Increase the stock price by $.25 to $70.25 and recalculate the value of the put and call options.

If the stock price is increased by $.25, then the call price is $7.3527 and the put price is $8.4938.

C. For both the call and put options, calculate DELTA as the change in the value of the option divided by the change in the value of the stock.

Call DELTA

$(7.3527 - 7.2201) / 0.25 = 0.5304$

Put DELTA

$(8.4938 - 8.6111) / 0.25 = -0.4692$

D. Decrease the stock price by $.25 to $69.75 and recalculate the value of the put and call options.

If the stock price is decreased by $.25, then the call price is $7.0887 and the put price is $8.7298.

E. For both the call and put options, calculate DELTA as the change in the value of the option divided by the change in the value of the stock.

Call DELTA

$(7.2201 - 7.0887)/0.25 = 0.5256$

Put DELTA

$(8.6111 - 8.7298)/0.25 = -0.4748$

F. For both the call and put options, calculate GAMMA as the difference between the DELTA associated with a stock price increase and the DELTA associated with a stock price decrease divided by the change in the value of the stock.

Call GAMMA

$(0.5304 - 0.5256)/0.5 = 0.0096$

Put GAMMA

$(-0.4692 - (-0.4748))/0.5 = .0112$

G. Increase the risk-free interest rate by 25 basis points to 10.25 percent per annum and recalculate the value of the put and call options.

If the interest rate is increased by 25 basis points to 10.25 percent, then the call price is $7.2568 and the put price is $8.5599.

H. For both the call and put options, calculate RHO as the change in the value of the option divided by the change in the risk-free interest rate.

Call RHO

$(7.2568 - 7.2201)/0.0025 = 14.68$

Put RHO

$(8.5599 - 8.6111)/0.0025 = -20.48$

I. Increase the volatility of the underlying stock to 44 percent and recalculate the value of the put and call options.

If the volatility is increased to 44 percent, then the call price is $8.0019 and the put price is $9.3930.

J. For both the call and put options, calculate VEGA as the change in the value of the option divided by the change in the volatility of the stock.

Call VEGA

$(8.0019 - 7.2201)/0.04 = 19.5450$

Put VEGA

$(9.3930 - 8.6111)/0.04 = 19.5475$

K. Decrease the life of the option by 10 percent to 162 days and recalculate the value of the put and call options.

If the life of the option is decreased by 10 percent to 162 days, then the call price is $6.6721 and the put price is $8.4161.

L. For both the call and put options, calculate THETA as the difference in the value of the option with 162 days to expiration less the value of the option with 180 days to expiration divided by the passage of time.

Call THETA

$(6.6721 - 7.2201)/(18/365) = -11.1122$

Put THETA

$(8.4161 - 8.6111)/(18/365) = -3.9542$

21. Consider a stock that trades for $75. A put and a call on this stock both have an exercise price of $70, and they expire in 145 days. The risk-free rate is 9 percent per annum and the standard deviation of return for the stock is 0.35. Assume that the stock pays a continuous dividend of 4 percent.

A. What are the prices of a European call and put option written on this stock according to Merton's model?

$$d_1^M = \frac{\ln(75/70) + \left(\left[0.09 - 0.04 + 0.5\left(0.35^2\right)\right](0.3973)\right)}{0.35 \sqrt{0.3973}} = 0.5131$$

$$d_2^M = 0.5131 - 0.35 \sqrt{0.3973} = 0.2925$$

$$N\left(d_1^M\right) = 0.696056 \quad N\left(d_2^M\right) = 0.615045$$

$$c^M = e^{-\delta(T-t)} S_t N\left(d_1^M\right) - Xe^{-r(T-t)} N_2\left(d^M\right)$$

$$c^M = e^{-0.04(0.3973)} 75 \times 0.696056 - 70e^{-0.09(0.3973)} \times 0.615045 = \$9.84$$

$$N\left(-d_1^M\right) = 0.303944 \quad N\left(-d_2^M\right) = 0.384955$$

$$p^M = Xe^{-r(T-t)} N\left(-d_2^M\right) - e^{-\delta(T-t)} S_t N\left(-d_1^M\right)$$

$$p^M = 70e^{-0.09(0.3973)} \times 0.384955 - e^{-0.04(0.3973)} 75 \times 0.303944 = \$3.56$$

The call price is \$9.8402, and the put price is \$3.5641.

B. Increase the stock price by \$.25 to \$75.25 and recalculate the value of the put and call options.

When the stock price is increased by \$.25, then the call price is \$10.0121 and the put price is \$3.4899.

C. For both the call and put options, calculate DELTA as the change in the value of the option divided by the change in the value of the stock.

Call DELTA   **Put DELTA**

(10.0121 − 9.8402) /0.25 = 0.6876   (3.4899 − 3.5641) /0.25 = −0.2968

D. Decrease the stock price by \$.25 to \$74.75 and recalculate the value of the put and call options.

If the stock price is decreased by \$.25, then the call price is \$9.6696 and the put price is \$3.6395.

E. Calculate DELTA for both the call and put options as the change in the value of the option divided by the change in the value of the stock.

Call DELTA   **Put DELTA**

(9.8402 − 9.6696) /0.25 = 0.6824   (3.5641 − 3.6395) /0.25 = −0.3016

F. Calculate GAMMA for both the call and put options as the difference between the DELTA associated with a stock price increase and the DELTA associated with a stock price decrease divided by the change in the value of the stock.

Call GAMMA   **Put GAMMA**

(0.6876 − 0.6824) /0.5 = 0.0104   (−0.2968 − (−0.3016)) /0.5 = 0.0096

G. Increase the risk-free interest rate by 25 basis points to 9.25 percent per annum and recalculate the value of the put and call options.

When the interest rate is increased by 25 basis points to 9.25 percent, then the call price is \$9.8815 and the put price is \$3.5383.

H. Calculate RHO for both the call and put options as the change in the value of the option divided by the change in the risk-free interest rate.

Call RHO　　　　　　　　　　　　**Put RHO**

(9.8815 – 9.8402) /0.0025 = 16.5200　　(3.5383 – 3.5641) /0.0025 = –10.32

I. Increase the volatility of the underlying stock to 38.5 percent and recalculate the value of the put and call options.

When the volatility is increased to 38.5 percent, the call price is \$10.4136 and the put price is \$4.1374.

J. Calculate VEGA for both the call and put options as the change in the value of the option divided by the change in the volatility of the stock.

Call VEGA　　　　　　　　　　　　**Put VEGA**

(10.4136 – 9.8402) /0.035 = 16.3829　　(4.1374 – 3.5641) /0.035 = 16.3800

K. Decrease the life of the option by 20 percent to 116 days and recalculate the value of the put and call options.

When the life of the option is decreased by 20 percent to 116 days, then the call price is \$9.1028 and the put price is \$3.0764.

L. Calculate THETA for both the call and put options as the difference in the value of the option with 116 days to expiration less the value of the option with 145 days to expiration divided by the passage of time.

Call THETA　　　　　　　　　　　　**Put THETA**

(9.1028 – 9.8402) / (29/365) = –9.2811　　(3.0764 – 3.5641) / (29/365) = –6.1383

22. CSM is trading at \$78 and has an annualized standard deviation of return of 30 percent. CSM is expected to pay a dividend equal to 3 percent of the value of its stock price in 70 days. The current risk-free rate of interest is 7 percent per annum. Options written on this stock have an exercise price of \$80 and expire in 120 days.

A. Using a four-period binomial model, calculate the values of European put and call options written on CSM.

$$U = e^{\sigma\sqrt{\Delta t}} = e^{0.3\sqrt{30/365}} = 1.0898$$

$$D = 1/U = 1/1.0898 = 0.9176$$

$$\pi_U = \frac{e^{r\Delta t} - D}{U - D} = \frac{e^{0.07 \times 30/365} - 0.9176}{1.0898 - 0.9176} = 0.5120 \quad \pi_D = 1 - 0.5120 = 0.4880$$

$$e^{-r\Delta t} = 0.9943$$

Stock price tree

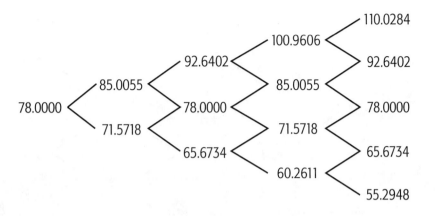

The stock prices in the tree must be adjusted for the dividend to be paid in 70 days before we can calculate the value of the options. Therefore, the stock prices in the tree in periods three and four must be adjusted downward by one minus the dividend yield paid by the firm $(1 - 3\%)$.

Dividend-adjusted stock price tree

Put price tree

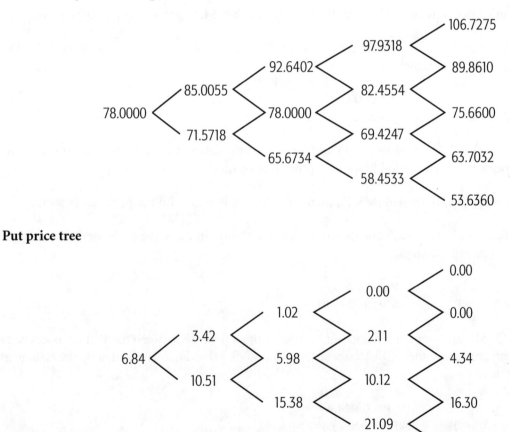

The price of the put option is $6.84.

Call price tree

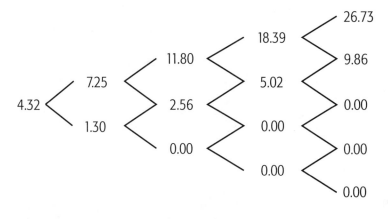

The price of the call option is $4.32.

B. Increase the stock price by $.25 to $78.25 and recalculate the value of the put and call options using the recursive procedure (single-period binomial option pricing model).

When the stock price is increased by $.25, then the call price is $4.42 and the put price is $6.69.

C. Calculate DELTA for both the call and put options as the change in the value of the option divided by the change in the value of the stock.

Call DELTA   **Put DELTA**
(4.42 – 4.32) /0.25 = 0.40   (6.69 – 6.84) /0.25 = –0.60

D. Decrease the stock price by $.25 to $77.75 and recalculate the value of the put and call options using the recursive procedure (single-period binomial option pricing model).

When the stock price is decreased by $.25, then the call price is $4.22 and the put price is $6.99.

E. Calculate DELTA for both the call and put options as the change in the value of the option divided by the change in the value of the stock.

Call DELTA   **Put DELTA**
(4.32 – 4.22) /0.25 = 0.40   (6.69 – 6.84) /0.25 = –0.60

F. Calculate GAMMA for both the call and put options as the difference between the DELTA associated with a stock price increase and the DELTA associated with a stock price decrease divided by the change in the value of the stock.

Call GAMMA   **Put GAMMA**
(0.3869 – 0.3869) /0.5 = 0   (–0.5831 – (–0.5831)) /0.5 = 0

Calculating the price of each option to two decimal places using a four-period binomial process to model the price movements in a stock over a 90-day period produces symmetric price changes in the value of the options. There is not sufficient information in our modeling process to capture the nonlinearity of the pricing function for small symmetric changes in the stock price. This generates a value of zero for GAMMA.

G. Increase the risk-free interest rate by 20 basis points to 7.20 percent per annum and recalculate the value of the put and call options using the recursive procedure (single-period binomial option pricing model).

When the interest rate is increased by 20 basis points to 7.20 percent, then the call price is $4.34 and the put price is $6.81.

H. Calculate RHO for both the call and put options as the change in the value of the option divided by the change in the risk-free interest rate.

Call RHO   **Put RHO**

$(4.34 - 4.32)/0.002 = 10$ $(6.81 - 6.84)/0.002 = -15$

I. Increase the volatility of the underlying stock to 33 percent and recalculate the value of the put and call options using the recursive procedure (single-period binomial option pricing model).

When the volatility is increased to 33 percent, then the call price is $4.83 and the put price is $7.35.

J. Calculate VEGA for both the call and put options as the change in the value of the option divided by the change in the volatility of the stock.

Call VEGA   **Put VEGA**

$(4.83 - 4.32)/0.03 = 17$ $(7.35 - 6.84)/0.03 = 17$

K. Notice that each branch in the binomial tree represents the passage of time. That is, as one moves forward through the branches in a binomial tree, the life of the option wastes away. Also notice that the initial stock price of $78 reappears in the middle of the second branch of the tree. Using the parameter values for U, D, π_U, π_D, Δt, and $e^{-r\Delta t}$ calculated using the initial information given, recalculate the value of the call and put options using a **two-period** model. Assume that the dividend will be paid before period one and make the appropriate adjustments to the stock price tree. That is, calculate the option prices after 60 days, assuming that the stock price is unchanged.

$$U = e^{\sigma\sqrt{\Delta t}} = e^{0.3\sqrt{30/365}} = 1.0898$$

$$D = 1/U = 1/1.0898 = 0.9176$$

$$\pi_U = \frac{e^{r\Delta t} - D}{U - D} = \frac{e^{0.07 \times 30/365} - 0.9176}{1.0898 - 0.9176} = 0.5120 \quad \pi_D = 1 - 0.5120 = 0.4880$$

$$e^{-r\Delta t} = 0.9943$$

Dividend-adjusted stock price tree

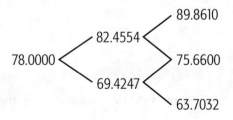

Call price tree

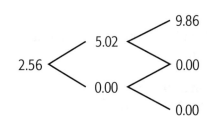

Put price tree

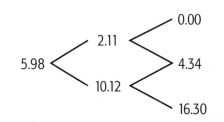

The call price is $2.56, and the put price is $5.98.

L. Calculate THETA for both the call and put options as the difference in the value of the option with two periods to expiration less the value of the option with four periods to expiration divided by twice the passage of time associated with each branch in the tree, that is, $2 \times \Delta t$.

Call THETA

$(2.56 - 4.32) / [2 \times (30/365)] = -10.7067$

Put THETA

$(5.98 - 6.84) / [2 \times (30/365)] = -5.2317$

23. DCC exports high-speed digital switching networks, and their largest and most important clients are in Asia. A recent financial crisis in Asia has diminished the prospects of new sales to the Asian market in the near term. However, you believe that DCC is a good investment for the long term. A quick check of Quote.com reveals that DCC is trading at $78.625 per share. Your previous calculation of the historical volatility for DCC indicated an annual standard deviation of return of 27 percent, but examining the implied volatility of several DCC options reveals an increase in annual volatility to 32 percent. There are two traded options series that expire in 245 days. The options have $75 and $80 strike prices respectively. The current 245-day risk-free interest rate is 4.75 percent per annum, and you hold 2,000 shares of DCC.

	X = 75		X = 80	
	Call	**Put**	**Call**	**Put**
DELTA	0.6674	−0.3326	0.574	−0.426
GAMMA	0.0176	0.0176	0.019	0.019
THETA	−7.5372	−4.0865	−7.7495	−4.0687
VEGA	23.4015	23.4015	25.2551	25.2551
RHO	27.6835	−21.0792	24.4395	−27.574

A. Construct a portfolio that is DELTA- and GAMMA-neutral using the call options written on DCC.

The investor owns 2,000 shares of DCC. An option contract extends the right to buy or sell 100 shares of the underlying stock at the strike price. Thus, by scaling the stock position by 100, we can convert the stock position to a scale that matches a single option contract. On a scaled basis, the shareholder has a long position in 20 = 2000/100, contract units of stock. The investor must determine how many $75 call options and $80 call options to hold to create a portfolio that is DELTA- and GAMMA-neutral. The DELTA of the stock, DELTA$_s$, is one, and the GAMMA of the stock, GAMMA$_s$, is zero.

$$N_s \text{ DELTA}_s + N_{75} \text{ DELTA}_{75} + N_{80} \text{ DELTA}_{80} = 0$$
$$N_s \text{ GAMMA}_s + N_{75} \text{ GAMMA}_{75} + N_{80} \text{ GAMMA}_{80} = 0$$

$$20 \times 1 + N_{75}(0.6674) + N_{80}(0.5740) = 0$$
$$20 \times 0 + N_{75}(0.0176) + N_{80}(0.0190) = 0$$

We must solve the equation for N_{75} and N_{80} subject to the constraint that the DELTA of the portfolio is −20 and the GAMMA is 0.

$$N_{75}(0.6674) + N_{80}(0.5740) = -20$$
$$N_{75}(0.0176) + N_{80}(0.0190) = 0$$

$$N_{75} = -147.39$$
$$N_{80} = 136.53$$

To create a portfolio with a DELTA of −20 and a GAMMA of 0, the investor must sell 147.39 of the $75 call option contracts and purchase 136.53 of the $80 call option contracts.

B. Construct a portfolio that is DELTA- and GAMMA-neutral using the put options written on DCC.

The investor owns 2,000 shares of DCC. An option contract extends the right to buy or sell 100 shares of the underlying stock at the strike price. Thus, by scaling the stock position by 100, we can convert the stock position to a scale that matches a single option contract. On a scaled basis, the shareholder has a long position in 20 = 2000/100, contract units of stock. The investor must determine how many $75 put options and $80 put options to hold to create a portfolio that is DELTA- and GAMMA-neutral. The DELTA of the stock, DELTA_s, is one, and the GAMMA of the stock, GAMMA_s, is zero.

$$N_s \text{ DELTA}_s + N_{75} \text{ DELTA}_{75} + N_{80} \text{ DELTA}_{80} = 0$$
$$N_s \text{ GAMMA}_s + N_{75} \text{ GAMMA}_{75} + N_{80} \text{ GAMMA}_{80} = 0$$

$$20 \times 1 + N_{75}(-0.3326) + N_{80}(-0.4260) = 0$$
$$20 \times 0 + N_{75}(0.0176) + N_{80}(0.0190) = 0$$

We must solve the equation for N_{75} and N_{80} subject to the constraint that the DELTA of the portfolio is −20 and the GAMMA is 0.

$$N_{75}(-0.3326) + N_{80}(-0.426) = -20$$
$$N_{75}(0.0176) + N_{80}(0.0190) = 0$$

$$N_{75} = -322.53$$
$$N_{80} = 298.76$$

To create a portfolio with a DELTA of −20 and a GAMMA of 0, the investor must sell 322.53 of the $75 put option contracts and purchase 298.76 of the $80 put option contracts.

C. Construct a portfolio that is DELTA- and THETA-neutral using the call options written on DCC.

The investor owns 2,000 shares of DCC. An option contract extends the right to buy or sell 100 shares of the underlying stock at the strike price. Thus, by scaling the stock position by 100, we can convert the stock position to a scale that matches a single option contract. On a scaled basis, the shareholder has a long position in 20 = 2000/100, contract units of stock. The investor must determine how many $75 call options and $80 call options to hold to create a portfolio that is DELTA- and THETA-neutral. The DELTA of the stock, $DELTA_s$, is one, and the THETA of the stock, $THETA_s$, is zero.

$$N_s\ DELTA_s + N_{75}\ DELTA_{75} + N_{80}\ DELTA_{80} = 0$$
$$N_s\ THETA_s + N_{75}\ THETA_{75} + N_{80}\ THETA_{80} = 0$$

$$20 \times 1 + N_{75}\ (0.6674) + N_{80}\ (0.5740) = 0$$
$$20 \times 0 + N_{75}\ (-7.5372) + N_{80}\ (-7.7495) = 0$$

We must solve the equation for N_{75} and N_{80} subject to the constraint that the DELTA of the portfolio is −20 and the THETA is 0.

$$N_{75}\ (0.6674) + N_{80}\ (0.5740) = -20$$
$$N_{75}\ (-7.5372) + N_{80}\ (-7.7495) = 0$$

$$N_{75} = -183.28$$
$$N_{80} = 178.26$$

To create a portfolio with a DELTA of −20 and a THETA of 0, the investor must sell 183.28 of the $75 call option contracts and purchase 178.26 of the $80 call option contracts.

D. Construct a portfolio that is DELTA- and THETA-neutral using the put options written on DCC.

The investor owns 2,000 shares of DCC. An option contract extends the right to buy or sell 100 shares of the underlying stock at the strike price. Thus, by scaling the stock position by 100, we can convert the stock position to a scale that matches a single option contract. On a scaled basis, the shareholder has a long position in 20 = 2000/100, contract units of stock. The investor must determine how many $75 put options and $80 put options to hold to create a portfolio that is DELTA- and THETA-neutral. The DELTA of the stock, $DELTA_s$, is one, and the THETA of the stock, $THETA_s$, is zero.

$$N_s\ DELTA_s + N_{75}\ DELTA_{75} + N_{80}\ DELTA_{80} = 0$$
$$N_s\ THETA_s + N_{75}\ THETA_{75} + N_{80}\ THETA_{80} = 0$$

$$20 \times 1 + N_{75}\ (-0.3326) + N_{80}\ (-0.426) = 0$$
$$20 \times 0 + N_{75}\ (-4.0865) + N_{80}\ (-4.0687) = 0$$

We must solve the equation for N_{75} and N_{80} subject to the constraint that the DELTA of the portfolio is −20 and the THETA is 0.

$$N_{75}\ (-0.3326) + N_{80}\ (-0.426) = -20$$
$$N_{75}(-4.0865) + N_{80}\ (-4.0687) = 0$$

$$N_{75} = -209.94$$
$$N_{80} = 210.86$$

To create a portfolio with a DELTA of −20 and a THETA of 0, the investor must sell 209.94 of the $75 put option contracts and purchase 210.86 of the $80 put option contracts.

E. How effective do you expect the DELTA- and GAMMA-neutral hedges to be? Explain.

The effectiveness of the DELTA-, GAMMA-neutral hedges will be conditional on movements in DCC's stock price over the hedge period. If DCC's stock remains relatively constant during the hedge period, then the hedge should be effective. However, if DCC's stock price is volatile during the hedge period, which is very likely to happen, then it will be necessary to rebalance the portfolio periodically to maintain the effectiveness of the hedge.

24. Consider a stock, PRN, that trades for $24. A put and a call on this stock both have an exercise price of $22.50, and they expire in 45 days. The risk-free rate is 5.5 percent per annum, and the standard deviation of return for the stock is .28.

A. Calculate the price of the put and call option using the Black-Scholes model.

$$d_1 = \frac{\ln(24/22.5) + \left(\left[0.055 + 0.5\left(0.28^2\right)\right](0.1233)\right)}{0.28\sqrt{(0.1233)}} = 0.7746$$

$$d_2 = 0.7746 - 0.28\sqrt{(0.1233)} = -0.6763$$

$$N(d_1) = 0.780705 \quad N(d_2) = 0.750563$$

$$c = 24 \times 0.780705 - 22.5e^{-0.055 \times 0.1233} \times 0.750563 = \$1.96$$

$$p = c - S + Xe^{-r(T-t)} = \$1.96 - \$24 + \$22.5e^{-0.055 \times 0.1233} = \$.31$$

The call price is $1.96, and the put price is $.31.

Note: Use the following information for the remaining parts of this problem.
Suppose that you own 1,500 shares of PRN and you wish to hedge your investment in PRN using the traded PRN options. You are going on vacation in 45 days and want to use your shares to finance your vacation, so you do not want the value of your PRN shares to fall below $22.50.

B. Construct a hedge using a covered call strategy. In a covered call strategy, the investor sells call options to hedge against the risk of a stock price decline.

The investor owns 1,500 shares of PRN. An option contract extends the right to buy or sell 100 shares of the underlying stock at the strike price. Thus, by scaling the stock position by 100, we can convert the stock position to a scale that matches a single option contract. On a scaled basis, the shareholder has a long position in 15 = 1,500/100, contract units of stock. The investor wants to create a hedge position that expires in 45 days and the PRN options expire in 45 days. In this hedge, the investor will hold the option contracts to their expiration date and use the moneyness of the options to hedge the investment in PRN. The investor's objective is to create a price floor of $22.50 for the 1,500 shares of PRN. The minimum value desired for the PRN shares in 45 days is $33,750 = 1,500 × $22.50.

In this covered call hedge, the investor will sell one call option of every share of stock that he owns. On a scaled basis, the shareholder has a long position in 15 PRN contract units of stock. Thus, the investor should sell 15 PRN call options at $1.96. The cash inflow from the sale of the 15 call options is $2,940 = $1.96 × 15 × 100.

C. Construct a hedge using a protective put strategy. In a protective put strategy, the investor purchases put options to hedge against the risk of a stock price decline.

In this protective put hedge, the investor will buy one put option of every share of stock that he owns. On a scaled basis, the shareholder has a long position in 15 PRN shares. Thus, the investor should buy 15 PRN put options at $.31. The cash outflow from the purchase of the 15 put options is $465 = $.31 × 15 × 100.

D. If PRN is trading at $19 in 45 days, analyze and compare the effectiveness of the two alternative hedging strategies.

Covered call:
When PRN is trading at $19, the call options that the investor sold expire worthless. The investor keeps the proceeds of $2,940 from the sale of the call options. The investor's stock position is worth $28,500 = $19 × 1,500. The total value of the portfolio consisting of the stock position and the proceeds from the sale of the options is $31,440 = $28,500 + $2,940. Thus, the value of the portfolio is $2,310 less than the $33,750 minimum value for the portfolio established by the investor at the start of the hedge.

Protective put:
When PRN is trading at $19, the put options owned by the investor are in-the-money. The investor will exercise the 15 put options, selling 1,500, 15 × 100, shares of stock at $22.50 per share. The value of the investor's portfolio is $33,750, the minimum value for the portfolio established by the investor at the start of the hedge.

The covered call hedge strategy resulted in a loss of value to the investor's portfolio that was greater than the loss the investor was willing to accept at the start of the hedge period. The protective put strategy produced a portfolio that had a value that was equal to the minimum set by the investor at the start of the hedge.

E. If PRN is trading at $26 in 45 days, analyze and compare the effectiveness of the two alternative hedging strategies.

Covered call:
When PRN is trading at $26, the call options sold by the investor are in-the-money. The owner of the options will exercise the 15 call options against the investor. The investor will have to sell his 1,500 shares of PRN stock at $22.50 per share to the owner of the option. The investor will receive $33,750 from the sale of the stock. The proceeds of $2,940 from the sale of the call options plus the $33,750 from the sale of the stock result in a position that is worth $36,690. The value of 1,500 shares of PRN at $26 per share is $39,000. Thus, the investor incurs an opportunity cost of $2,310 from the sale of 15 PRN call options.

Protective put:
When PRN is trading at $26, the put options that the investor purchased expire worthless. The investor's stock position is worth $39,000, $26 × 1,500. The total value of the portfolio consisting of the stock position and the cost of the put options is $38,535, $39,000 − $465.

When the stock price exceeds the exercise price of an option at expiration, the investor incurs an opportunity cost when implementing a covered call hedge strategy. The protective put hedging strategy is not subject to this opportunity cost.

25. A friend, Audrey, holds a portfolio of 10,000 shares of Microsoft stock. In 60 days she needs at least $855,000 to pay for her new home. You suggest to Audrey that she can construct an insured portfolio using Microsoft stock options. You explain that an insured portfolio can be constructed several different ways, but the basic notion is to create a portfolio that consists of a long position in Microsoft's stock and a long position in put options written on Microsoft. If at the end of the hedge period Microsoft's stock is trading at a price below the strike price on the put option, Audrey has the right to sell her Microsoft stock to the owner of the put option for the strike price. Thus, at the end of the hedge period, Audrey has sufficient assets to cover her needs or obligations. This hedging strategy can be implemented using traded options. However, Audrey may not be able to find an option with the desired strike price or expiration

date. Dynamic hedging permits Audrey to overcome these limitations associated with traded option contracts. In dynamic hedging, Audrey constructs a portfolio that consists of a long position in stock and a long position in Treasury bills. As the underlying stock price changes, Audrey dynamically alters the allocation of assets in the portfolio between stock and Treasury bills. Therefore, we can view dynamic hedging as an asset allocation problem where Audrey determines how much of her resources are allocated to the stock, and how much of her resources are allocated to Treasury bills. The amount of resources available for investment is simply the current cash value of Audrey's stock position. The proportion of resources committed to the stock, w, are calculated as

$$\frac{SN(d_1)}{S + P} = w$$

where S is the current stock price, P is the price of the relevant put option, and $N(d_1)$ comes from the Black-Scholes model. The proportion of resources committed to the Treasury bill is $1 - w$.

A. Microsoft is currently trading at $90. The annualized risk-free interest rate on a 60-day Treasury bill is 5 percent. The current volatility of Microsoft's stock is 0.32. Audrey wishes to create an insured portfolio. Since she needs $855,000 in 60 days, she decides to establish a position in a 60-day Microsoft put option with an $85.50 strike price. Audrey calls her broker, who informs her there is no 60-day Microsoft put option with a strike price of $85.50. Thus, Audrey must construct a dynamic hedge to protect the value of her investment in Microsoft stock. Using the Black-Scholes model, calculate the value of a put option with an $85.50 strike price with 60 days to expiration. Determine the allocation of assets in Audrey's insured portfolio. That is, find the proportion of resources committed to Microsoft stock, w, and the proportion of resources committed to Treasury bills, $1 - w$. Determine the dollar amount of her resources committed to Microsoft stock, and the dollar amount of her resources committed to Treasury bills.

$$d_1 = \frac{\ln(90/85.5) + \left(\left[0.05 + .5\left(0.32^2\right)\right](0.1644)\right)}{0.32\sqrt{(0.1644)}} = 0.5236$$

$$d_2 = 0.5236 - 0.32\sqrt{(0.1644)} = 0.3938$$

$$N(d_1) = 0.699711 \quad N(d_2) = 0.653146$$

$$c = 90 \times 0.699711 - 85.5e^{-0.05 \times 0.1644} \times 0.653146 = \$7.59$$

$$p = c - S + Xe^{-r(T-t)} = \$7.59 - \$90 + \$85.5e^{-0.05 \times 0.1644} = \$2.39$$

The call price is $7.59, and the put price is $2.39. The proportion of resources committed to the stock is

$$w = \frac{S\,N(d_1)}{S + P} = \frac{\$90 \times 0.699711}{\$90 + \$2.39} = 0.6816$$

The proportion of resources committed to Treasury bills is

$$1 - w = 1 - 0.6816 = 0.3184$$

Audrey holds 10,000 shares of Microsoft with a market value of $90 per share, giving her a portfolio with a cash value of $900,000. Audrey will commit 68.16 percent of her resources to Microsoft stock and 31.84 percent of her resources to Treasury bills. Audrey holds $613,468 worth of Microsoft stock, $900,000 × 0.6816, and $286,532 worth of Treasury bills, $900,000 × 0.3184.

B. Twenty days later Microsoft is trading at $92. The annualized risk-free interest rate on a 40-day Treasury bill is 5 percent, and the volatility of Microsoft's stock is 0.32. Using the Black-Scholes model, calculate the value of a put option with an $85.50 strike price with 40 days to expiration. Determine the allocation of assets in Audrey's insured portfolio. That is, find the proportion of resources committed to Microsoft stock, w, and the proportion of resources committed to Treasury bills, $1 - w$.

$$d_1 = \frac{\ln(92/85.5) + \left(\left[0.05 + 0.5\left(0.32^2\right)\right](0.1096)\right)}{0.32\sqrt{(0.1096)}} = 0.7964$$

$$d_2 = 0.7964 - 0.32\sqrt{(0.1096)} = -0.6904$$

$$N(d_1) = 0.787092 \quad N(d_2) = 0.755041$$

$$c = 92 \times 0.787092 - 85.5e^{-0.05 \times 0.1096} \times 0.755041 = \$8.21$$

$$p = c - S + Xe^{-r(T-t)} = \$8.21 - \$92 + \$85.5e^{-0.05 \times 0.1096} = \$1.24$$

The call price is $8.21, and the put price is $1.24. The proportion of resources committed to the stock is

$$w = \frac{S\,N(d_1)}{S + P} = \frac{\$92 \times 0.787092}{\$92 + \$1.24} = 0.7766$$

The proportion of resources committed to Treasury bills is

$$1 - w = 1 - 0.7766 = 0.2234$$

C. Twenty days later Microsoft is trading at $86. The annualized risk-free interest rate on a 20-day Treasury bill is 5 percent, and the volatility of Microsoft's stock is 0.32. Using the Black-Scholes model, calculate the value of a put option with an $85.50 strike price with 20 days to expiration. Determine the allocation of assets in Audrey's insured portfolio. That is, find the proportion of resources committed to Microsoft stock, w, and the proportion of resources committed to Treasury bills, $1 - w$.

$$d_1 = \frac{\ln(86/85.5) + \left(\left[0.05 + 0.5\left(0.32^2\right)\right](0.0548)\right)}{0.32\sqrt{(0.0548)}} = 0.1519$$

$$d_2 = 0.1519 - 0.32\sqrt{(0.0548)} = 0.0770$$

$$N(d_1) = 0.560356 \quad N(d_2) = 0.530674$$

$$c = 86 \times 0.560356 - 85.5e^{-0.05 \times 0.0548} \times 0.530674 = \$2.94$$

$$p = c - S + Xe^{-r(T-t)} = \$2.94 - \$86 + \$85.5e^{-0.05 \times 0.0548} = \$2.21$$

The call price is $2.94, and the put price is $2.21. The proportion of resources committed to the stock is

$$w = \frac{S\,N(d_1)}{S + P} = \frac{\$86 \times 0.560356}{\$86 + \$2.21} = 0.5463$$

The proportion of resources committed to Treasury bills is

$$1 - w = 1 - 0.5463 = 0.4537$$

D. Discuss the adjustments Audrey has made in the allocation of resources between Microsoft stock and Treasury bills as Microsoft's stock price has changed.

In dynamic hedging, the investor's commitment to Microsoft stock increases as Microsoft's stock price increases and decreases as Microsoft's stock price decreases. With 60 days to the end of the hedge period, Audrey holds 68.16 percent of her resources in Microsoft stock. With 40 days to the end of the hedge period and Microsoft trading at $92, Audrey holds 77.66 percent of her resources in Microsoft stock. At 20 days to the end of the hedge period and Microsoft trading at $86, Audrey holds 54.63 percent of her resources in Microsoft stock. The trading strategy associated with dynamic hedging requires the investor to purchase additional Microsoft shares as the market price of the stock goes up and to sell additional Microsoft shares as the market price of the stock goes down. This buying of stock at successively higher prices and selling at successively lower prices is a direct cost of the insurance created.

American Option Pricing | 15

Answers to Questions and Problems

1. Explain why American and European calls on a nondividend stock always have the same value.

   An American option is just like a European option, except the American option carries the right of early exercise. Exercising a call before expiration discards the time value inherent in the option. The only off-setting benefit from early exercise arises from an attempt to capture a dividend. If there is no dividend, there is no incentive to early exercise, so the early exercise feature of an American call on a nondividend stock has no value.

2. Explain why American and European puts on a nondividend stock can have different values.

   The exercise value of a put is $X - S$. On a European put, this value cannot be captured until the expiration date. Therefore, before expiration, the value of the European put will be a function of the present value of these exercise proceeds: $e^{-r(T-t)}(X - S)$. The American put gives immediate access at any time to the full proceeds, $X - S$, through exercise. In certain circumstances, notably on puts that are deep-in-the-money with time remaining until expiration, this differential in exercise conditions can give the American put extra value over the corresponding European put, even in the absence of dividends.

3. Explain the circumstances that might make the early exercise of an American put on a nondividend stock desirable.

   Early exercise of an American put provides the holder with an immediate cash inflow of $X - S$. These proceeds can earn a return from the date of exercise to the expiration date that is not available on a European put. However, early exercise discards the time value of the put. Therefore, the early exercise decision requires trading off the sacrificed time value against the interest that can be earned by investing the exercise value from the date of exercise to the expiration date of the put. For deep-in-the-money puts with time remaining until expiration, the potential interest gained can exceed the time value of the put that is sacrificed.

4. What factors might make an owner exercise an American call?

   The key factor is an approaching dividend, and exercise of an American call should occur only at the moment before an ex-dividend date. The dividend must be "large" relative to the share price, and the call will typically also be deep-in-the-money.

5. Do dividends on the underlying stock make the early exercise of an American put more or less likely? Explain.

   Dividends make early exercise of an American put less likely. Dividends decrease the stock price and increase the exercise value of the put. Thus, the holder of the American put has an incentive to delay exercising and wait for the dividend payments.

6. Do dividends on the underlying stock make the early exercise of an American call more or less likely? Explain.

Dividends increase the likelihood of early exercise on an American call. In fact, if there are no dividends on the underlying stock, early exercise of an American call is irrational.

7. Explain the strategy behind the pseudo-American call pricing strategy.

In pseudo-American call pricing, the analysis treats the stock price as the current stock price reduced by the present value of all dividends to occur before the option expires. It then considers potential exercise just prior to each ex-dividend date, by reducing the exercise price by the present value of all dividends to be paid, including the imminent dividend. (The dividends are a reduction from the exercise price because they represent a cash inflow if the option is exercised.) For each dividend date, the analysis values a European option using the Black-Scholes model. The pseudo-American price is the maximum of these European option prices. Implicitly, the pricing strategy assumes exercise on the date that gives the highest European option price.

8. Consider a stock with a price of $140 and a standard deviation of 0.4. The stock will pay a dividend of $2 in 40 days and a second dividend of $2 in 130 days. The current risk-free rate of interest is 10 percent. An American call on this stock has an exercise price of $150 and expires in 100 days. What is the price of the call according to the pseudo-American approach?

First, notice that the second dividend is scheduled to be paid in 130 days, after the option expires. Therefore, the second dividend cannot affect the option price and it may be disregarded. To apply the pseudo-American model, we begin by subtracting the present value of the dividend from the stock price to form the adjusted stock price:

$$\text{Adjusted Stock Price} = \$140 - \$2e^{-0.10(40/365)} = \$138.02$$

For the single dividend date, we reduce the exercise price by the $2 of dividend so the adjusted exercise price is $148. Applying the Black-Scholes model with $S = \$138.02$, $E = \$148$, and $T - t = 40$ days gives a price of $4.05. Applying the Black-Scholes model with $S = \$138.02$, $E = \$150$, and $T - t = 100$ gives a price of $8.29. The higher price, $8.29, is the pseudo-American option price.

9. Could the exact American call pricing model be used to price the option in question 8? Explain.

Yes. Once we notice that the second dividend falls beyond the expiration date of the option, the exact American model fits exactly and gives a price of $8.28, almost the same as the pseudo-American price of $8.29.

10. Explain why the exact American call pricing model treats the call as an "option on an option."

The exact American model applies to call options on stocks with a single dividend occurring before the option expires. Early exercise of an American call is optimal only at the ex-dividend date. At the ex-dividend date, the holder of an American call has a choice: exercise and own the stock or do not exercise and hold what is then equivalent to a European option that expires at the original expiration date of the American call. (The option that results from not exercising is equivalent to a European call because there are no more dividends occurring before expiration.) Thus, the exact American call model recognizes that the call embodies an option to own a European option at the dividend date. It also embodies the right to acquire the stock at the stated exercise price at the ex-dividend date.

11. Explain the idea of a bivariate cumulative standardized normal distribution. What would be the cumulative probability of observing two variables both with a value of zero, assuming that the correlation between them was zero? Explain.

The bivariate cumulative distribution considers the probability of two standardized normal variates having values equal to or below a certain threshold at the same time given a certain correlation between the two. Consider first a univariate standardized normal variate. The probability of its value being zero or less equals the chance that it is below its mean of zero, which is 50 percent. Considering two such variates, with a zero correlation between them, the probability that both have a value of zero or less equals $0.5 \times 0.5 = 0.25$. If the two variables had a correlation other than zero, this probability would be different.

12. In the exact American call pricing model, explain why the model can compute the call price with only one dividend.

The exact American model uses the cumulative bivariate standardized normal distribution, which considers the correlation between a pair of variates. The formula, for example, evaluates the probability of not exercising and the option finishing in-the-money, and of not exercising and the option finishing out-of-the-money. If there were more dividends, the bivariate distribution would be inadequate to handle all of the possible combinations, and higher multivariate normal distributions would have to be considered. For these, no solution has yet been found.

13. What is the critical stock price in the exact American call pricing model?

The critical stock price, S^*, is the stock price that makes the call owner indifferent regarding exercise at the ex-dividend date. If the option is not exercised at the ex-dividend date, the American call effectively becomes a European call and the value is simply given by the Black-Scholes model. If the owner exercises, she receives the stock price, plus the dividend, less the exercise price. Therefore, where D_1 is the dividend, the critical stock price makes the following equation hold:

$$S^* + D_1 - X = \text{European Call}$$

14. Explain how the analytical approximation for American option values is analogous to the Merton model.

Both models pertain to underlying goods with a continuous dividend rate.

15. Explain the role of the critical stock price in the analytic approximation for an American call.

The critical stock price is the stock price that makes the owner of an American call indifferent regarding exercise. If the stock price exceeds the critical stock price, the owner should exercise. Otherwise, the option should not be exercised.

16. Why should an American call owner exercise if the stock price exceeds the critical price?

If the stock price exceeds the critical stock price, the owner should exercise to capture the exercise proceeds. These can be invested to earn a return from the date of exercise to the expiration of the option. The critical stock price is the price at which the benefits of earning that interest just equal the costs of discarding the time value of the option. If the stock price exceeds the critical stock price, the potential interest proceeds are worth more than the time value of the option, and the option should be exercised.

17. Consider the binomial model for an American call and put on a stock that pays no dividends. The current stock price is $120, and the exercise price for both the put and the call is $110. The standard deviation of the stock returns is 0.4, and the risk-free rate is 10 percent. The options expire in 120 days. Model the price of these options using a four-period tree. Draw the stock tree and the corresponding trees for the call and the put. Explain when, if ever, each option should be exercised. What is the value of a European call in this situation? Can you find the value of the European call without making a separate computation? Explain.

$U = 1.1215$; $D = 0.8917$; $\pi_U = 0.5073$. The American call is worth $18.93, while the American put is worth $5.48. With no dividend, the American call should not be exercised at any time. The put should be exercised if the stock price drops three times from $120.00 to $85.07. Then the exercisable proceeds would be $24.93, but the corresponding European put would be worth only $24.03. The asterisk in the option tree indicates a node at which exercise should occur.

Stock Price Lattice

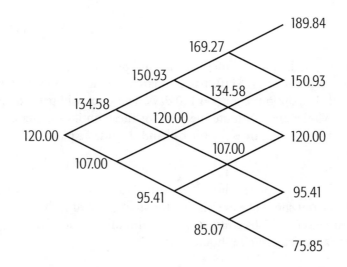

Call Price Lattice

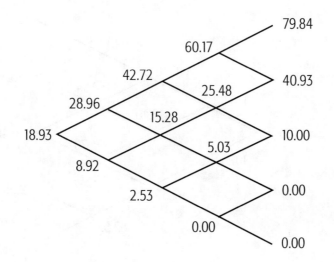

Put Price Lattice

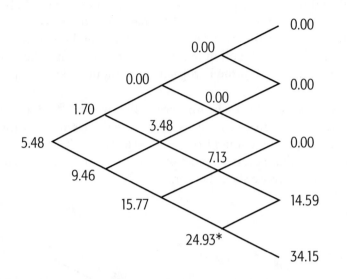

18. Consider the binomial model for an American call and put on a stock whose price is $120. The exercise price for both the put and the call is $110. The standard deviation of the stock returns is 0.4, and the risk-free rate is 10 percent. The options expire in 120 days. The stock will pay a dividend equal to 3 percent of its value in 50 days. Model and compute the price of these options using a four-period tree. Draw the stock tree and the corresponding trees for the call and the put. Explain when, if ever, each option should be exercised.

$U = 1.1215; D = 0.8917; \pi_U = 0.5073$. The call is worth $16.14, and the put is worth $6.28. The call should never be exercised. The put should be exercised if the stock price drops three straight times to $82.52. This gives exercisable proceeds of $27.48, compared to a computed value of $26.58. The asterisk in the option tree indicates a node at which exercise should occur.

Stock Price Lattice

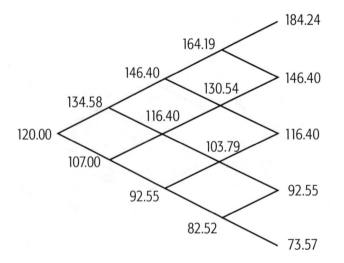

Call Price Lattice

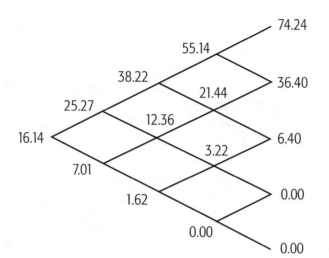

74.24
55.14
38.22
36.40
21.44
25.27
12.36
16.14
6.40
7.01
3.22
1.62
0.00
0.00
0.00
0.00

Put Price Lattice

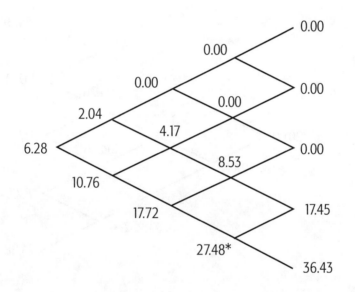

0.00
0.00
0.00
0.00
2.04
0.00
6.28
4.17
0.00
10.76
8.53
17.72
17.45
27.48*
36.43

19. Consider the binomial model for an American call and put on a stock whose price is $120. The exercise price for both the put and the call is $110. The standard deviation of the stock returns is 0.4, and the risk-free rate is 10 percent. The options expire in 120 days. The stock will pay a $3 dividend in 50 days. Model and compute the price of these options using a four-period tree. Draw the stock tree and the corresponding trees for the call and the put. Explain when, if ever, each option should be exercised.

$U = 1.1215$; $D = 0.8917$; $\pi_U = 0.5073$. The call is worth $16.63, while the put is worth $6.14. The call should never be exercised. The put should be exercised if the stock price drops three straight times to $82.97. This gives exercisable proceeds of $27.03, which exceeds the computed value of $26.13. The asterisk in the option tree indicates a node at which exercise should occur.

Stock Price Lattice

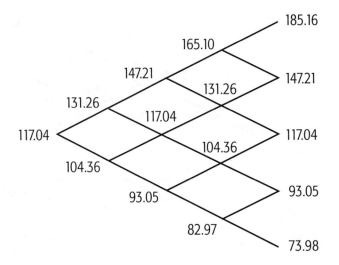

Adjusted Stock Price Lattice

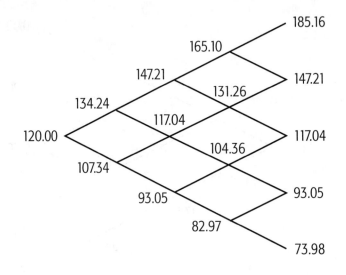

Call Price Lattice

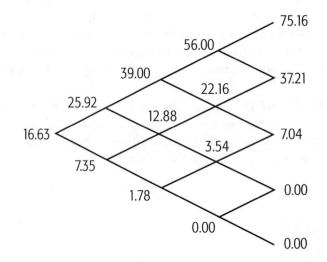

Put Price Lattice

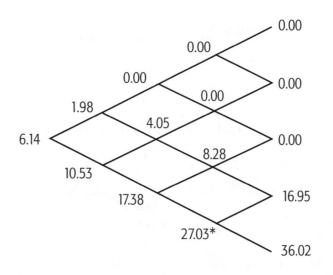

20. Consider the analytic approximation for American options. A stock sells for $130, has a standard deviation of 0.3, and pays a continuous dividend of 3 percent. An American call and put on this stock both have an exercise price of $130, and they both expire in 180 days. The risk-free rate is 12 percent. Find the value of the call and put according to this model. Demonstrate that you have found the correct critical stock price for both options.

For the call, the critical price is $S^* = \$604.08$. For the put, the critical price is $S^{**} = \$103.88$. To verify that these critical prices are correct, we need to show that they satisfy the following two equations.

Call: $\quad S^* - X = c_t(S^*, X, T - t) + \left\{1 - e^{-\delta(T-t)}N(d_1)\right\}(S^*/q_2)$

Put: $\quad X - S^{**} = p_t(S^{**}, X, T - t) - \left\{1 - e^{-\delta(T-t)}N(-d_1)\right\}(S^{**}/q_1)$

$$q_1 = \frac{1 - n - \sqrt{(n-1)^2 + 4k}}{2}$$

$$q_2 = \frac{1 - n + \sqrt{(n-1)^2 + 4k}}{2}$$

$$n = \frac{2(r - \delta)}{\sigma^2}, \quad k = \frac{2r}{\sigma^2\left(1 - e^{-r(T-t)}\right)}$$

With these values:

$$n = 2(.12 - 0.03)/(0.3 \times 0.3) = 2.00$$

$$k = (2 \times 0.12)/\left[0.3 \times 0.3\,(1 - 0.9425)\right] = 0.24/0.0052 = 46.4082$$

$$q_1 = \frac{1 - 2 - \sqrt{(2-1)^2 + 4(46.4082)}}{2} = -7.3307$$

$$q_2 = \frac{1 - 2 + \sqrt{(2-1)^2 + 4(46.4082)}}{2} = 6.3307$$

For the call, evaluating d_1 at the critical price for the call, $604.08, gives $d_1 = 35.4167$:

$$d_1 = \frac{\ln\left(\dfrac{604.08}{130}\right) + \left[.12 - .03 + .5(.3)(.3)\right]\left(\dfrac{180}{365}\right)}{.3\sqrt{\dfrac{180}{365}}} = 35.4167$$

For the put, evaluating d_1 at the critical price for the put, $103.88, gives $d_1 = -0.7487$:

$$d_1 = \frac{\ln\left(\dfrac{103.88}{130}\right) + \left[.12 - .03 + .5(.3)(.3)\right]\left(\dfrac{180}{365}\right)}{.3\sqrt{\dfrac{180}{365}}} = -.7487$$

For the call, $N(d_1) = N(35.4167) = 1.0000$, while for the put, $N(-d_1) = N(-27.0603) = 0.772981$. The prices of the corresponding European call and put, each evaluated at its critical price, are $472.68 and $22.74, respectively.

With these values, we now verify that the specified critical prices are correct. For the call:

$$604.08 - 130.00 = 474.08 = 472.68 + (.0147)(604.08/6.3307)$$

For the put:

$$130.00 - 103.88 = 26.12 = 22.74 - (.2384)(103.88/-7.3307)$$

21. An American call and put both have an exercise price of $100. An acquaintance asserts that the critical stock price for both options is $90 under the analytic approximation technique. Comment on this claim and explain your reasoning.

   Something is amiss. The critical price for a call must lie above the exercise price, while the critical price for a put must lie below the exercise price. Therefore, $90 might be the critical price for the put, but it cannot be the critical price for the call.

22. Consider a stock with a price of $80 and a standard deviation of 0.3. The stock will pay a $5 dividend in 70 days. The current risk-free rate of interest is 10 percent. Options written on this stock have an exercise price of $80 and expire in 120 days. Model and compute the price of these options using a four-period tree.

A. Draw the stock price trees.

$$U = e^{\sigma\sqrt{\Delta t}} = e^{0.3\sqrt{30/365}} = 1.0898$$

$$D = 1/U = 1/1.0898 = 0.9176$$

$$\pi_U = \frac{e^{r\Delta t} - D}{U - D} = \frac{e^{0.1 \times 30/365} - 0.9176}{1.0898 - 0.9176} = 0.5264 \quad \pi_D = 1 - 0.5264 = 0.4736$$

$$e^{-r\Delta t} = 0.9918$$

To construct the stock price tree necessary to calculate the value of this option, we must adjust the current stock price of $80 downward by the present value of the dividends to be received prior to the option's expiration. In this problem, the dividend of $5.00 will be paid in 70 days.

$$D_1 \, Xe^{-r(T-t)} = \$5.00 \times e^{-0.1 \times (70/365)} = \$4.9050$$

$$S' = \$80 - \$4.9050 = \$75.0950$$

Stock price tree

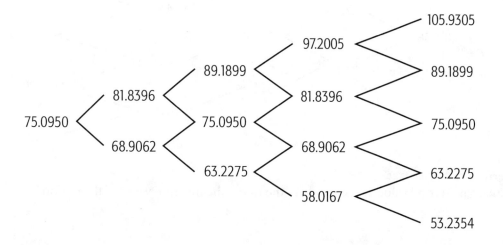

After constructing the stock price tree, the prices in the tree must be adjusted upward by the present value of the dividend yet to be received. That is, we must add the present value of $5.00 to be received in 40 days to the stock prices at node one, and we must add the present value of $5.00 to be received in 10 days to the stock prices at node two. Thus, we add $4.9050 to the node zero stock price, $4.9455 to the node one stock prices, and $4.9863 to the node two stock prices.

$$D_1 \, Xe^{-r(T-t)} = \$5.00 \times e^{-0.1 \times (70/365)} = \$4.9050$$

$$D_1 \, Xe^{-r(T-t)} = \$5.00 \times e^{-0.1 \times (40/365)} = \$4.9455$$

$$D_1 \, Xe^{-r(T-t)} = \$5.00 \times e^{-0.1 \times (10/365)} = \$4.9863$$

Dividend-adjusted stock price tree

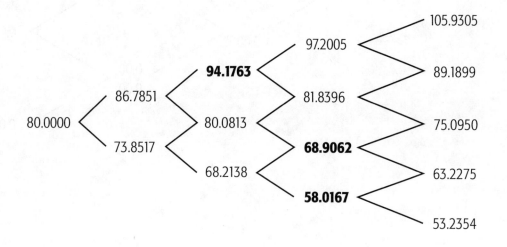

B. Calculate the values of European and American call and put options written on this stock. Value the options using the recursive procedure. Construct the price trees for each option.

European call price tree

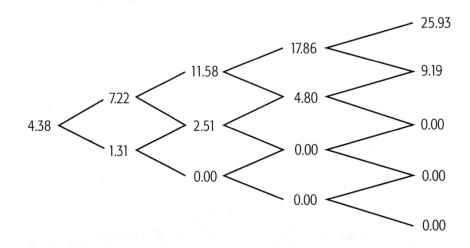

American call price tree

Note: The second value at each node in the tree is the intrinsic value of the option.

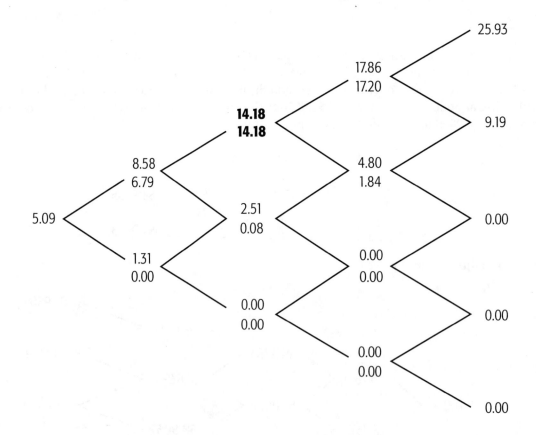

European put price tree

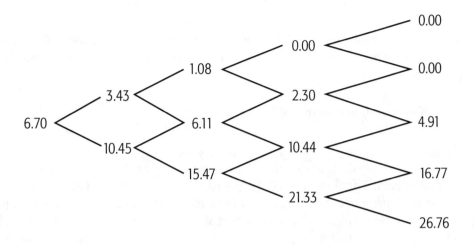

American put price tree
Note: The second value at each node in the tree is the intrinsic value of the option.

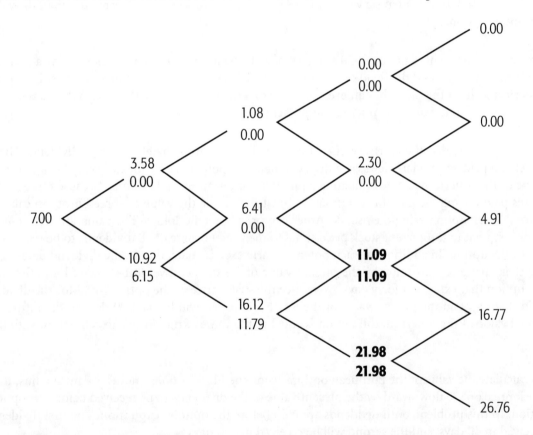

The prices for the American call and put options are $5.09 and $7.00, respectively. The prices for the corresponding European call and put options are $4.38 and $6.70.

C. Compare the prices of the European and American options. How much value does the right to exercise the option before expiration add to the value of the American options?

In both cases the American options are more valuable than the equivalent European options. The American call is worth $.71 more than the European call, and the American put is worth $.29 more than the European put.

D. Explain when, if ever, each option should be exercised.

Theory tells us that it will only be rational for the investor to exercise an American call option immediately before a dividend is paid, and that the rational exercise of an American put will occur immediately after a dividend is paid. The dividend will be paid in 70 days, which is between the second and third branches in the stock price tree used to value the options. Examination of both the stock price and option pricing trees reveals the following: The call option should be exercised early if the stock price rises to $94.18 after two periods. At this stock price, the intrinsic value of the American option, $14.18, is greater than the value of the European option, $11.58. The put option should be exercised if the stock price falls to $68.91 or lower. It should also be exercised at a stock price of $58.02 or less after three periods. At this stock price, $68.91, the intrinsic value of the American put option, $11.09, is greater than the value of the European option, $10.44.

23. Consider a stock with a price of $70 and a standard deviation of 0.4. The stock will pay a dividend of $2 in 40 days and a second dividend of $2 in 130 days. The current risk-free rate of interest is 10 percent. An American call on this stock has an exercise price of $75 and expires in 180 days. What is the price of the call according to the pseudo-American approach?

Theory suggests that the early exercise of a call will occur immediately before a dividend. The pseudo-American pricing "model" views each dividend date as a potential date for early exercise and estimates the value of the American call by evaluating a portfolio of European call options. Because there are two dividends paid during the life of the option, we must determine the value of three European call options to price this call option using the pseudo-American pricing methodology. The valuation technique requires an adjustment to the current stock price equal to the present value of all dividends to be received over the life of the option. In addition, at each potential early exercise date, that is, the dividend date, we decrease the strike price of the option by the present value of the dividend yet to be received. In other words, for the option that expires in forty days, we reduce the strike price of the option by $2 for the dividend to be paid that day, and the present value of the $2 dividend that will be paid 90 days in the future. The estimated value of the American call option is equal to the value of the European call option with the largest value.

To calculate the value of the European options using the Black-Scholes model, we must adjust the current stock price of $70 downward by the present value of the dividends to be received before the option's expiration. In this problem, both dividends are paid before the option's expiration. The first dividend will be received in 40 days, and the second will be received in 130 days.

$$D_1 \, Xe^{-r(T-t)} = \$2 \times e^{-0.1 \times (40/365)} \quad = \$1.98$$

$$D_2 \, Xe^{-r(T-t)} = \$2 \times e^{-0.1 \times (130/365)} \quad = \$1.93$$

$$S' = \$70 - \$1.98 - \$1.93 \quad = \$66.09$$

Option #1 that expires in 180 days

$$d_1 = \frac{\ln(66.09/75) + \left(\left[0.10 + 0.5\left(0.4^2\right)\right]\left(0.4932\right)\right)}{0.40\sqrt{(0.4932)}} = -0.1341$$

$$d_2 = -0.1341 - 0.40\sqrt{(0.4932)} = -0.4150$$

$$N(d_1) = 0.446650 \quad N(d_2) = 0.339061$$

$$c = 66.09 \times 0.446650 - 75e^{-0.1 \times 0.4932} \times 0.339061 = \$5.31$$

Option #2 that expires in 40 days

To calculate the value of the European option that expires in 40 days using the Black-Scholes model, we must decrease the strike price of the option, \$75, by the present value of the dividends to be received after 40 days, but before the option's expiration. In this case, both dividends are paid before the option's expiration. The first dividend will be received immediately and is equal to \$2, and the second \$2 dividend will be received in 90 days.

$$D_1 \; Xe^{-r(T-t)} = \$2 \times e^{-0.1 \times (90/365)} = \$1.95$$

$$X' = \$75 - \$2 - \$1.95 = \$71.05$$

$$d_1 = \frac{\ln(66.09/71.05) + \left(\left[0.10 + 0.5\left(0.4^2\right)\right]\left(0.1096\right)\right)}{0.40\sqrt{(0.1096)}} = -0.3972$$

$$d_2 = -0.3972 - 0.40\sqrt{(0.1096)} = -0.5296$$

$$N(d_1) = 0.345612 \quad N(d_2) = 0.298190$$

$$c = 66.09 \times 0.345612 - 71.05e^{-0.1 \times 0.1096} \times 0.298190 = \$1.89$$

Option #3 that expires in 130 days

To calculate the value of the European option that expires in 130 days using the Black-Scholes model, we must decrease the strike price of the option, \$75, by the amount of the dividends to be received prior to the option's expiration. In this case, the second dividend of \$2 is paid on day 130. Thus, the strike price of \$75 will be reduced by \$2 to \$73.

$$X' = \$75 - \$2 = \$73$$

$$d_1 = \frac{\ln(66.09/73) + \left(\left[0.10 + 0.5\left(0.4^2\right)\right]\left(0.3562\right)\right)}{0.40\sqrt{(0.3562)}} = -0.1479$$

$$d_2 = -0.1479 - 0.40\sqrt{(0.3562)} = -0.3866$$

$$N(d_1) = 0.441212 \quad N(d_2) = 0.349521$$

$$c = 66.09 \times 0.441212 - 73e^{-0.1 \times 0.3562} \times 0.349521 = \$4.54$$

The value of the American call using the pseudo-American pricing methodology is the largest of the three option values, $5.31.

$$C = \text{MAX } (\$5.31, \$1.89, \$4.54) = \$5.31$$

24. Consider a stock with a price of $140 and a standard deviation of 0.4. The stock will pay a dividend of $5 in 40 days and a second dividend of $5 in 130 days. The current risk-free rate of interest is 10 percent. An American call on this stock has an exercise price of $150 and expires in 100 days.

A. What is the price of the call according to the pseudo-American approach?

Theory suggests that the early exercise of a call will occur immediately before a dividend. The pseudo-American pricing "model" views each dividend date as a potential date for early exercise and estimates the value of the American call by evaluating a portfolio of European call options. Since there is only one dividend paid during the life of the option, we must determine the value of two European call options to price this call option using the pseudo-American pricing methodology. The valuation technique requires an adjustment to the current stock price equal to the present value of all dividends to be received over the life of the option. In addition, at each potential early exercise date, that is, the first dividend date, we decrease the strike price of the option by the present value of the dividend yet to be received before the option expires. The estimated value of the American call option is equal to the value of the European call option with the largest value.

To calculate the value of the European options using the Black-Scholes model, we must adjust the current stock price of $140 downward by the present value of the dividends to be received before the option's expiration. In this problem, the second dividend is paid after the option expires and is irrelevant in the pricing of this option. The dividend of $5 will be received in 40 days.

$$D_1 \, Xe^{-r(T-t)} = \$5 \times e^{-0.1 \times (40/365)} = \$4.95$$

$$S' = \$140 - \$4.95 = \$135.05$$

Option #1 that expires in 100 days

$$d_1 = \frac{\ln(135.05/150) + \left(\left[0.10 + 0.5\left(0.4^2\right)\right]\left(0.2740\right)\right)}{0.40 \sqrt{(0.2740)}} = -0.2658$$

$$d_2 = -0.2658 - 0.40 \sqrt{(0.2740)} = -0.4751$$

$$N(d_1) = 0.395212 \quad N(d_2) = 0.317348$$

$$c = 135.05 \times 0.395212 - 150e^{-0.1 \times 0.2740} \times 0.317348 = \$7.06$$

Option #2 that expires in 40 days

To calculate the value of the European option that expires in 40 days using the Black-Scholes model, we must decrease the strike price of the option, $150, by the amount of the dividends to be received after day 40 but before the option expires. In this case, the second dividend of $5 is paid on day 40. Thus, the strike price of $150 will be reduced by $5 to $145.

$$X' = \$150 - \$5 = \$145$$

$$d_1 = \frac{\ln(135.05/145) + \left(\left[0.10 + 0.5(0.4^2)\right](0.1096)\right)}{0.40\sqrt{(0.1096)}} - 0.3876$$

$$d_2 = -0.3876 - 0.40\sqrt{(0.1096)} = -0.5201$$

$$N(d_1) = 0.349143 \quad N(d_2) = 0.301514$$

$$c = 135.05 \times 0.349143 - 145e^{-0.1 \times 0.1096} \times 0.301514 = \$3.91$$

The value of the American call using the pseudo-American pricing methodology is the largest of the two option values, $7.06.

$$C = \text{MAX}\ (\$7.06, \$3.91) = \$7.06$$

B. What is the price of the call according to the compound option pricing model?

The first step necessary to value this American call option is to determine the critical stock price, S^*. The critical stock price is the stock price that makes the investor indifferent between holding an option until expiration, and exercising the option—thereby receiving the stock and the dividend. The critical stock price, S^*, is determined by solving the following equation, $S^* + D - X = c$, where the European call option, c, has a life of 60 days beginning 40 days in the future. That is, if the American call option is not exercised on the dividend date, then the investor holds an American call option written on a stock that does not pay a dividend. We can then value the American call option as a European call option. This option has 60 days until expiration, and we assume that the interest rate and the volatility of the stock remain constant. The critical stock price, S^*, is $170.90.

$$d_1 = \frac{\ln(170.90/150) + \left(\left[0.10 + 0.5\left(0.4^2\right)\right](60/365)\right)}{0.40 \sqrt{(60/365)}} = 0.9868$$

$$d_2 = 0.9868 - 0.40 \sqrt{60/365} = 0.8246$$

$$N(d_1) = 0.838127 \quad N(d_2) = .0795204$$

$$c = 170.90 \times 0.838127 - 150 e^{-0.1 \times 60/365} \times 0.795204 = \$25.90$$

$$S^* + D - X - c = 0 \quad \$170.90 + \$5 - \$150 - \$25.90 = 0$$

$$a_1 = \frac{\ln\left(\dfrac{140 - 5e^{-0.1(40/365)}}{150}\right) + \left[0.1 + 0.5(0.4)(0.4)\right](100/365)}{0.4 \sqrt{100/365}} = -0.2658$$

$$a_2 = -0.2658 - 0.4 \sqrt{100/365} = -0.4751$$

$$b_1 = \frac{\ln\left(\dfrac{140 - e^{-0.1(40/365)}}{170.90}\right) + \left[0.1 + 0.5(0.4)(0.4)\right](40/365)}{0.4 \sqrt{40/365}} = -1.6288$$

$$b_2 = -1.6288 - 0.4 \sqrt{40/365} = -1.7612$$

$$-\sqrt{\frac{t_1 - t}{T - t}} = -\sqrt{\frac{40}{180}} = -0.6325$$

$$N(b_1) = 0.051681 \quad N(b_2) = 0.039104$$

$$N_2\left[-0.2658; 1.6288; -0.6325\right] = 0.348740$$

$$N_2\left[-0.4751; 1.7612; -0.6325\right] = 0.283474$$

The price of the American call using the compound option pricing model is $7.10.

C. What is the critical stock price, S^*? Discuss the implications of this finding on the likelihood of exercising the call option early.

As computed earlier, the critical stock price is $170.90, which is $30.90 higher than the current stock price of $140. Thus, it is highly unlikely that the call option will be exercised early. That is, it is very unlikely that the stock price will rise $30.90 in forty days. Thus, the value of the early exercise premium is very small.

D. Compare the prices calculated using the three option pricing methods.

Since the critical stock price of $170.90 is $30.90 higher than the current stock price of $140, it is highly unlikely that the call option will be exercised early. That is, it is very unlikely that the stock price will rise $30.90 in forty days. In this problem, the approximations provided by the pseudo-American call option pricing model and the dividend-adjusted Black-Scholes European call pricing model are very close to the value produced by the compound option pricing model. Consequently, the prices for the American call options calculated using the three different option pricing models differ by four cents. Thus, the value of the right to exercise this option early is very small.

25. Consider the binomial model for an American call and put on a stock that pays no dividends. The current stock price is \$120, and the exercise price for both the put and the call is \$110. The standard deviation of the stock returns is 0.4, and the risk-free rate is 10 percent. The options expire in 120 days. Model the price of these options using a four-period tree.

A. Draw the stock price tree and the corresponding trees for the call and the put options.

$$U = e^{\sigma\sqrt{\Delta t}} = e^{0.4\sqrt{30/365}} = 1.1215$$

$$D = 1/U = 1/1.1215 = 0.8917$$

$$\pi_U = \frac{e^{r\Delta t} - D}{U - D} = \frac{e^{0.1 \times 30/365} - 0.8917}{1.1215 - 0.8917} = 0.5073 \quad \pi_D = 1 - 0.5073 = 0.4927$$

$$e^{-r\Delta t} = 0.9918$$

Stock price tree

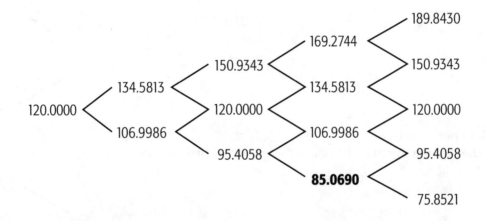

American call price tree
Note: The second value at each node in the tree is the intrinsic value of the option.

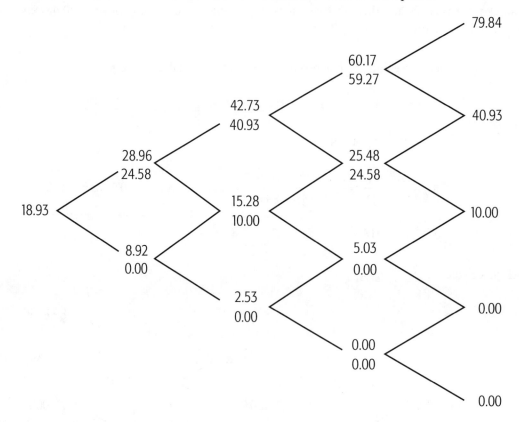

American put price tree
Note: The second value at each node in the tree is the intrinsic value of the option.

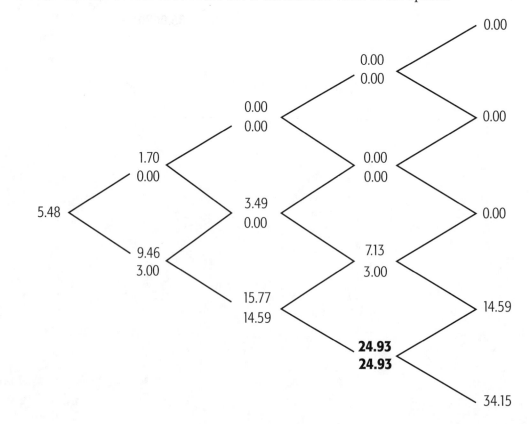

B. What is the value of each of the two options? Value the options using the recursive procedure.

The value of the American call option is $18.93, and the American put option is $5.48.

C. Explain when, if ever, each option should be exercised.

Since the stock underlying the options does not pay dividends, it would never be rational to exercise the American call early. However, this is not true for the American put option. If the stock price falls to $85.07, then the investor should exercise the option.

D. What is the value of a European call written on this stock? Can you find the value of the European call without making a separate computation? Explain.

Since exercising the American call early is not rational, the right to exercise the option before expiration is worthless. Thus, the price of the European call is the same as the price of the American call, $18.93.

26. Consider the binomial model for an American call and put on a stock whose price is $50. The exercise price for both the put and the call is $55. The standard deviation of the stock returns is 0.35, and the risk-free rate is 10 percent. The options expire in 160 days. The stock will pay a dividend equal to 4 percent of its value in 65 days. Model and compute the price of these options using a four-period tree.

A. Draw the stock price tree.

$$U = e^{\sigma\sqrt{\Delta t}} = e^{0.35\sqrt{40/365}} = 1.1228$$

$$D = 1/U = 1/1.1228 = 0.8906$$

$$\pi_U = \frac{e^{r\Delta t} - D}{U - D} = \frac{e^{0.1 \times 40/365} - 0.8906}{1.1228 - 0.8906} = 0.5185 \quad \pi_D = 1 - 0.5185 = 0.4815$$

$$e^{-r\Delta t} = 0.9891$$

Stock price tree

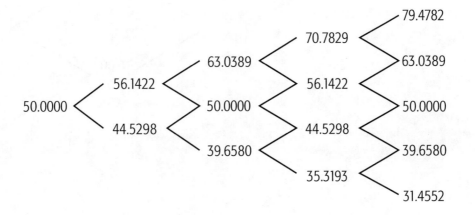

The stock prices in the tree must be adjusted for the dividend to be paid in 65 days before calculating the value of the options. Therefore, the stock prices in the tree in periods two, three, and four must be adjusted downward by one minus the dividend yield paid by the firm (1 − 4%).

Dividend-adjusted stock price tree

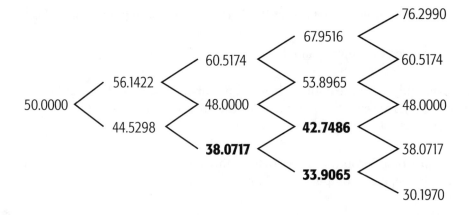

B. What is the value of each of the two options? Value the options using the recursive procedure. Draw the tree for each option.

Call option price tree
Note: The second value at each node in the tree is the intrinsic value of the option.

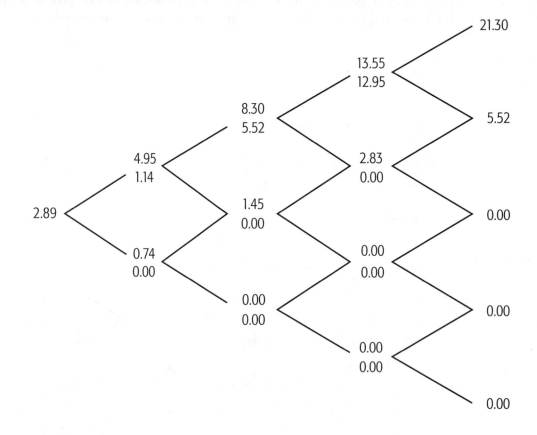

Put option price tree
Note: The second value at each node in the tree is the intrinsic value of the option.

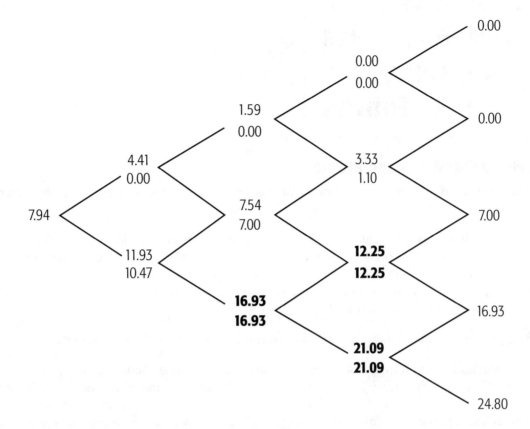

The price of the American call option is $2.89, and the price of the American put option is $7.94.

C. Explain when, if ever, each option should be exercised.

Theory tells us that it will only be rational for the investor to exercise an American call option immediately before a dividend is paid, and that the rational exercise of an American put will occur immediately after a dividend is paid. The dividend will be paid in 65 days, which is between the first and second branches in the stock price tree used to value the options. Examination of both the stock price and option pricing trees reveals the following. The call option should not be exercised early. The put option should be exercised if the stock price falls to $42.75 or lower after two periods. At the stock prices of $42.75, $38.07, and $33.91, the intrinsic values of the put options are greater than the value of the corresponding options, and the option should be exercised early if the stock price falls to these levels.

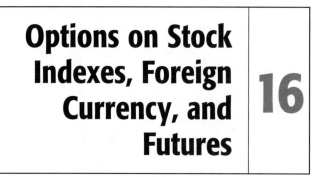

Options on Stock Indexes, Foreign Currency, and Futures

16

Answers to Questions and Problems

1. Explain why interest payments on a foreign currency can be treated as analogous to a dividend on a common stock.

   For a stock, dividends represent a leakage of value from the asset. If dividends were not paid, the stock price would continue to grow at a higher rate, compounding the value of the dividends. The same is true for a currency. The interest rate paid by a currency represents a leakage of value from the currency. Therefore, dividends from common stock and interest payments from a currency can be treated in the same way for option pricing purposes.

2. Why do we assume that the cost-of-carry for a futures is the same as the risk-free rate?

   For pricing options on futures, the important consideration is that the futures price follow the cost-of-carry relationship very closely. This adherence to the cost-of-carry model is much more important than the exact amount of the cost-of-carry. The option pricing model for futures does not work well if there is not an adherence to the cost-of-carry model. Thus, it is mainly a matter of convenience that we assume the cost-of-carry to equal the risk-free rate. In the real world, this assumption performs very well for financial futures, but it performs less well for futures on agricultural goods.

3. Explain how to adjust a price lattice for an underlying good that makes discrete payments.

   The text considers three types of dividend payments: constant proportional payments, occasional payments equal to a percentage of the asset value, and occasional payments of a fixed dollar amount. In every case, the presence of the dividend requires an adjustment in the stock price lattice. In essence, the nodes in the stock price lattice must be decreased by the present value of the dividends that will occur from the time represented by that node until the expiration of the option. Dividends occurring after the expiration date of the option play no role and may be disregarded. Once the stock price lattice has been adjusted to reflect the dividends, the corresponding lattice for the put or call can be worked through in the normal way to price the option correctly.

4. If a European and an American call on the same underlying good have different prices when all of the terms of the two options are identical, what does this difference reveal about the two options? What does it mean if the two options have identical prices?

   If the two have an identical price, it means that the early exercise feature of the American option has no value. Any difference in the prices will stem from the value associated with the early exercise privilege.

5. Consider an option on a futures contract within the context of the binomial model. Assume that the futures price is 100.00, that the risk-free interest rate is 10 percent, that the standard deviation of the

futures is .4, and that the futures expires in one year. Assuming that a call and a put on the futures also expire in one year, compute the binomial parameters U, D, and π_U. Now compute the expected futures price in one period. What does this reveal about the expected movement in futures prices?

$$U = e^{.4\sqrt{1}} = 1.4918; \quad D = \frac{1}{U} = .6703$$

$$\pi_U = \frac{e^{(.10 - .10)1} - .6703}{1.4918 - .6703} = .4013$$

The expected price movement is:

$$.4013\ (1.4918) + .5987\ (.6703) = 1.00$$

Thus, the futures price is not expected to change over the next year. In general, this will be true for futures. The futures price already impounds the expected price change in the asset between the current date and the expiration of the futures contract.

6. For a call and a put option on a foreign currency, compute the Merton model price, the binomial model price for a European option with three periods, the Barone-Adesi and Whaley model price, and the binomial model price with three periods for American options. Data are as follows: The foreign currency value is 2.5; the exercise price on all options is 2.0; the time until expiration is 90 days; the risk-free rate of interest is 7 percent; the foreign interest rate is 4 percent; the standard deviation of the foreign currency is .2.

The prices in the following table show that the American call and put have no exercise potential. The difference between the Merton and Whaley model put prices, on the one hand, and the binomial model put prices, on the other, is due to the very few periods being employed.

	Merton Model	European Binomial	Whaley Model	American Binomial
Call	.5104	.5097	.5104	.5097
Put	.0008	0	.0008	0

7. Consider a call and a put on a stock index. The index price is 500.00, and the two options expire in 120 days. The standard deviation of the index is .2, and the risk-free rate of interest is 7 percent. The two options have a common exercise price of 500.00. The stock index will pay a dividend of 20.00 index units in 40 days. Find the European and American option prices according to the binomial model, assuming two periods. Be sure to draw the lattices for the stock index and for all of the options that are being priced.

$$U = e^{.2\sqrt{\frac{60}{365}}} = 1.0845; \quad D = \frac{1}{1.0845} = .9221$$

$$\pi_U = \frac{1.0116 - .9221}{1.0845 - .9221} = .5510$$

As the following price lattices show, the European and American calls are worth $19.20. The European put is worth $27.67, and the American put is worth $30.21.

Stock Price Lattice

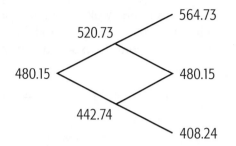

Adjusted Stock Price

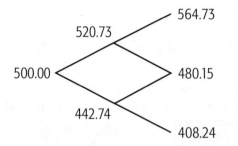

American and European Call Price

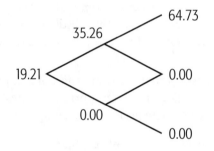

European Put Price

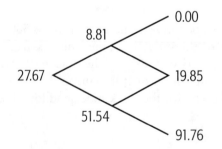

American Put Price

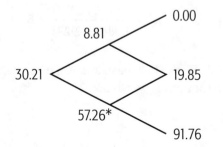

8. Consider two European calls and two European put options on a foreign currency. The exercise prices are $.90 and $1.00, giving a total of four options. All options expire in one year. The current risk-free rate is 8 percent, the foreign interest rate is 5 percent, and the standard deviation of the foreign currency is .3. The foreign currency is priced at $.80. Find all four option prices according to the Merton model. Compare the ratio of the option prices to the ratio of the exercise prices. What does this show?

With $X = \$.90$, the call is worth $.0640, and the put is worth $.1338. With $X = \$1.00$, the call is worth $.0392, and the put is worth $.2014. Comparing the ratio of the option prices to the ratio of exercise prices shows that the call is more sensitive to a change in the exercise price than is the put. A change of about 10 percent in the exercise price causes about a 63 percent change in the call price, but only about a 51 percent change in the put price.

The Options Approach to Corporate Securities | 17

Answers to Questions and Problems

1. Explain why common stock is itself like a call option. In the option analysis of common stock, what plays the role of the exercise price and what plays the role of the underlying stock?

Common stock is like a call option on the entire firm. To see how this can be the case, consider a firm with a single bond issue outstanding and assume that the bond is a pure discount bond. When the bond matures, the common stockholders have a choice: They can pay the bondholders the promised payment, or they can surrender the firm to the bondholders. If the firm is worth more than the amount due to the bondholders, the stock owners will pay the bondholders and keep the excess. If the firm is worth less than the amount due to the bondholders, the stock owners will abandon the firm to the bond owners.

In this situation, the amount due to the bond owners plays the role of the exercise price. The maturity date of the bond is the expiration date of the call option represented by the common stock. The common stock is like a call option. At expiration, the stock owners can exercise their call option by paying the claim of the bondholders (the exercise price). Upon exercising, the stockholders receive the underlying asset (the entire firm).

2. Consider a firm that issues a pure discount bond that matures in one year and has a face value of $1,000,000. Analyze the payoffs that the bondholders will receive in option pricing terms, assuming the only other security in the firm is common stock.

When the bond matures, the stock owners decide whether to pay the bonds or surrender the firm to the bondholders in lieu of payment. If the value of the firm exceeds the amount owed to the bond owners, $1,000,000, the bondholders receive full payment and the stock owners retain the excess. If the firm's value is less than the promised payment, the stock owners abandon the firm and the bondholders receive a payment equal to the value of the entire firm. However, by hypothesis, this is less than the promised payment of $1,000,000. This pattern of payment is like the payments on a short put position with an exercise price that equals the face value of the bond. However, a short position in a put can give a payoff at expiration that is negative. This is not true of a bond. The worst payoff for the bond is zero. Therefore, the payoff has the same pattern as a short position in a put with an exercise price that equals the face value of the bond plus a long position in a riskless bond.

3. Consider a firm with common stock and a pure discount bond as its financing. The total value of the firm is $1,000,000. There are 10,000 shares of common stock priced at $70 per share. The bond matures in ten years and has a total face value of $500,000. What is the interest rate on the bond, assuming annual compounding? Would the interest rate become higher or lower if the volatility of the firm's cash flows increases?

The $1,000,000 value of the firm equals the sum of the stock and bond values. As the outstanding stock is worth $700,000, the bonds must be worth $300,000. Therefore, the interest rate is 5.24 percent. If the volatility of the firm's cash flows increases, the total value of the firm will not change. However, because the common stock can be analyzed as a call option on the firm, the value of the common stock must increase. This means that the value of the bonds must decrease. If the bond value decreases, its yield must increase. This makes sense, because the bonds should be worth less if the firm's cash flows become more risky.

4. A firm has a capital structure consisting of common stock and a single bond. The managers of the firm are considering a major capital investment that will be financed from internally generated funds. The project can be initiated in two ways, one with a high fixed cost component and the other with a low fixed cost component. Although both technologies have the same expected value, the high fixed cost approach has the potential for greater payoffs. (If the product is successful, the high fixed cost approach gives much lower total costs for large production levels.) What does option theory suggest about the choice the managers should make? Explain.

Assuming that the managers perform in the interest of their shareholders, they must make the decision that increases the value of the stock. As the stock represents a call option on the total firm value, the managers should prefer the higher operating leverage/higher operating risk strategy.

5. In a firm with common stock, senior debt, and subordinated debt, assume that both debt instruments mature at the same time. What is the necessary condition on the value of the firm at maturity for each security holder to receive at least some payment? With two classes of debt, does option theory counsel managers to increase the riskiness of the firm's operations? Would there be any difference on this point between a firm with a single debt issue and two debt issues? Which bondholders would tend to be more risk-averse as far as choosing a risk level for the firm's operations? Explain.

For the senior debtholders to receive some payment, the value of the firm must exceed zero. For the subordinated debtholders to receive some payment, the value of the firm must exceed the total owed to the senior debtholders. For the common stockholders to receive any payment, the value of the firm must exceed the amount owed on both classes of debt. If the managers perform in the interest of the stockholders, the mere presence of two classes of debt does not suggest a change in operating policy. The stockholders get paid only after all the bondholders are paid, so it does not matter to the stockholders how the debt is split up, but only how much the total amount of debt payments is. Given that the junior debtholders have already purchased the junior debt, they are (by revealed preference) more risk-tolerant than the holders of the senior debt. However, increasing operating risk transfers wealth away from bondholders to stockholders. Thus, the junior debtholders would probably prefer a low-risk operating strategy if funds would be certain to sufficiently cover their holdings. However, consider an operating policy that would only generate enough cash to pay the senior debtholders. In this situation, it is clear that the junior debtholders would prefer a more risky operating policy that might give sufficient payoffs to repay their obligations.

6. Consider a firm financed solely by common stock and a single callable bond issue. Assume that the bond is a pure discount bond. Is there any circumstance in which the firm should call the bond before the maturity date? Would such an exercise of the firm's call option discard the time premium? Explain.

The stockholders should wait until the maturity date. The stockholders' situation here is analogous to a call on a nondividend stock. Early payment of the bond discards the time premium inherent in the option they hold.

7. Consider a firm financed only by common stock and a convertible bond issue. When should the bondholders exercise? Explain. If the common shares pay a dividend, could it make sense for the bondholders to exercise before the bond matures? Explain by relating your answer to our discussion of the exercise of American calls on dividend-paying stocks.

If the common stock pays no dividend, the bondholders should not exercise until the last possible date. However, if the stock pays a sufficiently large dividend, it might pay the bondholders to convert earlier.

The bondholder holds a call option on the firm's shares. If those shares pay dividends, then they are leaking value. The bondholders must decide whether it is worthwhile to discard the time premium in favor of securing the dividend. This is exactly analogous to the problem faced by the holder of an American call option on a dividend paying stock.

8. Warrants are often used to compensate top executives in firms. Often these warrants cannot be exercised until a distant expiration date. This form of compensation is used to align the manager's incentives with the maximization of the shareholders' wealth. Explain how the manager's receiving warrants might thwart the efforts to change his or her incentives.

 If a manager holds warrants, and the value of these warrants is large relative to other forms of compensation, the manager will focus on maximizing the value of the firm at the expiration date of the warrants. This incentive might be incompatible with making decisions that will increase the value of the firm at other dates. For example, if markets are not perfect, then the value of the shares might not fully reflect a good decision to make a large capital budgeting outlay. Therefore, the manager might forego the investment in order to enhance the share price on the critical date for the manager.

9. In preparation for the CFA exam, you have been watching *Trading Places*. During your most recent viewing of the movie, you were struck by the notion that creating a call option on frozen concentrated orange juice would be possible. Describe the process of creating a synthetic call option on frozen concentrated orange juice using the frozen concentrated orange juice futures contract. Be sure to discuss the information necessary to create the synthetic option.

 To create a synthetic call option on frozen concentrated orange juice, we must model the dynamics of the spot market price of orange juice. We could do this using either a binomial process or a stochastic process. Once we have modeled the dynamics of the spot price of orange juice, we can determine the appropriate hedge ratio for an initial position in the futures contract on frozen concentrated orange juice. That is, once we have determined the values of the five parameters necessary to value a call option—the strike price, the time until expiration, the risk-free interest rate, the spot market price, and the volatility of the spot market price—we can determine the dynamics of our position in the futures contract on frozen concentrated orange juice. With this information we will be able to determine our position in a Treasury bill. We will alter our position in the frozen concentrated orange juice futures contract and Treasury bill position as the spot price of orange juice changes. We will increase our position in the futures on frozen concentrated orange juice as the spot price of orange juice increases, and we will decrease our position in the futures on frozen concentrated orange juice as the spot price of orange juice decreases.

10. In automobile lease arrangements, the lessee has the right to buy the car from the manufacturer for a fixed price at the expiration of the lease. Assume that the lease in question matures in three years, and there are no tax advantages to leasing the car.

A. Describe the positions of the automobile manufacturer and the car owner.

 The car owner decides whether to purchase the car at the end of the contract. Therefore, the consumer is long the call option. Thus, the manufacturer has written a call option to the "purchaser" of the car.

B. Explain how such an option could be valued. Explain how you might estimate the parameters necessary to value this option. Be sure to discuss the factors complicating the valuation of this option.

 The right to purchase the car at the end of the lease period is a long-term European call option. The purchase price for the car is the strike price of the option, and the option expires in three years. At the end of the lease the lessee will decide whether to purchase the car or return it to the auto dealer. If the purchase price of the car is less than the market price for an equivalent automobile, that is, the option is in-the-money, then the lessee will purchase the car.

To value this option we need to know the strike price on the option, the time until expiration of the option, the relevant risk-free rate of interest, the spot price of the auto, and the volatility of the price of the auto. The strike price of the option and the expiration date of the option are clearly specified in the lease agreement. If we assume that we can create a riskless hedge between a synthetic call and the call attached to the lease, then we can use the appropriate three-year Treasury security rate as the risk-free interest rate in the pricing of the option. If we are not able to construct this riskless position, then we should not use a pricing model that assumes that it is possible to price the asset in a risk-neutral economy, that is, the Black-Scholes model. In this case we must use a risk-adjusted pricing model where we would value the option as the discounted value of the expected payoffs associated with the contract. To do this we would have to assess the probability of the set of possible payoffs associated with the option, calculate the expected payoffs, and discount the expected payoffs using an appropriate risk-adjusted return. Determination of the appropriate risk-adjusted rate of return would be the most difficult aspect of this problem. An appropriate proxy would be the market rate on three-year auto loans for an individual of the same risk class as the purchaser of the car.

The contract gives the "car buyer" the right to purchase a three-year-old automobile at the end of three years. Determining the spot price of the equivalent three-year-old automobile will be difficult, particularly for a consumer. The auto manufacturer will have access to information about the market for autos nationwide, while consumers may have access to information about the local automobile market. We need to know the market price of an auto with the same characteristics as the leased car. This value may not exist if the car in question is a new model, as there are no three-year-old versions of this car in the market. If there are autos that are perceived to be close substitutes for the car in question in the market, we can use the price of used versions of this car as a proxy for the spot price of the used car. The decision to purchase a particular auto is a consumption decision, and individual consumption preferences change over time as one's wealth and tastes change. The existence of cars perceived as close substitutes will be influenced by the tastes of consumers. Once the appropriate price series has been created, the price series can be used to calculate the historical volatility in the price of three-year-old automobiles. We implicitly assume that consumer tastes and demands will not change over the three-year life of the option. Determination of implied volatility would be difficult, as there is no market for options written on autos.

C. Explain why automobile manufacturers would bundle this right with the automobile lease.

Consider an alternative lease contract that requires the car "owner" to return the car to the manufacturer at the end of the lease period. In this contract, the car "owner" knows that the asset must be returned to the manufacturer in three years. Essentially the car owner has a long position in an in-the-money put option. The car "owner" has the right to return, put, the car to the manufacturer in three years whatever the condition of the car. This right is most valuable to the car "owner" when the car is returned very poor condition.

With the purchase option, the incentives of the car "owner" change. With the purchase option, the car "owner" has a stake in the condition of the car. Assume that the car is still desired or demanded by consumers at the end of the lease. The lessee influences/controls the quality of the car via his driving and maintenance habits over the life of the lease. If the lessee has an ownership stake in the car via the right to purchase the car, then the lessee is less likely to engage in moral hazard and purposely run down the value of the car. The lessee knows that his behaviors will influence the moneyness of the option contract. If the lessee does not choose to purchase the car, the condition of the leased car returned to the manufacturer should be on average higher than the condition of a car returned to the manufacturer in an environment that did not permit the purchase of the car. In addition, the right to purchase a car at a fixed price at the end of the lease provides a price benchmark for the used car at the end of the lease period. By revealing the purchase price of the car at the start of the lease, the informed manufacturer is signaling the market regarding the manufacturer's expectations about the value of the car at the end of the lease. This price benchmark should decrease the impact of depreciation on the market value of all similar cars regardless of whether the car was leased or purchased. This right increases the value of the car to potential purchasers and lessors and increases the probability of selling/leasing cars initially.

D. Does the presence of the right to purchase the car at the expiration of the lease increase the price of the lease? Explain.

If we assume that the auto manufacturer is in the business of selling new cars, not used cars, then the manufacturer has an incentive to set the purchase price of the car at a level that increases the probability, at the margin, that the lessee will purchase the car at the end of the lease. The existence of the right to purchase the auto at the end of the lease increases the probability that the condition of cars returned to the manufacturer is higher than the condition of cars returned to the manufacturer when such a purchase option is not available. Thus, if a manufacturer has a car returned, it will be of higher quality and easier to dispose of. The manufacturer clearly benefits from the existence of this right. The key issue is, does the consumer have to pay for the right to purchase the car at the end of the lease? The answer depends on the car in question and the market environment at the time of the sale of the auto. Does the manufacturer need this added benefit to sell the car initially? If economic conditions, consumer preferences, and competitive conditions are such that the manufacturer must provide a nonprice inducement to attract customers to the car, then the consumer is not likely to have to pay for this right. That is, if a consumer perceives two cars as equivalent and the manufacturers of the cars are offering the same lease terms with the exception that one is offering the right to purchase, then the consumer is likely to be induced to lease the car with the right to purchase the car at the end of the lease.

11. A developer has purchased 60 acres of rural property just north of Augusta, Georgia, to develop a golf course. The golf course development will also include a housing development. To generate operating capital, the developer is selling rights. The rights give the holder of the contract the right to purchase lots in the housing development for a fixed price. Each lot in the housing development is half an acre. The agreements expire six months after they are signed. The developer is offering the following inducement. A potential homeowner can purchase a lot for $25,000 at the end of six months if the homeowner enters the contract this week. The purchase price for a lot increases to $40,000 on all contracts signed after this week. The developer has asked you to price the rights to purchase property in the development. Explain how you would value these options. Discuss the factors that make the valuation of this contract difficult.

Real estate is a fixed asset. It is not transportable. The desirable characteristics of the asset cannot be transferred to another asset or location. The value of a particular piece of property is determined by its location and the demand for the property. The supply of property is fixed and controlled by the owner of the property. The value of the property will be influenced by the perception and tastes of potential home buyers, and by the perception of the existence of comparable substitute housing locations. Thus, we have the problem of pricing an asset that is in limited supply where the demand for the asset is strongly influenced by consumer preferences.

Assuming that we can create a riskless hedge between a synthetic call option and the call option being offered by the developer would not be appropriate. Thus, we should not use a pricing model that assumes that it is possible to price the asset in a risk-neutral economy, that is, the Black-Scholes model or the binomial model as we have developed it in the text. To price this option we must use a risk-adjusted pricing model where the value of the option is the present value of the expected payoffs associated with the contract. To do this we must assess the probability of the set of possible payoffs associated with the option, calculate the expected payoffs, and discount the expected payoffs using an appropriate risk-adjusted return. An appropriate proxy for the discount rate would be the six-month rate on consumer credit from a bank. The payoff on the option would be the difference between the market value of the property and the purchase price of the property, $25,000. To estimate the expected payoffs on the option, we would have to estimate the demand for the property. If consumers perceive that there is comparable real estate in the area, then the market price for this property can be used in evaluating the payoffs associated with the option. If consumers perceive that there is no comparable real estate in the area and there is considerable demand for the property, then one must estimate the premium that must be paid to purchase this property to evaluate the payoffs associated with the option.

12. Kevin is employed by Farm State Insurance. It is Kevin's job to develop a pricing model to price automobile insurance. Farm State Insurance will offer accident insurance policies to drivers of all ages, in all states. The insurance policies will be renewable semiannually. The policies only cover accidents and do not cover the theft of the vehicle. Several different deductibles will be offered to prospective policyholders. Model the auto insurance as an option. Discuss the pricing of this type of insurance policy and the construction of the insurance policies offered to drivers.

The insured has the right to make a claim against the insurance company anytime during the life of the contract, which in this case is six months. If there is an accident involving the driver, then the insurance company makes a payment. The amount of the payment is the difference between the dollar amount of the deductible and the dollar value of the claim against the insurance company. Since the insurance company is making a payment, the insurance company has effectively written a put option to the insured. This option is different from a stock option in that in order to make a claim against the insurance company, the insured must be involved in an accident. Assuming the insured does not intend to file a fraudulent claim against the firm, most policyholders have an incentive to avoid accidents. Being involved in an accident puts an individual at risk of serious injury.

Kevin's job is to determine the semi-annual premium on the different insurance policies offered to drivers. Assuming that we can create a riskless hedge between a synthetic put option and the put option being offered by Farm State would not be appropriate. Thus, we should not use a pricing model that assumes that it is possible to price the asset in a risk-neutral economy, that is, the Black-Scholes model. To price this option, we must use a risk-adjusted pricing model where the value of the option is the present value of the expected payoffs associated with the contract. Kevin must determine the expected payouts for a particular insured group during a six-month contract period, and discount those expected payouts at the firm's cost of capital. To price these policies, Kevin will need historical information about the distribution of claims for firms providing automobile insurance in the same state and region, and for the industry in general. Kevin must know the amount that the firm will pay if the insured is involved in an accident. This will be influenced by the types of automobiles being insured, the age of the drivers being insured, whether the driver has taken driver's training, and the location of the insured. Kevin must assess the probability of making a payout for a particular group of policyholders. An important part of the classification system used in the pricing of the policies will be the driving history of the insured. A key right of the insurance company will be the right to refuse coverage to a particular individual. Another important consideration is the size of the deducible that the insured chooses. The deductible represents the amount of risk that the individual is willing to self-insure, and can be viewed by the insurance company as a signal concerning the risk-taking preferences of the policyholder. Thus, the same policy with different deductibles will have different prices.

13. Your bank is thinking of offering a new product to small businesses. This product will allow a customer to borrow up to $50,000 at a fixed rate of interest. This line of credit has a life span of two years. The customer can draw against the credit line as many times as he or she wants over the life of the contract. However, the minimum amount that may be borrowed is $5,000. Once the customer has borrowed funds, he or she has up to one year to repay the loan. This contract has a fixed life and a fixed interest rate. The small business person gains access to the line of credit by paying an up-front fee. It is your job to price the contract and determine the amount of the up-front fee. Model the fixed rate line of credit as an option. Explain when an investor is likely to use this line of credit.

The small businessperson has the right to borrow anytime during a two-year period up to $50,000. By exercising this right, the customer obtains cash. When the owner of a put option written on common stock exercises the put, he or she too receives cash. Thus, the bank has effectively written a put option. Not only does the businessperson have the right to borrow funds, he or she has the right to choose the timing of the borrowing. Thus, the small businessperson has a multiple option. Both these options need to be valued in the pricing of the line of credit. The customer will exercise this line of credit when the cost of funds associated with the line of credit is less than the cost of funds available from other sources. One characteristic of a "normal" small business is that the firm does not generally have the same access to the capital markets as a larger firm does. Thus, it is not likely that the firm could issue commercial paper or a long-term bond as an alternative source of funding. It is more likely that the small businessperson is going to draw on the line of credit. In addition, temporary fluctuations in the firm's cash flows are likely to have a significant impact on the borrowing activities of the small businessperson.

14. The local junior service league is organizing a fund-raiser for the local homeless shelter. The owner of the Hallmark card shop in town has donated the grand prize of four Beanie Babies. These are not just any Beanie Babies. They are Garcia, Peace, Erin, and Princess Bear, the most famous and valuable retired Beanie Babies. However, in your state, it is a felony to operate a raffle. So rather than raffling off the grand prize, the junior service league must sell rights to the public that permit the "winner" of the raffle to purchase the grand prize at a retail price of $6.99 per baby. The "winner" will be randomly selected from among all entrants. It is your job to price the raffle tickets to be offered for sale. Explain how you would value these tickets.

One lucky individual is going to own a deep-in-the-money European call option. Each contestant is donating funds for the right to purchase a valuable asset at a below market price. Using the Black-Scholes model to price these rights would be appropriate if we can create a riskless hedge between a synthetic call option and the call option being offered in the raffle. However, that is not the case. Thus, we should not use a pricing model that assumes that it is possible to price the asset in a risk-neutral economy, that is, the Black-Scholes model. Valuation of the right can be determined as the present value of the expected payouts associated with the right. The underlying assets, the four Beanie Babies, are in fixed supply. There are a limited number of the Beanie Babies that are available in the market. The market for the Beanie Babies is an over-the-counter market. The market price of the Beanie Babies is determined by the consumer demand for the toys. The demand is driven by the preferences of a set of collectors who are willing to pay to buy the toys. The easiest way to determine the market value of the four Beanie Babies is to search the electronic auction markets that are part of the Internet. One can obtain from several of these markets estimates of the current value of the Beanie Babies. From this information, the payoff on a raffle ticket can be easily determined. The probability of winning is a function of the number of raffle tickets sold. The fewer the number of tickets sold, the higher the probability of winning and the higher the price of the raffle ticket. A short-term interest rate, with a maturity equal to the length of the time until the drawing for the raffle winner, should be used to discount the payoffs. Given the present value of the payoffs, one can determine the price of a raffle ticket.

15. Debt contracts represent fixed claims against the cash flows of a firm, while an equity contract entitles the shareholder to claim against the residual cash flows of the firm. The small firm in question has one shareholder, the entrepreneur who started and runs the firm. The firm's debt consists of loans from the local commercial bank. The firm's primary source of revenues is exports to Singapore. Because of the Asian financial crisis, the firm is facing considerable reduction in cash flows. The manager/entrepreneur has two investment projects. One is a safe project that will only generate sufficient cash flows to cover the firm's debt obligations. The other project is considerably more risky, but if successful will generate twice the firm's normal annual revenue. Which project do you expect the entrepreneur to undertake? Explain.

We can model the entrepreneur's position in the firm as a long position in an out-of-the-money European call option on his firm. The bank has effectively written the call option to the entrepreneur. The entrepreneur can purchase the firm from the bank by repaying his loans to the bank. If the entrepreneur defaults, the bank acquires the assets of the firm. The entrepreneur makes the operating decisions for the firm that affect both the riskiness and cash flows of the firm. The entrepreneur must choose between two projects. The safe project covers the entrepreneur's obligations to the bank, but the project leaves nothing for the entrepreneur. The risky project has the potential to generate large payoffs to the entrepreneur. The bank has a fixed claim against the assets of the firm, so if the risky project is successful, the bank will not share the gains from the project with the entrepreneur. However, the bank shares the additional risk with the entrepreneur. The entrepreneur has an incentive to engage in moral hazard and undertake the risky project. The entrepreneur has an undiversified portfolio and is bearing the full risk of ownership that comes from being the sole owner of the firm. Since the owner of the firm holds an out-of-the-money call and can affect the moneyness of the call by his choice of an investment project, the entrepreneur is likely to pick the high-risk project. In addition, by choosing the high-risk project, the entrepreneur can share risk with the bank without sharing the gains that may result from the investment project.

16. You have just been hired as CFO for a medium-sized manufacturing firm. The SEC requires your firm to report the value of the stock option contracts awarded to employees in your annual 10K report. Your firm has issued stock options to its executives. The options generally have a strike price that is slightly higher than the firm's stock price when they are offered. The options can be exercised anytime during the life of the option. If the options are exercised, the firm issues new treasury stock. Executives often exercise these options well before the expiration date of the option. The options issued to executives cannot be sold to any other party, and the options automatically expire if the executive leaves the firm. The majority of the options awarded to executives have had a life of three years. It is your job to value the options awarded by your firm. Explain why the firm would choose to compensate its executives with options. Explain how you would value these options. Discuss the possible reasons why an executive might choose to exercise these options early.

A corporation is usually managed by professional managers. In many corporations, these professional managers do not hold any of the firm's shares. Or if the manager does own shares, it is not a significant percentage of the shares outstanding. In this situation there is a clear separation between the management and ownership of the firm. The managers of the firm make all the operating decisions for the firm. These operating decisions affect the firm's cash flows and the riskiness of the firm. The purpose of the stock options is to align the interests of the shareholders and the managers of the firm by making the managers co-owners of the firm. Giving managers an equity stake in the firm creates an environment where managers have incentive to make decisions that maximize the value of their shares. Maximizing the value of the managers' shares also increases the wealth of the other owners of the firm. The executive stock options are not marketable. Thus the managers cannot sell the options to capture the intrinsic value and time premium associated with the options. The only way to capture the gain associated with a stock price increase is to exercise the option. The manager, like an owner of an American option written on a dividend paying stock, may choose to exercise the option to capture the dividends associated with the stock. Because the manager is an insider and has access to proprietary firm-specific information, the manager may choose to exercise an option to take advantage of his or her knowledge. For example, suppose the manager has access to negative information about an investment project that has not reached the market and has not been incorporated in the firm's stock price. The manager has an incentive to exercise the call options and to sell the stock in the market to capitalize on the value of this information through the sale of the overvalued shares. Nominally the valuation of the stock options should be straightforward and can be accomplished using the traditional pricing models used to value traded options. However, the fact that the options are not a marketable asset should adversely affect the value of the contract. Not being able to sell the option should reduce the value of the option to the manager. The question remains as to the size of this reduction in value.

17. WCS has enjoyed massive growth in the last decade and is in the process of constructing a new eighty-story corporate headquarters building. This construction project is early in the planning stage. The management of WCS has a choice between two technologies for the heating and cooling plant for the building. The choice is between a heating and cooling plant that burns only oil and one that burns either oil or natural gas. That is, the latter heating and cooling plant can be converted from oil burning to a natural gas fueled facility after a fixed cost expenditure of $50,000. Although the dual fuel plant has greater initial cost, it offers management greater flexibility in the future. In making the choice between the two heating and cooling plants, the firm's managers must assess the value of this operating option. Evaluate this investment decision facing the managers of WCS as an option. Assume that natural gas comes from domestic suppliers and heating oil is supplied in the global oil market.

    The dual fuel heating and cooling plant has option-like characteristics. Anytime in the future the management of WCS can choose to convert the heating and cooling plant of its headquarters building from oil to natural gas. The fixed cost of conversion is $50,000 and is equivalent to the strike price on an American option. Thus, by choosing to invest in this type of technology, the managers have a valuable right that may or may not be exercised in the future. When choosing the cheaper single fuel technology heating and cooling plant, the managers give up the right to convert the heating and cooling plant from oil to natural gas at a low cost in the future. If the single fuel technology is chosen, then in order to make the conversion from oil to natural gas, the entire heating and cooling plant must be replaced. The cost of the re-engineering of the heating and cooling plant will be significantly greater than the fixed cost of conversion associated with the dual fuel technology.

    The value of the right to convert the dual fuel plant from oil to natural gas will be dependent on the relative cost and volatility of the two fuels. The management of WCS must formulate expectations regarding the future prices of the two fuels as part of the valuation of the conversion right. To complete this task, WCS's managers must consider the sources of supply for the two fuels. The decision to supply oil to the world market involves both an economic and political decision. The supply of oil is often constrained for political reasons. If the managers of WCS expect the supply of oil to be limited in the future, the value of the conversion right increases. Another set of issues that must be evaluated by the managers of WCS is environmental. If the natural gas technology is more environmentally friendly and the managers of WCS expect government regulation to impose tighter constraints on pollution in the future, then the value of the conversion right will increase.

18. You are evaluating DOG as a potential target for acquisition. DOG has capital structure that consists of common stock and a convertible bond. The bond matures in 10 years, and upon conversion by a bondholder, the firm must issue additional shares of stock. Describe the bondholders' position. Discuss the valuation of the convertible bond. Explain when the bondholders should exercise their option. If DOG pays a dividend, would it be rational for the bondholders to exercise their option before the bond matures? Explain by relating your answer to the decision to exercise an American call option on a dividend paying stock.

    From the perspective of the bondholder, a long position in a convertible bond can be viewed as a position in a straight bond plus a position in an American call option. That is, it is the bondholder who has the right to convert the debt position to an equity position in the firm anytime over the life of the bond. The convertible bond can be valued as the value of a straight bond plus the value of an American call option. The American call option written on DOG shares can be valued using the standard American call option pricing methodologies.

When the value of the firm gets sufficiently high, the bondholder will exercise the option and convert his bond into an equity position in the firm. That is, the bondholder will convert the fixed payoff associated with the bond position into a variable payoff associated with the ownership of stock. If DOG does not pay dividends, then the bondholder should wait until the bond is about to mature to decide whether to convert the bond to an equity position in the firm. Exercising the option before this date results in the loss of the time premium of the option. However, if DOG becomes a target for acquisition and the stockholders are going to gain by receiving a premium as payment for their shares, then exercising their option would be rational for the bondholders. By exercising the option, the bondholder can share in the gains associated with the acquisition.

If DOG pays a dividend, then the decision to exercise the option early will be dependent on the size of the dividend paid. If the dividend is sufficiently large, then the bondholders can be induced to exercise early. Exercising the option entitles the bondholder to the stream of dividends paid by the firm. The decision to exercise early will be influenced by the size of the dividends, the timing of the dividends relative to the maturity of the bond, and the level of the market interest rates. The decision faced by the bondholder is the same as the decision faced by the owner of an American call option written on a dividend paying stock.

Value of a Convertible Bond at Maturity

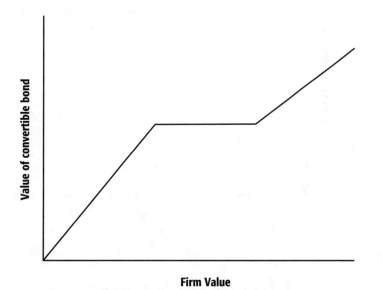

Suppose the bond also has a call provision. The call provision gives the firm's managers the right to call the bond after five years at a premium to par. Discuss the impact of the introduction of the call provision to the bond contract on the decision by the owners of the bond to convert the bond to stock prior to expiration of the bond contract.

The right to call the bond is held by the firm. So the bondholder has written the call provision to the managers of the firm. That is, the managers of the firm decide whether to call the bond prior to the bond's maturity. This short call option position places a ceiling on the potential gains available to bondholders from converting from a debt position in the firm to an equity position in the firm. Without the call provision, bondholders have no incentive to exercise the bond early unless the dividend paid by the firm is sufficiently large. When interest rates fall and the value of the bond rises, bondholders have an incentive to wait until the bond's maturity to convert the bond. When the call feature is introduced, the bondholders bear the risk of waiting to convert the bond. In this low interest rate environment, the firm's managers have an incentive to call the bond immediately and replace it with lower cost debt provided the bond has less than five years of life remaining. If the managers call the bond prior to the bondholders' conversion of the bond, the bondholders lose the upside potential associated with equity ownership. Thus bondholders have an incentive to convert early if they expect the managers of the firm to call the bond. Again, if DOG becomes a target for acquisition and the stockholders are going to gain by receiving a premium as payment for their shares, then it would be rational for the bondholders to exercise their options and convert their debt to equity. Upon conversion, the bondholders can share in the gains associated with the acquisition.

Value of a Callable Convertible Bond

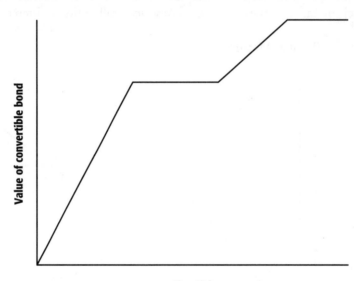

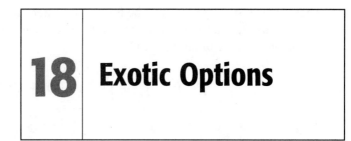

18 | Exotic Options

Answers to Questions and Problems

1. Using the following parameter values, find the price of a forward-start put: $S = 100$; $X = 100$; $T - t = 1$ year; $\sigma = 0.2$; $r = 0.1$; $\delta = 0.05$; $tg = 0.5$.

The first step is to value a plain vanilla put on the grant date, which is in one-half year. At that time, the put will have a half year remaining until expiration. Therefore,

$$d_1^M = \frac{\ln\left(\dfrac{100}{100}\right) + \left[0.1 - 0.05 + 0.5(0.2)(0.2)\right](0.5)}{0.2\sqrt{0.5}} = 0.247487$$

$$d_2^M = 0.247487 - 0.141421 = 0.106066$$

$$p_{tg}^M = Xe^{-r(T-t)}\, N\left(-d_2^M\right) - e^{-\delta(T-t)}\, S_t N\left(-d_1^M\right)$$

$$= 100e^{-.1(0.5)}\, N(-0.106066) - e^{-0.05(0.5)}\, 100\, N(-0.247487)$$

$$= 100e^{-.1(0.5)}\, 0.457765 - e^{-0.05(0.5)}\, 100\, (0.402266)$$

$$= 4.3106$$

Forward-Start Put $= e^{-\delta(tg - t)} P_{tg}^M = e^{-.05(.5)}\, 4.3106 = 4.2042$

2. Price all four types of compound options assuming the following parameter values: $S = 100$; $\sigma = 0.4$; $r = 0.1$; $\delta = 0.05$; $X = 100$; $x = 8$; $T = 1$ year; $te = 0.25$ years.

The first, and most difficult, step is to find the critical prices for the underlying calls and puts. For underlying calls, we have:

$$S^* e^{-\delta(T-te)}\, N(z) - Xe^{-r(T-te)}\, N\left(z - \sigma\sqrt{T - te}\right) - x = 0$$

For underlying puts, the critical stock price satisfies the following relationship:

$$S^* e^{-\delta(T-te)}\, N(-z) + Xe^{-r(T-te)}\, N\left(-z + \sigma\sqrt{T - te}\right) - x = 0$$

where:

$$z = \frac{\ln\left(\dfrac{S^*}{X}\right) + \left(r - \delta + 0.5\sigma^2\right)(T - te)}{\sigma\sqrt{T - te}}$$

These critical stock prices must be found by an iterative search. The critical stock price for an underlying call is 86.6162, and for an underlying put the critical stock price is 110.1995. These values can be verified as follows, first for underlying calls:

$$z = \frac{\ln\left(\frac{86.6152}{100}\right) + \left(0.1 - 0.05 + 0.5(0.4)(0.4)\right)(0.75)}{0.4\sqrt{0.75}} = -0.133353$$

Therefore,

$$N(z) = -0.133353; \quad N\left(z - \sigma\sqrt{T - te}\right) = -0.479763$$

Thus, we verify that 86.6152 is the correct critical stock price for underlying calls:

$$86.6152 \, e^{-0.05 \, (0.75)} \, 0.446957 - 100 \, e^{-0.1 \, (0.75)} \, 0.315698 - 8 = 0$$

The same verification can be performed for underlying puts.

Before computing the actual option values, we must compute other intermediate results:

$$w_1 = \frac{\ln\left(\frac{S}{S^*}\right) + \left(r - \delta + 0.5\sigma^2\right)(te - t)}{\sigma\sqrt{te - t}}$$

$$w_2 = \frac{\ln\left(\frac{S}{X}\right) + \left(r - \delta + 0.5\sigma^2\right)(T - t)}{\sigma\sqrt{T - t}}$$

With our sample values, $w_1 = 0.880974$ for underlying calls, and $w_1 = -0.323111$ for underlying puts. The other intermediate variables are invariant across all option types: $w_2 = 0.325000$; $\rho = 0.5$. We also need the following bivariate cumulative normal probabilities for compound options on underlying calls:

$$N_2\left(w_1; w_2; \rho\right) = N_2\left(0.880974; 0.325; 0.5\right)$$

$$= 0.564506$$

$$N_2\left(w_1 - \sigma\sqrt{te - t}; w_2 - \sigma\sqrt{T - t}; \rho\right) = N_2(0.680974; -0.075; 0.5)$$

$$= 0.416949$$

$$N_2\left(-w_1; w_2; -\rho\right) = N_2\left(-0.880974; 0.325; -0.5\right)$$

$$= 0.062904$$

$$N_2\left(-w_1 + \sigma\sqrt{te - t}; w_2 - \sigma\sqrt{T - t}; -\rho\right) = N_2\left(-0.680974; -0.075; -0.5\right)$$

$$= 0.053158$$

$$N\left(w_1 - \sigma\sqrt{te - t}\right) = N(0.680974) = 0.752056$$

$$N\left(-w_1 + \sigma\sqrt{te - t}\right) = N(-0.680974) = 0.247944$$

For convenience, we also note:

$$Se^{-\delta(T-t)} = 100\ e^{-0.05\ (1)} = 95.122942$$

$$Xe^{-r(T-t)} = 100\ e^{-0.1(1)} = 90.483742$$

$$xe^{-r(te-t)} = 8\ e^{-0.1(0.25)} = 7.802479$$

With all of these preliminary calculations out of the way, we are ready to compute the price of compound options on underlying calls from our pricing formulas:

$$CC_t = Se^{-\delta(T-t)}\ N_2\big(w_1; w_2; \rho\big) -$$

$$Xe^{-r(T-t)}\ N_2\left(w_1 - \sigma\sqrt{te-t};\ w_2 - \sigma\sqrt{T-t};\ \rho\right) -$$

$$xe^{-r(te-t)}\ N\left(w_1 - \sigma\sqrt{te-t}\right)$$

$$PC_t = -Se^{-\delta(T-t)}\ N_2\big(-w_1; w_2; -\rho\big) +$$

$$Xe^{-r(T-t)}\ N_2\left(-w_1 + \sigma\sqrt{te-t};\ w_2 - \sigma\sqrt{T-t};\ -\rho\right) +$$

$$xe^{-r(te-t)}\ N\left(-w_1 + \sigma\sqrt{te-t}\right)$$

$$CC_t = 95.122942(0.564506) - 90.483742(0.416949) - 7.802479(0.752056)$$

$$= 10.1024$$

$$PC_t = -95.122942(0.062904) + 90.483742(0.053158) + 7.802479(0.247944)$$

$$= 0.7608$$

We now turn to the pricing of compound options on underlying puts. Earlier we noted that the critical price is 110.1995 and the appropriate value for w_1 is –0.323111. The probabilities that we need for the underlying puts are:

$$N_2\left(-w_1;-w_2;\rho\right)=N_2\left(0.323111;-0.325;0.5\right)$$

$$=0.305486$$

$$N_2\left(-w_1+\sigma\sqrt{te-t};-w_2+\sigma\sqrt{T-t};\rho\right)=N_2\left(0.523111;0.075;0.5\right)$$

$$=0.442964$$

$$N_2\left(w_1;-w_2;-\rho\right)=N_2\left(-0.323111;-0.325;-0.5\right)$$

$$=0.067104$$

$$N_2\left(w_1-\sigma\sqrt{te-t};-w_2+\sigma\sqrt{T-t};-\rho\right)=N_2\left(-0.523111;0.075;-0.5\right)$$

$$=0.086930$$

$$N\left(-w_1+\sigma\sqrt{te-t}\right)=N\left(0.523111\right)$$

$$=0.699552$$

$$N\left(w_1-\sigma\sqrt{te-t}\right)=N\left(-0.523111\right)$$

$$=0.300448$$

We can now apply our formulas to compute the values of the compound options on underlying puts.

$$CP_t=-Se^{-\delta(T-t)}\,N_2\left(-w_1;-w_2;\rho\right)+$$
$$e^{-r(T-t)}\,N_2\left(-w_1+\sigma\sqrt{te-t};-w_2+\sigma\sqrt{T-t};\rho\right)-$$
$$xe^{-r(te-t)}\,N\left(-w_1+\sigma\sqrt{te-t}\right)$$
$$PP_t=Se^{-\delta(T-t)}\,N_2\left(w_1;-w_2;-\rho\right)-$$
$$e^{-r(T-t)}\,N_2\left(w_1-\sigma\sqrt{te-t};-w_2+\sigma\sqrt{T-t};-\rho\right)+$$
$$xe^{-r(te-t)}\,N\left(w_1-\sigma\sqrt{te-t}\right)$$

$$CP_t=-95.122942(0.305486)+90.483742(0.442964)-7.802479(0.699552)=5.5641$$

$$PP_t=95.122942(0.067104)-90.483742(0.086930)+7.802479(0.300448)=0.8617$$

3. Price a simple chooser option based on the following parameter values: $S=100$; $X=100$; $T=1$ year; $\sigma=0.5$; $r=0.1$; $\delta=0.05$; $tc=0.5$ years. By comparing this result with that of the example chooser in the sample text, what can you conclude about the influence of the stock's risk on the value of the chooser?

To price the chooser, we must first compute the following parameters:

$$w_1 = \frac{\ln\left(\dfrac{S}{X}\right) + \left(r - \delta + 0.5\sigma^2\right)(T - t)}{\sigma\sqrt{T - t}}$$

$$= \frac{\ln\left(\dfrac{100}{100}\right) + \left(0.1 - 0.05 + 0.5(0.5)(0.5)\right)(1.0)}{0.5\sqrt{1.0}}$$

$$= 0.35$$

$$w_2 = \frac{\ln\left(\dfrac{S}{X}\right) + \left(r - \delta\right)(T - t) + 0.5\,\sigma^2\,(tc - t)}{\sigma\sqrt{tc - t}}$$

$$= \frac{\ln\left(\dfrac{100}{100}\right) + \left(0.1 - 0.05\right)(1.0) + 0.5\,(0.5)\,(0.5)\,(0.5)}{0.5\sqrt{0.5}}$$

$$= 0.318198$$

$$N(w_1) = N(0.35) = 0.636831$$

$$N(-w_2) = N(-0.318198) = 0.375167$$

$$N\left(w_1 - \sigma\sqrt{T - t}\right) = N(0.35 - 0.5) = 0.440382$$

$$N\left(-w_2 + \sigma\sqrt{tc - t}\right) = N(-0.318198 + 0.353553) = 0.514102$$

Noting for convenience:

$$Se^{-\delta(T - t)} = 100\ e^{-0.05\ (1.0)} = 95.122942$$

$$Xe^{-r(T - t)} = 100\ e^{-0.1(1.0)} = 90.483742$$

We now compute the value of the chooser according to our valuation formula:

$$Chooser_t = Se^{-\delta(T - t)}N(w_1) - Xe^{-r(T - t)}\,N\left(w_1 - \sigma\sqrt{T - t}\right) +$$
$$Xe^{-r(T - t)}\,N\left(-w_2 + \sigma\sqrt{tc - t}\right) - Se^{-\delta(T - t)}N(-w_2)$$

$$Chooser_t = (95.122942)(0.636831) - 90.483742(0.440382)$$

$$+\ 90.483742(0.514102) - 95.122942(0.375167)$$

$$= 31.5606$$

The higher the volatility, the greater the value of the chooser option.

4. Find the value of a down-and-in put with: $S = 100$; $X = 100$; $(T - t) = 1$ year; $\sigma = 0.3$; $r = 0.1$; $\delta = 0.05$; BARR = 97; and REBATE = 2.

We begin by computing a host of intermediate values:

$$\lambda = \frac{r - \delta + 0.5\,\sigma^2}{\sigma^2} = 1.055556$$

$$w_2 = \frac{\ln\left(\dfrac{S}{BARR}\right)}{\sigma\sqrt{T-t}} + \lambda\,\sigma\,\sqrt{T-t} = 0.418197$$

$$w_3 = \frac{\ln\left(\dfrac{BARR^2}{SX}\right)}{\sigma\sqrt{T-t}} + \lambda\,\sigma\,\sqrt{T-t} = 0.113605$$

$$w_4 = \frac{\ln\left(\dfrac{BARR}{S}\right)}{\sigma\sqrt{T-t}} + \lambda\,\sigma\,\sqrt{T-t} = 0.215136$$

$$N\left(-w_2 + \sigma\sqrt{T-t}\right) = N(-0.118197) = 0.452956$$

$$N(-w_2) = N(-0.418197) = 0.337901$$

$$N\left(w_4 - \sigma\sqrt{T-t}\right) = N(-0.084864) = 0.466185$$

$$N(w_4) = N(0.215136) = 0.585169$$

$$N\left(w_3 - \sigma\sqrt{T-t}\right) = N(-0.186395) = 0.426067$$

$$N(w_3) = N(0.113605) = 0.545225$$

$$N\left(w_2 - \sigma\sqrt{T-t}\right) = N(0.118197) = 0.547044$$

$$Xe^{-r(T-t)} = 90.483742$$

$$Se^{-\delta(T-t)} = 95.122942$$

$$\left(\frac{BARR}{S}\right)^{2\lambda} = 0.937721$$

$$\left(\frac{BARR}{S}\right)^{2\lambda-2} = 0.996621$$

$$REBATE\ e^{-r(T-t)} = 1.809675$$

Using the equations from Table 18.2:

DP2 = 90.483742 (0.452956) − 95.122942 (0.337901) = 8.843017
DP3 = 90.483742 (0.996621) (0.466185) − 95.122942 (0.937721) (0.585169)
    = − 10.156731
DP4 = 90.483742 (0.996621) (0.426067) − 95.122942 (0.937721) (0.545225)
    = −10.211536
DP5 = 1.809675 [0.547044 − 0.996621 (0.466185)] = 0.149179

Finally, if $X > \text{BARR}$, then from Table 18.5:

$$\text{DIP} = \text{DP2} + \text{DP3} - \text{DP4} + \text{DP5}$$

$$= 8.843017 + 10.156731 + 10.211536 + 0.149179$$

$$= 9.0468$$

5. Consider a cash-or-nothing call and put, with common parameter values: $S = 100$; $X = 110$; $T - t = 0.5$ years; $\sigma = 0.4$; $r = 0.1$; $\delta = 0.0$; and $Z = 200$. What is the value of each option? What is the value of a long position in both options? Which items of information given above are not needed to value the portfolio of the two options?

As the first step, we need to determine:

$$d_2^M = \frac{\ln\left(\dfrac{S_t}{X}\right) + \left(r - \delta + .5\sigma^2\right)(T - t)}{\sigma\sqrt{T - t}} - \sigma\sqrt{T - t}$$

$$= \frac{\ln\left(\dfrac{100}{110}\right) + \left[0.1 - 0.0 + 0.5(0.4)(0.4)\right](0.5)}{0.4\sqrt{0.5}} - 0.4\sqrt{0.5}$$

$$= -0.301617$$

$N(d_2^M) = N(-0.301617) = 0.3481472$ and $N(-d_2^M) = N(0.301617) = 0.618528$. Therefore,

$$\text{CONC}_t = Ze^{-r(T - t)} N(d_2^M) = 200\ e^{-0.1(0.5)}\ (0.381472) = 72.5735$$

$$\text{CONP}_t = Ze^{-r(T - t)} N(-d_2^M) = 200\ e^{-0.1(0.5)}\ (0.618528) = 117.6724$$

The value of d_2^M and the associated probabilities are not necessary to value a portfolio of a cash-or-nothing call and put. The portfolio will pay the cash amount Z at expiration, so the portfolio must be worth the present value of Z at all times:

$$\text{CONC}_t + \text{CONP}_t = Ze^{-r(T - t)} = 72.5735 + 117.6724 = 190.2459$$

6. Consider an asset-or-nothing call and put, with common parameter values: $S = 100$; $X = 110$; $T - t = 0.5$ years; $\sigma = 0.4$; $r = 0.1$; and $\delta = 0.0$. What is the value of each option? What is the value of a long position in both options? Which items of information given above are not needed to value the portfolio of the two options?

First, we compute the value of d_1^M and its associated probabilities:

$$d_1 = \frac{\ln\left(\dfrac{S_t}{X}\right) + \left(r - \delta + .5\sigma^2\right)(T - t)}{\sigma\sqrt{T - t}}$$

$$= \frac{\ln\left(\dfrac{100}{110}\right) + \left(0.1 - 0.0 + .5\,(0.4)(0.4)\right)(0.5)}{0.4\sqrt{0.5}}$$

$$= -0.018774$$

$N(d_1{}^M) = 0.492511$ and $N(-d_1{}^M) = 0.507490$. Thus,

$$\text{AONC}_t = e^{-\delta(T-t)}\, S_t N(d_1{}^M) = e^{-0.0(0.5)}\, 100\,(0.492511) = 49.2510$$

$$\text{AONP}_t = e^{-\delta(T-t)}\, S_t N(-d_1{}^M) = e^{-0.0(0.5)}\, 100\,(0.507484) = 50.7490$$

The value of a portfolio of a call and put will pay the asset at expiration, thus the value of the portfolio is:

$$\text{AONC}_t + \text{AONP}_t = e^{-\delta(T-t)}\, S_t = e^{-0.0(0.5)}\, 100 = 100$$

Therefore, valuing the portfolio does not require knowledge of $d_1{}^M$ and its associated probabilities.

7. Value a gap call with: $S = 100$; $X = 100$; $T - t = 0.5$ years; $\sigma = 0.5$; $r = 0.1$; $\delta = 0.03$; and $g = 7$.

The value of a gap call is:

$$\text{GAPC}_t = e^{-\delta(T-t)}\, S_t N(d_1{}^M) - (X + g)\, e^{-r(T-t)}\, N(d_2{}^M)$$

Therefore, we first compute $d_1{}^M$, $d_2{}^M$, and their associated probabilities:

$$d_1^M = \frac{\ln\left(\dfrac{100}{100}\right) + \left[0.1 - 0.03 + 0.5\,(0.5)(0.5)\right](0.5)}{0.5\sqrt{0.5}} = 0.275772$$

$$d_2^M = d_1^M - \sigma\sqrt{T - t} = 0.275772 - 0.5\sqrt{0.5} = -0.077782$$

$N(d_1{}^M) = N(0.275772) = 0.608638$, and $N(d_2{}^M) = N(-0.077782) = 0.469001$. Therefore,

$$\text{GAPC}_t = e^{-0.03\,(0.5)}\, 100\,(0.608638) - (100 + 7)\, e^{-0.1(0.5)}\,(0.469001)$$

$$= 12.2221$$

8. Value a supershare with: $S = 100$; $X_L = 95$; $X_H = 110$; $T - t = 0.5$ years; $\sigma = 0.2$; $r = 0.1$; $\delta = 0.05$. By comparing this calculation with the sample supershare of the text, what can you conclude about the value of supershares and the value $X_H - X_L$?

The valuation formula, shown below, requires computing w_L and w_H.

$$SS = \frac{Se^{-\delta(T-t)}}{X_L}\left[N(w_L) - N(w_H)\right]$$

$$w_L = \frac{\ln\left(\dfrac{S}{X_L}\right) + \left(r - \delta + 0.5\sigma^2\right)(T-t)}{\sigma\sqrt{T-t}}$$

$$= \frac{\ln\left(\dfrac{100}{95}\right) + \left[0.1 - 0.05 + 0.5\,(0.2)(0.2)\right]0.5}{0.2\sqrt{0.5}}$$

$$= 0.610186$$

and:

$$w_H = \frac{\ln\left(\dfrac{S}{X_H}\right) + \left(r - \delta + 0.5\sigma^2\right)(T-t)}{\sigma\sqrt{T-t}}$$

$$= \frac{\ln\left(\dfrac{100}{110}\right) + \left[0.1 - 0.05 + 0.5\,(0.2)(0.2)\right](0.5)}{0.2\sqrt{0.5}}$$

$$= -0.426457$$

$N(0.610186) = 0.729131$, and $N(-0.426457) = 0.334887$.

$$SS = \frac{100e^{-0.05(0.5)}}{95}\left[0.729131 - 0.334887\right] = 0.4047$$

For the text example and this problem, all parameters are the same except for the payoff range. In the text example, the payoff range ran from 100 to 105 with a supershare value of 0.1332, while in this problem it runs from 95 to 105, with a supershare value of 0.4047. Thus, the larger the payoff range, the greater the value of the supershare. This only makes sense, because the broader the payoff range, the greater the chance that the supershare will finish in-the-money. Notice that it is not only the size of the range, but its location. For instance, if the range ran from 0 to 25, the bounds would be wider, but this supershare would be worth zero.

9. Find the value of a lookback call and put with the common parameters: $S = 110$; $T - t = 1$ year; $\sigma = 0.25$; $r = 0.08$; and $\delta = 0.0$. For the call, MINPRI = 80. For the put, MAXPRI = 130.

Computing the value of a lookback call requires the following intermediate values:

$$b = \ln\left(\frac{S}{\text{MINPRI}}\right) = \ln\left(\frac{110}{80}\right) = 0.318454$$

$$\mu = r - \delta - 0.5\sigma^2 = 0.08 - 0.0 - 0.5\,(0.25)\,(0.25) = 0.048750$$

$$\lambda = \frac{0.5\sigma^2}{r - \delta} = \frac{0.5\,(0.25)\,(0.25)}{0.08 - 0.0} = 0.390625$$

$$S e^{-\delta(T-t)} = 110\,e^{-0.0(1)} = 110$$

$$\text{MINPRI}\,e^{-r(T-t)} = 80\,e^{-0.08(1.0)} = 73.849308$$

$$N\left(\frac{b + \mu\,(T-t)}{\sigma\,\sqrt{T-t}}\right) = N\left(\frac{0.318454 + 0.048750\,(1.0)}{0.25\,\sqrt{1.0}}\right) = 0.929058$$

$$N\left(\frac{-b + \mu\,(T-t)}{\sigma\,\sqrt{T-t}}\right) = N\left(\frac{-0.318454 + 0.048750\,(1.0)}{0.25\,\sqrt{1.0}}\right) = 0.140335$$

$$N\left(\frac{-b - \mu\,(T-t) - \sigma^2\,(T-t)}{\sigma\,\sqrt{T-t}}\right) =$$

$$N\left(\frac{-0.318454 - 0.048750\,(1.0) - (0.25)\,(0.25)\,(1.0)}{0.25\,\sqrt{1.0}}\right) = 0.042824$$

The valuation formula for a lookback call is:

$$\text{LBC} = S e^{-\delta(T-t)} - \text{MINPRI}\,e^{-r(T-t)}\,N\left(\frac{b + \mu\,(T-t)}{\sigma\,\sqrt{T-t}}\right)$$

$$+ \text{MINPRI}\,e^{-r(T-t)}\,\lambda\,e^{b(1-1/\lambda)}\,N\left(\frac{-b + \mu\,(T-t)}{\sigma\,\sqrt{T-t}}\right)$$

$$- S e^{-\delta(T-t)}\,(1+\lambda)\,N\left(\frac{-b - \mu\,(T-t) - \sigma^2\,(T-t)}{\sigma\,\sqrt{T-t}}\right)$$

Applying this to our values gives:

$$\text{LBC} = 110 - 73.849308\,(.929058)$$

$$+ 73.849308\,(0.237688)\,(0.140335) - 110\,(1.390625)\,(0.042824)$$

$$= 37.3023$$

To value the lookback put, we use many of the same intermediate values. However, for the lookback put, the b term is different:

$$b = \ln\left(\frac{S}{\text{MAXPRI}}\right) = \ln\left(\frac{110}{130}\right) = -0.167054$$

The cumulative normal values are:

$$N\left(\frac{-b-\mu\,(T-t)}{\sigma\sqrt{T-t}}\right)=$$

$$N\left(\frac{0.167054-0.048750\,(1.0)}{0.25\sqrt{1.0}}\right)=0.681971$$

$$N\left(\frac{b-\mu\,(T-t)}{\sigma\sqrt{T-t}}\right)=$$

$$N\left(\frac{-0.167054-0.048750\,(1.0)}{0.25\sqrt{1.0}}\right)=0.194009$$

$$N\left(\frac{b+\mu\,(T-t)+\sigma^2\,(T-t)}{\sigma\sqrt{T-t}}\right)=$$

$$N\left(\frac{-0.167054+0.048750\,(1.0)+(0.25)\,(0.25)\,(1.0)}{0.25\sqrt{1.0}}\right)=-0.223216$$

We also note that:

$$\text{MAXPRI}e^{-r(T-t)}=120.005125$$

The valuation formula for the lookback put is:

$$\begin{aligned}
\text{LBP} = {} & -Se^{-\delta(T-t)}+\text{MAXPRI}e^{-r(T-t)}N\left(\frac{-b-\mu\,(T-t)}{\sigma\sqrt{T-t}}\right)\\[4pt]
& -\text{MAXPRI}\,e^{-r(T-t)}\,\lambda\,e^{b(1-1/\lambda)}\,N\left(\frac{b-\mu\,(T-t)}{\sigma\sqrt{T-t}}\right)\\[4pt]
& +Se^{-\delta(T-t)}\,(1+\lambda)\,N\left(\frac{b+\mu\,(T-t)+\sigma^2\,(T-t)}{\sigma\sqrt{T-t}}\right)
\end{aligned}$$

With our values, we have:

$$\text{LBP} = -110 + 120.005125\,(0.681971)$$

$$-120.005125\,(0.506920)\,(0.194009) + 110\,(1.390625)\,(0.411683)$$

$$= -110 + 81.840015 - 11.802140 + 62.974634$$

$$= 23.0125$$

10. Find the value of an average price option with these common parameters: $S = 100$; $X = 90$; $\sigma = 0.2$; $r = 0.1$; $\delta = 0.05$; $t_0 = 0.0$; $t_1 = 0.5$; $t_2 = 0.5$; and $A = 95$. Compute the value of the option with observations every two days, $h = 2/365$. Now compute the value of the option assuming continuous observation, that

is, $h = 0$. Compare these results with the sample option of the chapter. What does this suggest about the value of the option and the frequency of observation?

$$W = A^{\left(\frac{t_1}{t_1 + t_2 + h}\right)} S^{\left(\frac{t_2 + h}{t_1 + t_2 + h}\right)}$$

$$= 95^{\left(\frac{0.5}{0.5 + 0.5 + 0.005479}\right)} 100^{\left(\frac{0.5 + 0.005479}{0.5 + 0.5 + 0.005479}\right)}$$

$$= 97.481565$$

$$M = \left(t_0 + t_2 \frac{t_2 + h}{2(t_1 + t_2 + h)}\right)\left[r - \delta - 0.5\sigma^2\right]$$

$$= \left(0.0 + 0.5 \frac{0.5 + 0.005479}{2(0.5 + 0.5 + 0.005479)}\right)\left[0.1 - 0.05 - 0.5(0.2)(0.2)\right]$$

$$= 0.003770$$

$$\Sigma^2 = t_0 + \left(\frac{t_2(t_2 + h)(2t_2 + h)}{6(t_1 + t_2 + h)^2}\right)\sigma^2$$

$$= 0.0 + \left(\frac{0.5(0.5 + 0.005497)[2(0.5) + 0.005497]}{6(0.5 + 0.5 + 0.005497)^2}\right)(0.2)(0.2)$$

$$= 0.001676$$

$$w_1 = \frac{\ln\left(\frac{W}{X}\right) + M}{\Sigma} + \Sigma$$

$$= \frac{\ln\left(\frac{97.481565}{90}\right) + 0.003770}{0.040936} + 0.040936$$

$$= 2.083730$$

We note that $N(w_1) = 0.981408$, and $N(w_1 - \Sigma) = 0.979464$. The valuation formula for an average price option is:

$$AVGPRI = We^{-r(T-t)} e^{(M + 0.5\Sigma2)} N(w_1) - Xe^{-r(T-t)} N(w_1 - \Sigma)$$

The price of our example option is:

$$AVGPRI = (97.481565)\ e^{-0.1(0.5)}\ e^{[0.003770 + 0.5(0.001676)]}\ (0.981408)$$

$$-90\ e^{-0.1(0.5)}\ (0.979464)$$

$$= 91.423703 - 83.852548$$

$$= 7.5711$$

We now compute the price of the same option with $h = 0$.

$$W = A^{\left(\frac{t_1}{t_1 + t_2 + h}\right)} S^{\left(\frac{t_2 + h}{t_1 + t_2 + h}\right)}$$

$$= 95^{\left(\frac{0.5}{0.5 + 0.5}\right)} 100^{\left(\frac{0.5}{0.5 + 0.5}\right)}$$

$$= 97.46794$$

$$M = \left(t_0 + t_2 \frac{t_2 + h}{2\left(t_1 + t_2 + h\right)}\right)\left[r - \delta - 0.5\sigma^2\right]$$

$$= \left(0.0 + 0.5 \frac{0.5}{2\left(0.5 + 0.5\right)}\right)\left[0.1 - 0.05 - 0.5\left(0.2\right)\left(0.2\right)\right]$$

$$= 0.003750$$

$$\Sigma^2 = t_0 + \left(\frac{t_2\left(t_2 + h\right)\left(2\,t_2 + h\right)}{6\left(t_1 + t_2 + h\right)^2}\right)\sigma^2$$

$$= 0.0 + \left(\frac{0.5\left(0.5\right)\left[2\left(0.5\right)\right]}{6\left(0.5 + 0.5\right)^2}\right)\left(0.2\right)\left(0.2\right)$$

$$= 0.001667$$

$$w_1 = \frac{\ln\left(\dfrac{W}{X}\right) + M}{\Sigma} + \Sigma$$

$$= \frac{\ln\left(\dfrac{97.46794}{90}\right) + 0.003750}{0.040829} + 0.040829$$

$$= 2.085264$$

$N(w_1) = 0.981477$, and $N(w_1 - \Sigma) = 0.979545$. The price of our example option with continuous observation is:

$$\text{AVGPRI} = \left(97.46794\right) e^{-0.1(0.5)} e^{\left[0.003750 + 0.5\left(0.001667\right)\right]} \left(0.981477\right)$$

$$-90\ e^{-0.1(0.5)}\left(0.979545\right)$$

$$= 91.415066 - 83.859482$$

$$= 7.5556$$

For the example average price option of the text and these problems, we find that the value of the option is: 7.5556 with continuous observation; 7.5634 with observations every day; and 7.5711 with observations every second day. This suggests that the price of the average option varies inversely with the observation frequency, but that the effect is quite small.

11. Consider an exchange option with the following common parameter values: $S_1 = 100$; $S_2 = 100$; $\sigma_1 = 0.3$; $\sigma_2 = 0.2$; $\delta_1 = 0.05$; $\delta_2 = 0.05$; $T - t = 0.5$ years. Compute the value of this exchange option with $\rho = 0.0$ and $\rho = 0.7$. Compare your results with those for the sample exchange option in the chapter. What do these results suggest about the value of exchange options as a function of the correlation between the two assets?

We begin by computing intermediate values as follows:

$$\Sigma^2 = \sigma_1^2 + \sigma_2^2 - 2\rho\,\sigma_1\,\sigma_2$$

$$= 0.3\,(0.3) + 0.2\,(0.2) - 2\,(0.0)\,(0.3)\,(0.2)$$

$$= 0.13$$

$$w_1 = \frac{\ln\left(\dfrac{S_2}{S_1}\right) + \left(\delta_1 - \delta_2 + 0.5\,\Sigma^2\right)(T-t)}{\Sigma\sqrt{T-t}}$$

$$= \frac{\ln\left(\dfrac{100}{100}\right) + \left[0.05 - 0.05 + 0.5\,(0.13)\right](0.5)}{\sqrt{0.13}\,\sqrt{0.5}}$$

$$= 0.127475$$

$$w_2 = \frac{\ln\left(\dfrac{S_2}{S_1}\right) + \left(\delta_1 - \delta_2 + 0.5\Sigma^2\right)(T-t)}{\Sigma\sqrt{T-t}} - \Sigma\sqrt{T-t}$$

$$= \frac{\ln\dfrac{100}{100} + \left[0.05 - 0.05 + 0.5\,(0.13)\right](0.5)}{\sqrt{0.13}\,\sqrt{0.5}} - \sqrt{0.13}\,\sqrt{0.5}$$

$$= -0.127475$$

With these values, $N(w_1) = 0.550718$, and $N(w_2 = 0.449282$. The valuation equation is:

$$\text{EXOPT} = S_2\,e^{-\delta_2(T-t)}\,N(w_1) - S_1\,e^{-\delta_1(T-t)}\,N(w_2)$$

$$\text{EXOPT} = 100\,e^{-0.05(0.5)}\,0.550718 - 100\,e^{-0.05(0.5)}\,0.449282$$

$$= 53.712072 - 43.818919$$

$$= 9.8932$$

We now compute the value of the same option with $\rho = 0.7$.

$$\Sigma^2 = \sigma_1^2 + \sigma_2^2 - 2\rho\,\sigma_1\,\sigma_2$$

$$= 0.3\,(0.3) + 0.2\,(0.2) - 2\,(0.7)\,(0.3)\,(0.2)$$

$$= 0.046$$

$$w_1 = \frac{\ln\left(\dfrac{S_2}{S_1}\right) + \left(\delta_1 - \delta_2 + 0.5\,\Sigma^2\right)(T - t)}{\Sigma\sqrt{T - t}}$$

$$= \frac{\ln\left(\dfrac{100}{100}\right) + \left[0.05 - 0.05 + 0.5\,(0.046)\right](0.5)}{\sqrt{0.046}\,\sqrt{0.5}}$$

$$= 0.075829$$

$$w_2 = \frac{\ln\left(\dfrac{S_2}{S_1}\right) + \left(\delta_1 - \delta_2 + 0.5\,\Sigma^2\right)(T - t)}{\Sigma\sqrt{T - t}} - \Sigma\sqrt{T - t}$$

$$= \frac{\ln\left(\dfrac{100}{100}\right) + \left[0.05 - 0.05 + 0.5\,(0.046)\right](0.5)}{\sqrt{0.046}\,\sqrt{0.5}} - \sqrt{0.046}\,\sqrt{0.5}$$

$$= -0.075829$$

With these values, $N(w_1) = 0.530223$, and $N(w_2) = 0.469777$. Therefore,

$$\text{EXOPT} = 100\ e^{-0.05(0.5)}\ 0.530223 - 100\ e^{-0.05(0.5)}\ 0.469777$$

$$= 51.713175 - 45.817134$$

$$= 5.8960$$

For these parameter values, but differing correlations, we have values as follows: for $\rho = 0.0$, the price is 9.8932; for $\rho = 0.5$, the price is 7.2687 as shown in the text; and for $\rho = 0.7$, the price is 5.8960. Therefore, the price of the option varies inversely with the correlation.

For rainbow options, consider these parameter values: $S_1 = 100$; $S_2 = 100$; $X = 95$; $T - t = 0.5$ years; $\sigma_1 = 0.4$; $\sigma_2 = 0.5$; $r = 0.06$; $\delta_1 = 0.02$; $\delta_2 = 0.03$; and $\rho = 0.2$. (Interpret $X = 95$ as the exercise price or as the cash payment depending on the type of option.) Use this information for problems 12–18.

All of the following problems rely on some common values that we compute here and use in the specific solutions below.

$$\Sigma^2 = \sigma_1^2 + \sigma_2^2 - 2\rho\,\sigma_1\,\sigma_2 = 0.4\,(0.4) + 0.5\,(0.5) - 2\,(0.2)\,(0.4)\,(0.5) = 0.33$$

$$\rho_1 = \frac{\rho\,\sigma_2 - \sigma_1}{\Sigma} = \frac{0.2\,(0.5) - 0.4}{\sqrt{0.33}} = -0.522233$$

$$\rho_2 = \frac{\rho\,\sigma_1 - \sigma_2}{\Sigma} = \frac{0.2\,(0.4) - 0.5}{\sqrt{0.33}} = -0.731126$$

$$w_1 = \frac{\ln\left(\dfrac{S_1}{X}\right) + \left(r - \delta_1 + 0.5\,\sigma_1^2\right)(T-t)}{\sigma_1 \sqrt{T-t}}$$

$$= \frac{\ln\left(\dfrac{100}{95}\right) + \left[0.06 - 0.02 + 0.5\,(0.4)\,(0.4)\right](0.5)}{0.4\,\sqrt{0.5}}$$

$$= 0.393481$$

$$w_2 = \frac{\ln\left(\dfrac{S_2}{X}\right) + \left(r - \delta_2 + 0.5\,\sigma_2^2\right)(T-t)}{\sigma_2 \sqrt{T-t}}$$

$$= \frac{\ln\left(\dfrac{100}{95}\right) + \left[0.06 - 0.03 + 0.5\,(0.5)\,(0.5)\right](0.5)}{0.5\,\sqrt{0.5}}$$

$$= 0.364282$$

$$w_3 = \frac{\ln\left(\dfrac{S_1}{S_2}\right) + \left(\delta_2 - \delta_1 + 0.5\,\Sigma^2\right)(T-t)}{\Sigma \sqrt{T-t}}$$

$$= \frac{\ln\left(\dfrac{100}{100}\right) + \left[0.03 - 0.02 + 0.5\,(0.33)\right](0.5)}{\sqrt{0.33}\,\sqrt{0.5}}$$

$$= 0.215410$$

$$w_4 = \frac{\ln\left(\dfrac{S_2}{S_1}\right) + \left(\delta_1 - \delta_2 + 0.5\,\Sigma^2\right)(T-t)}{\Sigma \sqrt{T-t}}$$

$$= \frac{\ln\left(\dfrac{100}{100}\right) + \left[0.02 - 0.03 + 0.5\,(0.33)\right](0.5)}{\sqrt{0.33}\,\sqrt{0.5}}$$

$$= 0.190792$$

The basic evaluation units that we require are:

Q1.　$S_1\, e^{-\delta_1 (T-t)}\left\{ N(w_3) - N_2\left(-w_1; w_3; \rho_1\right)\right\}$

Q2.　$S_2\, e^{-\delta_2 (T-t)}\left\{ N(w_4) - N_2\left(-w_2; w_4; \rho_2\right)\right\}$

Q3.　$X e^{-r(T-t)}\, N_2\left(-w_1 + \sigma_1 \sqrt{T-t}; -w_2 + \sigma_2 \sqrt{T-t}; \rho\right)$

To evaluate Q1–Q3, we need the following intermediate values:

$$S_1 e^{-\delta_1 (T-t)} = 100\, e^{-0.02\,(0.5)} \quad = \quad 99.004983$$

$$S_2 e^{-\delta_2 (T-t)} = 100\, e^{-0.03\,(0.5)} \quad = \quad 98.511194$$

$$Xe^{-r(T-t)} = 95\, e^{-0.06\,(0.5)} \quad = \quad 92.192326$$

$$N(w_3) = N(0.215410) \quad = \quad 0.585276$$

$$N(w_4) = N(0.190792) \quad = \quad 0.575656$$

$$N_2\left(-w_1; w_3; \rho_1\right) \quad =$$

$$N_2\left(-0.393481; 0.215410; -0.522233\right) \quad = \quad 0.122795$$

$$N_2\left(-w_2; w_4; \rho_2\right) \quad =$$

$$N_2\left(-0.364282; 0.190792; -0.731126\right) \quad = \quad 0.084427$$

$$N_2\left(-w_1 + \sigma_1 \sqrt{T-t}; -w_2 + \sigma_2 \sqrt{T-t}; \rho\right) \quad =$$

$$N_2\left(-0.393481 + 0.4\sqrt{0.5}; -0.364282 + 0.5\sqrt{0.5}; 0.2\right) \quad = \quad 0.257875$$

Using the previous intermediate results, we now compute Q1–Q3:

$$Q1 = S_1\, e^{-\delta_1 (T-t)} \left\{ N(w_3) - N_2\left(-w_1; w_3; \rho_1\right) \right\}$$

$$= 99.004983\,(0.585276 - 0.122795)$$

$$= 45.787924$$

$$Q2 = S_2\, e^{-\delta_2 (T-t)} \left\{ N(w_4) - N_2\left(-w_2; w_4; \rho_2\right) \right\}$$

$$= 98.511194\,(0.575656 - 0.084427)$$

$$= 48.391555$$

$$Q3 = Xe^{-r(T-t)}\, N_2\left(-w_1 + \sigma_1 \sqrt{T-t}; -w_2 + \sigma_2 \sqrt{T-t}; \rho\right)$$

$$= 92.192326\,(0.257875)$$

$$= 23.774096$$

12. Find the value of an option on the best of two assets and cash.

$$\text{BEST3} = Q1 + Q2 + Q3 = 45.787924 + 48.391555 + 23.774096 = 117.9536$$

13. Find the value of an option on the better of two assets.

The valuation equation is CBETTER = BEST3, given that $X = 0$. If $X = 0$, several values computed above must be adjusted. First, Q3 = 0. However, w_1 and w_2 both change as well. Each has X alone in its denominator, thus w_1 and w_2 are both infinite. These are important in the computation of the bivariate cumulative normal values. For present purposes, within the context of the unit normal distribution, let these variables be set equal to 10.0. As shown below, the large values of w_1 and w_2 force the bivariate probabilities to zero.

$$Xe^{-r(T-t)} = 0 \ e^{-0.06(0.5)} = 0.0$$

$$N_2(-w_1; w_3; \rho_1) = N_2 \ (-10.0; 0.215410; -0.522233) = 0.0$$

$$N_2(-w_2; w_4; \rho_2) = N_2 \ (-10.0; 0.190792; -0.731126) = 0.0$$

These affect the computation of Q1 and Q2 as follows:

$$Q1 = S_1 \ e^{-\delta_1 (T-t)} \left\{ N(w_3) - N_2 \ (-w_1; w_3; \rho_1) \right\}$$
$$= 99.004983 \, (0.585276 - 0.0)$$
$$= 57.945254$$

$$Q2 = S_2 \ e^{-\delta_2 (T-t)} \left\{ N(w_4) - N_2 \ (-w_2; w_4; \rho_2) \right\}$$
$$= 98.511194 \, (0.575656 - 0.0)$$
$$= 56.708521$$

Therefore, CBETTER = Q1 + Q2 + Q3 = 57.945254 + 56.708521 + 0 = 114.6538.

14. Find the value of a call on the maximum of two assets.

$$\text{CMAX} = \text{BEST3} - Xe^{-r(T-t)} = Q1 + Q2 + Q3 - Xe^{-r(T-t)} = 117.9536 - 92.192326 = 25.761249$$

15. Find the value of a put on the maximum of two assets.

$$\text{PMAX} = \text{CMAX} - \text{CBETTER} + Xe^{-r(T-t)} = 25.761249 - 114.6538 + 92.192326 = 3.2998$$

16. Find the value of a call on the minimum of two assets.

$$\text{CMIN} = C_t^M(S_1) + C_t^M(S_2) - \text{CMAX} = 14.4949 + 16.7708 - 25.761249 = 5.504451$$

17. Find the value of a call on the worse of two assets.

$$\text{CWORSE} = C_t^M(S_1) + C_t^M(S_2) - \text{CBETTER, given that } X = 0$$
$$= 99.004983 + 98.511194 - 114.6538 = 82.8624$$

18. Find the value of a put on the minimum of two assets.

$$\text{PMIN} = \text{CMIN} - \text{CWORSE} + Xe^{-r(T-t)} = 5.504451 - 82.8624 + 92.192326 = 14.8344$$

Interest Rate Options

Answers to Questions and Problems

1. Explain the relationship among mortgage-backed securities, mortgage pass-throughs, and collateralized mortgage obligations.

   The mortgage-backed security (MBS) is a security that gives the security owner rights to cash flows from mortgages that underlie the MBS. The MBS comes in two basic types: mortgage pass-through securities and collateralized mortgage obligations. The owner of a pass-through owns a fractional share of the entire pool of mortgages that underlie the pass-through security. The owner of a pass-through participates in all the cash flows from the underlying mortgage pool. A collateralized mortgage obligation (CMO) is another type of MBS. A CMO is created by decomposing the cash flows from a pool of mortgages. For example, some CMOs are backed by interest-only payments from a pool of mortgages, while other CMOs might be backed by principal-only payments from the same mortgage pool.

2. Explain the similarities and differences between the zero-coupon yield curve and the implied forward yield curve.

   Both the zero-coupon yield curve and the forward yield curve show rates of interest that apply to single future payments. The rates from both curves can be used to discount a single payment from a distant future date to an earlier date. The zero-coupon yield curve gives discount rates for discounting a distant payment to the present. The rates from the forward curve are essentially rates for discounting a distant payment from its payment date to a time one period earlier. For example, if the forward curve has annual rates, the forward rate for a period from year 7 to year 8 could be used to discount a payment to be received at year 8 back to year 7. Together, the single-period forward rates that constitute the forward yield curve can be used to discount a distant payment back to any earlier time.

3. Given the zero-coupon yield curve, explain how to find the implied forward yield curve.

   The forward rate between any two periods is a function of the zero-coupon discount rates for a horizon from the present to the initiation point of the forward rate and the zero-coupon rates for a horizon from the present to the termination date of the forward rate. For example, consider a single-period forward rate from year 5 to year 6. This forward rate can be found by using the zero-coupon yield curve to find the zero-coupon factors for years 5 and 6, $Z_{0,5}$ and $Z_{0,6}$. The forward rate factor for this period, $FRF_{5,6}$, is given by:

$$FRF_{5,6} = \frac{Z_{0,6}}{Z_{0,5}}$$

   Given the set of one-period *FRF*s, the elements of the forward yield curve can be found quite easily, because the one-period forward rate is simply the one-period *FRF* minus 1:

$$1 + FR_{n,\,n+1} = FRF_{n,\,n+1}$$

In general, for any forward rate factor for a period beginning at time x and ending at time y, we have:

$$FRF_{x,y} = \frac{Z_{0,y}}{Z_{0,x}}$$

4. Given the implied forward yield curve, explain how to find the zero-coupon yield curve.

The forward yield curve consists of all one-period forward rates. For a horizon of n periods, the zero-coupon factor is:

$$Z_{0,n} = FRF_{0,1} \times FRF_{1,2} \times \ldots FRF_{n-1,n}$$

The n-period zero-coupon yield is:

$$n\text{-Period Zero-Coupon Yield} = \sqrt[n]{Z_{0,n}}$$

5. Given the par yield curve, explain how to find the zero-coupon yield curve.

Finding the zero-coupon yield curve requires the technique of bootstrapping detailed in the text. Bootstrapping uses the sequence of par yields to find the zero-coupon factors for each maturity covered by the yield curve. Given the sequence of zero-coupon factors, the zero-coupon yields that constitute the zero-coupon yield curve are found as in the answer to the previous question.

In bootstrapping, we begin by noting that the short-term (one-period) par yield is the same as the zero-coupon yield for one period. This gives the information necessary to find the zero-coupon factor for two periods. Let R_n indicate the n-period par yield. Because each R_n is from the par yield curve, the coupon rate on an n-period instrument must be R_n. Therefore, assuming a par value on a bond of 100, we have for the two-period case:

$$100 = \frac{R_2 \times 100}{Z_{0,1}} + \frac{100 + R_2 \times 100}{Z_{0,2}}$$

Recalling that the one-period par yield is the same as the one-period zero-coupon yield, we can solve this equation for $Z_{0,2}$. We then repeat the process. For a three-period horizon, we solve:

$$100 = \frac{R_3 \times 100}{Z_{0,1}} + \frac{R_3 \times 100}{Z_{0,2}} + \frac{100 + R_3 \times 100}{Z_{0,3}}$$

We repeat this process until all zero-coupon factors are found.

6. How does Equation 19.2 differ from the usual bond pricing formula?

The usual bond pricing formula discounts all cash flows from a bond at a single rate, the yield-to-maturity of the bond. In Equation 19.2, each cash flow from the bond is discounted at the zero-coupon rate appropriate for the time until the particular cash flow is to be paid.

7. Explain how to create a forward rate agreement for Treasuries using Treasury strips. Specifically, how would you create a forward rate agreement to cover a period from five to eight years in the future? Assume the five-year zero-coupon rate is 7 percent and the eight-year zero-coupon rate is 7.3 percent. Assume also that you wish to take a long position in the FRA, with a transaction amount of $1,000,000. (That is, the market value of the strips traded will be $1,000,000.)

When a T-bond is stripped, each cash flow from the bond is treated as a security. Therefore, a stripped T-bond is a portfolio of zero-coupon bonds. A forward rate agreement to cover any particular period can be constituted by two zero-coupon instruments, one maturing at the beginning of the forward rate period, one maturing at the end of the forward rate period. In a forward rate agreement, no cash flow occurs at the time of contracting. Instead, a cash flow occurs at the expiration of the forward agreement.

For a period from five to eight years in the future, one can create a forward rate agreement by buying and selling a five-year and an eight-year zero, with both having the same market value. Given the information in the question, we have:

$$Z_{0,5} = (1 + 0.07)^5 = 1.402552$$

$$Z_{0,8} = (1 + 0.073)^8 = 1.757105$$

These zero-coupon factors imply principal amounts as follows to have market values of $1,000,000:

$$\$1,000,000 \times Z_{0,5} = \$1,000,000 \times 1.402552 = \$1,402,552$$

$$\$1,000,000 \times Z_{0,8} = \$1,000,000 \times 1.757105 = \$1,757,105$$

To create a long FRA position, one should transact as follows:

Buy 8-year zero-coupon with principal amount of $1,757,105 at $1,000,000.
Sell 5-year zero-coupon with principal amount of $1,402,552 at $1,000,000.

These two transactions require zero initial cash flow. At year 5, the 5-year zero will mature, and the trader will owe $1,402,552. This is the forward price of the FRA to cover years 5 to 8. Notice that this will be an FRA that is determined and settled in advance.

8. Assume that you wish to conduct an OAS analysis of a callable corporate bond with an 18-year maturity that is callable in seven years. You cannot find any Treasury bond that matches the cash flows of the callable bond. Explain how you might proceed with your analysis.

You can create a surrogate T-bond using strips. First, determine the exact amounts and timing of the cash flows on the corporate bond. Second, find the zero-coupon Treasury instrument that best matches each cash flow. Third, create a portfolio of those zeros that match the desired, but unavailable, T-bond. Fourth, price the portfolio of strips. Fifth, find the yield-to-maturity of the surrogate bond. This effectively provides the desired T-bond to allow the OAS analysis to proceed.

9. In various incarnations of the Black model in this chapter, we saw that the role of the stock price in the Black-Scholes-Merton model could be played alternately by the futures price, the forward bond price, and the forward LIBOR interest rate. What underlying assumptions unite these various proxies for the stock price and allow the application of the Black model?

The implicit assumption is that these different measures (the futures price, the forward bond price, and the forward LIBOR interest rate) are all assumed to have a log-normal distribution at the expiration date of the option.

10. What does it mean for an interest rate agreement to be "determined in advance and settled in arrears"?

By convention, most interest rate agreements are determined in advance and paid in arrears. The rate on an FRA is determined in advance, that is, at the time the agreement matures and the underlying loan begins. The FRA is settled in arrears, meaning that the cash flow on the FRA occurs at the maturity of the instrument presumed to underlie the FRA. For example, consider a three-month FRA to cover a period extending from five to eight months in the future. The contract is initiated at time zero, the present. The gain or loss on the contract is determined in advance—at the beginning of the period covered by the FRA—which is at month 5. The agreement is settled in arrears—at the maturity date of the underlying instrument—which is at month 8.

11. You are examining a horizon extending from six through nine months in the future. For this period, an FRA is available, as well as calls and puts on LIBOR. Assume that you enter an FRA to receive-fixed and pay LIBOR. You also buy a call on LIBOR and sell a put on LIBOR for the same period, with strike rates equal to the rate on the FRA. All instruments have the same notional amount. Explain the economic import of your transactions. Can the totality of your transactions be analyzed as some simpler instrument? If so, what?

An FRA is equivalent to a portfolio of a call and put on LIBOR, assuming matching time periods and notional amounts. A receive-fixed/pay LIBOR FRA can be replicated by a long put/short call portfolio. In the terms of the question, the FRA is a receive-fixed/pay LIBOR position. The long call/short put portfolio is equivalent to a pay-fixed/receive LIBOR FRA. With all of these transactions, the net economic effect of the transactions is zero. There should be no net cash flows at the time of contracting or at the expiration date of the FRA and options. All this transacting amounts to nothing, except perhaps transaction costs.

12. For a future period, the FRA rate is 8 percent. Consider the following varieties of a "collarlet" (caplet plus floorlet) for this loan. Assume that the periods and notional amounts of the options match the terms of the FRA.

A. A collarlet gives an 8–8 percent collar on the loan. How much should the collarlet cost?

This collarlet is equivalent to an FRA with a contract rate of 8 percent. Since the FRA rate stated in the question is also 8 percent, this collarlet should be costless.

B. A 7.8–7.9 percent collarlet is costless. How should you respond as an arbitrageur?

A collarlet with an 8 percent strike rate should be costless, and represents a firm commitment at 8 percent, like an FRA at 8 percent. This collarlet guarantees a rate not less than 7.8 percent and not higher than 7.9 percent. With an FRA rate of 8 percent prevailing, this collarlet has positive economic value. Therefore, since it is costless, the arbitrageur should buy the call and sell the put to acquire the collarlet, and should enter an FRA as the receive-fixed party.

The following figure shows the payoffs from the collarlet as the solid line and the receive-fixed FRA as the dotted line. No matter what LIBOR prevails at the expiration of the options and the FRA, the arbitrageur makes a profit. The profit is equal to the sum of the FRA line and the collarlet line (times the unspecified fraction of the year times the unspecified notional amount). Graphically, the figure shows that this sum is positive no matter what the Observed LIBOR happens to be.

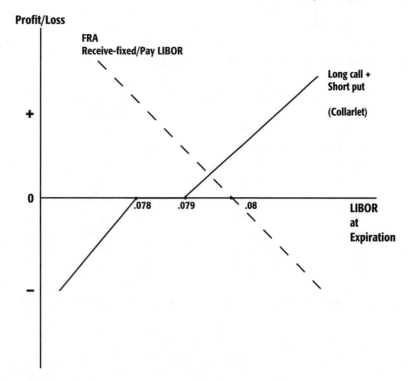

C. An 8.2–8.5 percent collarlet is fairly priced. What can you infer about its cost?

The collarlet represents a commitment to finance at a rate not higher than 8.5 percent and not lower than 8.2 percent. Since the prevailing FRA rate is 8 percent, taking the collarlet is worse than the FRA. Therefore, rational prices must be such that the collarlet has a negative price—that is, the cost of buying the call and selling the put should give a cash inflow. Said another way, the put must be worth more than the call.

D. A 7.5–7.8 percent collarlet is fairly priced. What can you infer about its cost?

This collarlet gives a financing opportunity of not less than 7.5 percent, but not more than 7.8 percent. These are excellent terms in an environment with an FRA rate of 8 percent. Therefore, this collarlet must have a positive cost. The cost of the call exceeds the cost of the put.

Maturity (years)	Yield Curve #1 (par annual yields)	Yield Curve #2 (par annual yields)
1	0.0500	0.1200
2	0.0540	0.1196
3	0.0545	0.1191
4	0.0552	0.1171
5	0.0564	0.1130
6	0.0594	0.1105
7	0.0652	0.1070
8	0.0666	0.1035
9	0.0714	0.0992
10	0.0772	0.0953

13. Using the yield data in the table above, interpret Yield Curve #1 as the par yield curve. Complete the following table by finding all zero-coupon factors and by finding all one-year forward rate factors. Also, find all four-year forward rates. Assume annual compounding throughout.

Maturity (years)	Par Yield	Zero-Coupon Factor	One-Year Forward Rate Factors
1	0.0500	1.050000	1.050000
2	0.0540	1.111145	1.058233
3	0.0545	1.172909	1.055586
4	0.0552	1.240408	1.057549
5	0.0564	1.317252	1.061950
6	0.0594	1.419450	1.077584
7	0.0652	1.576568	1.110690
8	0.0666	1.702647	1.079970
9	0.0714	1.921525	1.128551
10	0.0772	2.237349	1.164361

To find the four-year forward rates, we first find all four-year forward rate factors:

$$FRF_{0,4} = \frac{Z_{0,4}}{Z_{0,0}} = \frac{1.240408}{1.000000} = 1.240408$$

$$FRF_{1,5} = \frac{Z_{0,5}}{Z_{0,1}} = \frac{1.317252}{1.050000} = 1.254526$$

$$FRF_{2,6} = \frac{Z_{0,6}}{Z_{0,2}} = \frac{1.419450}{1.111145} = 1.277466$$

$$FRF_{3,7} = \frac{Z_{0,7}}{Z_{0,3}} = \frac{1.576568}{1.172909} = 1.344152$$

$$FRF_{4,8} = \frac{Z_{0,8}}{Z_{0,4}} = \frac{1.702647}{1.240408} = 1.372651$$

$$FRF_{5,9} = \frac{Z_{0,9}}{Z_{0,5}} = \frac{1.921525}{1.317252} = 1.458738$$

$$FRF_{6,10} = \frac{Z_{0,10}}{Z_{0,6}} = \frac{2.237349}{1.419450} = 1.576208$$

Given the various four-year FRFs above, each four-year forward rate is the fourth root of the four-year FRF minus 1, as given in the following table:

Starting Date	Ending Date	Four-Year FRF	Four-Year Forward Rate
0	4	1.240408	0.055337
1	5	1.254526	0.058327
2	6	1.277466	0.063132
3	7	1.344152	0.076743
4	8	1.372651	0.082406
5	9	1.458738	0.098991
6	10	1.576208	0.120478

14. Using the yield data in the table above, interpret Yield Curve #2 as the zero-coupon yield curve. Find all zero-coupon factors. Find the par yield curve. Assume annual compounding throughout.

If the elements of Yield Curve #2 are zero-coupon yields, the zero-coupon factors are found by adding 1 to the yield and raising the quantity to a power reflecting the number of periods that equals the maturity of the rate, as follows:

$$Z_{0,1} = 1.12$$

$$Z_{0,2} = (1.1196)^2 = 1.253504$$

$$Z_{0,3} = (1.1191)^3 = 1.401544$$

$$Z_{0,4} = (1.1171)^4 = 1.557285$$

$$Z_{0,5} = (1.1130)^5 = 1.707953$$

$$Z_{0,6} = (1.1105)^6 = 1.875475$$

$$Z_{0,7} = (1.1070)^7 = 2.037198$$

$$Z_{0,8} = (1.1035)^8 = 2.198764$$

$$Z_{0,9} = (1.0992)^9 = 2.342559$$

$$Z_{0,10} = (1.0953)^{10} = 2.485026$$

We now use the zero-coupon factors to find the par yields for each maturity, assuming a par value of $1,000. To find the par yield, we need to find the coupon, $COUP$, and the corresponding coupon rate on the bond that gives a market value of $1,000, when each cash flow from the bond is discounted by the appropriate zero-coupon factor. In essence, we apply the bond pricing equation:

$$1,000 = \sum_{n=1}^{N} \frac{COUP_n}{Z_{0,n}} + \frac{1,000}{Z_{0,N}}$$

$$COUP_n = \frac{1,000 - \dfrac{1,000}{Z_{0,N}}}{\displaystyle\sum_{n=1}^{N} \dfrac{1}{Z_{0,n}}}$$

As an example, consider the five-year maturity:

$$Z_{0,5} = 1.707953$$

$$\sum_{n=1}^{5} \frac{1}{Z_{0,n}} = 3.631759$$

$$1,000 = COUP_t \times 3.631759 + \frac{1,000}{1.707953}$$

$$COUP_t = 114.13$$

The coupon is 114.13, for a coupon rate of 11.413 percent for the five-year maturity. This coupon rate is the par yield. The following table gives the result for the entire yield curve:

Maturity	$Z_{0,n}$	$\dfrac{1}{Z_{0,n}}$	$\displaystyle\sum_{n=1}^{N}\dfrac{1}{Z_{0,n}}$	$1{,}000 - \dfrac{1{,}000}{Z_{0,n}}$	Coupon	Coupon Rate (percent)
1	1.120000	0.892857	0.892857	107.142857	120.00	12.000
2	1.253504	0.797764	1.690621	202.236291	119.62	11.962
3	1.401544	0.713499	2.404120	286.501173	119.17	11.917
4	1.557285	0.642143	3.046263	357.856783	117.47	11.747
5	1.707953	0.585496	3.631759	414.503795	114.13	11.413
6	1.875475	0.533198	4.164957	466.801744	112.08	11.208
7	2.037198	0.490870	4.655828	509.129697	109.35	10.935
8	2.198764	0.454801	5.110629	545.199030	106.68	10.668
9	2.342559	0.426884	5.537512	573.116408	103.50	10.350
10	2.485026	0.402410	5.939922	597.589723	100.61	10.061

15. Using the yield data in the table above, interpret Yield Curve #1 as the zero-coupon yield curve. Find the price of an 8 percent annual coupon bond that matures in eight years. A callable bond with a price of 98.75 percent of par matures in eight years and has a coupon of 8 percent. Find the OAS between these bonds.

The following table gives the intermediate calculations for pricing the bond:

Maturity	Zero-Coupon Rate	Zero-Coupon Factor	Bond Cash Flow	Present Value of Cash Flow
1	0.0500	1.050000	80	76.1905
2	0.0540	1.110916	80	72.0126
3	0.0545	1.172573	80	68.2261
4	0.0552	1.239764	80	64.5284
5	0.0564	1.315655	80	60.8062
6	0.0594	1.413708	80	56.5888
7	0.0652	1.556030	80	51.4129
8	0.0666	1.674992	1080	644.7794

Bond Price = 1094.5449

For the OAS analysis, we need to find the yield spread to add to the zero-coupon rates that will give this bond a price of 98.75 percent of par. In terms of the preceding table, it will be the amount to add to the zero-coupon rate in the second column. The following table shows various spreads and the resulting price. The OAS analysis can proceed by trial and error until the computed yield-adjusted T-bond price equals the callable bond price of 98.75.

Spread	Resulting Bond Price
0.050000	826.7478
0.030000	922.0697
0.010000	1032.6465
0.020000	975.2822
0.019000	980.8258
0.017000	992.0389
0.018000	986.4112
0.017800	987.5334
0.017810	987.4772
0.017805	987.5053
0.017806	987.4997

A spread of 0.017806 gives a bond price of 987.4997 ≈ 987.500. The OAS is 178.06 basis points.

16. A T-bond futures contract matures in five months, and the corresponding T-bond futures option expires in four months. The current futures price is 103.50. The yield curve is flat at 7 percent. Assume continuous compounding. The standard deviation of the T-bond futures price is 0.2835. The strike price for both a call and a put is 100.00. Using the Black model, find the price of the call and the put.

Applying the Black model from Equation 19.5, we first compute d_1^F and d_2^F:

$$d_1^F = \frac{\ln\left(\dfrac{F_t}{X}\right) + \left(.5\sigma^2\right)(T-t)}{\sigma\sqrt{T-t}} = \frac{\ln\left(\dfrac{103.50}{100}\right) + \left(0.5 \times 0.2835^2\right)(0.3333)}{0.2835 \times \sqrt{0.3333}} = 0.292022$$

$$d_2^F = d_1^F - \sigma\sqrt{T-t} = 0.292022 - 0.163671 = 0.128351$$

Finding the cumulative normal values for the put and call, we have $N(d_1^F) = 0.614865$; $N(d_2^F) = 0.551065$; $N(-d_1^F) = 0.385135$; and $N(-d_2^F) = 0.448935$.

Assuming continuous discounting at the rate of 7.00 percent, we have:

$$c_t^F = e^{-r(T-t)}\left[F_t N\left(d_1^F\right) - X N\left(d_2^F\right)\right]$$

$$= e^{-0.07(0.3333)}\left[103.50\left(0.614865\right) - 100\left(0.551065\right)\right]$$

$$= 8.3353$$

$$p_t^F = e^{-r(T-t)}\left[X N\left(-d_2^F\right) - F_t N\left(-d_1^F\right)\right]$$

$$= e^{-0.07(0.3333)}\left[100\left(0.448935\right) - 103.50\left(0.385135\right)\right]$$

$$= 4.9160$$

17. Consider European call and put options on a Treasury bond with a coupon of 6 percent paid semiannually that matures in 40 months and has a par value of $1,000. The current term structure environment is given by the downward-sloping yields of Table 19.7. Use these yields and monthly compounding throughout. Both the call and put expire in three months. The call has an exercise price of $970, and the put has an exercise price of $1,010. The standard deviation of Treasury yields is given as follows: one-year maturity, 0.30; two-year maturity, 0.28; three-year maturity, 0.25; and five-year maturity, 0.19. (Use linear interpolation to find the appropriate yield volatility for the maturity of this bond.) Find the prices of the call and put options.

We begin by finding the actual cash price of the bond, and then the forward price of the bond in three months when the options expire. The following table gives the relevant cash flow and discounting information:

Month	Cash Flow	Zero-Coupon Factor	PV of Cash Flow
4	30	1.0262	29.2341
10	30	1.0661	28.1399
16	30	1.1066	27.1101
22	30	1.1478	26.1370
28	30	1.1896	25.2186
34	30	1.2318	24.3546
40	1030	1.2745	808.1601
			Total = 968.3543

The actual bond price is 968.3543, assuming a par value of 1000. $Z_{0,3} = 1.0196$. Therefore, the forward bond price when the options expire in three months is:

$$968.3543 \times 1.0196 = 987.3340$$

We next need to find the volatility of the forward bond price. To do so, we first need to find the Macaulay duration for the forward bond, which requires finding the monthly yield-to-maturity consistent with the forward bond price. We value the forward bond at month 3, finding the yield-to-maturity for the forward bond at the point, and finding the duration of the forward bond at that point as well. Viewed from the perspective of month 3, the remaining timing and cash flows are given in the following table:

Month	Cash Flow	PV of Cash Flow	Weighted PV of Cash Flow
1	30	29.8192	29.8192
7	30	28.7573	201.3011
13	30	27.7332	360.5313
19	30	26.7455	508.1649
25	30	25.7930	644.8261
31	30	24.8745	771.1091
37	1030	823.6101	30,473.5720
		Computed Forward Bond Price = 987.3328	Sum = 32,989.3237

With a forward bond price of 987.3340, the monthly yield to maturity on the forward bond, found by trial and error, is 0.006062, which gives a computed forward bond price of $987.3328 \approx 987.3340$, as shown in the third column of the table. The fourth column gives the present values of the cash flows weighted by the number of months until each cash flow is received, all from the perspective of month 3. The Macaulay's duration, D, is the sum of these weighted cash flows, 32989.3237, divided by the forward bond price, 987.3340:

$$D = \frac{32,989.3237}{987.3340} = 33.4125 \text{ months}$$

The modified Macaulay's duration, MD, of the forward bond is:

$$MD = \frac{D}{1+r} = \frac{33.4125}{1.006062} = 33.2112 \text{ months} = 2.7676 \text{ years}$$

We are now ready to find the standard deviation of the forward bond price, σ_P. We know that the three-year yield volatility is 0.25 and the five-year volatility is 0.19. The linearly interpolated volatility for a 40-month maturity is:

$$0.25 \times (20/24) + 0.19 \times (4/24) = 0.24$$

The monthly yield to maturity for the forward bond is 0.006062, implying an annualized yield of 0.075219, assuming monthly compounding. Therefore,

$$\sigma_P \approx MD \, r \, \sigma_r = 2.7676 \times 0.075219 \times 0.24 = 0.049962$$

We now have (finally!) all of the required inputs for the Black model. The forward bond price is 987.3340; the time to expiration is three months, or 0.25 years; the exercise price for the call is 970; the exercise price for the put is 1010; the standard deviation of the forward price is 0.049962; and the three-month factor is 1.0196. We begin by computing the d_1^F and d_2^F terms for the call:

$$d_1^F = \frac{\ln\left(\frac{F_t}{X}\right) + \left(.5\sigma^2\right)(T-t)}{\sigma\sqrt{T-t}}$$

$$= \frac{\ln\left(\frac{987.3340}{970.00}\right) + \left(0.5 \times 0.049962^2\right)(0.25)}{0.049962 \times \sqrt{0.25}}$$

$$= 0.721522$$

$$d_2^F = d_1^F - \sigma\sqrt{T-t}$$

$$= 0.721522 - 0.024981$$

$$= 0.696541$$

The cumulative normal terms that we require for the call are: $N(d_1^F) = N(0.721522) = 0.764706$; $N(d_2^F) = N(0.696541) = 0.756955$. The value of the call is

$$c_t^F = \frac{1}{1.0196}\left[F_t N\left(d_1^F\right) - X N\left(d_2^F\right)\right]$$

$$= 0.980777\left[987.3340\left(0.764706\right) - 970\left(0.756955\right)\right]$$

$$= 20.374543$$

As the put has a different exercise price, we must compute the d_1 and d_2 terms for it separately:

$$d_1^F = \frac{\ln\left(\frac{F_t}{X}\right) + \left(.5\sigma^2\right)(T-t)}{\sigma\sqrt{T-t}}$$

$$= \frac{\ln\left(\frac{987.3340}{1010.00}\right) + \left(0.5 \times 0.049962^2\right)(0.25)}{0.049962 \times \sqrt{0.25}}$$

$$= -0.896089$$

$$d_2^F = d_1^F - \sigma\sqrt{T-t}$$

$$= -0.896089 - 0.024981$$

$$= -0.921070$$

The cumulative normal terms that we require for the put are: $N(-d_1{}^F) = N(0.896089) = 0.814897$; $N(-d_2{}^F) = N(0.921070) = 0.821493$. The value of the put is

$$p_t^F = \frac{1}{1.0196}\left[XN\left(-d_2^F\right) - F_t\,N\left(-d_1^F\right)\right]$$

$$= 0.980777\left[1010\left(0.821493\right) - 987.3340\left(0.814897\right)\right]$$

$$= 24.649289$$

18. A call and put on three-month LIBOR expire in seven months. The yield curve environment is given by the upward-sloping yield curve of Table 19.7. The notional principal for the option is $100,000,000. The standard deviation of the three-month forward rate is 0.24. Assuming the strike rate on both the put and the call is 5.6 percent, price the two options. What would the prices be if the options were determined and paid in advance? Assume monthly compounding throughout.

We first need to find the forward rate that underlies the option. This would be the forward rate to cover the time from the expiration of the option at month 7 out to the maturity of the underlying instrument, which is month 10:

$$FRF_{7,10} = \frac{Z_{0,10}}{Z_{0,7}} = \frac{1.0493}{1.0339} = 1.014895$$

This forward rate factor covers three months, so the annualized *FRF* is:

$$1.014895^4 = 1.060925$$

for a forward rate of interest of 0.060925. We begin by computing the d_1 and d_2 terms with the relevant cumulative probabilities:

$$d_1^{LIBOR} = \frac{\ln\left(\dfrac{FLIBOR_t}{SR}\right) + \left(.5\,\sigma^2\right)\left(T - t\right)}{\sigma\,\sqrt{T - t}}$$

$$= \frac{\ln\left(\dfrac{0.060925}{0.0560}\right) + 0.5\left(0.24\right)^2\left(0.5833\right)}{0.24\,\sqrt{0.5833}}$$

$$= 0.551512$$

$$d_2^{LIBOR} = d_1^{LIBOR} - \sigma\,\sqrt{T - t}$$

$$= 0.551512 - 0.183298 = 0.368214$$

The relevant cumulative probabilities are: $N(d_1{}^{LIBOR}) = N(0.551512) = 0.709359$; $N(d_2{}^{LIBOR}) = N(0.368214) = 0.643643$; $N(-d_1{}^{LIBOR}) = N(-0.551512) = 0.290641$; and $N(-d_2{}^{LIBOR}) = N(-0.368214) = 0.356357$.

$$c_t^{FLIBOR} = NP \times FRAC \times \frac{1}{Z_{t,T+FRAC}} \left[FLIBOR_t \ N\!\left(d_1^{LIBOR}\right) - SR \ N\!\left(d_2^{LIBOR}\right) \right]$$

$$= \$100{,}000{,}000 \times 0.25 \times \frac{1}{1.0493} \left[0.060925 \left(0.709359\right) - 0.0560 \left(0.643643\right) \right]$$

$$= \$170{,}916.07$$

$$p_t^{LIBOR} = NP \times FRAC \times \frac{1}{Z_{t,T+FRAC}} \left[SR \ N\!\left(-d_2^{LIBOR}\right) - FLIBOR_t \ N\!\left(-d_1^{LIBOR}\right) \right]$$

$$= \$100{,}000{,}000 \times 0.25 \times \frac{1}{1.0493} \left[0.0560 \left(0.356357\right) - 0.060925 \left(0.290641\right) \right]$$

$$= \$53{,}575.93$$

If the option is determined and paid in advance, the option payoffs will occur at month 7, so the zero-coupon factor will be 1.0339. The resulting call and put values are $173,461.87 and $54,373.95, respectively.

19. Consider the downward-sloping yield curve of Table 19.7. Find $FRF_{11,17}$. Find $FRA_{11,17}$ assuming monthly compounding. For a call and put on six-month LIBOR that both expire in eleven months, what is the value of a long call/short put portfolio with a strike rate of 6.00 percent and a notional principal of $20,000,000? Assume that the standard deviation of the six-month forward rate is 0.27. How would you construct a riskless bond from the put, call, and FRA? How does this relate to forward put-call parity?

$$FRF_{11,17} = \frac{Z_{0,17}}{Z_{0,11}} = \frac{1.1134}{1.0728} = 1.037845$$

As this is a factor for six months, the corresponding forward rate is:

$$FRA_{11,17} = 1.037845^2 - 1 = 0.077122$$

We next make the intermediate computations to price the option.

$$d_1^{LIBOR} = \frac{\ln\!\left(\dfrac{FLIBOR_t}{SR}\right) + \left(.5\,\sigma^2\right)(T-t)}{\sigma\,\sqrt{T-t}}$$

$$= \frac{\ln\!\left(\dfrac{0.077122}{0.06}\right) + 0.5\left(0.27\right)^2\left(0.9167\right)}{0.27\,\sqrt{0.9167}}$$

$$= 1.100374$$

$$d_2^{LIBOR} = d_1^{LIBOR} - \sigma\,\sqrt{T-t}$$

$$= 1.100374 - 0.258510 = 0.841864$$

The relevant cumulative probabilities are: $N(d_1^{LIBOR}) = N(1.100374) = 0.864415$; $N(d_2^{LIBOR}) = N(0.841864) = 0.800068$; $N(-d_1^{LIBOR}) = N(-1.100374) = 0.135585$; and $N(-d_2^{LIBOR}) = N(-0.841864) = 0.199932$. The option prices are:

$$c_t^{FLIBOR} = NP \times FRAC \times \frac{1}{Z_{t,T+FRAC}} \left[FLIBOR_t \, N\!\left(d_1^{LIBOR}\right) - SR \, N\!\left(d_2^{LIBOR}\right) \right]$$

$$= \$20,000,000 \times 0.5 \times \frac{1}{1.1134} \left[0.077122\,(0.864415) - 0.06\,(0.800068) \right]$$

$$= \$167,606.73$$

$$p_t^{LIBOR} = NP \times FRAC \times \frac{1}{Z_{t,T+FRAC}} \left[SR \, N\!\left(-d_2^{LIBOR}\right) - FLIBOR_t \, N\!\left(-d_1^{LIBOR}\right) \right]$$

$$= \$20,000,000 \times 0.5 \times \frac{1}{1.1134} \left[0.06\,(0.199932) - 0.077122\,(0.135585) \right]$$

$$= \$13,825.52$$

The long call/short put portfolio with a common strike rate of 0.06 is equivalent to an FRA with a rate of 6 percent. The actual rate in the market for this FRA is 0.077122. One could create a riskless investment by buying the call, selling the put, and entering an FRA to receive-fixed at 0.077122. These transactions will have a payoff in 17 months of:

$$(0.077122 - 0.06) \times \$20,000,000 \times 0.5 = \$171,220.00$$

The present value of this payoff is $\$171,220/1.1134 = \$153,781.21$. This is exactly the cost of the long call/short put payoff. Thus, these transactions synthesize a risk-free bond, and this technique is just a straightforward application of forward put-call parity.

20. The upward-sloping term structure of Table 19.7 prevails. Consider a loan based on six-month LIBOR with a maturity of 24 months and a loan amount of $100,000,000. The loan is to start immediately. Assume that the standard deviation of all relevant interest rates is 0.23.

A. What is the cost of capping this loan at 7 percent?

The loan will have determination dates at months 0, 6, 12, and 18, with corresponding payment dates at 6, 12, 18, and 24 months. Therefore, we need the zero-coupon factors corresponding to each payment date, and we need the forward rates corresponding to each determination date. The zero-coupon factors are: $Z_{0,6} = 1.0289$; $Z_{0,12} = 1.0599$; $Z_{0,18} = 1.0931$; $Z_{0,24} = 1.1287$. The forward rate factors are:

$$FRF_{0,6} = Z_{0,6} = 1.0289$$

$$FRF_{6,12} = \frac{Z_{0,12}}{Z_{0,6}} = \frac{1.0599}{1.0289} = 1.030129$$

$$FRF_{12,18} = \frac{Z_{0,18}}{Z_{0,12}} = \frac{1.0931}{1.0599} = 1.031324$$

$$FRF_{18,24} = \frac{Z_{0,24}}{Z_{0,18}} = \frac{1.1287}{1.0931} = 1.032568$$

These are semi-annual FRFs, so squaring each and subtracting 1.0 gives the annualized forward rates to cover each period as: $FR_{0,6} = 0.058635$; $FR_{6,12} = 0.061166$; $FR_{12,18} = 0.063629$; $FR_{18,24} = 0.066197$.

With these figures, we now turn to pricing the cap, which consists of four call options on LIBOR. The first matures immediately; the other three mature in 6, 12, and 18 months. The following table presents the salient intermediate results:

Option Expiration	Forward Rate	Zero-Coupon Factor	d_1	d_2	$N(d_1)$	$N(d_2)$
0	0.058635	1.0289	−99.99	−99.99	0.00	0.00
6	0.061166	1.0599	−0.748173	−0.910807	0.227178	0.181198
12	0.063629	1.0931	−0.299895	−0.529895	0.382129	0.298092
18	0.066197	1.1287	−0.057457	−0.339148	0.477091	0.367249

Note: The forward rate begins at the option expiration and continues for six months. The zero-coupon factor is for the option expiration plus the six months until the payment is received.

The first option has a strike rate of 7 percent and is at expiration in an environment where the market rate is 0.058635, so it is worthless. The pricing problem is to price the other three calls. We price the option expiring in one year as an example. First, we calculate the d_1 and d_2 terms and their cumulative probabilities:

$$d_1^{LIBOR} = \frac{\ln\left(\dfrac{FLIBOR_t}{SR}\right) + (.5\sigma^2)(T-t)}{\sigma\sqrt{T-t}}$$

$$= \frac{\ln\left(\dfrac{0.063629}{0.07}\right) + 0.5(0.23)^2(1.0)}{0.23\sqrt{1.0}}$$

$$= -0.299895$$

$$d_2^{LIBOR} = d_1^{LIBOR} - \sigma\sqrt{T-t}$$

$$= -0.299895 - 0.23 = -0.529895$$

$N(d_1) = N(-0.299895) = 0.382129$, and $N(d_2) = N(-0.529895) = 0.298092$. The value of the option expiring in 12 months is:

$$c_t^{FLIBOR} = NP \times FRAC \times \frac{1}{Z_{t,T+FRAC}}\left[FLIBOR_t\, N(d_1^{LIBOR}) - SR\, N(d_2^{LIBOR})\right]$$

$$= \$100{,}000{,}000 \times 0.5 \times \frac{1}{1.0931}\left[0.063629(0.382129) - 0.07(0.298092)\right]$$

$$= \$157{,}718.70$$

Applying the same calculations, we find that the option that expires in six months is worth $57,159.95 and the option that expires in 18 months is worth $260,234.57. Given that the first option is worthless, the total cost of capping the loan at 7 percent equals the value of these three calls, for a total of $475,110.95.

B. What is the cost of a floor for this loan at 6 percent?

A floor at 6 percent consists of four put options. The analysis parallels that just applied to the calls, except the first option will have considerable value. We consider it first. By selling this first call, the initiator of the floor agrees to pay the floor rate of 6 percent even though the prevailing rate for the first six months is 0.058635. For the owner of the put, the payoff will occur in six months and will be:

$$(0.06 - 0.058635) \times \$100,000,000 \times 0.5 = \$68,250$$

The value of the put is the present value of this payoff that occurs in six months, which is $\$68,250/1.0289$ $= \$66,332.98$.

The other puts can be priced using the Black model. As with the call options, the intermediate calculations are shown in the following table:

Option Expiration	Forward Rate	Zero-Coupon Factor	d_1	d_2	$N(-d_1)$	$N(-d_2)$
0	0.058635	1.0289	N/A	N/A	N/A	N/A
6	0.061166	1.0599	0.199662	0.037027	0.420873	0.485232
12	0.063629	1.0931	0.370325	0.140325	0.355570	0.444202
18	0.066197	1.1287	0.489776	0.208084	0.312146	0.417582

Note: The forward rate begins at the option expiration and continues for six months. The zero-coupon factor is for the option expiration plus the six months until the payment is received.

Again, as an example, we show the computations for the put expiring in one year:

$$d_1^{LIBOR} = \frac{\ln\left(\dfrac{FLIBOR_t}{SR}\right) + \left(.5\,\sigma^2\right)(T-t)}{\sigma\sqrt{T-t}}$$

$$= \frac{\ln\left(\dfrac{0.063629}{0.06}\right) + 0.5\left(0.23\right)^2(1.0)}{0.23\sqrt{1.0}}$$

$$= 0.370325$$

$$d_2^{LIBOR} = d_1^{LIBOR} - \sigma\sqrt{T-t}$$

$$= 0.370325 - 0.23 = 0.140325$$

$N(-d_1) = N(-0.370325) = 0.355570$; $N(-d_2) = N(-0.140325) = 0.444202$. The value of the put is:

$$p_t^{LIBOR} = NP \times FRAC \times \frac{1}{Z_{t,T+FRAC}}\left[SR\,N\left(-d_2^{LIBOR}\right) - FLIBOR_t\,N\left(-d_1^{LIBOR}\right)\right]$$

$$= \$100,000,000 \times 0.5 \times \frac{1}{1.0931}\left[0.06\left(0.444202\right) - 0.063629\left(0.355570\right)\right]$$

$$= \$184,224.76$$

The put expiring in six months is worth $\$159,015.40$, while the put expiring in 18 months is worth $\$194,548.73$. Together the four puts are worth $\$604,121.87$. Therefore, faced with this yield curve environment, the borrower should receive a payment of $\$604,127.87$ for agreeing to accept a floating rate that cannot go below 6 percent.

C. What is the cost of a 5 –7.5 percent collar for this loan?

The collar consists of a portfolio of puts and calls. The calls have a strike rate of 7.5 percent, while the puts have a strike rate of 5 percent. The first expiration date is immediate, and with a prevailing 6-month rate of 0.058635, both the call and the put are out-of-the-money and expire worthless. They can be ignored. For the calls, we have:

Option Expiration	Forward Rate	Zero-Coupon Factor	d_1	d_2	$N(d_1)$	$N(d_2)$
0	0.058635	1.0289	N/A	N/A	N/A	N/A
6	0.061166	1.0599	−1.172393	−1.335028	0.120520	0.090934
12	0.063629	1.0931	−0.599864	−0.829864	0.274298	0.203308
18	0.066197	1.1287	−0.302381	−0.584072	0.381181	0.279586

Note: The forward rate begins at the option expiration and continues for six months. The zero-coupon factor is for the option expiration plus the six months until the payment is received.

For the puts, the intermediate calculations are:

Option Expiration	Forward Rate	Zero-Coupon Factor	d_1	d_2	$N(-d_1)$	$N(-d_2)$
0	0.058635	1.0289	N/A	N/A	N/A	N/A
6	0.061166	1.0599	1.320712	1.158078	0.093299	0.123416
12	0.063629	1.0931	1.163028	0.933028	0.122409	0.175403
18	0.066197	1.1287	1.137015	0.855323	0.127766	0.196186

Note: The forward rate begins at the option expiration and continues for six months. The zero-coupon factor is for the option expiration plus the six months until the payment is received.

With these intermediate values, the corresponding option values are shown in the following table:

Option Expiration	Call Value	Put Value	Collarlet Value
6	$26,025.12	$21,893.68	$4,131.44
12	100,871.25	44,889.35	55,981.90
18	188,893.84	59,873.00	129,020.84
Totals	$315,790.21	$126,656.03	$189,134.18

The cost of placing a 5–7.5 percent collar on the loan is $189,134.18.

The Swaps Market: Introduction 20

Answers to Questions and Problems

1. Explain the differences between a plain vanilla interest rate swap and a plain vanilla currency swap.

In a plain vanilla interest rate swap, one party pays a fixed rate of interest based on a given nominal amount, while the second party pays a floating rate of interest based on the same nominal amount. No principal is exchanged in the agreement. In a plain vanilla foreign currency swap, there are three different sets of cash flows. First, at the initiation of the swap, the two parties actually do exchange cash. Second, the parties make periodic interest payments to each other during the life of the swap agreement. In the plain vanilla currency swap, one party typically pays dollars at a floating rate, and the payer of the nondollar currency pays a fixed rate. Third, at the termination of the swap, the parties again exchange the principal.

2. Explain the role that the notional principal plays in understanding interest rate swap transactions. Why is this principal amount regarded as only notional? How does it compare with a deliverable instrument in the interest rate futures market?

The deliverable instrument in the interest rate futures market is like the notional principal in determining the scale of the daily settlement cash flows on the futures contracts. For many futures, however, actual delivery is possible but also avoidable. With an interest rate swap, the notional principal is not ever delivered. If we think of the Eurodollar futures contract, which is only cash-settled, the analogy between the notional principal and the underlying $1,000,000 Eurodollar deposit on a futures is quite close.

In interest rate swaps, all of the cash flows are based on a notional amount—notional, because the notional principal is not actually paid. This is essentially a matter of convenience in helping to conceptualize the transaction. The entire contract could be stated without regard to the principal amount. One definition of *notional* is "existing in idea only."

3. Consider a plain vanilla interest rate swap. Explain how the practice of net payments works.

In a typical interest rate swap, each party is scheduled to make payments to the other at certain dates. For the fixed payer, these amounts are certain, but the payments that the floating payer will have to make are unknown at the outset of the transaction. In each period, each party will owe a payment to the other. Rather than make two payments, the party owing the greater amount simply pays the difference between the two obligations.

4. Assume that you are a money manager seeking to increase the yield on your portfolio and that you expect short-term interest rates to rise more than the yield curve would suggest. Would you rather pay a fixed long-term rate and receive a floating short rate, or the other way around? Explain your reasoning.

You would prefer to pay a fixed long-term rate and receive a floating short-term rate. The initial short-term rate that you receive will merely be the spot rate that prevails today. However, if your hunch is correct, the short-term rate will rise more than the market expects, and you will then receive that higher rate. Because your payments are fixed, you will reap a profit from your insight.

5. Assume that the yield curve is flat, that the swaps market is efficient, and that two equally creditworthy counterparties engage in an interest rate swap. Who should pay the higher rate, the party that pays a floating short-term rate or the party that pays a fixed long-term rate? Explain.

They should pay the same. If the yield curve is flat, short-term rates equal long-term rates. Barring a change in rates, the two parties should pay the same amounts to each other in each period. If interest rates change, however, the payments will no longer be the same. If interest rates rise, the party paying the floating payment will lose; if rates fall, the floating payer will benefit.

6. In a currency swap, counterparties exchange the same sums at the beginning and the end of the swap period. Explain how this practice relates to the custom of making interest payments during the life of the swap agreement.

At the outset, the two parties exchange cash denominated in two currencies. Each party pays interest on the currency it receives from the other. Thus, the exchange of currencies is the basis for computing all of the interest payments that will be made over the life of the agreement. The interest payments can be either fixed or floating on both sides of the swap.

7. Explain why a currency swap is also called an "exchange of borrowings."

In a currency swap, both parties pay and both parties receive actual cash at the outset of the transaction. In effect, each has borrowed from the other, so they have exchanged borrowings.

8. What are the two major kinds of swap facilitators? What is the key difference between the roles they play?

They are swap brokers and swap bankers (swap dealers). The swap broker helps complete a swap by bringing counterparties together and perhaps by providing consulting services. The swap broker does not take a financial position in the transaction. By contrast, a swap banker or swap dealer will take a financial position to help the two parties complete their transaction. As the swap market has developed, the swap dealer has come to predominate. Most swap facilitators today are swap dealers who willingly act as counterparties to swaps.

9. In the context of interest rate swaps, "basis risk" is the risk arising from an unanticipated change in the yield relationship between the two instruments involved in the swap. Explain how basis risk affects a swap dealer. Does it affect a swap broker the same way? Explain.

Basis risk affects a swap dealer because it changes the gross profit margin that the dealer will receive. For example, assume that a swap dealer agrees to pay LIBOR and receive the two-year T-note rate plus 60 basis points. This agreement is based upon the yield spread between LIBOR and the two-year T-note when the swap is initiated. This spread can change due to shifts in the term structure, but it can also change due to political disturbances or other causes. Basis risk arises from changes of the second kind. For example, political unrest in Europe might cause LIBOR to rise relative to U.S. Treasury rates. In our example, the dealer would have to pay a higher rate without receiving any correlatively higher rate. This problem does not affect the swap broker, because the swap broker does not take a risk position in the transaction.

10. Assume a swap dealer attempts to function as a pure financial intermediary avoiding all interest rate risk. Explain how such a dealer may yet come to bear interest rate risk.

Ideally, a pure financial intermediary would take no risk position in the transactions it helps to consummate. In the real world, however, there are few things that are pure. A swap dealer might wish to avoid all risk positions, but swap dealers enter many transactions that are likely to leave the dealer with an unbalanced portfolio and an exposure to interest rate risk. Thus, even risk-averse swap dealers often find themselves with undesired risk positions that must be hedged away.

11. Two parties enter an interest rate swap paid in arrears on the following terms: a seven-year tenor, annual payments, $100 million notional principal, a fixed rate of 6.75 percent, with LIBOR as the floating rate. Assume that the following LIBOR spot rates are observed at each of the following dates. From the perspective of the receive-fixed side of the deal, what is the cash flow at each payment date of the swap? What role does the swap rate observed at the termination of the swap (year 7) play in the analysis?

Year (Date of Observation)	One-Year LIBOR (Rate Actually Observed)	Receive Fixed Cash Flow
0	0.0680	$0
1	0.0575	$6,750,000 – $6,800,000 = –$50,000
2	0.0875	$6,750,000 – $5,750,000 = $1,000,000
3	0.0674	$6,750,000 – $8,750,000 = –$2,000,000
4	0.0600	$6,750,000 – $6,740,000 = $10,000
5	0.0700	$6,750,000 – $6,000,000 = $750,000
6	0.0655	$6,750,000 – $7,000,000 = –$250,000
7	0.0685	$6,750,000 – $6,550,000 = $200,000

The observation of LIBOR at year 7 when the swap terminates plays no role in the analysis of the swap, as it affects no payment. This is the case, because each floating payment on the swap is "determined in advance and paid in arrears."

12. A plain vanilla foreign currency swap has just been arranged between parties ABC and XYZ. ABC has agreed to pay dollars based on LIBOR, while XYZ will pay British pounds at a fixed rate of 7 percent. The current exchange rate is £1 = $1.65. The notional principal is £100 million = $165 million. The tenor of the swap is seven years, and the swap has annual payments paid in arrears. Complete the following table showing the **periodic** cash outflows only for each party at each relevant period of the swap. (Ignore the exchange of principal.)

Year of Observation	LIBOR Rate Observed (%)	XYZ Sterling Pay Outflows	ABC Dollar Pay Outflows
0	6.5800	0	0
1	5.870	£7,000,000	0.0658 × $165,000,000 = $10,857,000
2	6.745	£7,000,000	0.0587 × $165,000,000 = $9,685,500
3	6.550	£7,000,000	0.06745 × $165,000,000 = $11,129,250
4	6.100	£7,000,000	0.0655 × $165,000,000 = $10,807,500
5	6.800	£7,000,000	0.0610 × $165,000,000 = $10,065,000
6	6.350	£7,000,000	0.0680 × $165,000,000 = $11,220,000
7	6.450	£7,000,000	0.0635 × $165,000,000 = $10,477,500

13. A swap dealer holds the following portfolio of interest rate swaps, all with annual payments, all with floating payments equal to LIBOR.

Swap	Notional Principal ($ million)	Tenor (years)	Fixed Rate (%)	Dealer's Position
A	20	3	7.000	Receive-Fixed
B	30	5	6.500	Pay-Fixed
C	25	4	7.250	Pay-Fixed
D	50	7	7.300	Receive-Fixed
E	10	2	6.750	Receive-Fixed

A. Complete the following table showing the dealer's position for each payment in each year. For example, the entry for a given year t and a given swap with a fixed rate of 8 percent, and a notional principal of $15 million, would be of the form: $(LIBOR_{t-1} - 8.00) \times \$15,000,000$.

The Swap Dealer's Anticipated Cash Flows

Year	Swap A	Swap B	Swap C	Swap D	Swap E	Dealer's Net Position
1	$1,400,000 − LIBOR$_0$ × $20,000,000	−$1,950,000 + LIBOR$_0$ × $30,000,000	−$1,812,500 + LIBOR$_0$ × $25,000,000	$3,650,000 − LIBOR$_0$ × $50,000,000	$675,000 − LIBOR$_0$ × $10,000,000	$1,962,500 − LIBOR$_0$ × $25,000,000
2	$1,400,000 − LIBOR$_1$ × $20,000,000	−$1,950,000 + LIBOR$_1$ × $30,000,000	−$1,812,500 + LIBOR$_1$ × $25,000,000	$3,650,000 − LIBOR$_1$ × $50,000,000	$675,000 − LIBOR$_1$ × $10,000,000	$1,962,500 − LIBOR$_1$ × $25,000,000
3	$1,400,000 − LIBOR$_2$ × $20,000,000	−$1,950,000 + LIBOR$_2$ × $30,000,000	−$1,812,500 + LIBOR$_2$ × $25,000,000	$3,650,000 − LIBOR$_2$ × $50,000,000	0	$1,287,500 − LIBOR$_2$ × $15,000,000
4	0	−$1,950,000 + LIBOR$_3$ × $30,000,000	−$1,812,500 + LIBOR$_3$ × $25,000,000	$3,650,000 − LIBOR$_3$ × $50,000,000	0	−$112,500 + LIBOR$_3$ × $5,000,000
5	0	−$1,950,000 + LIBOR$_4$ × $30,000,000	0	$3,650,000 − LIBOR$_4$ × $50,000,000	0	$1,700,000 − LIBOR$_4$ × $20,000,000
6	0	0	0	$3,650,000 − LIBOR$_5$ × $50,000,000	0	$3,650,000 − LIBOR$_5$ × $50,000,000
7	0	0	0	$3,650,000 − LIBOR$_6$ × $50,000,000	0	$3,650,000 − LIBOR$_6$ × $50,000,000

B. Appraise the dealer's net risk position.

Across the years, the dealer's current position appears to be weighted toward the receive-fixed side of the swap market. But the dealer's ultimate exposure depends on the LIBOR rates that materialize. For example, in year 1, a $LIBOR_0$ higher than (about) 8 percent gives a net outflow for the year. If LIBOR rates are in the range of the dealer's fixed rate commitments (6.5 to 7.3 percent), then the dealer's position is weighted toward the receive-fixed side of the deal. The major risk facing the dealer is rising LIBOR rates.

C. Recommend transactions that the dealer might use to reduce the net risk.

The dealer needs to protect against rising short-term rates, particularly in the more distant horizon. In the ordinary conduct of swap dealing, the dealer could reduce exposure by acting as the pay-fixed counterparty. This would be particularly desirable for swaps with a tenor of 6–7 years. The dealer might also consider using Eurodollar futures to hedge some of the risk. For example, by selling Eurodollar futures with expirations that match the existing cash flows, the dealer could reduce interest rate risk. Note that any such effort would only protect against rate changes that arise in the future. To fully appraise the risk exposure of this dealer, it would be helpful to know the current term structure.

14. Consider the swap indication schedule shown in the table below. Two parties, A and B, arrange a plain vanilla interest rate swap with the Bank as intermediary. In effect, A and B are counterparties to each other as described below, but their individual swaps are actually negotiated with the Bank. Party A enters a receive-fixed plain vanilla swap, while Party B enters a pay-fixed plain vanilla swap. Both swaps have a notional principal of $50 million and a five-year tenor. Both swaps have annual payments made in arrears.

Sample Swap Indication Pricing
Bank's Fixed Rates: (T-Note Rate Plus Indicated Basis Points)

Maturity (years)	Bank Pays	Bank Receives	T-Note Yields (%)
1	23	27	5.74
2	29	33	5.67
3	33	37	5.60
4	37	40	5.55
5	40	44	5.49

A. For each of the parties, state exactly the commitment that they undertake in their swap agreements.

Party A will receive a fixed rate of the 5-year T-Note rate plus 40 basis points, which equals 5.89 percent of a $50 million notional principal. Thus, the fixed inflow will be $2,945,000 each year. In return, Party A will pay (in arrears) LIBOR × $50,000,000. Party B will pay a fixed rate equal to the T-Note yield of 5.49 percent plus 44 basis points, which equals 5.93 percent of a $50 million notional principal. This fixed payment will be $2,965,000 each year. In return, Party B will receive (in arrears) LIBOR × $50,000,000.

B. What net cash flows will the Bank anticipate at each relevant date? What interest rate risk does the Bank face?

For each year t, the net cash flow for the bank will be:

$$\$2,965,000 - \$2,945,000 + LIBOR_{t-1} \times \$50,000,000 - LIBOR_{t-1} \times \$50,000,000 = \$20,000$$

Based on these two deals, the bank does not face interest rate risk.

C. In the event of default by either party, analyze the interest rate risk position of the Bank.

Default by either party exposes the bank to interest rate risk. If Party A, the receive-fixed counterparty to the bank, defaults, the bank is left to honor its commitments to Party B. This means that the bank must receive-fixed/pay-floating, so the bank is exposed to rising interest rates. If Party B defaults, the bank is left only with its pay-fixed/receive-floating obligations to Party A. If Party B defaults, the bank is exposed to interest rate risk from falling rates.

15. What is the difference between a seasonal and a roller coaster swap?

In a seasonal swap, the notional principal varies according to a fixed plan, typically rising and falling according to a regular plan. In a roller coaster swap, the notional principal of the swap first increases and then amortizes to zero over the remaining life of the swap.

16. Compare and contrast an accreting and an amortizing swap.

In an amortizing swap, the notional principal is reduced over time, while the notional principal in an accreting swap increases over time. Generally, these changes in notional principal occur on a schedule established when the swap agreement is negotiated.

17. "An equity swap is nothing but a commodity swap." Do you agree or disagree with this statement? Explain.

In essence, the statement is correct. A commodity swap involves one party making payments that are fixed relative to the price of a commodity and the other party making payments that float with the value of the underlying commodity. In an equity swap, the agreement has the same structure, except the underlying commodity may be thought of as a stock index or a stock portfolio.

18. Consider two plain vanilla interest rate swaps that have the same notional principal, the same fixed rate, and the same initial floating rate. One swap has a tenor of five years, while the second has a tenor of ten years. Assume that you take a pay-fixed position in the ten-year swap and a receive-fixed position in the five-year swap. What kind of instrument do these transactions create? Explain, assuming that the term structure is flat. What difference would it make if the term structure were not flat?

The net payment from these swaps during the first five years is zero, because the two exactly cancel each other. In each period, the pay-fixed swap requires a fixed payment and a floating receipt. By contrast, the receive-fixed swap generates a fixed receipt and a floating payment. The fixed payments are the same, and the floating payments are the same during the first five years. The pair of swaps, therefore, generates no cash flows in the first five years. After the tenor of the five-year swap, a five-year pay-fixed swap remains. Therefore, from the point of view of the initial contracting, the pair of swaps is equivalent to a forward pay-fixed swap with a tenor of five years that is to be initiated in five years. Notice that this outcome results from the fact that the yield curve is flat, as evidenced by the same fixed rate on two swaps with different tenors. If the term structure were not flat, at least one of the swaps would be an off-market swap, since they both have the same fixed rate. Therefore, you would have to make or receive an up-front payment on each swap that was an off-market swap.

19. "A swaption is essentially a portfolio of options on futures or options on forwards." Is this statement correct? Explain.

This is false. A swaption is a single option on a swap agreement, not a portfolio of options. The swaption may also be regarded as a single option on a portfolio of forward contracts. However, the swap agreement may be viewed as a portfolio of forward contracts.

20. Generally, political unrest in Europe is accompanied by an increase in the yield differential between Eurocurrency deposit rates and U.S. T-bill rates. Explain how to construct a basis swap to profit from such a development. Explain how this might be related to a TED spread in futures.

In a basis swap, both parties make floating rate payments, but the payments are tied to different indexes. Thus, to exploit generally unexpected political turmoil in Europe, one might agree to pay based on U.S. T-bill rates and to receive based on Eurocurrency deposit rates. In a TED spread in the futures market, one trades a T-bill futures contract against a Eurodollar futures contract. In this specific case, a trader would sell the Eurodollar futures and buy the T-bill futures to exploit a widening yield differential. This kind of swap is also known as a cross-currency basis swap when the Eurocurrency is not a Eurodollar.

21. Using interest rate swaps based on U.S. Treasury instruments, explain how to create a yield curve swap that will profit if the yield curve has an upward slope and the curve steepens. Explain how this might be related to the NOB spread in futures.

To profit from steepening yield curve, a trader could agree to receive floating payments based on the yield of a long-term instrument (such as a T-bond) and to make floating payments based on the yield of a short-term instrument (such as a T-bill). If the yield curve steepens, the rate received, the long-term rate, will rise more than the rate being paid, the short-term rate. In the NOB trade in the futures market, a trader trades a T-note futures contract against a T-bond futures contract. Thus, to profit from a steepening yield curve, the trader would sell T-bond futures and buy T-note futures. (The NOB trade is discussed in Chapter 5.)

22. Explain how two fixed-for-floating foreign currency swaps might be combined to create a fixed-for-fixed foreign currency swap.

Two fixed-for-floating currency swaps can be combined to created a fixed-for-fixed swap. Assume that in one swap a firm pays floating payments in Currency A and receives fixed payments in Currency B. The firm also has a second swap in which it makes fixed payments in Currency C and receives floating payments in Currency A. Assuming that these two swaps have the same notional amount, the payments in Currency A offset each other. This leaves the firm receiving fixed payments in Currency B and making fixed payments in Currency A.

Answers to Questions and Problems

1. A trader buys a bond that pays an annual coupon based on LIBOR with a principal amount of $10 million. The actual payment in each year depends on the level of LIBOR observed one year previously. The same trader simultaneously sells a $10 million dollar bond that pays a fixed rate of 7 percent interest and also has an annual coupon. Both bonds have a maturity of five years and are priced at par. The trader also enters a pay-fixed interest rate swap with annual payments, a tenor of five years, and a notional principal of $10 million. For the swap, the fixed rate is 7 percent and the floating rate is LIBOR. The swap also pays in arrears.

A. Construct a time line for each bond showing the payments associated with the bond.

FRN Time Line:

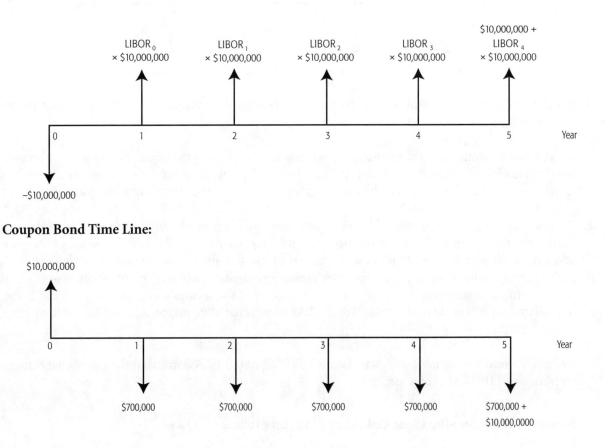

B. Construct a time line showing the net payments resulting from the two bonds.

Bond Portfolio Time Line:

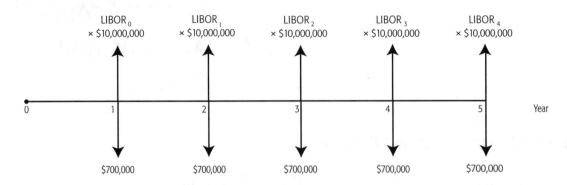

C. Construct a time line showing the payments for the swap.

Pay-Fixed Swap Time Line:

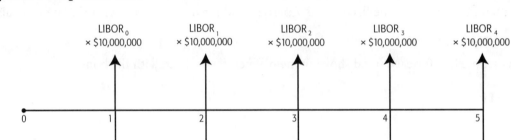

D. Based on the two time lines from parts B and C, what conclusion can you draw regarding the relationship between swaps and bond portfolios?

A plain vanilla swap can be constructed or synthesized by a bond portfolio. This is the case, because the bond portfolio and the swap have identical cash flows. This suggests that the prices of bonds can be used to value swaps, and that swaps can be used to transform cash flow patterns on bond portfolios.

2. Assume that today is December 17, 1998. A firm enters a plain vanilla interest rate swap as the receive-fixed party on a swap with a tenor of one year, quarterly payments at the end of the next four quarters, and a notional principal of $25 million. At the same time, this firm buys a strip of Eurodollar futures for the next four contracts, with 25 contracts per expiration. (Ignore daily settlement; in other words, assume that all futures-related cash flows occur at the expiration of the futures contract, which occurs at the end of each quarter.) At present, $t = 0$, the LIBOR yield curve is flat at 8 percent, and the fixed rate on the swap is also 8 percent.

A. Complete the following table using our familiar $LIBOR_t$ notation. Assume that the Eurodollar futures rate converges to LIBOR at expiration.

Quarter	Net Receive-Fixed Swap Cash Flow	Net Long Futures Cash Flow
0	0	0
1	$(0.08 - LIBOR_0)/4 \times \$25,000,000$	$(0.08 - LIBOR_1)/4 \times \$25,000,000$
2	$(0.08 - LIBOR_1)/4 \times \$25,000,000$	$(0.08 - LIBOR_2)/4 \times \$25,000,000$
3	$(0.08 - LIBOR_2)/4 \times \$25,000,000$	$(0.08 - LIBOR_3)/4 \times \$25,000,000$
4	$(0.08 - LIBOR_3)/4 \times \$25,000,000$	$(0.08 - LIBOR_4)/4 \times \$25,000,000$

All of the futures contracts should be entered at 8 percent, because the yield curve is flat. The payoff on each futures depends on the deviation of spot LIBOR at expiration from the initial futures rate of 8 percent. With daily settlement being considered, the actual flows would have been the same on the futures, but they would have been incurred piecemeal as the futures approached expiration.

B. If this swap had been a determined-in-advance/paid-in-advance swap, what would be the payment at $t = 3$ on the swap?

The payment would be:

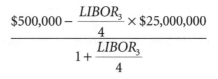

$$\frac{\$500,000 - \dfrac{LIBOR_3}{4} \times \$25,000,000}{1 + \dfrac{LIBOR_3}{4}}$$

C. What conclusion can you draw regarding the relationship between a plain vanilla interest rate swap and a strip of Eurodollar futures?

A strip of Eurodollar futures is very similar to an interest rate swap. However, while they may be conceptually very close, there are important differences in the timing of cash flows, as the table in part A shows. As the answer to part B shows, the Eurodollar strip is even closer to a determined-in-advance/paid-in-advance swap. Even then, the cash flow for the futures and swap are not quite identical. When we consider daily settlement on the futures, the equivalence is degraded even more. Still, a Eurodollar strip and a plain vanilla swap are very similar.

3. Consider a plain vanilla swap from the point of view of the pay-fixed counterparty. The swap has a tenor of five years with annual payments, a notional principal of $50 million, payments in arrears, a floating rate of LIBOR, and a fixed rate of 7 percent. Assume that the pay-fixed counterparty buys a call option with an expiration date of two years. If the call is in-the-money, it pays the observed LIBOR on that date minus 7 percent on a notional principal of $50 million. The pay-fixed party also sells a similar put option: two-year expiration, $50 million notional principal. If the put is in-the-money, the payoff equals 7 percent minus observed LIBOR times the notional principal. In each case, the rate is observed in two years, with the payment date actually occurring one year later. Bearing in mind that the rates observed at year 2 determine the actual cash flow at year 3 on the swap, put, and call:

A. Complete the following table showing the pay-fixed side of the swap, the long call, and the short put for the payment at year 3 as a function of LIBOR observed at year 2.

Payment at Year 3

$LIBOR_2$	Pay-Fixed Net Swap Payment	Long Call Payoff	Short Put Payoff
0.05	$-\$3,500,000 + 0.05 \times \$50,000,000 =$ $-\$1,000,000$	0	$-(0.07 - 0.05) \times \$50,000,000 =$ $-\$1,000,000$
0.06	$-\$3,500,000 + 0.06 \times \$50,000,000 =$ $-\$500,000$	0	$-(0.06 - 0.05) \times \$50,000,000 =$ $-\$500,000$
0.07	$-\$3,500,000 + 0.07 \times \$50,000,000 = \$0$	0	0
0.08	$-\$3,500,000 + 0.08 \times \$50,000,000 =$ $\$500,000$	$(0.08 - 0.07) \times \$50,000,000 =$ $\$500,000$	0
0.09	$-\$3,500,000 + 0.09 \times \$50,000,000 =$ $\$1,000,000$	$(0.09 - 0.07) \times \$50,000,000 =$ $\$1,000,000$	0

B. What does this table show about the relationship between a single swap payment and the call/put portfolio of options?

A single payment on a plain vanilla interest rate swap is equivalent to a call/put portfolio suitably adjusted as to timing and notional principal. A pay-fixed payment is equivalent to a long call/short put portfolio, while a receive-fixed payment is equivalent to a short call/long put portfolio.

C. What does the table show about an entire swap and a possible portfolio of options?

A plain vanilla interest rate swap can be replicated as a strip of call/put portfolios, with each portfolio corresponding to a single payment. This foreshadows the next chapter, which discusses caps (strips of interest rate calls), floors (strips of interest rate puts), and collars (strips of put/call portfolios).

D. If the swap had been a receive-fixed swap, what option position would have replicated the swap payment at year 3?

The same options, but with a short call/long put portfolio, would be equivalent to the receive-fixed payment.

4. Explain how an interest rate swap can be analyzed as a strip of futures. What are some limitations of this analysis?

We have already noted that a swap may be regarded as a portfolio of forward contracts. A swap may also be thought of as a portfolio of forward contracts, or FRAs. For example, a swap agreement with quarterly payments based on Eurodollar deposit rates is essentially similar to a strip of Eurodollar futures contracts in which the futures maturities match the payment dates on the swap. However, a strip of FRAs can exactly replicate the cash flows of a swap, while a strip of futures cannot. The futures contracts involve daily settlement cash flows, for instance, but an FRA and a swap do not. A strip of futures is unlikely to have expiration dates that exactly match the payment dates of a swap, particularly since Eurodollar futures have just four expiration dates per year for the main contracts on the March, June, September, December cycle. Also, swaps are generally paid in arrears, whereas futures are paid as they approach expiration through daily settlement.

5. Today the following rates may be observed: $FRA_{0,3} = 0.0600$; $FRA_{3,6} = 0.0595$; $FRA_{6,9} = 0.0592$; $FRA_{9,12} = 0.0590$; $FRA_{12,15} = 0.0590$; $FRA_{15,18} = 0.0588$; $FRA_{18,21} = 0.0587$; $FRA_{21,24} = 0.0586$, where the subscripts pertain to months. Consider a plain vanilla swap with a tenor of two years, quarterly payments, and a notional principal of $10 million.

A. Compute the discount rates for each payment date on the swap.

$$Z_{0,3} = 1 + FRA_{0,3}/4 = 1 + 0.0600/4 = 1.01500$$

$$Z_{0,6} = Z_{0,3}(1 + FRA_{3,6}/4) = 1.015(1 + 0.0595/4) = 1.030098$$

$$Z_{0,9} = Z_{0,6}(1 + FRA_{6,9}/4) = 1.030098(1 + 0.0592/4) = 1.045343$$

$$Z_{0,12} = Z_{0,9}(1 + FRA_{9,12}/4) = 1.045343(1 + 0.0590/4) = 1.060762$$

$$Z_{0,15} = Z_{0,12}(1 + FRA_{12,15}/4) = 1.060762(1 + 0.0590/4) = 1.076409$$

$$Z_{0,18} = Z_{0,15}(1 + FRA_{15,18}/4) = 1.076409(1 + 0.0588/4) = 1.092232$$

$$Z_{0,21} = Z_{0,18}(1 + FRA_{18,21}/4) = 1.092232(1 + 0.0587/4) = 1.108260$$

$$Z_{0,24} = Z_{0,21}(1 + FRA_{21,24}/4) = 1.108260(1 + 0.0586/4) = 1.124496$$

B. Find the *SFR* for this swap.

$$SFR = \frac{\displaystyle\sum_{n=1}^{N} \frac{FRA_{(n-1)\times MON, n\times MON}}{Z_{0,n\times MON}}}{\displaystyle\sum_{n=1}^{N} \frac{1}{Z_{0,n\times MON}}}$$

For our swap, $MON = 3$. Dealing with the numerator and denominator separately, we have:

$$NUMERATOR = \frac{0.0600}{1.01500} + \frac{0.0595}{1.030098} + \frac{0.0592}{1.045343} + \frac{0.0590}{1.060762}$$

$$+ \frac{0.0590}{1.076409} + \frac{0.0588}{1.092232} + \frac{0.0587}{1.108260} + \frac{0.0586}{1.124496}$$

$$= 0.059113 + 0.057761 + 0.056632 + 0.055620$$

$$+ 0.054812 + 0.053835 + 0.052966 + 0.052112$$

$$= 0.442851$$

$$DENOMINATOR = \frac{1}{1.01500} + \frac{1}{1.030098} + \frac{1}{1.045343} + \frac{1}{1.060762}$$

$$+ \frac{1}{1.076409} + \frac{1}{1.092232} + \frac{1}{1.108260} + \frac{1}{1.124496}$$

$$= 0.985222 + 0.970781 + 0.956624 + 0.942719$$

$$+ 0.929015 + 0.915556 + 0.902315 + 0.889287$$

$$= 7.491519$$

$$SFR = \frac{NUMERATOR}{DENOMINATOR} = \frac{0.442851}{7.491519} = 0.059114$$

C. Find the *APPROXSFR* for this swap.

$$(1 + APPROXSFR)^{T} = \prod_{n=1}^{N}\left(1 + FRA_{(n-1)\times MON, n\times MON}\right)^{PART}$$

$$= \left(1.0600^{0.25}\right)\left(1.0595^{0.25}\right)\left(1.0592^{0.25}\right)\left(1.0590^{0.25}\right)$$
$$\left(1.0590^{0.25}\right)\left(1.0588^{0.25}\right)\left(1.0587^{0.25}\right)\left(1.0586^{0.25}\right)$$

$$= 1.121693$$

$$APPROXSFR = 0.059100$$

D. Assume that the same swap is to be negotiated as an off-market swap in which the receive-fixed party will receive 7 percent. What payment at the initiation of the swap will make the transaction a fair deal?

The swap will be a "fair deal" if the present values of the two sides of the swap are equal. We have just found that the *SFR* for the plain vanilla swap is less than 6 percent. If the swap is to be negotiated with a fixed rate of 7 percent, the fixed rate payer will be paying too much. To make the off-market swap a fair deal, the receive-fixed party must make, and the pay-fixed party must receive, a payment of X. The present values of the payments made by the receive-fixed party, including our payment X, are:

$$X + PART \times NP \times$$

$$\left(\frac{FRA_{0,3}}{Z_{0,3}} + \frac{FRA_{3,6}}{Z_{0,6}} + \frac{FRA_{6,9}}{Z_{0,9}} + \frac{FRA_{9,12}}{Z_{0,12}} + \frac{FRA_{12,15}}{Z_{0,15}} + \frac{FRA_{15,18}}{Z_{0,18}} + \frac{FRA_{18,21}}{Z_{0,21}} + \frac{FRA_{21,24}}{Z_{0,24}} \right)$$

For the pay-fixed party, now paying 7 percent, the present value will be:

$$PART \times NP \times 0.07 \times$$

$$\left(\frac{1}{Z_{0,3}} + \frac{1}{Z_{0,6}} + \frac{1}{Z_{0,9}} + \frac{1}{Z_{0,12}} + \frac{1}{Z_{0,15}} + \frac{1}{Z_{0,18}} + \frac{1}{Z_{0,21}} + \frac{1}{Z_{0,24}} \right)$$

For both of these terms, we have already found the quantities in parentheses in part B of the question, where we found the *SFR* for the plain vanilla swap. They are equal to the *NUMERATOR* and *DENOMINATOR* computed there. Therefore, the fair deal will meet the condition:

$$X + PART \times NP \times 0.442851 = PART \times NP \times 0.07 \times 7.491519$$

From the statement of the question, we know: $PART = 0.25$ and $NP = \$10,000,000$. Therefore, we have:

$$X = 0.25 \times \$10,000,000 \left[0.07 (7.491519) - 0.442851 \right] = \$203,888$$

The receive-fixed party must pay the pay-fixed party \$203,888 at the outset of the swap to make the off-market swap a fair deal. This \$203,888 compensates the pay-fixed party for paying about 1 percent per annum more than the *SFR* on a plain vanilla swap. This makes sense intuitively, because the pay-fixed party is paying about 1 percent over the *SFR* on \$10,000,000 for each of two years, or something over \$100,000 per year.

6. Today in the market you observe the following discount rates, where the subscripts indicate months: $Z_{0,3}$ = 1.0240; $Z_{0,6}$ = 1.0475; $Z_{0,9}$ = 1.0735; $Z_{0,12}$ = 1.0976; $Z_{0,15}$ = 1.1193; $Z_{0,18}$ = 1.1472; $Z_{0,21}$ = 1.1655; $Z_{0,24}$ = 1.1872. Compute all possible three-month FRA rates.

$$1.0240 = 1 + FRA_{0,3}/4; \quad FRA_{0,3} = 4 \times 0.0240 = 0.09600$$

In general, for FRAs to cover a fraction of the year equal to *PART*, where $a > 0$:

$$FRA_{a,b} = \left(\frac{Z_{0,b}}{Z_{0,a}} - 1 \right) PART$$

Therefore,

$$FRA_{3,6} = (Z_{0,6}/Z_{0,3} - 1) \times 4 = (1.0475 / 1.0240 - 1) \times 4 = 0.091797$$
$$FRA_{6,9} = (Z_{0,9}/Z_{0,6} - 1) \times 4 = (1.0735/1.0475 - 1) \times 4 = 0.099284$$
$$FRA_{9,12} = (Z_{0,12}/Z_{0,9} - 1) \times 4 = (1.0976/1.0735 - 1) \times 4 = 0.089800$$
$$FRA_{12,15} = (Z_{0,15}/Z_{0,12} - 1) \times 4 = (1.1193/1.0976 - 1) \times 4 = 0.079082$$

$$FRA_{15, 18} = (Z_{0, 18}/Z_{0, 15} - 1) \times 4 = (1.1472/1.1193 - 1) \times 4 = 0.099705$$
$$FRA_{18, 21} = (Z_{0, 21}/Z_{0, 18} - 1) \times 4 = (1.1655/1.1472 - 1) \times 4 = 0.063808$$
$$FRA_{21, 24} = (Z_{0, 24}/Z_{0, 21} - 1) \times 4 = (1.1872/1.1655 - 1) \times 4 = 0.074474$$

7. A zero-coupon swap is a swap in which the fixed rate is zero. Instead of making periodic coupon payments, the fixed rate payer makes a single large payment at the termination of the swap. Zero-coupon swaps may be either interest rate swaps in any currency (with no exchange of principal) or foreign currency swaps (with the customary exchange of principal). Using one zero-coupon swap (either an interest rate or a foreign currency swap), and one bond of any type, construct a synthetic zero-coupon bond that pays German marks, and has a principal amount of DM 100 million and a maturity of five years. The German mark yield curve is flat at 6.3 percent. Assume annual payments throughout.

A. Find the cash flows associated with the German zero and draw a time line for this instrument.

With a flat yield curve at 6.3 percent and annual compounding, the five-year zero-coupon factor is $(1.063)^5 = 1.357270$. A zero-coupon bond to pay DM 100,000,000 in five years would cost DM 73,677,296.

Zero-Coupon DM Bond:

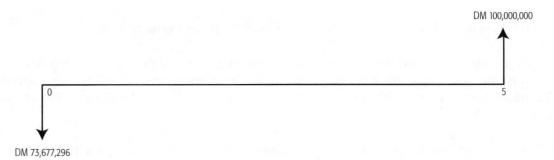

B. Draw time lines for the two instruments that will replicate the German zero, showing the cash flow amounts at each time, under the assumption of constant interest rates.

DM FRN:

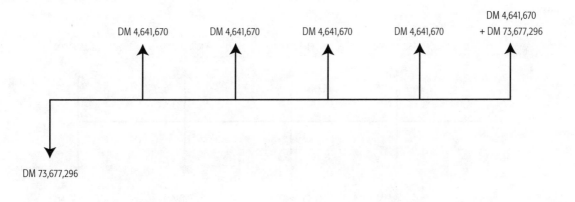

Zero-Coupon Receive-Fixed DM Interest Rate Swap:

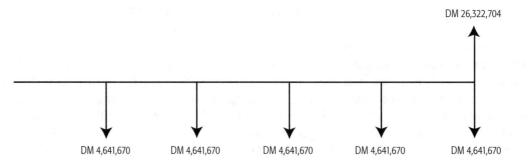

C. State the transactions necessary to replicate the German zero.

Replicating the DM zero-coupon bond can be accomplished by buying a DM FRN with a maturity of five years and with an initial outlay of DM 73,677,296. At present rates, the annual coupon payment would be DM 4,641,670. Also, one would enter a DM zero-coupon interest rate swap to receive a fixed payment at the termination of the swap in the amount of DM 26,322,704 and to make five floating rate payments at annual intervals. At present rates, the annual floating payment would be DM 4,641,670.

D. Explain how the replication you have created still works if interest rates change.

If rates change, the floating payments will vary on both the FRN and the zero-coupon interest rate swap. However, they will still be the same quantity on the two instruments and will still exactly offset each other. Therefore, the replication will be maintained with a net outflow at $t = 0$ of DM 73,677,296 and a net inflow at $t = 5$ of DM 100,000,000.

8. Consider an already existing fixed-for-fixed foreign currency swap that was negotiated at an exchange rate of $1 = ¥111 with a notional principal of $100 million = ¥11.1 billion yen. The swap has quarterly payments and a remaining tenor of one year. The dollar fixed rate is 7 percent, and the yen fixed rate is 6.8 percent. Assume that the following foreign exchange rates are observed now, where $_{\$,¥}FX_{x,y}$ is the value of the dollar in terms of yen for a contract initiated at month x with delivery at month y: $_{\$,¥}FX_{0,3} = 115$; $_{\$,¥}FX_{0,6} = 117$; $_{\$,¥}FX_{0,9} = 119$; $_{\$,¥}FX_{0,12} = 120$.

A. Prepare a time line showing the remaining payments on the swap from the point of view of the dollar payer.

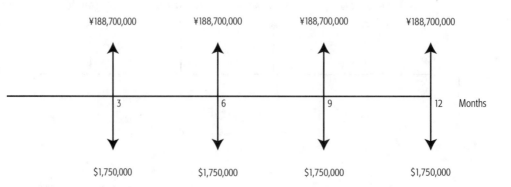

B. Calculate the present value of the swap from the point of view of the dollar payer if the following U.S. interest rates hold: $FRA_{0,3} = 0.0635$; $FRA_{3,6} = 0.0640$; $FRA_{6,9} = 0.0642$; $FRA_{9,12} = 0.0645$.

Given the forward exchange rates stated above, the dollar value of each of the four yen payments is:

Payment 1: ¥188,700,000/115 = $1,640,870
Payment 2: ¥188,700,000/117 = $1,612,821
Payment 3: ¥188,700,000/119 = $1,585,714
Payment 4: ¥188,700,000/120 = $1,572,500

The net dollar payments from the point of view of the dollar payer are:

Net Payment 1: = $1,640,870 − $1,750,000 = −$109,130
Net Payment 2: = $1,612,821 − $1,750,000 = −$137,179
Net Payment 3: = $1,585,714 − $1,750,000 = −$164,286
Net Payment 4: = $1,572,500 − $1,750,000 = −$177,500

The discount rates are as follows:

$Z_{0,3} = 1 + 0.0635/4 = 1.015875$
$Z_{0,6} = 1.015875\ (1 + 0.0640/4) = 1.032129$
$Z_{0,9} = 1.032129\ (1 + 0.0642/4) = 1.048695$
$Z_{0,12} = 1.048695\ (1 + 0.0645/4) = 1.065605$

From the point of view of the dollar payer, the present value (PV) of the remaining swap commitment is:

$$PV = \frac{-\$109,130}{1.015875} - \frac{\$137,179}{1.032129} - \frac{\$164,286}{1.048695} - \frac{\$177,500}{1.065605}$$

$$= -\$107,425 - \$132,909 - \$156,658 - \$166,572$$

$$= -\$563,564$$

C. How does the solution of this problem relate to the interest rate parity theorem?

The solution evaluated the swap from the point of view of the U.S. dollar payer. In doing so, each yen cash flow was converted into dollars at the foreign exchange forward rate corresponding to the timing of the yen flow. These converted dollars were then discounted at the U.S. dollar rate. In essence, the combination of the U.S. interest rate with the forward foreign exchange rate takes account of the interest rate parity between the dollar and the yen. The solution did not need to confront the yen interest rates directly, because they were effectively considered by using the U.S. interest rate and the forward foreign exchange rates.

9. Today you observe the following U.S. interest rates: $FRA_{0,3} = 0.0650$; $FRA_{3,6} = 0.0655$; $FRA_{6,9} = 0.0659$; $FRA_{9,12} = 0.0661$, where the subscripts pertain to months. Consider a plain vanilla interest rate swap with quarterly payments and a tenor of one year with a notional principal of $50 million and a zero-cost collar that parallels this swap, having four payments and a remaining life of one year, with a notional principal of $50 million. The collar has a common strike rate of 6.5 percent for the put (floor) and the call (cap).

A. Without computation, determine whether the collar is fairly priced. Explain.

The collar cannot be fairly priced, since the strike rate is 6.50 percent, the price of the collar is zero, and the term structure lies above that rate. Because rates start at 6.5 percent and rise from there, the SFR must exceed 6.50 percent, and the zero-cost collar should have a strike rate that equals the SFR.

B. Find the SFR for a plain vanilla swap.

The discount rates are as follows:

$$Z_{0,3} = 1 + 0.0650/4 = 1.016250$$
$$Z_{0,6} = 1.016250 \ (1 + 0.0655/4) = 1.032891$$
$$Z_{0,9} = 1.032891 \ (1 + 0.0659/4) = 1.049908$$
$$Z_{0,12} = 1.049908 \ (1 + 0.0661/4) = 1.067258$$

Next, we apply Equation 20.5, treating the numerator and denominator separately for convenience:

$$NUMERATOR = \frac{0.0650}{1.016250} + \frac{0.0655}{1.032891} + \frac{0.0659}{1.049908} + \frac{0.0661}{1.067258} = 0.252076$$

$$DENOMINATOR = \frac{1}{1.016250} + \frac{1}{1.032891} + \frac{1}{1.049908} + \frac{1}{1.067258} = 3.841611$$

$$SFR = \frac{0.252076}{3.841611} = 0.065617$$

C. Explain an arbitrage strategy based on the facts presented, being sure to state the transactions you would make to exploit the arbitrage.

A long call/short put option portfolio with both options having a common strike rate pays (LIBOR – strike rate) × notional principal. A plain vanilla pay-fixed interest rate swap pays (LIBOR – SFR) × notional principal. These values would require adjustment for swaps with payment intervals other than one year. In our problem, the common strike rate is 6.5 percent, the SFR is 6.5617 percent, and payments occur quarterly.

If we buy the zero-cost collar with a strike rate of 6.5 percent and sell the pay-fixed swap with an SFR of 6.5617 percent, our cost will be zero. (Selling a pay-fixed swap is equivalent to entering a receive-fixed swap.) The payoff on a single date will be as follows:

Collar: (LIBOR/4 – 0.065/4) × \$50,000,000
Receive-Fixed Swap: (0.065617/4 – LIBOR/4) × \$50,000,000
Combined Position: (0.065617/4 – 0.065/4) × \$50,000,000 = \$7,712.50

Therefore, this arbitrage strategy will yield four inflows of \$7,712.50 with no outflows.

D. Compute the present value of your arbitrage transactions.

$$PV = \frac{\$7,712.50}{1.016250} + \frac{\$7,712.50}{1.032891} + \frac{\$7,712.50}{1.049908} + \frac{\$7,712.50}{1.067258} = \$29,628.43$$

10. For a fairly priced plain vanilla swap with annual payments and a tenor of five years, the fixed rate is 6.44 percent. The yield curve is flat. You also are aware of two bonds available in the marketplace, each with annual coupon payments and maturities of five years. The first is a coupon bond with a coupon rate of 8.25 percent. The second is an FRN paying LIBOR + 2 percent. Assume zero default risk for all instruments.

A. Without computation, but by inspecting the information given, which bond should be worth more?

With a flat yield curve, all FRA rates and discount rates will be equal to the fairly priced swap fixed rate of 6.44 percent. The FRN will, therefore, pay 8.44 percent, so it should be worth more than the coupon bond paying 8.25 percent.

B. Compute the no-arbitrage price difference between the two bonds.

Assuming a par value of 100 on both bonds, the FRN will pay 8.44 − 8.25 = 0.19 more each period. Therefore, the price differential should be equal to the present value of those flows, discounted at the rate of 6.44 percent.

$$PV = \frac{0.19}{1.0644} + \frac{0.19}{1.0644^2} + \frac{0.19}{1.0644^3} + \frac{0.19}{1.0644^4} + \frac{0.19}{1.0644^5} = 0.790859$$

C. Explain what arbitrage transactions you would enter if the price difference between the bonds were 6 percent of par. (Assume that the truly more valuable bond is priced higher than the truly less valuable bond, but the price difference is 6 percent instead of the no-arbitrage price difference you found in part B of this question.) Draw a time line for each instrument assuming a par value of 100. Hint: You will need a third instrument, some kind of interest rate swap, to ensure that the transaction is an arbitrage opportunity rather than a speculation.

The price difference should be 0.79 percent of par, not 6 percent. Therefore, if the FRN is priced so much higher than the coupon bond, we can create an arbitrage opportunity by selling the overpriced instrument and buying the underpriced one. This requires selling the FRN and buying the coupon bond. Doing only this leaves a risk exposure and is not arbitrage, however.

Instead, the arbitrageur should: sell the FRN, buy the coupon bond, and initiate a pay-fixed plain vanilla interest rate swap, as shown below, in a diagram assuming par values of 100 on each instrument:

Sell FRN:

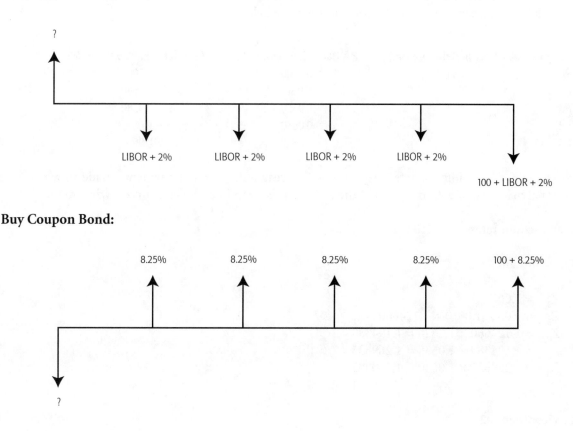

Buy Coupon Bond:

Initiate Pay-Fixed Swap:

The prices of the bonds are unknown, but the price difference is 6 percent of par by assumption, so there is a net inflow of 6 percent of par at $t = 0$. At each coupon date, the net cash flow is:

$$-\text{LIBOR} - 2\% + 8.25\% + \text{LIBOR} - 6.44\% = -0.19\%$$

As we have already seen, the present value of those five coupon flows is 0.790859 percent of par. At maturity of the bonds, 100 percent of par is due on the FRN and 100 percent of par is received on the coupon bond for a net zero payment. Therefore, the arbitrage has a present value of 6 percent of par from the price differential of the bonds, less 0.790859 percent of par for the coupon outflows. Also, this is an arbitrage because all uncertainty has been eliminated with respect to interest rates.

11. Consider two term structure environments, one in which the yield curve rises and one in which the yield curve falls by the same amount, as shown in the table below.

Maturity (subscripts pertain to years)	FRA Rates Environment #1	FRA Rates Environment #2
$FRA_{0,1}$	0.0600	0.0600
$FRA_{1,2}$	0.0610	0.0590
$FRA_{2,3}$	0.0620	0.0580
$FRA_{3,4}$	0.0630	0.0570
$FRA_{4,5}$	0.0640	0.0560

A. For a plain vanilla interest rate swap with a five-year tenor, annual payments made in arrears, and a notional principal of $30 million, find the *SFR* for this swap in each yield curve environment.

The discount rates are as follows:

Environment #1

$Z_{0,1} = 1.06$
$Z_{0,2} = 1.06 \times 1.0610 = 1.124660$
$Z_{0,3} = 1.124660 \times 1.0620 = 1.194389$
$Z_{0,4} = 1.194389 \times 1.0630 = 1.269635$
$Z_{0,5} = 1.269635 \times 1.0640 = 1.350892$

Environment #2

$Z_{0,1} = 1.06$
$Z_{0,2} = 1.06 \times 1.0590 = 1.122540$
$Z_{0,3} = 1.122540 \times 1.0580 = 1.187647$

$$Z_{0,4} = 1.187647 \times 1.0570 = 1.255343$$
$$Z_{0,5} = 1.255343 \times 1.0560 = 1.325642$$

For the two environments, the *SFR*s are:

$$SFR_1 = \frac{\dfrac{0.0600}{1.06} + \dfrac{0.0610}{1.124660} + \dfrac{0.0620}{1.194389} + \dfrac{0.0630}{1.269635} + \dfrac{0.0640}{1.350892}}{\dfrac{1}{1.06} + \dfrac{1}{1.124660} + \dfrac{1}{1.194389} + \dfrac{1}{1.269635} + \dfrac{1}{1.350892}} = 0.061879$$

$$SFR_2 = \frac{\dfrac{0.0600}{1.06} + \dfrac{0.0590}{1.122540} + \dfrac{0.0580}{1.187647} + \dfrac{0.0570}{1.255343} + \dfrac{0.0560}{1.325642}}{\dfrac{1}{1.06} + \dfrac{1}{1.122540} + \dfrac{1}{1.187647} + \dfrac{1}{1.255343} + \dfrac{1}{1.325642}} = 0.058112$$

B. Find the present value of each payment from the point of view of the pay-fixed party in each environment. Find the sum of the present value of the payments in each environment.

Present Value of Pay-Fixed Cash Flows–Environment #1

Payment #	Amount	Zero-Coupon Factor	Present Value
1	$(-0.061879 + 0.06) \times \$30,000,000 = -\$56,370.72$	1.06	−$53,179.92
2	$(-0.061879 + 0.0610) \times \$30,000,000 = -\$26,370.72$	1.124660	−$23,447.72
3	$(-0.061879 + 0.0620) \times \$30,000,000 = \$3,630.00$	1.194389	$3,038.61
4	$(-0.061879 + 0.0630) \times \$30,000,000 = \$33,629.28$	1.269635	$26,487.35
5	$(-0.061879 + 0.0640) \times \$30,000,000 = \$63,629.28$	1.350892	$47,101.68

Present Value of Pay-Fixed Cash Flows–Environment #2

Payment #	Amount	Zero-Coupon Factor	Present Value
1	$(-0.058112 + 0.06) \times \$30,000,000 = \$56,647.89$	1.06	$53,441.41
2	$(-0.058112 + 0.0590) \times \$30,000,000 = \$26,647.89$	1.12254	$23,738.93
3	$(-0.058112 + 0.0580) \times \$30,000,000 = -\$3,352.11$	1.187647	−$2,822.48
4	$(-0.058112 + 0.0570) \times \$30,000,000 = -\$33,352.11$	1.255343	−$26,568.12
5	$(-0.058112 + 0.0560) \times \$30,000,000 = -\$63,352.11$	1.325642	−$47,789.74

The present values necessarily sum to zero in each environment.

C. Evaluate the default risk on these two swaps from the point of view of a swap bank in which the swap bank pays fixed, assuming a relatively stable yield curve environment.

As with any fairly priced plain vanilla swap, the present value of all the payments is zero when the swap is initiated. However, the pattern of positive and negative present value payments is quite different. From the point of view of the pay-fixed party, the positive present value payments occur later in Environment #1 and earlier in Environment #2. This suggests that Environment #1 is riskier for a pay-fixed party, because the pay-fixed party expects to lose on the early payments and make it up on the later. If the pay-fixed party suffers a default after two payments in Environment #1, for example, he never gets any positive present value payments. This contrasts markedly with Environment #2.

D. Explain how any observed difference in default risk from the point of view of the bank might affect the bank's pricing of the swap.

A rising yield curve (Environment #1) exposes a pay-fixed party to greater default risk than a falling yield curve environment, because of the timing of positive and negative present value cash flows in each situation. Therefore, we might expect a swap dealer to demand slightly more favorable terms to take the pay-fixed side of a swap in a rising yield curve environment.

Note: The remaining questions all use the same interest rate data, the same foreign exchange data, the same notional principal, and the same tenor.

Interest Rate Data: Problem 12
Foreign Exchange Data: Problem 13
Swap Terms: Semiannual payments; $100,000,000 = ¥13,350,000,000 notional principal
Tenor: 5 years

12. The following data pertain to U.S. and Japanese interest rates over the next five years for semiannual periods. Complete the following tables.

U.S. Rates

Maturity (Semiannual Periods)	Annualized Par Yield	Zero-Coupon Factor	Forward Rate Factor
1	0.067700	1.03385000	1.03385000
2	0.068504	1.06969145	1.03466794
3	0.069367	1.10776466	1.03559271
4	0.070146	1.14800662	1.03632717
5	0.070294	1.18872682	1.03547035
6	0.071231	1.23416869	1.03822735
7	0.071893	1.28132127	1.03820594
8	0.071988	1.32793480	1.03637926
9	0.072105	1.37654384	1.03660499
10	0.072293	1.42770275	1.03716475

Japanese Rates

Maturity (Semiannual Periods)	Annualized Par Yield	Zero-Coupon Factor	Forward Rate Factor
1	0.048327	1.02416350	1.02416350
2	0.049302	1.04992199	1.02515076
3	0.049428	1.07600705	1.02484475
4	0.050119	1.10414448	1.02614986
5	0.050766	1.13369515	1.02676341
6	0.051651	1.16569027	1.02822197
7	0.052546	1.19976103	1.02922797
8	0.053157	1.23451641	1.02896859
9	0.053170	1.26740872	1.02664388
10	0.053356	1.30243902	1.02763931

Values for these tables were found by applying the bootstrapping method.

13. Find the foreign exchange rates between the U.S. dollar and the Japanese yen for the next ten semiannual periods consistent with the interest rates of problem 12, and complete the following table.

Dollar/Yen Exchange Rates

Maturity (Semiannual Periods)	$ per Yen	Yen per $
0	0.00749064	133.500000
1	0.00756148	132.249192
2	0.00763168	131.032725
3	0.00771172	129.672796
4	0.00778820	128.399336

5	0.00785425	127.319667
6	0.00793067	126.092691
7	0.00799985	125.002294
8	0.00805747	124.108458
9	0.00813565	122.915856
10	0.00821106	121.786982

Given the spot exchange rates and the term structures for the two countries, the forward exchange rates of the dollar versus the yen can be found by applying the interest rate parity theorem. As an example, we compute the value of the dollar in terms of yen for a horizon of 3.5 years (7 semiannual periods). From Equation 21.1, we have:

$$_x Z_{t, T} = {}_{x, y}FX_{t, t} \times {}_y Z_{t, T} \times {}_{y, x}FX_{t, T}$$

In terms of our example, we have:

$_x Z_{t, T}$ = the 7-period zero-coupon factor for the United States = 1.28132127
$_{x, y}FX_{t, t}$ = the spot exchange rate = 133.5
$_y Z_{t, T}$ = the 7-period zero-coupon factor for Japan = 1.19976103
$_{y, x}FX_{t, T}$ = the unknown foreign exchange forward rate = 125.0022935

The table shows all of the resulting calculations.

14. Based on the U.S. rates of problem 12, find the *SFR* for a plain vanilla U.S. interest rate swap with a tenor of five years, semiannual payments, and a notional principal of $100,000,000.

For a plain vanilla interest rate swap, the *SFR* is given by Equation 21.13:

$$SFR = \frac{\sum_{n=1}^{N} \dfrac{FRA_{(n-1) \times MON, n \times MON}}{Z_{0, n \times MON}}}{\sum_{n=1}^{N} \dfrac{1}{Z_{0, n \times MON}}}$$

The following table shows the intermediate computations:

U.S. Rates

Maturity (Semiannual Periods)	Zero-Coupon Factor	$1/(Z_{0, t})$	Forward Rate $FRA_{t-1, t}$	$FRA_{t-1, t}/Z_{0, t}$
1	1.03385000	0.96725831	0.03385000	0.03274169
2	1.06969145	0.93484902	0.03466794	0.03240929
3	1.10776466	0.90271881	0.03559271	0.03213021
4	1.14800662	0.87107512	0.03632717	0.03164369
5	1.18872682	0.84123617	0.03547035	0.02983894
6	1.23416869	0.81026201	0.03822735	0.03097417
7	1.28132127	0.78044439	0.03820594	0.02981761
8	1.32793480	0.75304902	0.03637926	0.02739537
9	1.37654384	0.72645707	0.03660499	0.02659195
10	1.42770275	0.70042591	0.03716475	0.02603115
SUMS		8.28777582		0.29957408

For the plain vanilla swap, the semiannual *SFR* = 0.29957408/0.828777582 = 0.03614650, so the annualized *SFR* equals 2 × 0.03614650 = 0.07229300. Note also that the *SFR* on the swap will equal the coupon rate on a fixed coupon bond of the same maturity that trades at par. From the completed table of problem 12, that rate is 0.072293.

15. Based on the Japanese rates of problem 12, find the *SFR* for a plain vanilla Japanese interest rate swap with a tenor of five years, a notional principal of ¥13,350,000,000, and semiannual payments.

   The *SFR* on the swap will equal the coupon rate on a fixed coupon bond of the same maturity that trades at par. From the completed table of problem 12, that rate is 0.053356. It can also be computed directly as illustrated for the U.S. swap in the preceding problem.

16. Complete the following tables, based on the U.S. and Japanese interest rates of problem 12, the foreign exchange rates of question 13, and the *SFR*s computed in questions 14 and 15. The following letters correspond to column labels in the tables.

A. Cash flows on a U.S. semiannual coupon bond with a five-year maturity, a par value of $100,000,000, which trades at par.

B. The cash flows consistent with the term structure of problem 12 for a semiannual U.S. dollar floating rate bond with a par value of $100,000,000 and a maturity of five years.

C. The cash flows on the receive-fixed side of the U.S. dollar interest rate swap computed in question 14.

D. The cash flows consistent with the term structure on the pay-floating side of the U.S. dollar interest rate swap computed in question 14.

E. The cash flows on a Japanese semiannual coupon bond with a five-year maturity, a par value of ¥13,350,000,000, which trades at par.

F. The cash flows consistent with the term structure of problem 12 on a semiannual Japanese yen floating rate bond with a par value of ¥13,350,000,000 and a maturity of five years.

G. The cash flows on the pay-fixed side of the Japanese yen interest rate swap computed in question 15.

H. The cash flows on the pay-floating side of the Japanese yen interest rate swap computed in question 15.

U.S. Instruments

Maturity (Semiannual Periods)	A Buy Semiannual Bond	B Sell FRN	C Receive-Fixed Interest Rate Swap	D Pay-Floating Interest Rate Swap
0	−$100,000,000	$100,000,000	$0	$0
1	3,614,650	−3,385,000	3,614,650	−3,385,000
2	3,614,650	−3,466,794	3,614,650	−3,466,750
3	3,614,650	−3,559,271	3,614,650	−3,559,346
4	3,614,650	−3,632,717	3,614,650	−3,632,720
5	3,614,650	−3,547,035	3,614,650	−3,547,017
6	3,614,650	−3,822,735	3,614,650	−3,822,745
7	3,614,650	−3,820,594	3,614,650	−3,820,546
8	3,614,650	−3,637,926	3,614,650	−3,637,964
9	3,614,650	−3,660,499	3,614,650	−3,660,495
10	103,614,650	−103,716,475	3,614,650	−3,716,481
Present Value of Cash Flows	0	0	$29,957,408	−$29,957,408

Japanese Instruments

Maturity (Semiannual Periods)	E Buy Semiannual Bond	F Sell FRN	G Receive-Fixed Interest Rate Swap	H Pay-Floating Interest Rate Swap
0	−¥13,350,000,000	¥13,350,000,000	¥0	¥0
1	356,151,300	−322,589,400	356,151,300	−322,589,400
2	356,151,300	−335,765,850	356,151,300	−335,765,850
3	356,151,300	−331,680,750	356,151,300	−331,680,750
4	356,151,300	−349,102,500	356,151,300	−349,102,500
5	356,151,300	−357,286,050	356,151,300	−357,286,050
6	356,151,300	−376,763,700	356,151,300	−376,763,700
7	356,151,300	−390,193,800	356,151,300	−390,193,800
8	356,151,300	−386,736,150	356,151,300	−386,736,150
9	356,151,300	−355,697,400	356,151,300	−355,697,400
10	13,706,151,300	−13,718,980,650	356,151,300	−368,980,650
Present Value of Cash Flows	0	0	¥3,099,999,852	¥3,099,999,852

For the floating instruments, the cash flow consistent with the term structure equals the forward rate times the notional principal, being careful to adjust the floating rate for the periodicity of the swap payments. We already have the semiannual FRFs in the table for problem 12. So, using those forward rates and the notional principal of $100,000,000, the following table gives the payments on the U.S. dollar FRN:

U.S. Rates

Maturity (Semiannual Periods)	Forward Rate $FRA_{t-1,\,t}$	Floating Payment $FRA_{t-1,\,t} \times NP$
1	0.03385000	3,385,000
2	0.03466794	3,466,794
3	0.03559271	3,559,271
4	0.03632717	3,632,717
5	0.03547035	3,547,035
6	0.03822735	3,822,735
7	0.03820594	3,820,594
8	0.03637926	3,637,926
9	0.03660499	3,660,499
10	0.03716475	3,716,475

For the floating rate payments on the Japanese bond, the Japanese forward rates are used, along with the notional principal of ¥13,350,000,000.

Japanese Rates

Maturity (Semiannual Periods)	Forward Rate $FRA_{t-1,\,t}$	Floating Payment $FRA_{t-1,\,t} \times NP$
1	0.02416350	322,582,725
2	0.02515076	335,762,646
3	0.02484475	331,677,412
4	0.02614986	349,100,631
5	0.02676341	357,291,524
6	0.02822197	376,763,299
7	0.02922797	390,193,399
8	0.02896859	386,730,677
9	0.02664388	355,695,798
10	0.02763931	368,984,789

Note that the present values of the two sides of the swap are the same, as they must be for fairly priced swaps.

17. Based on the tables of the preceding question, explain how a U.S. dollar plain vanilla receive-fixed interest rate swap is equivalent to a portfolio of bonds. Show how to replicate the swap position with a bond portfolio.

As the first table in question 16 shows, if we buy the semiannual bond and sell the FRN, the resulting cash flows are identical to the cash flows on the receive-fixed swap.

18. Explain the transactions necessary to replicate a U.S. dollar plain vanilla receive-fixed swap as a portfolio of FRAs.

An interest rate swap is a portfolio of off-market FRAs. To replicate the receive-fixed swap, one would enter 10 off-market FRAs. In each, one would contract to receive $3,614,650 and to pay the forward rate times the half-year periodicity of the swap payments, times the notional principal. The floating rate payments implied by the term structure appear in column D of the table in problem 16.

19. Based on the previous calculations, complete the following tables detailing the cash flows for a fixed-for-fixed currency swap. What is the expected present value benefit or loss on the periodic payments for the dollar payer? What is the expected present value benefit or loss on the reexchange of principal for the dollar payer? Explain the portfolio of capital market instruments that would replicate this fixed-for-fixed swap from the point of view of the dollar payer.

Fixed-for-Fixed Currency Swap–Dollar Payer Perspective

Date (Semiannual period)	Actual Cash Flows		Dollar Value of Cash Flows	
	Receipts	Payments	Receipts	Payments
0	$100,000,000	¥13,350,000,000	$100,000,000	$100,000,000
1	¥356,151,300	$3,614,650	2,693,032	3,614,650
2	¥356,151,300	$3,614,650	2,718,033	3,614,650
3	¥356,151,300	$3,614,650	2,746,538	3,614,650
4	¥356,151,300	$3,614,650	2,773,778	3,614,650
5	¥356,151,300	$3,614,650	2,797,300	3,614,650
6	¥356,151,300	$3,614,650	2,824,520	3,614,650
7	¥356,151,300	$3,614,650	2,849,158	3,614,650
8	¥356,151,300	$3,614,650	2,869,678	3,614,650
9	¥356,151,300	$3,614,650	2,897,521	3,614,650
10	¥356,151,300	$3,614,650	2,924,379	3,614,650
10	¥13,350,000,000	$100,000,000	$109,617,627	$100,000,000

Fixed-for-Fixed Currency Swap–Dollar Payer Perspective

Present Value of Cash Flows

Date (Semiannual Periods)	Receipts	Payments	Net
0	$100,000,000	$100,000,000	0
1	2,604,858	3,496,300	−891,443
2	2,540,951	3,379,152	−838,201
3	2,479,352	3,263,013	−783,661
4	2,416,169	3,148,632	−732,463
5	2,353,190	3,040,774	−687,584
6	2,288,601	2,928,814	−640,212
7	2,223,609	2,821,033	−597,424

8	2,161,008	2,722,009	−561,000
9	2,104,925	2,625,888	−520,963
10	2,048,311	2,531,795	−483,484
10	76,779,026	70,042,591	6,736,435
SUMS	$200,000,000	$200,000,000	0

The dollar payer expects to lose a total of $6,736,436 on the periodic payments in present value terms (the sum of the first 11 elements in the final column of the table) and make up the same amount on the reexchange of principal (the last element of the final column). The dollar payer could replicate her swap by buying a yen-denominated coupon bond and by issuing a dollar-denominated coupon bond, both of the appropriate principal and timing.

20. Consider again the fixed-for-fixed currency swap of the preceding question. Explain how this swap could be replicated in the foreign exchange forward market, detailing the FOREX forward contracts necessary to replicate the swap.

A fixed-for-fixed currency swap can be replicated by a portfolio of foreign exchange transactions. First, in the spot market, the dollar payer would exchange ¥13,350,000,000 for $100,000,000 at the prevailing spot rate. Next, the dollar payer would require a sequence or strip of 10 off-market FOREX forward transactions to pay $3,614,650 and receive ¥356,151,300 each six months for the next five years. Finally, the dollar payer would need a forward contract to pay ¥13,350,000,000 and receive $100,000,000 at the end of the five years. This would also be an off-market transaction. The cumbersome nature of these transactions, and the fact that the replication requires so many off-market FOREX forwards, indicates the operational advantage of the swap contract.

21. Explain how a plain vanilla dollar-pay currency swap can be replicated using capital market instruments as the key elements of the replicating portfolio. Illustrate the replicating cash flows in a table.

To synthesize a plain vanilla dollar-pay currency swap one buys a Japanese coupon bond and sells a dollar-denominated FRN. At initiation, the yen bond costs ¥13,350,000,000 and the sale of the dollar bond yields an inflow of $100,000,000. Each semi-annual period, the trader receives ¥356,151,300 and pays U.S. six-month LIBOR $\times$ 0.5 $\times$ $100,000,000. At period 10, in addition to the periodic payment, the trader receives ¥13,350,000,000 and pays $100,000,000. As the table shows, these are exactly the cash flows on a plain vanilla dollar-pay currency swap.

	Synthesizing Instruments		Synthesized Currency Swap	
Semiannual Periods	**Buy Japanese Coupon Bond**	**Sell FRN $ Bond**	**Receipts**	**Payments**
0	−¥13,350,000,000	$100,000,000	$100,000,000	−¥13,350,000,000
1	356,151,300	−3,385,000	¥356,151,300	−$3,385,000
2	356,151,300	−3,466,750	¥356,151,300	−$3,466,750
3	356,151,300	−3,559,346	¥356,151,300	−$3,559,346
4	356,151,300	−3,632,720	¥356,151,300	−$3,632,720
5	356,151,300	−3,547,017	¥356,151,300	−$3,547,017
6	356,151,300	−3,822,745	¥356,151,300	−$3,822,745
7	356,151,300	−3,820,546	¥356,151,300	−$3,820,546
8	356,151,300	−3,637,964	¥356,151,300	−$3,637,964
9	356,151,300	−3,660,495	¥356,151,300	−$3,660,495
10	356,151,300	−3,716,481	¥356,151,300	−$3,716,481
10	¥13,350,000,000	−$100,000,000	¥13,350,000,000	−$100,000,000

22. Explain how a yen fixed-pay plain vanilla currency swap could be replicated by combining two other swaps. Prepare a table showing the replicating cash flows.

A plain vanilla currency swap can be replicated by a fixed-for-fixed currency swap, combined with a plain vanilla interest rate swap. If a party enters the dollar pay-fixed swap that we have analyzed and also enters a plain vanilla interest rate swap, the cash flows would be as shown in the following table:

Synthetic Plain Vanilla Currency Swap–Dollar Payer Perspective

Date (Semiannual Period)	Dollar-Pay Fixed-for-Fixed Currency Swap		Receive-Fixed Interest Rate Swap		Resulting Synthetic Plain Vanilla Currency Swap	
	Receipts	Payments	Receipts	Payments	Receipts	Payments
0	$100,000,000	¥13,350,000,000	$0	$0	$100,000,000	¥13,350,000,000
1	¥356,151,300	$3,614,650	3,614,650	−3,385,000	¥356,151,300	−3,385,000
2	¥356,151,300	$3,614,650	3,614,650	−3,466,750	¥356,151,300	−3,466,750
3	¥356,151,300	$3,614,650	3,614,650	−3,559,346	¥356,151,300	−3,559,346
4	¥356,151,300	$3,614,650	3,614,650	−3,632,720	¥356,151,300	−3,632,720
5	¥356,151,300	$3,614,650	3,614,650	−3,547,017	¥356,151,300	−3,547,017
6	¥356,151,300	$3,614,650	3,614,650	−3,822,745	¥356,151,300	−3,822,745
7	¥356,151,300	$3,614,650	3,614,650	−3,820,546	¥356,151,300	−3,820,546
8	¥356,151,300	$3,614,650	3,614,650	−3,637,964	¥356,151,300	−3,637,964
9	¥356,151,300	$3,614,650	3,614,650	−3,660,495	¥356,151,300	−3,660,495
10	¥356,151,300	$3,614,650	3,614,650	−3,716,481	¥356,151,300	−3,716,481
10	¥13,350,000,000	$100,000,000	$0	$0	¥13,350,000,000	$100,000,000

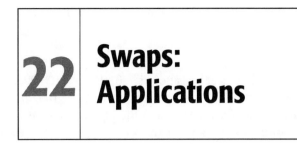

22 Swaps: Applications

Answers to Questions and Problems

1. At present, you observe the following rates: $FRA_{0,1}$ = 5.25 percent and $FRA_{1,2}$ = 5.70 percent, where the subscripts refer to years. You also observe prices on calls and puts on one-year LIBOR that expire in one year, with payment the following year. For a call on LIBOR with a strike rate of 5.70 percent, the price is 150 basis points. The corresponding put has a strike rate of 5.70 percent, and a cost of 143 basis points.

A. Explain how these prices represent an arbitrage opportunity. Draw a diagram illustrating the arbitrage opportunity.

From the forward put-call parity relationship, we know that a long FRA position is equivalent to a long call/short put portfolio with matching quantities and dates. Therefore, the cost of a long call/short put portfolio with a common strike rate equal to the FRA rate should be zero. In our situation, the long call/short put portfolio costs 7 basis points, the difference between the call cost and the put cost. Therefore, we can sell the option portfolio (sell the call and buy the put) and take a long position in the FRA. As the diagram shows, at expiration, the short call/long put portfolio and the long FRA will have exactly offsetting payoffs, for a net zero payoff.

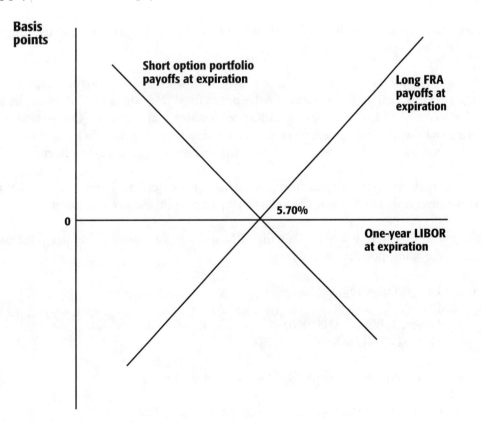

B. Assuming a notional principal of $100 million, state the transactions that you would enter to secure the arbitrage profit.

> $t = 0$
> Sell 1 call for 150 basis points = $0.0150 \times \$100,000,000 = +\$1,500,000$.
> Buy 1 put for 143 basis points = $0.0143 \times \$100,000,000 = -\$1,430,000$.
> Enter a pay-fixed position in the FRA on one-year LIBOR with a one-year maturity at a contract rate of 5.70 percent.
> Net Cash Flow: + $70,000

> $t = 1$
> There will be a net zero obligation no matter what the one-year spot rate for LIBOR is.
>   Consider two examples, with one-year LIBOR at 5.60 and 5.80 percent:
> *LIBOR = 5.60 percent*
> Call expires worthless.
> Long put is worth $(0.0570 - 0.0560) \times \$100,000,000 = +\$100,000$.
> FRA obligation is $(-0.057 + 0.056) \times \$100,000,000 = -\$100,000$.
> Net Obligation: 0

> *LIBOR = 5.80 percent*
> Short call is exercised against arbitrageur: $(0.0580 - 0.0570) \times \$100,000,000 = -\$100,000$.
> Put expires worthless.
> Pay-fixed FRA pays $(0.0580 - 0.0570) \times \$100,000,000 = +\$100,000$.
> Net Obligation: 0

C. Compute the present value of the arbitrage profit.

The present value of the arbitrage profit is $70,000, because it is received immediately at the time of contracting and no other cash flows are incurred.

2. An inverse floating rate note, or inverse floater, is a debt instrument with a floating rate that moves inversely with market rates. Generally, an inverse floater pays a fixed rate minus LIBOR. Consider an FRN with a principal amount of $50 million paying LIBOR with a five-year maturity. Consider also a plain vanilla interest rate swap with a fixed rate of 7 percent, a floating rate equal to LIBOR, a notional principal of $100 million, and a tenor of five years. For both instruments assume annual payments.

A. Explain how to construct the inverse floater from the instruments described above. Assume that there is no floor rate on the inverse floater. What is the net annual payment on the inverse floater?

To construct the inverse floater, one should issue the FRN and initiate a swap as the pay-fixed party. An annual payment on the whole position would be:

On the FRN:	Pay LIBOR × $50,000,000
On the swap:	Pay $7,000,000
	Receive LIBOR × $100,000,000
Net Payment:	$7,000,000 – LIBOR × $50,000,000

B. Compute the value of a net annual payment if LIBOR is 5.5 or 6.5 percent.

LIBOR = 5.5 percent:	$7,000,000 – 0.055 × $50,000,000 = $4,250,000
LIBOR = 6.5 percent:	$7,000,000 – 0.065 × $50,000,000 = $3,750,000

This shows that the construction is an inverse floater; as rates rise, the payment drops.

C. What happens to this instrument if LIBOR exceeds 14 percent?

As an example, let LIBOR equal 15 percent. Then the cash flow is:

$$\$7,000,000 - 0.15 \times \$50,000,000 = -\$500,000$$

The bond, instead of giving payments, requires payments. The breakeven point is 14 percent. We might say that the inverse floater sank. Typically, inverse floaters have a minimum 0 percent coupon payment so that they cannot really "sink" as in this situation. This also indicates why the fixed rate is set so high relative to LIBOR —to provide buoyancy.

D. Explain how to construct an inverse floater from a fixed rate bond and a plain vanilla swap.

One can create an inverse floater by buying a fixed rate bond and initiating a receive-fixed plain vanilla swap. The total periodic cash flow on the constructed inverse floater will consist of a fixed coupon inflow on the bond, C, a fixed inflow on the swap, $SFR \times NP$, and a floating outflow on the swap, LIBOR $\times NP$. This gives a total periodic cash flow of:

$$C + SFR \times NP - \text{LIBOR} \times NP$$

The size of this cash flow will vary inversely with LIBOR, showing that it is an inverse floater.

E. What modifications to the analysis would be required to replicate an inverse floater with a floor rate?

To replicate the floor that inverse floaters typically feature, one would need a swaption as well as the other instruments. Consider the inverse floater from the buyer's perspective. With a floor, the buyer is guaranteed to receive a rate no less than the floor rate. Therefore, the owner of the inverse floater needs a receiver swaption with a fixed rate equal to the floor rate on the inverse floater. When the rate on the inverse floater goes below the floor, the owner of the inverse floater continues to receive the low floating rate. With the receiver swaption, the floater owner can exercise the swaption to pay the floating rate and receive the fixed rate. The receipt of the floating rate on the inverse floater and the payment of the floating rate upon exercise of the swaption offset each other, leaving the owner of the inverse floater and swaption receiving a fixed rate equal to the floor rate.

3. A portfolio manager handles a Japanese equity portfolio for her clients, who are principally long-term dollar-based investors seeking exposure to the Japanese economy. The current value of the portfolio is $1.5 billion, and the spot exchange rate is $1 = ¥125. The portfolio pays an annual dividend of 3 percent. However, the quarterly distributions are weighted heavily toward the last quarter, with a mix of approximately 20-20-20-40 percent across the four quarters. The manager feels that her clients, many of whom rely on dollar income from the portfolio, would appreciate a dollar income stream less subject to foreign exchange risk. Therefore, the portfolio manager would like to reduce the exchange rate risk associated with the dividend payments while retaining the equity exposure to the Japanese market and while retaining the foreign exchange exposure on the principal. For the purpose of this analysis, we assume that the dividend payments are made on the last day of each quarter and that we are presently approaching year end. The manager has invited you to make proposals for avoiding this exchange rate risk over a horizon of three years. Note that the problem is not the uneven amounts of the dividends across quarters, but the foreign exchange risk of those payments.

A. Briefly compare and contrast the merits of using futures, FOREX forwards, or a swap to solve this problem.

The quarterly yen payments are ¥1.125 billion for the smaller quarters and ¥2.250 billion for the large quarter. Evaluated at the spot exchange rate, the dollar value of these payments is about $9,000,000 and

$18,000,000, respectively. Hedging the exchange risk would essentially involve selling the yen receipts forward in favor of dollars.

The futures market would be a conceptually appropriate vehicle for this task, except the hedging horizon is three years and foreign exchange futures are really viable only for a horizon of one year. Therefore, futures can provide only part of the solution at best. The risk could also be hedged by entering twelve FOREX forward contracts, one for each dividend payment over the next three years. A plain vanilla foreign currency swap is available with the necessary tenor, but it has two drawbacks. First, it involves an exchange of principal, which really is not needed in this context. Second, the dividend payments have a seasonal character that is not amenable to a plain vanilla swap.

B. Explain how you would address this problem by using at least one swap among the instruments you would recommend.

One might approach this problem with a fixed-for-fixed seasonal foreign currency swap with no exchange of principal. The problem does not provide information on prevailing forward FOREX rates, but the swap could be established to provide ¥1.125 billion for each of the next three quarters, followed by ¥2.250 billion for the fourth quarter, each payment being in exchange for a fixed dollar amount that reflects current FOREX forward rates. The last two years of the swap would repeat the pattern of the first year. Alternatively, one might go to the FOREX forward market.

4. Assume you can borrow at a fixed rate for ten years for 11 percent or that you can borrow at a floating rate of LIBOR plus 40 basis points for ten years. Assume also that LIBOR stands at 10.60 percent. Under these circumstances, your financial advisor states: "The all-in cost is the same on both deals—11 percent. Therefore, the two are equivalent, and one should be indifferent between these two financing alternatives." How would you react? Explain.

Your financial advisor is naive, because she is neglecting the shape of the term structure. Her advice would have some foundation if the yield curve were flat at 11 percent. In this situation, the expected cost on the two alternatives would be the same. However, the short-term strategy still involves risks (and opportunities) that the fixed rate strategy does not possess.

5. A firm needs to secure fixed rate financing of $40 million for a horizon of five years. It is considering two alternatives that seem equally attractive to management in terms of the instruments involved. Thus, the choice revolves solely around the relative cost. Alternative A is to issue a straight bond with annual coupon payments. The bond would sell at par, the firm would net 98 percent of the sale proceeds, and the coupon rate would be 7 percent. Administrative costs would be $30,000 for each coupon payment, and would be payable on the payment date. Under Alternative B, the firm would engage in a sequence of one-year financings, obtained at the prevailing rate each year, with each annual financing in the amount of $40 million. The firm would pair this financing with a pay-fixed interest rate swap. The firm's investment bank has guaranteed to make this sequence of loans at LIBOR, but would charge a fee of 15 basis points on each loan amount, payable at each loan date. The investment bank would also take the receive-fixed side of the swap that the firm needs with a fixed rate of 7.3 percent. The two alternatives differ slightly in the dollar amount of funds that they would provide, but this difference can be ignored. What is the all-in cost for each alternative?

We first need to set out all of the cash flows from each alternative as shown in the following table:

Cash Flows for the Two Financing Alternatives

Year	A	B-Bond	B-Swap	B-Net
0	+0.98 × ($40,000,000)	$40,000,000		$40,000,000
		− 0.0015 × ($40,000,000)		− 0.0015 × ($40,000,000)

1	$- 0.07 \times (\$40,000,000)$ $- \$30,000$	$\$40,000,000$ $- 0.0015 \times (\$40,000,000)$ $- \text{LIBOR} \times \$40,000,000$ $- \$40,000,000$	$(\text{LIBOR} - 0.073) \times$ $\$40,000,000$	$- (0.0015 + 0.073) \times$ $\$40,000,000$
2	$- 0.07 \times (\$40,000,000)$ $- \$30,000$	$\$40,000,000$ $- 0.0015 \times (\$40,000,000)$ $- \text{LIBOR} \times \$40,000,000 -$ $\$40,000,000$	$(\text{LIBOR} - 0.073) \times$ $\$40,000,000$	$- (0.0015 + 0.073) \times$ $\$40,000,000$
3	$- 0.07 \times (\$40,000,000)$ $- \$30,000$	$\$40,000,000$ $- 0.0015 \times (\$40,000,000)$ $- \text{LIBOR} \times \$40,000,000$ $- \$40,000,000$	$(\text{LIBOR} - 0.073) \times$ $\$40,000,000$	$- (0.0015 + 0.073) \times$ $\$40,000,000$
4	$- 0.07 \times (\$40,000,000)$ $- \$30,000$	$\$40,000,000$ $- 0.0015 \times (\$40,000,000)$ $- \text{LIBOR} \times \$40,000,000 -$ $\$40,000,000$	$(\text{LIBOR} - 0.073) \times$ $\$40,000,000$	$- (0.0015 + 0.073) \times$ $\$40,000,000$
5	$- 0.07 \times (\$40,000,000)$ $- \$30,000 - \$40,000,000$	$- \text{LIBOR} \times \$40,000,000$ $- \$40,000,000$	$(\text{LIBOR} - 0.073) \times$ $\$40,000,000$	$- (0.073) \times \$40,000,000$ $- \$40,000,000$

The following table summarizes and consolidates all of the cash flow information for the two alternatives and shows the IRRs for each alternative. The financing alternative using a sequence of FRNs and a swap saves about 11 basis points per year.

Net Flows and IRRs for Each Alternative

Year	Net Flows–Alternative A	Net Flows–Alternative B
0	39,200,000	39,940,000
1	−2,830,000	−2,980,000
2	−2,830,000	−2,980,000
3	−2,830,000	−2,980,000
4	−2,830,000	−2,980,000
5	−42,830,000	−42,920,000
	IRR 0.075703	IRR 0.074612

6. Today the following rates may be observed: $FRA_{0,3} = 0.0600$; $FRA_{3,6} = 0.0595$; $FRA_{6,9} = 0.0592$; $FRA_{9,12} = 0.0590$; $FRA_{12,15} = 0.0590$; $FRA_{15,18} = 0.0588$; $FRA_{18,21} = 0.0587$; $FRA_{21,24} = 0.0586$, where the subscripts pertain to months. Consider a two-year plain vanilla interest rate swap with quarterly payments, and also consider a forward interest rate swap to be initiated in twelve months, with quarterly payments, a notional principal of $20 million, and a tenor of twelve months.

A. Without computing the *SFR* for the forward swap, compare and contrast the *SFR* for the plain vanilla swap of the previous question with the *SFR* for the forward swap. What should the relationship be between the two *SFRs*?

The FRA rates for the second year are lower than those for the first year, so the forward swap should have a lower *SFR* than the swap covering both years.

B. Find the *SFR* for the forward swap.

We first find the zero-coupon factors that pertain to the forward swap:

$$Z_{0,3} = 1 + FRA_{0,3}/4 = 1 + 0.0600/4 = 1.01500$$
$$Z_{0,6} = Z_{0,3}(1 + FRA_{3,6}/4) = 1.015(1 + 0.0595/4) = 1.030098$$

$$Z_{0,9} = Z_{0,6} (1 + FRA_{6,9}/4) = 1.030098 (1 + 0.0592/4) = 1.045343$$
$$Z_{0,12} = Z_{0,9} (1 + FRA_{9,12}/4) = 1.045343 (1 + 0.0590/4) = 1.060762$$
$$Z_{0,15} = Z_{0,12} (1 + FRA_{12,15}/4) = 1.060762 (1 + 0.0590/4) = 1.076409$$
$$Z_{0,18} = Z_{0,15} (1 + FRA_{15,18}/4) = 1.076409 (1 + 0.0588/4) = 1.092232$$
$$Z_{0,21} = Z_{0,18} (1 + FRA_{18,21}/4) = 1.092232 (1 + 0.0587/4) = 1.108260$$
$$Z_{0,24} = Z_{0,21} (1 + FRA_{21,24}/4) = 1.108260 (1 + 0.0586/4) = 1.124496$$

To find the *SFR* for the forward swap, we observe that both sides of the swap must have the same present value at the time the swap is initiated:

$$PART \times NP \left(\frac{FRA_{12,15}}{Z_{0,15}} + \frac{FRA_{15,18}}{Z_{0,18}} + \frac{FRA_{18,21}}{Z_{0,21}} + \frac{FRA_{21,24}}{Z_{0,24}} \right) =$$

$$PART \times NP \times SFR \left(\frac{1}{Z_{0,15}} + \frac{1}{Z_{0,18}} + \frac{1}{Z_{0,21}} + \frac{1}{Z_{0,24}} \right)$$

Therefore,

$$SFR = \frac{\dfrac{FRA_{12,15}}{Z_{0,15}} + \dfrac{FRA_{15,18}}{Z_{0,18}} + \dfrac{FRA_{18,21}}{Z_{0,21}} + \dfrac{FRA_{21,24}}{Z_{0,24}}}{\dfrac{1}{Z_{0,15}} + \dfrac{1}{Z_{0,18}} + \dfrac{1}{Z_{0,21}} + \dfrac{1}{Z_{0,24}}}$$

$$= \frac{\dfrac{0.0590}{1.076409} + \dfrac{0.0588}{1.092232} + \dfrac{0.0587}{1.108260} + \dfrac{0.0586}{1.124496}}{\dfrac{1}{1.076409} + \dfrac{1}{1.092232} + \dfrac{1}{1.108260} + \dfrac{1}{1.124496}}$$

$$SFR = \frac{0.054812 + 0.053835 + 0.052966 + 0.052122}{0.929015 + 0.915556 + 0.902315 + 0.889287} = \frac{0.213725}{3.636173} = 0.058777$$

C. Assume that today the following rates are observed: $FRA_{0,3} = 0.0590$; $FRA_{3,6} = 0.0588$; $FRA_{6,9} = 0.0587$; $FRA_{9,12} = 0.0586$, where the subscripts pertain to months. What would be the *SFR* for a plain vanilla swap based on these rates, assuming a tenor of one year and quarterly payments? Explain.

First, we find the zero-coupon factors:

$$Z_{0,3} = 1 + 0.0590/4 = 1.014750$$
$$Z_{0,6} = 1.014750 \times (1 + 0.0588/4) = 1.029667$$
$$Z_{0,9} = 1.029667 \times (1 + 0.0587/4) = 1.044777$$
$$Z_{0,12} = 1.044777 \times (1 + 0.0586/4) = 1.060083$$

Next, we apply Equation 22.15, treating the numerator and denominator separately for convenience:

$$NUMERATOR = \frac{0.0590}{1.014750} + \frac{0.0588}{1.029667} + \frac{0.0587}{1.044777} + \frac{0.0586}{1.060083} = 0.226711$$

$$DENOMINATOR = \frac{1}{1.014750} + \frac{1}{1.029667} + \frac{1}{1.044777} + \frac{1}{1.060083} = 3.857117$$

$$SFR = \frac{0.226711}{3.857117} = 0.058777$$

The forward swap that we considered earlier and this plain vanilla swap have exactly the same pattern of rates. In other words, the four rates in this plain vanilla swap are the same as the last four FRA rates on our original swap. Therefore, the plain vanilla swap and a forward swap will have the same *SFR*.

7. Consider an amortizing interest rate swap with an initial notional principal of $50 million, annual payments, and a tenor of five years that is negotiated today. The notional principal is $50 million for the first payment, and then drops $10 million per year. FRA rates covering the tenor of this swap are as follows, where the subscripts indicate years: $FRA_{0,1} = 0.0600$; $FRA_{1,2} = 0.0615$; $FRA_{2,3} = 0.0623$; $FRA_{3,4} = 0.0628$; $FRA_{4,5} = 0.0633$.

A. Assuming that Equation 22.15 does not pertain to an amortizing swap, which numbered equation from the chapter is best suited to computing the *SFR* for this amortizing swap? Explain.

Equation 22.16 works best, because it allows for the notional principal to be different for each payment on the swap.

B. Find the relevant zero-coupon factors for each of the payments in the swap.

$$Z_{0,1} = 1 + FRA_{0,1} = 1.0600$$
$$Z_{0,2} = Z_{0,1}(1 + FRA_{1,2}) = 1.0600\,(1.0615) = 1.125190$$
$$Z_{0,3} = Z_{0,2}(1 + FRA_{2,3}) = 1.125190\,(1.0623) = 1.195289$$
$$Z_{0,4} = Z_{0,3}(1 + FRA_{3,4}) = 1.195289\,(1.0628) = 1.270354$$
$$Z_{0,5} = Z_{0,4}(1 + FRA_{4,5}) = 1.270354\,(1.0633) = 1.350767$$

C. Compute the *SFR* for this swap.

Letting NP_t = the payment at year t, we have: $NP_1 = \$50,000,000$; $NP_2 = \$40,000,000$; $NP_3 = \$30,000,000$; $NP_4 = \$20,000,000$; $NP_5 = \$10,000,000$. Therefore, the *SFR* must satisfy this equation:

$$\frac{FRA_{0,1} \times NP_1}{Z_{0,1}} + \frac{FRA_{1,2} \times NP_2}{Z_{0,2}} +$$

$$\frac{FRA_{2,3} \times NP_3}{Z_{0,3}} + \frac{FRA_{3,4} \times NP_4}{Z_{0,4}} + \frac{FRA_{4,5} \times NP_5}{Z_{0,5}} =$$

$$SFR\left(\frac{NP_1}{Z_{0,1}} + \frac{NP_2}{Z_{0,2}} + \frac{NP_3}{Z_{0,3}} + \frac{NP_4}{Z_{0,4}} + \frac{NP_5}{Z_{0,5}}\right)$$

Treating the numerator and denominator separately, we have:

$$SFR = \frac{NUMERATOR}{DENOMINATOR}$$

where:

$$NUMERATOR =$$

$$\frac{0.0600 \times \$50,000,000}{1.0600} + \frac{0.0615 \times \$40,000,000}{1.125190} +$$

$$\frac{0.0623 \times \$30,000,000}{1.195289} + \frac{0.0628 \times \$20,000,000}{1.270354} + \frac{0.0633 \times \$10,000,000}{1.350767}$$

$$= \$2,830,189 + \$2,186,297 + \$1,563,639 + \$988,701 + \$468,623$$

$$= \$8,037,488$$

$$DENOMINATOR =$$

$$\frac{\$50,000,000}{1.0600} + \frac{\$40,000,000}{1.125190} + \frac{\$30,000,000}{1.195289} + \frac{\$20,000,000}{1.270354} + \frac{\$10,000,000}{1.350767}$$

$$= \$47,169,811 + \$35,549,552 + \$25,098,533 + \$15,743,643 + \$7,403,201$$

$$= \$130,964,740$$

$$SFR = \frac{\$8,037,448}{\$130,964,740} = 0.061371$$

Note: The following interest rate data for the United States and Britain are used in almost all of the remaining problems. These data cover the next 10 years by semiannual periods.

8. Complete the following table for U.S. interest rates.

U.S. Interest Rates

Semiannual Periods	Annualized Par Yield	Semiannual Par Yield	Zero-Coupon Factor	Forward Rate Factor
1	0.055329	0.027665	1.027665	1.027665
2	0.055682	0.027841	1.056462	1.028022
3	0.056260	0.028130	1.086817	1.028733
4	0.057375	0.028688	1.119922	1.030461
5	0.057944	0.028972	1.153741	1.030197
6	0.057961	0.028981	1.187231	1.029027
7	0.059389	0.029695	1.228150	1.034466
8	0.059813	0.029907	1.266943	1.031587
9	0.059910	0.029955	1.305460	1.030401
10	0.060649	0.030325	1.350134	1.034221
11	0.060982	0.030491	1.393981	1.032476
12	0.061214	0.030607	1.438803	1.032154
13	0.061532	0.030766	1.486458	1.033121
14	0.061702	0.030851	1.534379	1.032238
15	0.062721	0.031361	1.596588	1.040544
16	0.063835	0.031918	1.665192	1.042969
17	0.064431	0.032216	1.729578	1.038666

18	0.064785	0.032393	1.792790	1.036547
19	0.066198	0.033099	1.884719	1.051277
20	0.066626	0.033313	1.958708	1.039258

9. Complete the following table for British interest rates.

British Interest Rates

Semiannual Periods	Annualized Par Yield	Semiannual Par Yield	Zero-Coupon Factor	Forward Rate Factor
1	0.053832	0.026916	1.026916	1.026916
2	0.054334	0.027167	1.055079	1.027425
3	0.056197	0.028099	1.086778	1.030044
4	0.057242	0.028621	1.119689	1.030284
5	0.058987	0.029494	1.156934	1.033264
6	0.059890	0.029945	1.194448	1.032425
7	0.061010	0.030505	1.235377	1.034266
8	0.062106	0.031053	1.279148	1.035431
9	0.062947	0.031474	1.324413	1.035387
10	0.064515	0.032258	1.378273	1.040667
11	0.064558	0.032279	1.423121	1.032539
12	0.066683	0.033342	1.491341	1.047937
13	0.067310	0.033655	1.548687	1.038453
14	0.068090	0.034045	1.611660	1.040662
15	0.069823	0.034912	1.694301	1.051277
16	0.069891	0.034946	1.754696	1.035646
17	0.070146	0.035073	1.821253	1.037931
18	0.070253	0.035127	1.887592	1.036425
19	0.071105	0.035553	1.975971	1.046821
20	0.071393	0.035697	2.054628	1.039807

10. Consider a forward interest rate swap on British rates from the perspective of time zero. The forward swap has semiannual payments, and the first payment will be made in three years. The swap has a tenor of five years and a notional principal of £100,000,000. From the perspective of time zero, find the *SFR* for this forward swap. If we were to treat the forward swap as an immediate swap, at what time would the swap be valued? From that point in time, treat the forward swap as an immediate swap and determine the *SFR*. Show that the two *SFR*s computed are the same.

First, from time zero, the following table shows the cash flows on the forward swap, and various intermediate calculations for the analysis:

Forward Swap Analysis Standpoint of Time Zero

Period	Zero-Coupon Factor, $Z_{0,t}$	Forward Rate Factor, $FRF_{t-1,t}$	$1/Z_{0,t}$	$FR_{t-1,t}/Z_{0,t}$
6	1.194448	1.032425	0.837207	0.027146
7	1.235377	1.034266	0.809469	0.027737
8	1.279148	1.035431	0.781770	0.027699
9	1.324413	1.035387	0.755051	0.026719
10	1.378273	1.040667	0.725546	0.029506
11	1.423121	1.032539	0.702681	0.022865
12	1.491341	1.047937	0.670537	0.032144
13	1.548687	1.038453	0.645708	0.024829
14	1.611660	1.040662	0.620478	0.025230
15	1.694301	1.051277	0.590214	0.030264
SUMS			7.138663	0.274139

As we have noted, a forward swap can be priced using the plain vanilla swap equation, Equation 21.13:

$$SFR = \frac{\sum_{n=1}^{N} \dfrac{FRA_{(n-1)\times MON, n\times MON}}{Z_{0, n\times MON}}}{\sum_{n=1}^{N} \dfrac{1}{Z_{0, n\times MON}}} = \frac{0.274139}{7.138663} = 0.038402$$

This is expressed in semiannual terms, so the annualized rate is twice as large, or 0.076804.

We can also price this swap from the point of view of a swap that is immediately negotiated. If the first payment is to occur at year 3, we price the swap from the standpoint of time 2.5 years. Where the subscripts refer to semiannual periods, we have $Z_{0,5} = 1.156934$ from the table in question 9.

Forward Swap Analysis Standpoint of Time 2.5 Years

Period	Zero-Coupon Factor, $Z_{0, t} / Z_{0, 5}$	Forward Rate Factor, $FRF_{t-1, t}$	$\dfrac{1}{\dfrac{Z_{0,t}}{Z_{0,5}}}$	$\dfrac{FR_{t-1, t}}{\dfrac{Z_{0,t}}{Z_{0,5}}}$
6	1.032425	1.032425	0.968593	0.031407
7	1.067802	1.034266	0.936503	0.032090
8	1.105636	1.035431	0.904457	0.032046
9	1.144761	1.035387	0.873545	0.030912
10	1.191315	1.040667	0.839408	0.034136
11	1.230080	1.032539	0.812955	0.026453
12	1.289046	1.047937	0.775768	0.037188
13	1.338613	1.038453	0.747042	0.028726
14	1.393044	1.040662	0.717852	0.029189
15	1.464475	1.051277	0.682839	0.035014
SUMS			8.258962	0.317161

$$SFR = \frac{0.317161}{8.258962} = 0.038402$$

This is the same answer we found from the standpoint of time zero.

11. In the United States, a retailer is faced with a seasonal cash flow pattern over the next five years. The retailer has determined to enter a pay-fixed seasonal swap with a tenor of five years. In the first part of each year, the notional principal will be $50,000,000. In the second half of each year, the notional principal will be $75,000,000. Determine the *SFR* for this seasonal swap, and complete the following table.

Seasonal Swap Cash Flows

Semiannual Periods	Notional Principal	Fixed Payment	Implied Floating Payment
1	$50,000,000	1,517,950	1,383,250
2	$75,000,000	2,276,925	2,101,650
3	$50,000,000	1,517,950	1,436,650
4	$75,000,000	2,276,925	2,284,575
5	$50,000,000	1,517,950	1,509,850
6	$75,000,000	2,276,925	2,177,025
7	$50,000,000	1,517,950	1,723,300
8	$75,000,000	2,276,925	2,369,025
9	$50,000,000	1,517,950	1,520,050
10	$75,000,000	2,276,925	2,566,575

Because the notional principal varies in a seasonal swap, we cannot use the plain vanilla pricing equation. Instead, we need to use Equation 22.16:

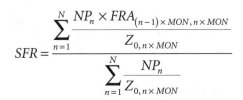

$$SFR = \frac{\sum_{n=1}^{N} \dfrac{NP_n \times FRA_{(n-1) \times MON, n \times MON}}{Z_{0, n \times MON}}}{\sum_{n=1}^{N} \dfrac{NP_n}{Z_{0, n \times MON}}}$$

The following table shows the intermediate calculations in applying Equation 22.16:

Seasonal Swap Analysis

Period	NP_t	$(NP_t \times FR_{t-1, t})/ Z_{0, t}$	$NP_t/ Z_{0, t}$
1	$50,000,000	1,346,013	48,653,987
2	$75,000,000	1,989,329	70,991,668
3	$50,000,000	1,321,888	46,005,905
4	$75,000,000	2,039,941	66,968,950
5	$50,000,000	1,308,656	43,337,283
6	$75,000,000	1,833,700	63,172,205
7	$50,000,000	1,403,167	40,711,639
8	$75,000,000	1,869,875	59,197,612
9	$50,000,000	1,164,379	38,300,676
10	$75,000,000	1,900,978	55,550,042
SUMS		16,177,925	532,889,967

$$SFR = \frac{16,177,925}{532,889,967} = 0.030359$$

This computed *SFR* is for a semiannual period. In annual terms, *SFR* = 0.060718. To complete the table showing the cash flows, we note that the fixed payment is just the semiannual *SFR* times the notional principal for the period. Each floating payment is the implied forward rate times the notional principal for the period.

12. In Great Britain, the manager of a fixed rate mortgage portfolio at a building society is quite satisfied with the composition of her portfolio, but she would like to protect the value of the portfolio from rising interest rates. The current market and principal value of the portfolio is £200,000,000. The mortgages in the portfolio are somewhat unusual in that they do not allow prepayment. However, the principal on the mortgages is being repaid over the next five years consistent with the schedule in the following table. The manager is considering two possible swaps to hedge the interest rate risk of the portfolio. First, the manager might initiate a plain vanilla interest rate swap with a notional principal of £100,000,000 and a tenor of five years. Alternatively, the manager is wondering if she might prefer an amortizing swap with a notional principal schedule that matches the table below and a tenor of five years.

Semiannual Periods	Notional Principal
1	£200,000,000
2	175,000,000
3	133,000,000
4	127,000,000
5	107,000,000
6	85,000,000
7	77,000,000
8	65,000,000
9	45,000,000
10	22,000,000

A. By inspecting the British interest rates, but without computation, which swap would have the higher *SFR*? Explain.

It is a close call by visual inspection, but the yield curve is rising and the plain vanilla swap has a higher notional principal in the later periods subject to the higher rate. Therefore, the plain vanilla swap probably has the higher rate.

B. Find the *SFR* for the plain vanilla swap.

Using the data from the table below:

$$SFR = \frac{0.274455}{8.508239} = 0.032258$$

Therefore, in annualized terms, the *SFR* is 0.064516.

C. Find the *SFR* for the amortizing swap.

For this amortizing swap, the notional principal varies, so that we must use Equation 22.16 and the calculations in the table below:

$$SFR = \frac{28,074,241}{923,158,660} = 0.030411$$

In annualized terms, *SFR* = 0.060822.

The following table presents the intermediate calculations useful in the *SFR* for both swaps.

British Building Society Amortizing Swap

Semiannual Periods	NP	$FRA_{t-1,t}$	$1/Z_{0,t}$	$FRA_{t-1,t}/Z_{0,t}$	$NP/Z_{0,t}$	$(NP \times FRA_{t-1,t})/Z_{0,t}$
1	£200,000,000	0.026916	0.973789	0.026211	194,757,896	5,242,104
2	175,000,000	0.027425	0.947796	0.025993	165,864,357	4,548,830
3	133,000,000	0.030044	0.920151	0.027645	122,380,100	3,676,788
4	127,000,000	0.030284	0.893105	0.027047	113,424,353	3,434,943
5	107,000,000	0.033264	0.864354	0.028752	92,485,829	3,076,449
6	85,000,000	0.032425	0.837207	0.027146	71,162,579	2,307,447
7	77,000,000	0.034266	0.809469	0.027737	62,329,151	2,135,771
8	65,000,000	0.035431	0.781770	0.027699	50,815,074	1,800,429
9	45,000,000	0.035387	0.755051	0.026719	33,977,317	1,202,355
10	22,000,000	0.040667	0.725546	0.029506	15,962,005	649,127
SUMS			8.508239	0.274455	923,158,660	28,074,241

D. Which of the two swaps would you recommend to the manager? Which side of the swap should the manager take? Explain.

The portfolio manager receives a fixed rate on the mortgages, so she needs a pay-fixed swap. This leaves a position in which the mortgage portfolio essentially earns a floating rate. Of the two swaps, the amortizing swap more closely matches the cash flows on the portfolio. Also, the amortizing swap has a lower fixed rate. Since she will be the fixed-rate payer, both considerations point toward the amortizing swap. The following table presents the intermediate calculations useful in finding the *SFR* for both swaps.

13. At time zero, the five-year forward FOREX rate is $1 = £0.580024. What is the current spot exchange rate to the nearest cent? Rounding the spot exchange rate to the nearest full cent, complete the following table.

10-period zero-coupon factor for the United States   = 1.350134
10-period zero-coupon factor for Great Britain   = 1.378273
10-period foreign exchange forward rate   = 0.580024

The proceeds of investing £1 for 10 semi-annual periods in Britain and then converting to dollars is:

$$£1 \times 1.378273 \times 1/0.580024 = \$2.376234$$

This must have the same value as converting £1 to dollars at the (unknown) spot rate and investing the proceeds at the dollar rate for the same period:

$$£1 \times SPOT \times 1.350134 = \$2.376234$$

Therefore, the spot rate is £1 = $1.76.

U.S. and British Foreign Exchange Rates

Semiannual Periods	$ per £	£ per $
0	1.760000	0.568182
1	1.761284	0.567768
2	1.762307	0.567438
3	1.760063	0.568161
4	1.760366	0.568064
5	1.755143	0.569754
6	1.749366	0.571636
7	1.749704	0.571525
8	1.743207	0.573655
9	1.734814	0.576431
10	1.724068	0.580024
11	1.723962	0.580059
12	1.697997	0.588929
13	1.689280	0.591968
14	1.675606	0.596799
15	1.658498	0.602955
16	1.670225	0.598722
17	1.671408	0.598298
18	1.671606	0.598227
19	1.678722	0.595691
20	1.677835	0.596006

14. At time zero, a British exporter has just entered a contract to supply Princess Diana memorabilia to a U.S. customer. The contract calls for the purchase of $50,000,000 worth of material each six months over the next four years. The U.S. customer will pay in dollars. The British exporter would like to avoid the foreign exchange risk inherent in this transaction, but is unsure whether to accept exposure to British interest rates. The exporter also needs additional financing to cope with this increase in business and is considering issuing a quanto note to provide the financing and to cope with the interest rate risk and possibly the foreign exchange risk inherent in the large new order. The quanto note the exporter is considering would be based on British LIBOR, would have payments in U.S. dollars, and would have terms that match the Princess Diana order. Specifically, the issue would be for $400,000,000, with semiannual interest-only payments, and would have a maturity of four years. The spot exchange rate is £1 = $1.760000.

A. Explain the interest rate and currency exposure that the British borrower would face if he issued the quanto note in conjunction with the Princess Diana cash flows.

From the Princess Diana order, the exporter has foreign exchange risk, because he will incur costs in British pounds to produce the merchandise, but will receive U.S. dollars in payment. By issuing a quanto note, the exporter will receive a large dollar inflow at time zero that involves some FOREX risk. However, the exporter could immediately convert those dollars to pounds at the spot rate. In addition, the periodic outflows on the quanto note will be in dollars. These outflows will largely offset the dollar inflows, helping to deal with the foreign exchange risk inherent in the Princess Diana order. However, there may be some residual foreign exchange risk due to a mismatch in the periodic flows. The interest rate risk position after issuing the quanto note is that the exporter is exposed to floating British interest rates, versus a fixed dollar receipt.

B. By visually comparing the British and U.S. yield curves, what can you infer about the likely spread? Price the quanto note. What spread should the exporter expect on the issuance?

The British rates are initially lower than the U.S. rates, but the British yield curve is more strongly upward sloping. Therefore, the spread should be close to zero. As the following calculations show, the spread is *very* narrow.

Fair pricing for the quanto note equates the $400,000,000 received at issuance versus the present value of the repayment stream. In the following equation, the LIBOR values can be thought of as representing the British forward rates that prevail at issuance. Alternatively, the actual cash flows on the quanto note will depend on the rates of British LIBOR that prevail on each determination date. Given the term structure information we already possess, the only unknown in this equation is the spread over or under British LIBOR ($SPRD$) on the note.

$$\$400{,}000{,}000 = \sum_{t=1}^{8} \frac{(\pounds\ LIBOR_t + SPRD) \times \$400{,}000{,}000}{Z_{0,t}} + \frac{\$400{,}000{,}000}{Z_{0,8}}$$

Notice that the principal amount does not affect the spread, as the preceding equation simplifies to:

$$1 - \frac{1}{Z_{0,8}} = \sum_{t=1}^{8} \frac{(\pounds\ LIBOR_t + SPRD)}{Z_{0,t}}$$

The left-hand term is 0.21069851. $SPRD$ is found by an iterative search to be −0.00115631. Therefore, the issuance should be at British LIBOR minus about 11 or 12 basis points. The following table illustrates the accuracy of the calculation:

The Quanto Note Spread Calculation

Semiannual Periods	$Z_{0,t}$	$\pounds\ FR_t$	$(\pounds\ FR_t + SPRD)/Z_{0,t}$
1	1.027665	0.026916	0.02506623
2	1.056462	0.027425	0.02486478
3	1.086817	0.030044	0.02658009
4	1.119922	0.030284	0.02600868
5	1.153741	0.033264	0.02782920
6	1.187231	0.032425	0.02633749
7	1.228150	0.034266	0.02695900
8	1.266943	0.035431	0.02705306
SUM			0.21069853

C. Complete the following table, identifying the implied dollar cash flows on the quanto note. How closely do these match the dollar inflows? What do you think of the proposed issuance size as a means of offsetting the foreign exchange risk?

The following table shows the quanto note outflows implied by the term structure and the difference. Considering the interest payments on the quanto note in isolation, the quanto note accounts for only about 20 percent of the dollar inflows, leaving roughly $35–40,000,000 mismatch. In addition, the quanto note creates a large mismatch in the final period when the principal is returned. At best, issuing the quanto note is only a partial solution to the FOREX risk.

Quanto Note Cash Flow Comparison

Semiannual Periods	Dollar Inflow from Sales	Implied Quanto Note Outflow	Net Dollar Flow
1	$50,000,000	10,303,876	39,696,124
2	$50,000,000	10,507,476	39,492,524
3	$50,000,000	11,555,076	38,444,924
4	$50,000,000	11,651,076	38,348,924
5	$50,000,000	12,843,076	37,156,924
6	$50,000,000	12,507,476	37,492,524
7	$50,000,000	13,243,876	36,756,124
8	$50,000,000	413,709,876	−363,709,876

D. The exporter is uncertain that the quanto note approach is correct, but is convinced that the U.S. provides the best capital pool for achieving his financing. An alternative approach is to issue a four-year semiannual payment, amortizing note in the U.S. for $350,000,000 at the fixed U.S. rate. Find the rate for this issuance that is compatible with the U.S. term structure, and complete the following table for the issuance amount of $350,000,000. Discuss the suitability of this approach in terms of avoiding the foreign exchange risk inherent in the Princess Diana project.

Amortizing Note Cash Flow Comparison–$350,000,000 Principal

Semiannual Periods	Dollar Inflow from Sales	Implied Note Outflow	Net Dollar Flow
1	$50,000,000	$49,678,870	+$321,130
2	$50,000,000	$49,678,870	$321,130
3	$50,000,000	$49,678,870	$321,130
4	$50,000,000	$49,678,870	$321,130
5	$50,000,000	$49,678,870	$321,130
6	$50,000,000	$49,678,870	$321,130
7	$50,000,000	$49,678,870	$321,130
8	$50,000,000	$49,678,870	$321,130

The payment on the amortizing note, *PAY*, is found as:

$$PAY = \frac{\$350,000,000}{\sum_{t=1}^{8} \frac{1}{Z_{0,t}}} = \$49,678,870$$

The yield to maturity on this note is the IRR of the cash flows. The semiannual IRR is 0.029139 for an issuance rate of 0.058279. Note that this is slightly less than the par yield (0.059813) for a four-year coupon bond, because the yield curve is rising and the amortized note has an effectively shorter maturity (duration) than a coupon bond. The amortizing note with a principal of $350,000,000 creates a dollar obligation that almost exactly offsets the $50,000,000 semiannual inflow, leaving the British exporter with a net dollar inflow of $321,130 semiannually.

E. As another alternative, the British exporter may just finance in England and confront the financial risk of the dollar inflows with a swap. That is, the British exporter is interested in swapping the eight $50,000,000 inflows against British pounds. Propose two alternative currency swaps in which the exporter pays his dollar receipts in exchange for British pounds. One swap gives the exporter a fixed British pound payment, while the other gives a floating payment. Price the fixed rate swap, and complete the following table detailing the cash flows on the floating rate swap.

These two swaps are currency annuity swaps, as there is no principal to be exchanged, but just a sequence of even dollar payments. In both swaps, the exporter will be paying the present value of the dollar flows discounted at the U.S. rate. In return, one swap will pay eight payments of a fixed amount in pounds that have a present value that equals that of the U.S. dollar cash flow stream. In the second swap, the exporter will receive a sequence of pound payments that depend on changes in British LIBOR. However, the table illustrates the payment stream consistent with the British term structure at the inception of the swap.

First, the present value of the dollar cash flow stream is:

$$PV = \$50,000,000 \times \sum_{t=1}^{8} \frac{1}{Z_{0,t}} = \$50,000,000 \times 7.045249 = \$352,262,450$$

With a spot exchange rate of £1 = $1.760000, the value of the dollar stream is £200,149,119. For the fixed British pound swap, the payment stream must have a present value of £200,149,119 when the payments are discounted according to the British term structure, with each payment, *PAY*, being given by:

$$PV = PAY \times \sum_{t=1}^{8} \frac{1}{Z_{0,t}}$$

$$£200,149,119 = PAY \times 7.027642$$

$$PAY = £28,480,267$$

For the swap that pays a floating rate in British pounds, the sequence of floating rate payments consistent with the British term structure must have a present value equal to the present value of the dollar inflows converted to British pounds at the spot rate, which is £200,149,119. Therefore, the British pound floating payments must be computed on a notional principal satisfying the following equation:

$$£200,149,119 = NP \times \sum_{t=1}^{8} \frac{FR_{t-1,t}}{Z_{0,t}}$$

$$NP = \frac{£200,149,119}{0.218230}$$

$$= £917,147,592$$

For example, the fifth payment, consistent with the British term structure, and as shown in the table, would be:

$$NP \times FR_{4,5} = £917,147,592 \times 0.033264 = £30,507,998$$

British Exporter's Currency Annuity Cash Flow Analysis

Semiannual Periods	$FR_{t-1,t}$	Implied British Pound Cash Inflow on Floating Rate Swap
1	0.026916	£24,685,945
2	0.027425	25,152,773
3	0.030044	27,554,782
4	0.030284	27,774,898
5	0.033264	30,507,998

6	0.032425	29,738,511
7	0.034266	31,426,979
8	0.035431	32,495,456

15. A U.S. oil field equipment manufacturer, DrillBit, is currently negotiating a contract with a Houston-based oil exploration firm, FindIt, for a medium-term contract to deliver equipment each six months for two years. The present is time zero. If the deal goes through, the first equipment will be delivered in six months, with payment for the equipment being made six months following delivery. The contract calls for four deliveries spaced six months apart, with equipment valued at $60,000,000 for each delivery. Most of DrillBit's financing is at a floating rate, so DrillBit is considering initiating a pay-fixed interest rate swap to match the cash flows on the FindIt deal. By entering this pay-fixed swap, DrillBit would agree to pay a sequence of four payments of $60,000,000 in return for a sequence of four payments tied to LIBOR of equal present value. The floating rate inflows on the swap would approximately match DrillBit's current floating rate debt obligations (not described here). So the swap would effectively convert DrillBit's existing financing position for a floating rate obligation to a fixed rate obligation. However, it is presently uncertain whether the deal with FindIt will be completed.

A. Describe the swap being proposed in detail with regard to its timing and cash flows. What is the implicit notional principal on which the floating payments must be computed? Complete the following table showing the cash flows on the swap consistent with the existing U.S. term structure.

Annuity Swap Cash Flow Analysis

Semiannual Periods	Fixed Payment	$FR_{t-1,t}$	$FR_{t-1,t}/Z_{0,t}$	Implied Floating Payment
2	$60,000,000	0.028022	0.026524	57,338,540
3	60,000,000	0.028733	0.026438	58,793,386
4	60,000,000	0.030461	0.027199	62,329,215
5	60,000,000	0.030197	0.026173	61,789,019

In terms of semiannual payments, the swap would consist of four payments of $60,000,000 at times 2, 3, 4, and 5 in return for a sequence of floating rate payments with a present value equal to the present value of the fixed rate payments, satisfying the following equation.

$$\$60,000,000 \times \sum_{t=2}^{5} \frac{1}{Z_{0,t}} = NP \times \sum_{t=2}^{5} \frac{FR_{t-1,t}}{Z_{0,t}}$$

$$\$60,000,000 \times 3.626339 = \$2,046,197,265 \times 0.106334$$

The present value of the fixed rate payments is $217,580,340, and the floating rate payments should be computed on a notional principal of $2,046,197,265. The implied floating rate payments are shown in the table.

B. What is the *SFR* on this swap?

This swap is a forward swap to cover periods 2–5. Therefore, it may be priced as a plain vanilla swap from the standpoint of time zero.

$$SFR = \frac{\sum_{t=2}^{T} \dfrac{FRA_{(t-1),t}}{Z_{0,t}}}{\sum_{t=2}^{T} \dfrac{1}{Z_{0,t}}} = \frac{0.106334}{3.626339} = 0.029323$$

In annualized terms, *SFR* = 0.058645.

C. Explain how DrillBit might structure a swaption now to match its needs described above if the deal goes through.

The swaption would be a payer swaption with an expiration of six months, semiannual payments, a tenor of two years, and a notional principal of $2,046,197,265. If the deal goes through, DrillBit could exercise the swaption to enter the swap analyzed in section A.

D. Price the swaption, assuming that the standard deviation of all interest rates is 0.22 and the strike rate is 6 percent.

The price of a payer swaption is given by Equation 22.32:

$$Payer\ Swaption_t = NP \times FRAC \times \left[SFR\ N(d_1) - SR\ N(d_2) \right] \sum_{n=1}^{N} \frac{1}{Z_{t,T_n}}$$

where:

$$d_1 = \frac{\ln\left(\dfrac{SFR_t}{SR}\right) + (.5\,\sigma^2)(T-t)}{\sigma\,\sqrt{T-t}}$$

$$d_2 = d_1 - \sigma\,\sqrt{T-t}$$

For our swap, the valuation date is time zero, $t = 0$, $SFR = 0.058645$, $FRAC = 0.5$, $SR = 0.06$, $\sigma = 0.22$, and $NP = \$2,046,197,265$. The payment dates are 2–5 semiannual periods from now, so:

$$\sum_{n=2}^{5} \frac{1}{Z_{0,T_n}} = 3.626339$$

$$d_1 = \frac{\ln\left(\dfrac{SFR_t}{SR}\right) + (.5\,\sigma^2)(T-t)}{\sigma\,\sqrt{T-t}}$$

$$= \frac{\ln\left(\dfrac{0.058645}{0.06}\right) + 0.5\,(0.22)^2\,(0.5)}{0.22\,(0.7071)}$$

$$= -0.069054$$

$$d_2 = d_1 - \sigma\,\sqrt{T-t}$$

$$= -0.069054 - 0.155563$$

$$= -0.224617$$

The cumulative normal values are: $N(d_1) = N(-0.069054) = 0.472473$; $N(d_2) = N(-0.224617) = 0.411139$.

$$Payer\ Swaption_t$$

$$= NP \times FRAC \times \left[SFR\ N(d_1) - SR\ N(d_2) \right] \sum_{n=1}^{N} \frac{1}{Z_{t,T_n}}$$

$$= \$2,046,197,265 \times 0.5 \times \left[0.058645 \times 0.472473 - 0.06 \times 0.411139 \right] \times 3.62633$$

$$= \$11,278,115$$

Therefore, the cost of the payer swaption is $11,278,115, which is 55.12 basis points.

16. A U.S. industrial firm, Sterling Industries, with a less than sterling credit rating, seeks new financing to upgrade its manufacturing facilities. Sterling has determined that it wants fixed rate financing without any foreign exchange exposure. Sterling needs to arrange its financing in two steps. First, it needs $175,000,000 at present in the form of a semiannual coupon bond with a maturity of six years. Second, as its modernization plans proceed, Sterling will need another $50,000,000 in financing at year 4. This too will be a semiannual coupon bond, and it will have a maturity of four years. Sterling has been exploring the possibilities for meeting its financing needs with investment bankers in both the United States and Great Britain and is considering several alternatives. It is now time zero, which is when Sterling will issue first financing. Although Sterling is sure that it wants its ultimate interest rate exposure to be as just described, Sterling's management remains open to alternative ways of achieving that exposure. Assuming, for the moment, that Sterling could issue at the rates shown in the U.S. yield curve, at what rates would it expect to issue its two financings? Unfortunately, given its credit rating, Sterling is unable to issue at the rates in the interest rate tables completed in problems 8 and 9. Instead, Sterling faces the following three alternatives for meeting its financing needs:

A. Issue a six-year semiannual coupon bond at prevailing rates plus 135 basis points with a principal of $175,000,000. Wait until year 4 and issue the second semiannual coupon bond. Sterling's U.S. investment banker indicates that Sterling can reasonably expect similar terms on its second financing, but that the spread will probably be only about 125 basis points, as the loan amount is substantially less. Flotation costs on both alternatives are estimated to be 120 basis points, payable at the time of flotation on each issue. This alternative involves some interest rate risk, but Sterling is willing to consider this alternative seriously if it is truly price-effective.

B. Issue an FRN with a principal amount of $175,000,000 and a six-year maturity at a spread of 110 basis points over the LIBOR rates in the table. Sterling's U.S. investment banker is also willing to commit to financing Sterling's residual needs itself for a commitment fee of 90 basis points for a second issuance of an FRN at year 4 in the amount of $50,000,000 with a maturity of four years. (This commitment would not be structured as an option, but as a firm commitment by both parties.) The FRN from the investment banker would also have the same 110 basis point spread over LIBOR, and the commitment fee would be payable at time zero. Flotation costs for any FRN will be 85 basis points, which is in addition to the spread and any commitment fee. Sterling is determined to have a fixed interest rate position. The investment banker agrees to act as counterparty for any necessary swap or swaps at the rates implied by the U.S. yield curve of the table for a fee of 45 basis points of the entire financing package ($175,000,000 + $50,000,000) payable immediately. Except for the fee, the swap will be fairly priced according to the term structure.

C. Through its British investment advisers, Sterling is also considering financing in England. Sterling can issue a British FRN with a six-year maturity at British LIBOR, from the table, plus 85 basis points. The flotation costs for the service of the British investment banking firm would be 80 basis points on an FRN. The British investment banker is willing to act as a counterparty to Sterling for any desired swap that it might need in conjunction with this financing. Sterling is interested in this financing alternative but concerned about how it will plan for and meet the second part of its financing need. The British advisor is unwilling to predict Sterling's access to British markets for the second part of its financing need. Sterling discusses the entire matter fully with its U.S. investment banker; the U.S. investment banker is willing to allow Sterling to have the commitment for the second tranche described in Alternative B above, without going through the U.S. investment banker for the immediate financing. The terms would be the same as described in Alternative B, except the commitment fee would be 105 basis points and the swap initiation fee would be 55 basis points if Sterling only takes that part of the deal. The U.S. investment banking firm is still willing to provide a swap for the entire deal, so the swap initiation fee would apply to the entire financing package that Sterling contemplates ($175,000,000 plus $50,000,000).

For each of the three financing plans, describe in detail the instruments that Sterling would issue and the swaps that it would enter. For each alternative, prepare a table showing the cash flows for each period and determine the all-in cost of each alternative. (For simplicity, ignore any swap cash flows in determining the all-in cost.) Which alternative would you adopt if you were Sterling's CEO? Explain.

If Sterling could issue at the rates implied by the U.S. yield curve in problem 8, it would expect to issue the six-year bond right now at a rate of 6.1214 percent, read directly from the table. If it were to wait until year 4 and issue a four-year bond, it would now expect to issue at the forward rate implied by the term structure from the standpoint of year 4. The dollar coupon, *COUP*, would have to satisfy this equation:

$$\$50,000,000 = COUP \times \sum_{t=9}^{16} \frac{1}{\dfrac{Z_{0,t}}{Z_{0,8}}} + \frac{\$50,000,000}{\dfrac{Z_{0,16}}{Z_{0,8}}}$$

$$= COUP \times 6.930697 + \$38,041,950$$

Therefore, the semiannual dollar coupon payment is: *COUP* = \$1,725,375. This implies a semiannual yield of 0.0345075 and an annualized yield of 0.069015.

Alternative A

To these rates from the yield curve, Sterling must add its risk premium. For its six-year bond, Sterling would issue at the yield curve rate of 6.1214 percent plus 135 basis points, or 0.074714. With that rate, the six-year coupon bond has the cash flows shown in the second column of the table for Alternative A. As computed above, the term structure implies a coupon rate for a four-year bond at time 4 to be 0.069015. Because Sterling would probably issue at a rate 125 basis points higher, the expected rate would be 0.081515, leading to the cash flows in the third column. The fourth column shows the flotation costs at 120 basis points of the principal amount. The final column aggregates the cash flows of the other columns. Finding the IRR of the final column of cash flows gives a semiannual yield to maturity of 0.039140, or 0.078280 in annual terms. Under Alternative A, Sterling already has fixed rate financing, so it will not need to enter the swap market.

Cash Flow Analysis
Sterling Industries, Financing Alternative A

Semiannual Periods	Issue Six-Year Coupon Bond	Implied Cash Flows for Second Bond	Flotation Costs	Total Cash Flow
0	175,000,000		−2,100,000	172,900,000
1	−6,537,475			−6,537,475
2	−6,537,475			−6,537,475
3	−6,537,475			−6,537,475
4	−6,537,475			−6,537,475
5	−6,537,475			−6,537,475
6	−6,537,475			−6,537,475
7	−6,537,475			−6,537,475
8	−6,537,475	50,000,000	−600,000	42,862,525
9	−6,537,475	−2,037,875		−8,575,350
10	−6,537,475	−2,037,875		−8,575,350
11	−6,537,475	−2,037,875		−8,575,350
12	−181,537,475	−2,037,875		−183,575,350
13		−2,037,875		−2,037,875
14		−2,037,875		−2,037,875
15		−2,037,875		−2,037,875
16		−52,037,875		−52,037,875

Alternative B

Under Alternative B, Sterling will meet its financing need by issuing at a floating rate and then using a swap to convert the floating rate financing to a fixed rate. The second column of the table for Alternative B shows the forward rates from the term structure, and Sterling will issue a six-year FRN at those semi-annual rates plus an annual spread of 110 basis points. This leads to the cash flows for the six-year FRN. For example, the cash flow at time 10 is a payment of $6,951,175, and the rate for this semiannual period is 0.034221. Adding half of Sterling's spread of 110 basis points implies a forward rate for period 10 of 0.039721. Applying this spread-adjusted forward rate to the principal of $175,000,000 gives the payment for period 10 that is consistent with the term structure: $0.039721 \times \$175,000,000 = \$6,951,175$. For the second FRN, to be issued at year 4 with a maturity of four years, the spread is estimated to be 110 basis points also, and the cash flows on the second bond were derived in the same way as those for the first. Flotation costs are 85 basis points, so the flotation cost for the first bond would be:

$$0.0085 \times \$175,000,000 = \$1,487,500$$

The commitment fee charged at time zero for the promise to issue the FRN at year 4 is 90 basis points. As the second FRN will be for $50,000,000, this fee is $450,000. In addition, the investment banker will charge a swap initiation fee of 45 basis points applied to the entire financing package, or $1,012,500. The final column shows the aggregate cash flows. The last column includes the swap initiation fees, but does not include the swap flows themselves because the swap is fairly priced. The IRR for these flows is 0.038292, implying an annualized yield of 0.076584.

Under Alternative B, the two different financings require different swap analyses. For the initial financing, Sterling would want a pay-fixed swap with cash flows to match the periodic cash flows for the first financing. Under this swap, Sterling would receive a floating payment each period that would match its obligation on the FRN and would make a fixed rate payment. If this were a plain vanilla swap, the *SFR* on this swap would match the yield on a par instrument with a maturity of six years, or 0.061214. The actual *SFR* on this swap would differ slightly, as the swap would have varying periodic cash flows. Similarly, for the second issuance, Sterling would require a pay-fixed forward swap to cover from year 4 to year 8. We have seen under Alternative A that the implied issuance rate for a coupon bond covering years 4 to 8 is 0.069015. Sterling's second swap would be at this rate plus the impact of the fees. These swaps would not affect the present value of the cash flows shown in the last column, as a fairly priced swap requires the exchange of cash flow streams with equal value at the time the swap is negotiated.

Cash Flow Analysis
Sterling Industries, Financing Alternative B

Semiannual Periods	Forward Rates	Issue Six-Year FRN	Issue Four-Year FRN at Year 4	Flotation Costs	Swap Initiation Fee	Commitment Fee	Total Cash Flow (Without Swap Flows)
0		175,000,000		−1,487,500	−1,012,500	−450,000	172,050,000
1	0.027665	−5,803,875					−5,803,875
2	0.028022	−5,866,350					−5,866,350
3	0.028733	−5,990,775					−5,990,775
4	0.030461	−6,293,175					−6,293,175
5	0.030197	−6,246,975					−6,246,975
6	0.029027	−6,042,225					−6,042,225
7	0.034466	−6,994,050					−6,994,050
8	0.031587	−6,490,225	50,000,000	−425,000			43,084,775
9	0.030401	−6,282,675	−1,795,050				−8,077,725
10	0.034221	−6,951,175	−1,986,050				−8,937,225
11	0.032476	−6,645,800	−1,898,800				−8,544,600
12	0.032154	−181,589,450	−1,882,700				−183,472,150
13	0.033121		−1,931,050				−1,931,050

14	0.032238	−1,886,900	−1,886,900
15	0.040544	−2,302,200	−2,302,200
16	0.042969	−52,423,450	−52,423,450

Alternative C

The third alternative involves financing in both the United States and Great Britain. The first issuance would be for £99,431,818 = $175,000,000 at the spot exchange rate of £1 = $1.760000. The following table shows the implied British pound cash flows at British floating rates for this issuance. The British issuance would be at a spread of 85 basis points over the British forward rates in the table. Thus, for the tenth period, as an example, the cash flow would be the forward rate, plus the semiannual spread times the British pound issuance amount:

$$(0.040667 + 0.00425) \times £99,431,818 = £4,466,179$$

At the tenth-period forward rate of exchange of £1 = $1.724068, the dollar equivalent of this flow would be $7,699,996, as shown in the final column of the table. We can then use the dollar equivalent flows for the subsequent portion of the analysis.

Cash Flow Analysis
Sterling Industries, Financing Alternative C, British FRN

Semiannual Periods	British Forward Rates	Exchange Rates	Cash Flows in British Pounds	Dollar Equivalent Cash Flows
0		1.760000	99,431,818	175,000,000
1	0.026916	1.761284	−3,098,892	−5,458,029
2	0.027425	1.762307	−3,149,503	−5,550,391
3	0.030044	1.760063	−3,409,915	−6,001,665
4	0.030284	1.760366	−3,433,778	−6,044,706
5	0.033264	1.755143	−3,730,085	−6,546,833
6	0.032425	1.749366	−3,646,662	−6,379,347
7	0.034266	1.749704	−3,829,716	−6,700,869
8	0.035431	1.743207	−3,945,554	−6,877,917
9	0.035387	1.734814	−3,941,179	−6,837,213
10	0.040667	1.724068	−4,466,179	−7,699,996
11	0.032539	1.723962	−3,657,997	−6,306,248
12	0.047937	1.697997	−104,620,866	−177,645,917

The following table shows the cash flow analysis for Alternative C. The third column of the table shows the dollar equivalent cash flows from the British issuance derived in the previous table. Under Alternative C, Sterling would make the second issuance through the investment banking firm, as in Alternative B. These fourth column cash flows are the same as those explored in Alternative B. The flotation cost on the British issuance is 80 basis points, or $1,400,000. For the second issuance through the U.S. investment banking firm, the flotation cost is now 85 basis points, or $425,000. The swap initiation fee is now 55 basis points (instead of the 45 basis points in Alternative B), for a total of:

$$(\$175,000,000 + \$50,000,000) \times 0.0055 = \$1,237,500$$

Finally, the commitment fee charged by the U.S. investment bank for the second issuance is 105 basis points on $50,000,000, or $525,000. The final column shows the total cash flow for the entire financing, without the swap flows. (Again, we can ignore the swap flows because the swap is fairly priced. We do need, however, to take into account the various fees associated with the swap.) The IRR for these flows is 0.037309, implying an annualized issuance cost of 0.074617. If Sterling were to adopt Alternative C, it would need to enter swaps. The financing in Alternative C is all at a floating rate. Therefore, Sterling would need to convert these floating obligations to fixed obligations by pay-fixed interest rate swaps. It would require a swap (or swaps) with varying cash flows.

Comparing the Alternatives

Alternative A is the simplest, but fails to give complete fixed rate financing. At 7.8280 percent it is also the most expensive. Because Sterling strongly desires fixed rate financing, Alternative A can be dropped from consideration. Alternative B costs about 17 basis points less than Alternative A at 7.6584 percent, and Alternative C is the cheapest at 7.4617 percent. Unfortunately, Alternative C is the most complicated, involving a foreign issuance and dealing through two investment banking firms. Both Alternatives B and C provide routes to fixed rate financing, so Sterling must decide if the added complications of Alternative C are worth bearing to save almost 20 basis points. Alternative C saves about $450,000 per year for six years while costing an extra $212,500 up-front. This substantial saving suggests that Alternative C is the preferable strategy.

Note: We ignored the cash flows on the swaps in computing the all-in costs on the grounds that a fairly priced swap has a zero *NPV*. However, with a shaped yield curve and varying periodic swap payments, the swap cash flows can still affect the all-in cost very slightly.

Use the following data on Mid-Continent National Bank for the remaining problems. Use the U.S. interest rate data from problem 8 above.

The asset/liability committee at Mid-Continent National Bank (MCNB) has recently been reconstituted and is beginning its analysis of the bank's financial position. The ALCO (asset/liability committee) is interested in using swaps and a duration-based approach to manage the bank's interest rate exposure. The following balance sheet shows MCNB's current position in market value terms.

Mid Continent National Bank
Stylized Balance Sheet–Market Values

Assets		Liabilities and Net Worth	
A: Cash	$73,000,000	E: Demand Deposits	$225,000,000
B: Marketable Securities (6-month maturity; yield 7%)	135,000,000	F: Three-Month Money Market Obligations (average yield 6.2%)	175,000,000
C: Amortizing Loans (10-year average maturity; semiannual payments; 8% average yield)	475,000,000	G: Six-Month Money Market Obligations (average yield 6.8%)	85,000,000
D: Commercial Loans (5-year average maturity; semiannual payments; 7.4% average yield; par value $235,000,000)	$248,415,824	H: FRN (4-year maturity; semiannual payments)	130,000,000
		I: Coupon Bond (7-year maturity; semiannual payments; 8.5% coupon; par value $180,000,000)	203,670,556
		Total Liabilities	$818,670,556
		Net Worth	$112,745,268
Total Assets	$931,415,824	Total Liabilities and Net Worth	$931,415,824

17. Using the zero-coupon factors for the United States from problem 8, find the payment on the amortizing loan. For balance sheet items C, D, and I, find the semiannual and annualized yield-to-maturity, and compute the Macaulay duration based on the yield-to-maturity (not the zero-coupon rates). For each of these items, prepare a table of the form shown below showing the computations.

Dollar Equivalent Cash Flow Analysis
Sterling Industries, Financing Alternative C

Semiannual Periods	U.S. Forward Rates	Dollar Equivalent of British Six-Year FRN	Issue Four-Year FRN at Year 4	Flotation Costs	Swap Initiation Fee	Commitment Fee	Total Cash Flow
0		175,000,000		-1,400,000	-1,237,500	-525,000	171,837,500
1	0.027665	-5,458,029					-5,458,029
2	0.028022	-5,550,391					-5,550,391
3	0.028733	-6,001,665					-6,001,665
4	0.030461	-6,044,706					-6,044,706
5	0.030197	-6,546,833					-6,546,833
6	0.029027	-6,379,347					-6,379,347
7	0.034466	-6,700,869					-6,700,869
8	0.031587	-6,877,917	50,000,000	-425,000			42,697,083
9	0.030401	-6,837,213	-1,795,050				-8,632,263
10	0.034221	-7,699,996	-1,986,050				-9,686,046
11	0.032476	-6,306,248	-1,898,800				-8,205,048
12	0.032154	-177,645,917	-1,882,700				-179,528,617
13	0.033121		-1,931,050				-1,931,050
14	0.032238		-1,886,900				-1,886,900
15	0.040544		-2,302,200				-2,302,200
16	0.042969		-52,423,450				-52,423,450

Duration Computation Worksheet

Semiannual Periods	Cash Flow	Present Value of Cash Flow	Weighted Present Value of Cash Flow
1			
2			
.			
.			
.			
Maturity			
SUMS			

The following table gives the yield-to-maturities for the various items, found by an iterative search using a spreadsheet:

Yield-to-Maturities

Balance Sheet Item	Semiannual Yield-to-Maturity	Annualized Yield-to-Maturity
Item C: Amortizing Loans	0.03135534	0.06271068
Item D: Commercial Loans	0.03029731	0.06059462
Item I: Coupon Bond	0.03079531	0.06159062

Duration Computation Worksheet
C: Amortizing Loans

Semiannual Periods	Cash Flow	Present Value of Cash Flow	Weighted Present Value of Cash Flow
1	32,328,875	31,346,010	31,346,010
2	32,328,875	30,393,027	60,786,053
3	32,328,875	29,469,016	88,407,047
4	32,328,875	28,573,096	114,292,385
5	32,328,875	27,704,415	138,522,075
6	32,328,875	26,862,143	161,172,860
7	32,328,875	26,045,479	182,318,350
8	32,328,875	25,253,642	202,029,136
9	32,328,875	24,485,879	220,372,910
10	32,328,875	23,741,457	237,414,575
11	32,328,875	23,019,668	253,216,348
12	32,328,875	22,319,822	267,837,868
13	32,328,875	21,641,253	281,336,295
14	32,328,875	20,983,315	293,766,403
15	32,328,875	20,345,378	305,180,674
16	32,328,875	19,726,837	315,629,386
17	32,328,875	19,127,100	325,160,698
18	32,328,875	18,545,596	333,820,735
19	32,328,875	17,981,772	341,653,665
20	32,328,875	17,435,089	348,701,774
SUMS		474,999,994	4,502,965,247

$$D = \frac{4,502,965,247}{475,000,000} = 9.48 \text{ semiannual periods} = 4.74 \text{ years}$$

Duration Computation Worksheet
Item D: Commercial Loans

Semiannual Periods	Cash Flow	Present Value of Cash Flow	Weighted Present Value of Cash Flow
1	8,695,000	8,439,312	8,439,312
2	8,695,000	8,191,142	16,382,284
3	8,695,000	7,950,270	23,850,811

4	8,695,000	7,716,482	30,865,926
5	8,695,000	7,489,568	37,447,839
6	8,695,000	7,269,327	43,615,961
7	8,695,000	7,055,562	49,388,935
8	8,695,000	6,848,084	54,784,669
9	8,695,000	6,646,706	59,820,357
10	243,695,000	180,809,381	1,808,093,810
SUMS		248,415,833	2,132,689,904

$$D = \frac{2,132,689,904}{248,415,824} = 8.59 \text{ semiannual periods} = 4.29 \text{ years}$$

FDuration Computation Worksheet
Item I: Coupon Bond

Semiannual Periods	Cash Flow	Present Value of Cash Flow	Weighted Present Value of Cash Flow
1	7,650,000	7,421,454	7,421,454
2	7,650,000	7,199,736	14,399,472
3	7,650,000	6,984,642	20,953,925
4	7,650,000	6,775,974	27,103,894
5	7,650,000	6,573,539	32,867,697
6	7,650,000	6,377,153	38,262,918
7	7,650,000	6,186,634	43,306,435
8	7,650,000	6,001,806	48,014,449
9	7,650,000	5,822,500	52,402,504
10	7,650,000	5,648,552	56,485,515
11	7,650,000	5,479,799	60,277,794
12	7,650,000	5,316,089	63,793,066
13	7,650,000	5,157,269	67,044,499
14	187,650,000	122,725,411	1,718,155,750
SUMS		203,670,557	2,250,489,372

$$D = \frac{2,250,489,372}{203,670,556} = 11.05 \text{ semiannual periods} = 5.52 \text{ years}$$

18. Complete the following table summarizing the durations for all of the balance sheet items for MCNB.

Summary of Durations for MCNB Balance Sheet Items

	Assets			Liabilities	
Item	Market Value	Duration (Years)	Item	Market Value	Duration (Years)
A: Cash	$73,000,000	0.00	E: Demand Deposits	$225,000,000	0.00
B: Marketable Securities	135,000,000	0.50	F: Three-Month Money Market	175,000,000	0.25
C: Amortizing Loans	475,000,000	4.74	G: Six-Month Money Market	85,000,000	0.50
D: Commercial Loans	248,415,824	4.29	H: FRN	130,000,000	0.50
			I: Coupon Bond	203,670,556	5.52

19. Compute the duration of the asset portfolio and the liability portfolio for MCNB individually.

$$D_A = \frac{\$73,000,000}{\$931,415,824}(0.00) + \frac{\$135,000,000}{\$931,415,824}(0.50)$$

$$+ \frac{\$475,000,000}{\$931,415,824}(4.74) + \frac{\$248,415,824}{\$931,415,824}(4.29)$$

$$= 0.000 + 0.0725 + 2.4173 + 1.1442$$

$$= 3.6340$$

$$D_L = \frac{\$225,000,000}{\$818,670,556}(0.00) + \frac{\$175,000,000}{\$818,670,556}(0.25)$$

$$+ \frac{\$85,000,000}{\$818,670,556}(0.50) + \frac{\$130,000,000}{\$818,670,556}(0.50)$$

$$+ \frac{\$203,670,556}{\$818,670,556}(5.52)$$

$$= 0.0000 + 0.0534 + 0.0519 + 0.0794 + 1.3733$$

$$= 1.5580$$

20. Find the duration gap for MCNB.

The duration gap, D_G, is given by Equation 22.3:

$$D_G = D_A - \frac{Total\ Liabilities}{Total\ Assets} D_L$$

$$D_G = 3.6340 - \frac{\$818,670,556}{\$931,415,824} \times 1.5580 = 2.2646$$

21. Find the durations for the fixed rate side and floating rate side of an eight-year plain vanilla interest rate swap in terms of semi annual periods and years. What are the durations of the receive-fixed and pay-fixed plain vanilla swap?

The fixed rate side of the swap is just an eight-year semiannual par coupon bond. From the table of problem 8, the par yield-to-maturity for an eight-year coupon bond is 0.063835, or 0.031918 in semiannual terms. The following table shows the duration computation.

Duration Computation Worksheet
Fixed Rate Side of Swap

Semiannual Periods	Cash Flow	Present Value of Cash Flow	Weighted Present Value of Cash Flow
1	31.9180	30.9308	30.9308
2	31.9180	29.9740	59.9481
3	31.9180	29.0469	87.1408
4	31.9180	28.1485	112.5939
5	31.9180	27.2778	136.3891
6	31.9180	26.4341	158.6046
7	31.9180	25.6165	179.3153
8	31.9180	24.8241	198.5931
9	31.9180	24.0563	216.5068
10	31.9180	23.3122	233.1223

11	31.9180	22.5912	248.5028
12	31.9180	21.8924	262.7088
13	31.9180	21.2153	275.7983
14	31.9180	20.5590	287.8267
15	31.9180	19.9231	298.8471
16	1031.9180	624.1977	9,987.1636
SUMS		1000.00	12,773.9920

$$D = \frac{12{,}773.9920}{1{,}000} = 12.7740 \text{ semiannual periods} = 6.3870 \text{ years}$$

The floating rate on the swap resets semiannually, so the duration of the floating rate side is 0.50 years.

Duration of a Receive-Fixed Swap

= Duration of Underlying Coupon Bond − Duration of Underlying Floating Rate Bond

= 6.3870 − 0.50

= 5.8870

Duration of a Pay-Fixed Swap

= Duration of Underlying Floating Rate Bond − Duration of Underlying Coupon Bond

= 0.50 − 6.3870

= −5.8870

22. Explain how to hedge the asset portfolio alone using this swap to give the combined asset portfolio/interest rate swap a duration of zero. Show your calculations.

Equation 22.2 gives a general rule for finding a hedge for a zero duration:

$$D_X \times MV_X + D_H \times MV_H{}^* = 0$$

where:
D_X = duration of position to be hedged
D_H = duration of hedging instrument
MV_X = market value of position to be hedged
$MV_H{}^*$ = market value of hedging vehicle

Because the asset portfolio has a positive duration, we will use a pay-fixed swap with a negative duration as the hedging vehicle:

$$3.6340 \times \$931{,}415{,}824 + -5.8870 \times MV_H{}^* = 0$$

Solving for $MV_H{}^*$, the notional principal for the swap, gives: $MV_H{}^* = \$574{,}955{,}853$. Therefore, to hedge the asset portfolio alone, MCNB should enter a pay-fixed swap with a notional principal of about $575,000,000.

23. Explain how to hedge the liability portfolio alone using this swap to give the combined liability portfolio/interest rate swap a duration of zero. Show your calculations.

To hedge the liability portfolio, we use the same approach:

$$D_X \times MV_X + D_H \times MV_H{}^* = 0$$

From the point of view of MCNB, the liability portfolio is, of course, a liability. Therefore, its duration is negative and the appropriate side of the swap is one that lengthens the duration of the liability portfolio from –1.5580 to zero. Therefore, a receive-fixed swap will be required:

$$-1.5580 \times \$818,670,556 + 5.8870 \times MV_H^* = 0$$

$$MV_H^* = \$216,661,921$$

To hedge the liability portfolio considered in isolation, MCNB should enter a receive-fixed swap with a notional principal of \$216,661,921.

24. Using the duration gap already computed, explain how to hedge the interest rate risk of the entire bank so that the bank plus swap position has a duration of zero.

The hedging equation for the duration gap approach is given by Equation 22.4:

$$D_G^* = D_G + D_S \left(\frac{MV_H^*}{Total\ Assets} \right)$$

where:

D_G^* = the desired duration gap
D_S = the duration of the swap
MV_H^* = the required market value (notional principal) for the swap

Hedging the entire bank to a zero duration position means $D_G^* = 0$. Since the duration gap is positive, a pay-fixed swap with its negative duration will be the hedging vehicle:

$$D_G + D_S \left(\frac{MV_H^*}{Total\ Assets} \right) = 0$$

$$2.2646 - 5.8870 \left(\frac{MV_H^*}{\$931,415,824} \right) = 0$$

$$MV_H^* = \$358,295,274$$

Hedging the entire bank to a duration of zero requires a pay-fixed swap with a notional principal of \$358,296,274. Notice that this is the same net result as hedging the asset portfolio separately with a pay-fixed swap with a notional principal of \$574,955,853 and hedging the liability portfolio separately with a receive-fixed swap with a notional principal of \$216,661,921. (Note: \$574,955,853 – \$216,661,921 = \$358,293,932. The difference between this result and \$358,296,274 is due to rounding.)

25. Using the duration gap approach, show how to set the duration of the entire bank plus swap position so that it has a duration of 2.0 years.

As the duration gap exceeds 2.0 years, we will need a pay-fixed swap with a notional principal given as:

$$D_G + D_S \left(\frac{MV_H^*}{Total\ Assets} \right) = 2$$

$$2.2646 - 5.8870 \left(\frac{MV_H^*}{\$931,415,824} \right) = 2$$

$$MV_H^* = \$41,863,874$$

26. Using the duration gap approach, show how to set the duration of the entire bank plus swap position so that it has a duration of 8.0 years. Compute the effect on MCNB's net worth if the yield curve shifted up or down by 50, 100, and 500 basis points, assuming that the average yield-to-maturity for the entire bank is 6.50 percent.

To set the duration gap to 8.0 years, we will need to lengthen the duration gap with a receive-fixed swap. The needed notional principal is:

$$D_G + D_S \left(\frac{MV_H^*}{Total\ Assets} \right) = 8$$

$$2.2646 + 5.8870 \left(\frac{MV_H^*}{\$931,415,824} \right) = 8$$

$$MV_H^* = \$907,430,324$$

For any interest-sensitive item, we can use the following duration price change formula to find the approximate price change for a given change in yields. The net worth of MCNB is $112,745,268. If the bank has an overall duration of 8.0 years and an average yield-to-maturity of 6.5 percent, the effect of a jump in interest rates of 50 basis points would be:

$$\Delta P = -D \frac{\Delta r}{1+r} P = -8 \frac{+0.0050}{1.065} \$112,745,268 = -\$4,234,564$$

Under this policy, a rise in rates of just 50 basis points would cause a loss of $4,234,564. The effects of a 100 and 500 basis point rise are:

$$\Delta P = -D \frac{\Delta r}{1+r} P = -8 \frac{+0.01}{1.065} \$112,745,268 = -\$8,469,128$$

$$\Delta P = -D \frac{\Delta r}{1+r} P = -8 \frac{+0.05}{1.065} \$112,745,268 = -\$42,345,641$$

As these computations show, the effect of a shift in rates is directly proportional. The loss from a 100 basis point rise was twice as large as the loss from a 50 basis point rise. Also, a very large jump in rates can be quite destructive of firm value, as the result of the 500 basis point rise indicates.

Solutions to Exercises for OPTION!

1. Consider a call and a put option on the same underlying stock. Both options have an exercise price of $75. The call costs $5, and the put costs $4. If you buy both the call and the put, what is the position called? Complete the following table showing the value and profits and losses at expiration.

Stock Price at Expiration	Position Value at Expiration	Position Profit at Expiration
$50	25.00	16.00
$65	10.00	1.00
$70	5.00	−4.00
$75	0.00	−9.00
$80	5.00	−4.00
$85	10.00	1.00
$90	15.00	6.00

The position is called a "straddle."

2. Consider a call and a put on the same underlying stock. Both options have the same exercise price of $50. The stock currently sells for $50. If you buy the stock, sell the put for $3, and buy the call for $4, complete the following table showing the value of the entire position and the profits and losses on the position at expiration.

Stock Price at Expiration	Position Value at Expiration	Position Profit at Expiration
$35	20	−31
$40	30	−21
$45	40	−11
$50	50	−1
$55	60	9
$60	70	19
$65	80	29

3. Consider two calls on the same underlying stock. The calls have the same expiration date and exercise prices of $80 and $90. If the calls cost $12 and $4, respectively, complete the following table showing the value of and profits on a bull spread at expiration using these two calls.

Stock Price at Expiration	Position Value at Expiration	Position Profit at Expiration
$70	0	−8
$75	0	−8
$80	0	−8
$85	5	−3
$90	10	2
$95	10	2
$100	10	2
$105	10	2
$110	10	2

4. Consider two puts on the same underlying stock. The puts have the same expiration date and exercise prices of $80 and $90. If the puts cost $4 and $12, respectively, complete the following table showing the value of and profits on a bull spread at expiration using these two puts.

Stock Price at Expiration	Position Value at Expiration	Position Profit at Expiration
$70	−10	−2
$75	−10	−2
$80	−10	−2
$85	−5	3
$90	0	8
$95	0	8
$100	0	8
$105	0	8
$110	0	8

5. Consider two calls on the same underlying stock. The calls have the same expiration date and exercise prices of $80 and $90. If the calls cost $12 and $4, respectively, complete the following table showing the value of and profits on a bear spread at expiration using these two calls.

Stock Price at Expiration	Position Value at Expiration	Position Profit at Expiration
$70	0	8
$75	0	8
$80	0	8
$85	−5	3
$90	−10	−2
$95	−10	−2
$100	−10	−2
$105	−10	−2
$110	−10	−2

6. Consider two puts on the same underlying stock. The puts have the same expiration date and exercise prices of $80 and $90. If the puts cost $4 and $12, respectively, complete the following table showing the value of and profits on a bear spread at expiration using these two puts.

Stock Price at Expiration	Position Value at Expiration	Position Profit at Expiration
$70	10	2
$75	10	2
$80	10	2
$85	5	−3
$90	0	−8
$95	0	−8
$100	0	−8
$105	0	−8
$110	0	−8

7. For the same underlying stock, three calls with the same expiration date have exercise prices of $30, $35, and $40. For a long butterfly spread, complete the following table showing the value of and profits on the position at expiration.

Stock Price at Expiration	Position Value at Expiration	Position Profit at Expiration
$20	0	0
$25	0	0
$30	0	0

$35	5	5
$40	0	0
$45	0	0
$50	0	0

8. For the same underlying stock, two calls with the same expiration date have exercise prices of $30 and $40 and cost $11 and $8, respectively. Using these options, create two bull ratio spreads, one with a 2:1 ratio and the other with a 3:1 ratio. Complete the following table for the profits on the two spreads.

Stock Price at Expiration	Profits on 2:1 Ratio Spread	Profits on 3:1 Ratio Spread
$20	−14.00	−25.00
$25	−14.00	−25.00
$30	−14.00	−25.00
$35	−4.00	−10.00
$40	6.00	5.00
$45	11.00	15.00
$50	16.00	25.00

9. A stock now sells at $70 and a put on this stock with an exercise price of $70 costs $4. Using these instruments, create an insured portfolio and complete the following table.

Stock Price at Expiration	Profits on Stock Alone	Profits on Insured Portfolio
$50	−20	−4
$55	−15	−4
$60	−10	−4
$65	−5	−4
$70	0	−4
$75	5	1
$80	10	6
$85	15	11
$90	20	16

10. A stock sells at $100, and a call and a put on this stock both expire in one year and have the same exercise price of $100. The risk-free rate of interest is 9 percent. For a position that is long the call, short the stock, and long a bond that pays $100 in one year, complete the following table. What can you infer from the table?

Stock Price at Expiration	Value of Combined Position	Value of Call − Put
$80	20	−20
$85	15	−15
$90	10	−10
$95	5	−5
$100	0	0
$105	0	5
$110	0	10
$115	0	15
$120	0	20

The long call/short put portfolio in the last column has the same profit and loss profile as the stock alone. The combined position of the middle column (long call/short stock/long bond) has the same value profile as a put. This is reasonable, because from put-call parity, the combined position constitutes a synthetic put.

11. Consider a call option that expires in one year and has an exercise price of $100. The underlying stock price is $150, and the risk-free rate of interest is 10 percent. From these facts alone, what can you say about the current price of the call option? Using these values in the Black-Scholes model, complete the following table. Draw a graph showing the price of this call as a function of the standard deviation using the values in the table. What does this show about the no-arbitrage bounds for the price of a call option?

Standard Deviation	Call Price
.9	77.36
.8	73.80
.7	70.35
.6	67.10
.5	64.18
.4	61.78
.3	60.17
.2	59.56
.1	59.52
.01	59.52

The price of a European call must always equal or exceed $S - X^{-r(T-t)}$. For this option, that quantity is $59.52. Therefore, from the indicated facts alone, we know that the call price must be at least $59.52. The table shows that the price of the call falls for lower values of the standard deviation. These values converge on $59.52. Thus, the table and the accompanying graph show that value above this boundary is due to the volatility of the underlying good.

12. Consider a put option that expires in one year and has an exercise price of $150. The underlying stock price is $100, and the risk-free rate of interest is 10 percent. From these facts alone, what can you say about the current price of the put option? Using these values in the Black-Scholes model, complete the following table. Draw a graph showing the price of this put as a function of the standard deviation using the values in the table. What does this show about the no-arbitrage bounds for the price of a put option?

Standard Deviation	Put Price
.9	60.96
.8	56.98

.7	52.99
.6	49.05
.5	45.22
.4	41.63
.3	38.52
.2	36.36
.1	35.73
.01	35.73

For a European put, the lower bound of value is $Xe^{-r(T-t)} - S$. For these values, this bound is $35.73, so the put price must equal or exceed this amount. As the standard deviation falls, the value of the put converges to this bound of $35.73. Therefore, any excess value above $35.73 is due to the volatility of the underlying good.

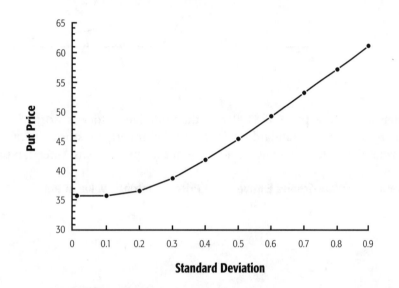

13. A put option has an exercise price of $100 and expires in one year. The risk-free rate of interest is 10 percent, and the standard deviation of the underlying stock is .2. Complete the following table. Explain what the table shows about the value of European versus American put options. Prepare a graph showing the put price and the intrinsic value of the put as a function of the stock price using the values in the table below.

Stock Price	Black-Scholes European Put Price	Intrinsic Value of Put
$80	13.27	20
$85	10.07	15
$90	7.43	10
$95	5.35	5
$100	3.75	0
$105	2.58	0
$110	1.73	0
$115	1.11	0
$120	.74	0

For puts deep-in-the-money, the price is less than the intrinsic value, because the put owner cannot exercise and obtain the intrinsic value. Rather, the put's value approximates the present value of the intrinsic value. For puts near-the-money or deep-in-the-money, the put's value exceeds the intrinsic value.

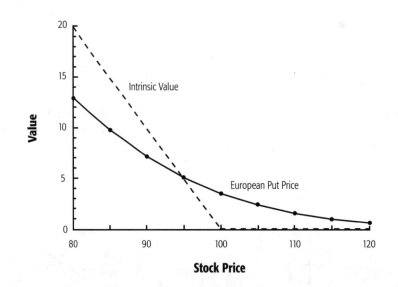

14. A put option has an exercise price of $100, and the underlying stock is worth $80. The risk-free rate of interest is 10 percent, and the standard deviation of the underlying stock is .2. Complete the following table. Explain what the table shows about the value of European versus American put options.

Days Until Expiration	Black-Scholes European Put Price	Intrinsic Value of Put
5	19.86	20
10	19.73	20
30	19.18	20
90	17.64	20
180	15.82	20
270	14.45	20
365	13.27	20

We know that the value of an American option must always equal or exceed its intrinsic value, so the American put price must always equal or exceed $20 in this example. For this deep-in-the-money European put, the price is near the intrinsic value with little time until expiration. However, when considerable time remains until expiration, the European put price is well below the intrinsic value.

15. Consider two call options on the same underlying stock. The calls have exercise prices of $80 and $90 and both expire in 150 days. The risk-free rate of interest is 8 percent, and the stock price is $100. Using the Black-Scholes model, complete the following table. What principle does the table illustrate regarding boundary conditions on call options?

Standard Deviation	Call Price $X = \$80$	Call Price $X = \$90$	Price Difference
.9	33.32	28.28	5.04
.8	31.38	26.05	5.33
.7	29.48	23.83	5.65
.6	27.66	21.62	6.04
.5	25.96	19.45	6.51
.4	24.46	17.34	7.12
.3	23.31	15.39	7.92

.2		22.68	13.77	8.91
.1		22.59	12.94	9.65
.01		22.59	12.91	9.68

As a no-arbitrage condition, the price difference between two calls on the same underlying good with the same expiration date can never exceed the difference in the two exercise prices. For the options in this problem, that difference is $10.00. As the table indicates, the price differential approaches the difference in the exercise prices as the standard deviation falls. With a standard deviation of .01, the price difference is $9.68. Even more exactly, we might note that both options approach the boundary price of $S - Xe^{-r(T-t)}$. Therefore, we know that the price differential must approach $(X_{90} - X_{80})e^{-r(T-t)} = \$10e^{-.08(150/365)} = \$9.68$.

16. Consider a call option with an exercise price of $80 that expires in 150 days. The risk-free rate of interest is 8 percent, and the stock price is $80. Using the Black-Scholes model, complete the following table. What principle does the table illustrate regarding the pricing of call options? Prepare a graph using the data in the table expressing the value of the call option as a function of the standard deviation.

Standard Deviation	Call Price
.9	19.19
.8	17.25
.7	15.30
.6	13.34
.5	11.37
.4	9.39
.3	7.41
.2	5.45
.1	3.57
.01	2.59

For an at-the-money call, the call price varies directly with the standard deviation of the underlying good. This principle holds for all calls regardless of their moneyness.

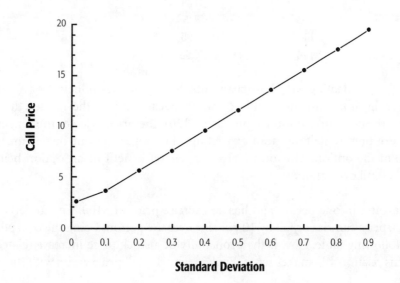

17. Consider two put options on the same underlying stock, with a standard deviation of .3. The puts have exercise prices of $80 and $90 and both expire in 150 days. The risk-free rate of interest is 8 percent, and the stock price is $60. Using the Black-Scholes model, complete the following table. What principle does the table illustrate regarding boundary conditions on put options?

Standard Deviation	Put Price X = $80	Put Price X = $90	Price Difference
.9	25.75	33.47	7.72
.8	24.25	32.06	7.81
.7	22.77	30.73	7.96
.6	21.36	29.52	8.16
.5	20.04	28.48	8.44
.4	18.88	27.69	8.81
.3	17.98	27.23	9.25
.2	17.49	27.09	9.60
.1	17.41	27.09	9.68
.01	17.41	27.09	9.68

The lower bound for a European put price is $Xe^{-r(T-t)} - S$, and the lower bound for the price difference between two European puts is the present value of the differences in the exercise prices. For our example, this is $10e^{-.08(150/365)} = \$9.68$. As the standard deviation becomes small, the options tend to their boundary price and the difference in prices tends to the present value of the difference in exercise prices of $9.68.

18. Consider two put options on the same underlying stock. The stock trades for $100. One put has an exercise price of $80, while the other has an exercise price of $120. The standard deviation of the stock is .3, and the risk-free rate of interest is 11 percent. Complete the following table. What does the completed table indicate about the influence of the time until expiration on the pricing of puts? Explain the difference in the price patterns for the two puts. Would call options exhibit the same kind of price pattern? Explain.

Days until Expiration	Put Price X = $80	Put Price X = $120
100	.31	17.93
120	.43	17.77
140	.56	17.63
160	.68	17.51
180	.80	17.39
200	.92	17.28
220	1.03	17.18
240	1.14	17.08
260	1.24	16.98

Assuming that we are dealing with European puts, for the at-the-money put ($X = \$80$), the put price is larger the longer the time remaining until expiration. Because it is at-the-money, there is no intrinsic value to consider. For the deep-in-the-money put ($X = \$120$), the price is lower the longer the term until expiration. The more time remaining until expiration, the longer the put owner must wait to capture the intrinsic value of the option. This outweighs the general benefit of an option being more valuable the longer the term until expiration.

19. A call option expires in one period and has an exercise price of $100. The underlying stock price is also $100. The stock price can rise or fall by 10 percent over the period. Using the one-period binomial model, complete the following table. How is the probability of a stock price increase related to the interest rate? Explain why this relationship makes sense. Explain why the call price varies with the interest rate as it does.

Interest Rate	Call Price	Probability of a Stock Price Increase
0.01	5.45	.55
0.02	5.88	.60
0.03	6.31	.65
0.04	6.73	.70
0.05	7.14	.75

0.06	7.55	.80
0.07	7.94	.85
0.08	8.33	.90
0.09	8.72	.95

The interest rate indicates the risk-free rate of return available in the economy. To warrant the risk of holding an option, the expected return must be higher than this risk-free rate. If the stock price can rise by only 10 percent, then an ever higher interest rate must require a greater probability of achieving the 10 percent jump in the stock price. If it did not, the expected return from holding the option would not equal the risk-free rate and the central criterion of a risk-neutral economy would be violated.

20. A stock currently trades at $140, and a call option on the stock has an exercise price of $150 and expires in one year. The standard deviation of the stock price is .3, and the risk-free rate of interest is 12 percent. What is the Black-Scholes price for this call option? Complete the following table using the multi-period binomial model. What is the relationship between prices from the binomial model and the Black-Scholes model? Explain.

Periods	Binomial Model Price
1	21.95
2	19.88
5	20.13
10	20.24
25	19.88
50	19.99
100	19.98
150	20.01
200	20.00

The Black-Scholes price is $19.99. As the number of periods increases, the binomial model price becomes virtually identical with the Black-Scholes price. This makes sense, because the Black-Scholes model assumes infinitely small periods by its continuous time framework. As the number of periods in the binomial model increases, the period length becomes smaller. This gives an improved approximation to the Black-Scholes framework.

21. A stock currently trades at $140, and a call option on the stock has an exercise price of $150 and expires in one year. The call price is $11, and the risk-free rate of interest is 12 percent. What is the standard deviation of the underlying stock? Complete the following table using the Black-Scholes model to find each price, and show the price to four decimals. What does the completed table show about the technique necessary to find the volatility when the other parameters are known?

Standard Deviation	Call Price	Error
0.01	6.96	−4.04
0.2	14.71	3.71
0.1	9.62	−1.38
0.15	12.11	1.11
0.125	10.84	−0.16
0.13	11.09	0.09
0.1275	10.97	−0.03
0.1285	11.02	0.02
0.1282	11.00	0.00

The standard deviation of the underlying stock is 0.128133. The table illustrates an iterative search for the implied standard deviation. The table illustrates the method of bisection—the next guess of the standard deviation is halfway between the two previous guesses. There are other fancier and more efficient search techniques available.

22. A stock trades for $75 and is expected to pay a dividend of $2 in 30 days. European call and put options on this stock expire in 90 days and have an exercise price of $75. The risk-free rate of interest is 7 percent, and the standard deviation of the stock is .3. Find the price of these options according to the Black-Scholes model, ignoring dividends. What are the values of these European options according to the adjustments to the Black-Scholes model for known dividends? Verify your answer by showing your own calculations.

    The call is worth $4.01, and the put is worth $4.72.

23. A stock trades at $40 and has a standard deviation of .4. The risk-free rate is 8 percent. A European call and put on this stock expire in 90 days. The exercise price for the call is $35, and the exercise price for the put is $45. Using the Merton model, complete the following table. What does the completed table show about the influence of dividends on call and put prices?

Continuous Dividend Rate	Call Price	Put Price
0.005	6.57	5.82
0.01	6.53	5.85
0.02	6.45	5.91
0.03	6.37	5.98
0.05	6.22	6.11
0.075	6.03	6.27
0.1	5.84	6.44
0.125	5.66	6.61
0.15	5.48	6.78

    Other factors held constant, an increasing dividend rate causes call prices to fall and put prices to rise.

24. A stock pays a continuous dividend of 3 percent and currently sells for $80. The risk-free rate of interest is 7 percent, and the standard deviation on the stock is .25. A European call and put on this stock both have an exercise price of $75 and expire in 180 days. Find the price of these options according to the Black-Scholes model (*i.e.*, ignoring the dividend) and the Merton model. Find the price of these options according to the binomial model with 5, 25, 50, 100, and 200 periods.

    Ignoring dividends, the Black-Scholes call and put prices are $9.93 and $2.38, respectively. The Merton call and put prices are $9.07 and $2.70, respectively. The following table shows the binomial call and put prices.

Periods	Call Price	Put Price
5	9.00	2.63
25	9.11	2.82
50	9.09	2.72
100	9.07	2.70
200	9.08	2.71

25. A stock pays a proportional dividend equal to 2 percent of its value in 150 days. The current stock price is $120, the risk-free rate is 9 percent, and the standard deviation of the stock is .2. A European call and put option on this stock both expire in 270 days and both have an exercise price of $120. Find the price of these options according to the Black-Scholes model (*i.e.*, ignoring the dividend) and the Merton model. Find the price of these options according to the binomial model with 5, 25, 50, 100, and 200 periods.

    The Black-Scholes call and put prices are $8.45 and $4.09, respectively. The Merton call and put prices are $7.83 and $4.46, respectively.

Periods	Call Price	Put Price
5	8.12	4.74
25	7.89	4.52
50	7.80	4.43
100	7.82	4.44
200	7.83	4.45

26. A stock will pay a cash dividend of $1.75 in 150 days. The current stock price is $120, the risk-free rate is 9 percent, and the standard deviation of the stock is .2. A European call and put option on this stock both expire in 270 days and both have an exercise price of $120. Find the price of these options according to the Black-Scholes model (*i.e.,* ignoring the dividend) and the Merton model. Find the price of these options according to the binomial model with 5, 25, 50, 100, and 200 periods.

The Black-Scholes call and put prices are $12.41 and $4.68, respectively. A dividend of $1.75 in 150 days is at a rate of $4.26 per year on a stock with a current price of $120. This implies a continuous dividend rate of $\delta = 0.0355$. The Merton call and put prices are $10.38 and $5.76, respectively.

Periods	Call Price	Put Price
5	11.56	5.52
25	11.32	5.99
50	11.31	5.99
100	11.30	5.98
200	11.29	5.98

27. A stock trades at $80 and has a standard deviation of .4. The risk-free rate of interest is 6 percent. A European call and put both expire in 100 days and have the same exercise price of $80. Complete the following table for the sensitivities of the two options.

Call

Stock	DELTA	THETA	VEGA	RHO	GAMMA
$60	.1169	−4.8821	6.1656	1.7405	.0156
$65	.2094	−7.8745	9.7886	3.3281	.0211
$70	.3247	−10.8194	13.1823	5.4626	.0245
$75	.4502	−13.0861	15.5392	7.9565	.0252
$80	.5727	−14.3025	16.4273	10.5551	.0234
$85	.6818	−14.4384	15.8727	13.0198	.0200
$90	.7721	−13.7135	14.2311	15.1819	.0160
$95	.8423	−12.4623	11.9840	16.9591	.0121
$100	.8942	−11.0048	9.5724	18.3424	.0087

Put

Stock	DELTA	THETA	VEGA	RHO	GAMMA
$60	−.8831	−.1603	6.1656	−19.8200	.0156
$65	−.7906	−3.1528	9.7886	−18.2324	.0211
$70	−.6753	−6.0976	13.1823	−16.0979	.0245
$75	−.5498	−8.3644	15.5392	−13.6040	.0252
$80	−.4273	−9.5818	16.4273	−11.0053	.0234
$85	−.3182	−9.7167	15.8727	−8.5407	.0200
$90	−.2279	−8.9918	14.2311	−6.3785	.0160
$95	−.1577	−7.7406	11.9840	−4.6013	.0121
$100	−.1058	−6.2831	9.5724	−3.2181	.0087

28. A stock trades at $80 and has a standard deviation of .4. The stock pays a continuous dividend of 3 percent. The risk-free rate of interest is 6 percent. A European call and put both expire in 100 days and have the same exercise price of $80. Complete the following table for the sensitivities of the two options.

Call

Stock	DELTA	THETA	VEGA	RHO	GAMMA
$60	.1084	−4.4159	5.8314	1.6172	.0148
$65	.1967	−7.1627	9.3979	3.1310	.0203
$70	.3082	−9.8589	12.8332	5.1953	.0239
$75	.4312	−11.8899	15.3247	7.6393	.0249
$80	.5527	−12.8817	16.3978	10.2179	.0234
$85	.6622	−12.7894	16.0253	12.6920	.0202
$90	.7538	−11.8264	14.5227	14.8865	.0164
$95	.8258	−10.3242	12.3542	16.7091	.0125
$100	.8795	−8.6077	9.9635	18.1417	.0091

Put

Stock	DELTA	THETA	VEGA	RHO	GAMMA
$60	−.8834	−1.4794	5.8314	−19.9432	.0148
$65	−.7952	−4.3750	9.3979	−18.4295	.0203
$70	−.6836	−7.2199	12.8332	−16.3652	.0239
$75	−.5606	−9.3997	15.3247	−13.9211	.0249
$80	−.4391	−10.5403	16.3978	−11.3426	.0234
$85	−.3296	−10.5968	16.0253	−8.8684	.0202
$90	−.2380	−9.7825	14.5227	−6.6740	.0164
$95	−.1660	−8.4291	12.3542	−4.8514	.0125
$100	−.1123	−6.8614	9.9635	−3.4188	.0091

29. Two stocks have the same standard deviation of .4, but Stock A is priced at $110, and Stock B trades for $100. The risk-free rate is 11 percent. Consider two call options written on these two stocks that both expire in 90 days. Call A has an exercise price of $110, while Call B has an exercise price of $100. Find the DELTAs for these two options. What is unusual about the result, and how can it be explained?

The DELTA for both options is .5932. The DELTAs are identical because the DELTA depends only on the ratio of the stock price to the exercise price, not the stock and exercise prices in isolation. This is clear from considering the formula for d^1, which includes the ratio S/X.

30. A stock trades for $50 and has a standard deviation of .4. A call on the stock has an exercise price of $40 and expires in 55 days. The risk-free rate is 8 percent. Find the DELTA for the call, and explain how to create a DELTA-neutral portfolio. (Assume that you are short one call.) Complete the following table.

The DELTA is .9444. If we are to be short one call, the DELTA-neutral portfolio will consist of the short call plus a long position in the stock of .9444 shares.

Stock Price	Call Price	Portfolio Value
$45	6.22	36.28
$46	7.05	36.39
$47	7.92	36.47
$48	8.82	36.51
$49	9.74	36.54
$50	10.67	36.55
$51	11.63	36.53
$52	12.59	36.52

$53	13.56	36.49
$54	14.54	36.46
$55	15.52	36.42

31. A stock trades for $50 and has a standard deviation of .4. A call on the stock has an exercise price of $40 and expires in 55 days. The risk-free rate is 8 percent. Find the DELTA for the call, and explain how to create a DELTA-neutral portfolio. (Assume that you are short one call.) Complete the following table showing how the value of the DELTA-neutral portfolio changes over time. Assume the stock price does not change. How do you account for the change in the value of the DELTA-neutral portfolio?

The DELTA is .9444. A DELTA-neutral portfolio that is short one call must be long DELTA shares, or .9444 shares, in this problem. While the portfolio is DELTA-neutral when created at day 55, it does not remain DELTA-neutral over time. Specifically, the price of the call must decay to its intrinsic value of $10 by expiration. This is reflected in the table. Therefore, the value of the portfolio must change.

Days until Expiration	Call Price	Portfolio Value
55	10.67	36.55
50	10.60	36.62
45	10.52	36.70
40	10.44	36.78
35	10.37	36.85
30	10.31	36.91
25	10.24	36.98
20	10.19	37.03
15	10.13	37.09
10	10.09	37.13
5	10.04	37.18

32. A stock trades for $100 and has a standard deviation of .3. A call on the stock has an exercise price of $100 and expires in 77 days. The risk-free rate is 8 percent. Find the DELTA for the call, and form a DELTA-neutral portfolio assuming that you are short one call. What is the GAMMA for the stock and for the call? Does the portfolio have a positive or negative GAMMA? Complete the following table. How do these values illustrate the GAMMA of the portfolio?

The DELTA is .5759, and the GAMMA is .0284. The DELTA-neutral portfolio consists of the short call plus a long position of .5759 shares. The GAMMA for the stock is zero, so the portfolio will have a GAMMA of −.0284, reflecting the short position in the call. The values in the table reflect the negative GAMMA of the portfolio because the portfolio value decreases at stock prices away from $100, the price used to establish the DELTA-neutral portfolio.

Stock Price	Call Price	Portfolio Value
$80	.36	45.71
$85	.94	48.01
$90	2.04	49.79
$95	3.81	50.90
$100	6.32	51.27
$105	9.54	50.93
$110	13.35	50.00
$115	17.61	48.62
$120	22.17	46.94

33. A stock with a standard deviation of .5 now trades for $100. Two calls on this stock both expire in 70 days and have exercise prices of $90 and $100. The risk-free rate is 10 percent. Find the DELTA and GAMMA

for both calls. Construct a portfolio that is long one share of stock and that is both DELTA-neutral and GAMMA-neutral. For the portfolio, complete the following table.

For the call with $X = \$90$, the DELTA is .7512 and the GAMMA is .0145. For the call with $X = \$100$, the DELTA is .5781 and the GAMMA is .0179. Recalling that the DELTA of a stock is 1.0 and the GAMMA of a stock is zero, and letting N_{90} and N_{100} be the number of calls with $X = \$90$ and $X = \$100$, respectively, a DELTA-neutral and GAMMA-neutral portfolio must meet the following two conditions:

DELTA-neutrality	$1 + .7512N_{90} + .5781N_{100} = 0$
GAMMA-neutrality	$.0145N_{90} + .0179N_{100} = 0$

Solving these two equations for two unknowns gives $N_{90} = -3.5350$ and $N_{100} = 2.8637$. Therefore, the DELTA-neutral and GAMMA-neutral portfolio will consist of: long 1 share, short 3.5350 calls with $X = \$90$, and long 2.8637 calls with $X = \$100$. At a stock price of $100, the two calls are worth $15.35 and $9.62, so the entire portfolio costs:

$$\$100 - 3.5350(\$15.35) + 2.8637(\$9.62) = \$73.29, \text{ when } \sigma = 0.5$$

Standard Deviation	Portfolio Value
.3	72.34
.35	72.82
.45	73.23
.5	73.29
.55	73.25
.6	73.16
.65	73.01
.7	72.83

34. A stock sells for $70, has a standard deviation of .3, and pays a 2 percent continuous dividend. The risk-free rate is 11 percent. Three calls on this stock all expire in 100 days and have exercise prices of $65, $70, and $75. Using these calls, construct a long position in a butterfly spread. What does the spread cost? Complete the following table for the profitability of the spread as a function of the stock price for the current time and for the expiration date. For the long position, is time decay beneficial or detrimental? Explain.

The three options cost $8.22, $5.20, and $3.05, for the $65, $70, and $75 exercise prices, respectively. Therefore, the spread, which is long one $65 call, short two $70 calls, and long one $75 call, costs $.87. Time decay is beneficial. If the stock price remains at $70, the value of the spread will go to $5.00 at expiration.

Stock Price	Profit with $T - t = 100$	Profit at Expiration
$50	−.76	−.87
$55	−.57	−.87
$60	−.28	−.87
$65	−.06	−.87
$70	.00	4.13
$75	−.11	−.87
$80	−.31	−.87
$85	−.51	−.87
$90	−.65	−.87

35. Consider a long position in a straddle with an exercise price of $50. The stock price is $80, and the standard deviation of the stock is .4. The risk-free rate is 6 percent, and the options expire in 180 days. What is the current price of the two options? Prepare a graph of the current value of the straddle as a function

of the stock price. On the same axes, graph the value of the straddle at expiration. Let the stock prices range from $30 to $70. As a first step to preparing the graph, complete the following table.

The call is worth $31.72, and the put is worth $.26.

Stock Price	Current Straddle Price	Straddle Price at Expiration
$30	18.92	20.00
$35	14.93	15.00
$40	12.12	10.00
$45	10.82	5.00
$50	11.06	0.00
$55	12.68	5.00
$60	15.38	10.00
$65	18.88	15.00
$70	22.93	20.00

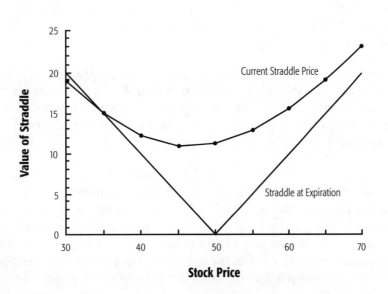

36. A stock trades at $50 and has a standard deviation of .3. The risk-free rate is 7 percent. An American and a European call on this stock both have an exercise price of $55, and both expire in 100 days. The stock will pay a dividend in 50 days, but the amount is uncertain. For the different possible dividend amounts shown in the table below, compute the exact American option price and the Black-Scholes model price with the known dividend adjustment. What kind of systematic difference do you notice in the pricing from the two models, if any?

Dividend Amount	Exact American	Black-Scholes Adjusted for Known Dividends
$.01	1.65	1.65
$.05	1.63	1.63
$.10	1.62	1.62
$.25	1.57	1.57
$.50	1.48	1.49
$1.00	1.34	1.33
$1.50	1.21	1.19
$2.00	1.10	1.06
$3.00	.93	.83

When the dividend is small relative to the value of the stock, the two models give the same answer to the penny. As the dividend becomes large relative to the stock price, the exact American price exceeds the Black-Scholes price adjusted for known dividends. This difference reflects the difference between American and European options, because as the dividend becomes larger, the early exercise privilege of an American option begins to have value.

37. A stock trades for $150 and has a standard deviation of .4. The risk-free rate of interest is 7 percent. Two dividends are expected. The first, due in 30 days, is $1.50, while the second, due in 150 days, is $2.00. Find the pseudo-American option price for a call that expires in 200 days with an exercise price of $140. Also, find the option price according to the Black-Scholes model adjusted for known dividends.

     The pseudo-American price is $23.13, and the Black-Scholes price adjusted for known dividends is also $23.13.

38. A stock with a standard deviation of .33 trades for $75. The risk-free rate is 6 percent. The stock pays a continuous dividend of 2 percent. An American call and put on this stock have an exercise price of $70 and both expire in 100 days. Find the price of these options using the analytic approximation of the American option price. What are the critical values for the call and the put? Using the Merton model, find the price of both options.

     The Merton model price for the call is $8.32, and for the put the price is $2.59. The analytic approximation gives a price of $8.32 for the call and $2.62 for the put. The critical price for the call is $237.23, while the critical price for the put is $53.39. The European and American call prices are the same (to the penny), because the current price of $75 is so far from the critical price for the call of $237.23. Therefore, the early exercise privilege of the American option has virtually no value.

39. A stock has a current price of $80 and a standard deviation of .3. The stock pays a continuous dividend of 3 percent. The risk-free rate is 7 percent. An American and a European call on this stock both expire in 200 days, and both have an exercise price of $70. Find the price of the American call according to the analytic approximation formula, and find the price of the European option according to the Merton model. What is the critical price for the American call? Complete the following table for the two options using the two respective models. Graph the price of the two options as a function of the stock price over the range from $60 to $100. Explain any particularly important features of the graph.

     According to both the Merton model and the analytic approximation, the price is $13.63. The critical price for the call is $191.02. The graphs are virtually identical, as the stock price is so far from the critical price and the early exercise feature has virtually no value. Only for stock prices above $90 does a difference in option values begin to emerge.

Stock Price	American Call According to the Analytic Approximation	European Call According to the Merton Model
$60	2.37	2.37
$65	4.25	4.25
$70	6.80	6.80
$75	9.96	9.96
$80	13.63	13.63
$85	17.71	17.70
$90	22.07	22.07
$95	26.64	26.63
$100	31.34	31.33

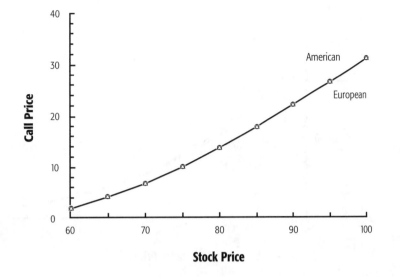

40. A stock has a current price of $70 and a standard deviation of .3. The risk-free rate is 7 percent. An American and a European put on this stock both expire in 200 days, and both have an exercise price of $80. Find the price of the American put according to the analytic approximation formula, and find the price of the European option according to the Merton model. What is the critical price for the American put? Complete the following table for the two options using the two respective models. Graph the price of the two options as a function of the stock price over the range from $60 to $100. Explain any particularly important features of the graph.

The put price according to the Merton model is $11.31, and according to the analytic approximation the price is $11.76. The critical price is $59.22. The American put is worth more than its intrinsic value in all instances shown in the table, while that is not true for the European put. Further, the price of the American put tends to its intrinsic value from above as the put becomes deep-in-the-money. For example, with a stock price of $60, the intrinsic value of the put is $20.00 and the value of the American put is $20.01. The price of the European put is often below its intrinsic value, due to the inability of exercise.

Stock Price	American Put According to the Analytic Approximation	European Put According to the Merton Model
$60	20.01	18.81
$65	15.52	14.80
$70	11.76	11.31
$75	8.68	8.39
$80	6.25	6.06
$85	4.40	4.27
$90	3.03	2.94
$95	2.05	1.98
$100	1.36	1.31

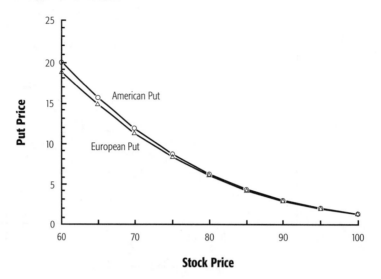

Stock Price

41. A stock has a current price of $80 and a standard deviation of .3. The risk-free rate is 7 percent. An American and a European call on this stock both expire in 200 days, and both have an exercise price of $70. The stock pays a continuous dividend of 3 percent. Find the price of the American call according to the analytic approximation formula, and find the price of the European option according to the Merton model. Complete the following table for the two options using the two respective models. How can you explain the price differentials reported in the table?

According to both the Merton model and the analytic approximation, the price is $13.63. The critical price for the call is $191.02. The option prices are virtually identical, as the stock price is so far from the critical price and the early exercise feature has virtually no value. Only for stock prices above $90 does a difference in option values begin to emerge.

Stock Price	American Call According to the Analytic Approximation	European Call According to the Merton Model
$60	2.37	2.37
$65	4.25	4.25
$70	6.80	6.80
$75	9.96	9.96
$80	13.63	13.63
$85	17.71	17.70
$90	22.07	22.07
$95	26.64	26.63
$100	31.34	31.33

42. A stock has a current price of $80 and a standard deviation of .3. The risk-free rate is 7 percent. An American and a European call on this stock both expire in 200 days, and both have an exercise price of $70. If the stock is to pay a dividend, it will be at a continuous rate, but the rate is uncertain. Alternative dividend rates are given in the table below. Find the price of the American call according to the analytic approximation formula, and find the price of the European option according to the Merton model for each dividend rate in the table. What do the price differentials in the table indicate about the importance of dividends for call pricing? For any of these dividend rates, should the American option be exercised now? If so, for which dividend rates?

The prices in the table show that the dividend becomes important as it becomes larger. At very low dividend rates, there is no difference, but a difference starts to emerge at the higher dividend rates. As the price of the American call always exceeds its intrinsic value, it should not be exercised. In fact, the critical value with δ = .05 is $120.01, so the stock price is very far below that critical value.

Dividend Rate	American Call According to the Analytic Approximation	European Call According to the Merton Model
0.001	14.64	14.64
0.005	14.50	14.50
0.01	14.32	14.32
0.02	13.98	13.98
0.03	13.63	13.63
0.04	13.30	13.29
0.05	13.00	12.96

43. A stock sells for $110 and has a standard deviation of .2. The risk-free rate is 7 percent. An American put on this stock has an exercise price of $120 and expires in 200 days. Using the binomial model for an American put and a European put, complete the following table. Should the American put be exercised now? Explain.

Number of Periods	American Put Price	European Put Price
1	10.00	9.81
2	11.27	10.30
5	11.08	9.66
10	10.97	9.63
25	11.01	9.68
50	11.03	9.73
100	11.03	9.74
200	11.03	9.75

The American put should be exercised only if its price equals its intrinsic value. This occurs only for a single-period model. For all other periods, the put price exceeds the intrinsic value. As the prices from the multi-period model are more reliable, the true price of the put is $11.03, and the put should not be exercised.

44. A stock sells for $110 and has a standard deviation of .2. The risk-free rate is 7 percent. An American put on this stock has an exercise price of $120 and expires in 200 days. Using the binomial model with 100 periods for an American put and a European put, complete the following table. From the table alone, what can you say about the correct exercise policy for the American put? Using the binomial model with 100 periods, find the exact stock price below which the American put should be exercised. Explain.

Stock Price	American Put Price	European Put Price
$90	30.00	25.77
$95	25.00	21.15
$100	20.00	16.87
$105	15.10	13.05
$110	11.30	9.74
$115	7.83	7.06
$120	5.38	4.90
$125	3.61	3.34
$130	2.34	2.19

From the table alone, we can say that the put should be exercised at a stock price of $100 or lower and that it should not be exercised at a stock price of $105 or higher. For stock prices of $100 or lower, the put price equals its intrinsic value, but for stock prices of $105 or higher, the put price exceeds its intrinsic value. By trial and error, it is possible to verify that the critical price, below which the put should be exercised, is $103.36. This is close to the analytical approximation critical price of $103.45.

45. The HOT100 stock index stands at 4000.00, and has a standard deviation of .20. The continuous dividend rate on the HOT100 is 3 percent, and the risk-free rate of interest is 5 percent. Using the Merton model, find the prices for the calls and puts shown in the table below.

Index Value	Call X = 4000.0 T − t = 180 days	Call X = 3750.0 T − t = 90 days	Put X = 4000.0 T − t = 180 days	Put X = 3750.0 T − t = 90 days
3500.0	53.54	55.77	507.52	285.62
3750.0	124.73	156.39	332.38	138.08
4000.0	239.45	320.89	200.77	54.42
4250.0	396.85	532.11	111.84	17.48
4500.0	588.98	767.42	57.64	4.63

46. The HOT100 stock index stands at 4000.00, and has a standard deviation of .20. The continuous dividend rate on the HOT100 is 3 percent, and the risk-free rate of interest is 5 percent. Using the Merton model, complete the table below for a call option with 180 days until expiration and an exercise price of $4,000.00.

Index Value	DELTA	THETA	VEGA	RHO	GAMMA
4500.0	.8239	−200.6818	769.1956	1,538.0251	.0004
4250.0	.7059	−242.1371	996.0760	1,283.6826	.0006
4000.0	.5477	−253.5453	1,093.3300	962.2793	.0007
3750.0	.3693	−220.9529	983.7842	621.5020	.0007
3500.0	.2058	−152.8179	695.7750	328.8437	.0006

47. The HOT100 stock index stands at 4000.00, and has a standard deviation of .20. The continuous dividend rate on the HOT100 is 3 percent, and the risk-free rate of interest is 5 percent. Using the Merton model, complete the table below for a put option with 180 days until expiration and an exercise price of $4,000.00.

Index Value	DELTA	THETA	VEGA	RHO	GAMMA
4500.0	−.1694	−138.5704	769.1956	−386.5329	.0004
4250.0	−.2795	−172.6359	996.0760	−640.8754	.0006
4000.0	−.4376	−176.6542	1,093.3300	−962.2793	.0007
3750.0	−.6160	−136.6720	983.7842	−1,303.0560	.0007
3500.0	−.7795	−61.1472	695.7750	−1,595.7143	.0006

48. The current dollar value of a German mark is $.6100, and the standard deviation of the mark is .25. The U.S. risk-free rate is 8 percent, while the German rate is 5 percent. European call and put options on the mark have an exercise price of $.6000 and expire in 250 days. What are these options worth today? If the German interest rate falls from 5 to 4 percent, what happens to the value of the options? Explain.

With δ = .05, the call is worth $.0592 and the put is worth $.0377. With δ = .04, the call is worth $.0617 and the put is worth $.0362. In effect, the foreign interest rate is like a dividend on a stock; it represents a leakage of value from the currency. Therefore, a lower dividend should raise the price of a call and diminish the price of a put. That is what happens in this example.

49. The current dollar value of a German mark is $.6100, and the standard deviation of the mark is .25. The U.S. risk-free rate is 8 percent, while the German rate is 5 percent. Consider an American and a European call on the mark with an exercise price of $.6000 that expires in 250 days. What are these options worth today? Should the American option be exercised now? If the German interest rate falls from 5 to 4 percent, what happens to the value of the options? Does it change the exercise decision? Explain.

With δ = .05, the European call is worth $.0592 and the American call is worth $.0593. With δ = .04, the European call is worth $.0617 and the American call is worth $.0617. In this example, the American call price always exceeds its intrinsic value, so it should not be exercised with either foreign interest rate.

50. Options now trade on the well-known widget futures contract. The current widget price is $100.00 per widget, and the futures price is $107.50. The futures contract expires in two years. The widget market is well-known for its strict adherence to cost-of-carry principles. The standard deviation of the futures price is .25. A European and an American call option on this futures have an exercise price of $105.00. What are the two options worth according to the Merton model and the analytic approximation for the American option? What would an American and a European put be worth, assuming they had the same contract terms?

The interest rate is .0362, because $100e^{.0362(2)} = \$107.50$, as the cost-of-carry model would imply. Therefore, the Merton call price is $15.06, and the American analytic call price is $15.43. The Merton put price is $12.74, and the American analytic put price is $13.04.

51. The text has assumed that the cost-of-carry equals the risk-free rate. Explain how **OPTION!** could be used to value a futures option if the cost-of-carry were less than or greater than the risk-free rate.

The module for futures option pricing requires that the interest rate and the cost-of-carry be identical. However, **OPTION!** could be used to price a futures option in this situation by using either the stock index or foreign currency modules, which allow differential rates. In the case of the stock index module, the dividend yield plays the role of the cost-of-carry, while the foreign interest rate acts as the cost-of-carry in the foreign currency option pricing model.

52. Using **OPTION!**, complete the following table for forward-start call and put options. Common parameters are: $S = 80$; $X = 75$; $T - t = 350$ days; $\sigma = 0.4$; $r = 0.08$; and $\delta = 0.03$. As the table indicates, the day of the grant, tg, varies. Taking the call as an example, what do the values in the table indicate about how the option price varies with tg?

tg in Days	Forward-Start Call	Forward-Start Put
50	14.9620	7.1697
100	13.8203	6.5087
150	12.5754	5.7478
200	11.1892	4.8489
250	9.5904	3.7407
300	7.6105	2.2549
349	4.8686	0.0004

As tg increases, the option has very little life after it is granted. Thus, the value of the underlying option approaches its intrinsic value, discounted to the present. The underlying call with the given parameters and one day until expiration is worth 5.0103, very close to its intrinsic value. If that option is not to be obtained for 349 days, the value of the forward start option is 5.0103 discounted at the dividend rate of 0.03, which is 4.8686.

53. Complete the following table for the compound options shown below. Common parameters are: $S = 100$; $\sigma = 0.3$; $r = 0.01$; $\delta = 0.04$; $X = 100$; $te = 100$ days; and $T - t = 365$ days. As the table indicates, the exercise price of the compound option varies.

Exercise Price of Compound Option	Call-on-Call	Call-on-Put	Put-on-Call	Put-on-Put
5	9.5718	4.2820	0.2967	0.6020
10	6.0915	1.7936	1.6812	2.9786
15	3.7224	0.6395	4.1770	6.6894
20	2.2038	0.1908	7.5233	11.1055
25	1.2702	0.0460	11.4546	15.8255
30	0.7149	0.0085	15.7641	20.6529
35	0.3937	0.0011	20.3078	25.5104

54. Complete the following table for the compound options shown below. Common parameters are: $S = 100$; $\sigma = 0.3$; $r = 0.01$; $\delta = 0.04$; $X = 100$; $x = 10$; and $T - t = 365$ days. As the table indicates, the expiration date of the compound option varies.

Expiration Date of Compound Option in Days	Call-on-Call	Call-on-Put	Put-on-Call	Put-on-Put
50	5.1384	1.0598	0.8623	2.3790
100	6.0915	1.7936	1.6812	2.9786
150	6.9037	2.4053	2.3610	3.4579
200	7.6388	2.9611	2.9655	3.8831
250	8.3346	3.4936	3.5325	4.2868
300	9.0248	4.0304	4.0957	4.6966
350	9.7665	4.6168	4.7121	5.1577

55. Consider a European straddle with the following parameters: $S = 50$; $X = 50$; $T - t = 365$ days; $\sigma = 0.5$; $r = 0.06$; and $\delta = 0.03$. What is the value of the straddle? Now consider a chooser option with the same parameters, but a varying choice date. Complete the table shown below. What does the table illustrate about the relationship between chooser prices and straddle prices?

Choice Date, tc, in Days	Chooser Value
0	10.1710
1	10.2493
50	13.0244
100	14.4635
150	15.5674
200	16.4954
250	17.3102
300	18.0441
350	18.7163
355	18.7807
360	18.8446
364	18.8953

The European call is worth 10.1710 and the European put is worth 8.7370, so the straddle is worth 18.9080. The table illustrates that the value of the chooser can range from the maximum price of either option in the straddle to the sum of the two options. If the choice must be made now, $tc = 0$, the chooser is worth 10.1710—just the value of the call. If the choice can be deferred until (almost) the expiration date, the chooser is worth 18.8953, just a hair under the value of the straddle itself.

56. Consider a European call and a European put with parameter values of: $X = 70$; $T - t = 180$ days; $\sigma = 0.25$; $r = 0.1$; and $\delta = 0.0$. What is the value of the call and put if $S = 80$? Now consider a down-and-in call and a down-and-in put, with $BARR = 80$ and $REBATE = 0.0$. Using these data, complete the following table. What do these results suggest about the value of barrier options relative to plain vanilla options?

Stock Price	Down-and-In Call	Down-and-In Put
120	0.1379	0.0016
100	1.7885	0.0504
90	5.4142	0.2405
85	8.9605	0.4974
83	10.8597	0.6571
82	11.9322	0.7532
81	13.0943	0.8616
80.10	14.2218	0.9709

80.01   14.3390   0.9824

The European call is worth 14.3520, while the European put is worth 0.9837. The barrier options will be worth the same as the underlying options if they hit the barrier. Consider the call first. For prices well above the barrier, there is little chance of hitting the barrier, so the option has little value. However, if the price is right at the barrier, say 80.01, the down-and-in call is worth about the same as the European call. For the down-and-in put, there is little value for all the prices shown in the table, as the down-and-in put is still way out-of-the-money even for the lowest price shown in the table. Thus, the call price is much more sensitive to the stock price that the put price for these values.

57. Consider an up-and-out call and an up-and-out put with the following common parameter values: $T - t = 180$ days; $\sigma = 0.2$; $r = 0.1$; $\delta = 0.03$; $BARR = 100$; and $REBATE = 0$. Complete the following table. What can you conclude from the completed table?

Stock Price	Up-and-Out Call X = 80	Up-and-Out Put X = 100
99	0.2733	0.6543
95	1.3940	3.4891
90	2.5741	7.4775
85	3.1139	11.8625
80	2.8546	16.5204
75	2.0297	21.3365
70	1.1034	26.2268

For a stock price near the barrier, say 99, both options are threatened with extinction, so each has little value. For stock prices below the barrier, the chance of extinction is less, so the value of the option will be more for that reason. However, we must also consider the likely payoffs. For the call, a low stock price reduces the chance of hitting the barrier, but it also implies little chance of a payoff. Thus, the call price is low for stock prices near the barrier and for stock prices below the exercise price. By contrast, the put fares very well for lower stock prices because a lower stock price reduces the risk of extinction from hitting the barrier and increases the payoff by being deeper-in-the-money.

58. Consider an up-and-out call and an up-and-out put with the following common parameter values: $S = 98$; $\sigma = 0.2$; $r = 0.1$; $\delta = 0.03$; $BARR = 100$; and $REBATE = 0$. Complete the following table, and interpret the results.

T – t in Days	Up-and-Out Call X = 80	Up-and-Out Put X = 100
1	16.9140	1.9809
2	14.4919	1.9639
5	10.1013	1.9233
10	6.9951	1.8735
20	4.5085	1.8011
50	2.2054	1.6582
100	1.1105	1.5026
300	0.2778	1.1489

With one day until expiration, the call should be worth an amount near its intrinsic value of 20. However, the up-and-out call is worth considerably less because of the chance that the barrier will be hit and the option will be worthless. Notice that the longer the term to expiration, the lower the price of the call, reflecting the increased chance of hitting the barrier the longer the time until expiration. This chance is very high, because the stock price is right at the barrier now. The put is just in-the-money, so its value should be close to its intrinsic value. However, there is a chance of hitting the barrier in the next day, so its price is somewhat lower than the correlative European put. Further, for longer terms to expiration, the put's value decreases, and it does so for two reasons. First, a longer term to expiration reduces the present value of the payoff. Second, a longer term to expiration increases the chance that the option will hit the barrier.

59. A supershare is written with the following parameters: $S = 100$; $T - t = 365$ days; $\sigma = 0.4$; $r = 0.1$; and $\delta = 0.06$. Complete the following table for this supershare, assuming the varying upper and lower bounds in the table. What does the table illustrate about the influence of the bounds on the prices of supershares?

X_L	X_H	Supershare
70	80	0.1060
80	90	0.1072
90	100	0.0999
95	105	0.0943
100	110	0.0879
110	120	0.0741
120	130	0.0606

For every row in the table, the difference between the upper and lower bounds is the same. Only the location differs. The location affects the value of the supershare in two ways. First, the probability that the stock price will lie in these bands differs. With an initial stock price of 100, there is little chance that the terminal stock price will lie in the range of 70 to 80, for example. Second, the payoff on a supershare is a proportion of the portfolio's value that varies with the lower bound. So, the lower the bound, given that the supershare pays, the greater the value of the supershare.

60. Consider two lookback calls with the following common parameters: $S = 100$; $T - t = 90$ days; $r = 0.06$; and $\delta = 0.0$. As the table indicates, the two calls are the same except one has $MINPRI = 50$, while the other has $MINPRI = 95$. Complete the following table and explain the differences in the prices of the two options.

Standard Deviation	Lookback Call $MINPRI = 50$	Lookback Call $MINPRI = 95$
0.1	50.7343	6.8623
0.2	50.7343	9.4658
0.3	50.7343	12.6941
0.4	50.7355	16.0141
0.5	50.7560	19.3036
0.6	50.8517	22.5234
0.9	52.1185	31.6506

The call with $MINPRI = 50$ is so deep-in-the-money that the volatility of the stock has very little effect on the price. By contrast, the call with $MINPRI = 95$ is just barely in-the-money, so its price is very sensitive to the standard deviation.

61. Consider an option to exchange one asset for another with $S_1 = 100$; $S_2 = 200$; $\delta_1 = 0.01$; $\delta_2 = 0.01$; $T - t = 90$ days; and $\rho = 0.0$. Complete the following table and interpret your results.

$\sigma_1 = \sigma_2$	Price of Exchange Option
0.5	100.1990
0.4	99.8408
0.3	99.7576
0.2	99.7537
0.1	99.7537
0.05	99.7537

The option is deep-in-the-money. For lower risk levels on the two assets, there is little chance that anything will change. Therefore, as the risk is lowered, the value of the option converges to the present value of the difference in the price of the two assets, discounted at the dividend rate.

62. A call on the maximum of two assets has the following parameters: $S_1 = 100$; $S_2 = 100$; $T - t = 365$ days; $r = 0.08$; $\delta_1 = 0.0$; $\delta_2 = 0.0$; $\rho = 0.0$. Complete the following table and interpret your results.

$\sigma_1 = \sigma_2$	Call Price	Put Price
0.5	40.7129	5.3919
0.4	33.6835	3.7248
0.3	26.7364	2.2484
0.2	19.9409	1.0062
0.1	13.4736	0.1480
0.05	10.5122	0.0035
0.01	8.2526	0.0000
0.001	7.7448	0.0000
0.0001	7.6940	0.0000

The owner of the call only needs one asset to rise in price, so the greater the volatility the better. If there is no volatility, then the call owner must expect to receive the asset worth 100 upon payment of the exercise price in one year. Thus, the value of the call becomes essentially the difference between the price of the asset and the present value of the exercise price, which is 7.68837. The value of the call with $\sigma = 0.0001$ is very close to that. The owner of the put must surrender the more valuable asset for the exercise price. If there is very little risk, the asset prices are unlikely to change, so the option will most likely expire worthless. If there is considerable risk, there is a good chance that one of the assets will have a price drop to bring the put into-the-money.

63. Consider a stock that now trades at $110 per share. A European call and put on this stock expire in 150 days and have a common exercise price of $90. The standard deviation of the stock is 0.4, and the stock pays a continuous dividend of 0.03. The risk-free rate is 0.07. Using **OPTION!,** find the price of the call and the put individually and the price of the call plus put portfolio. A standard chooser option also trades on the same stock. It too has an expiration date of 150 days and an exercise price of $90. Price this chooser option assuming that the choice date is in 149.99 days. Also price the chooser assuming the choice must be made in one day. Studying the prices of these options, what can you conclude about the relationship between standard chooser options and plain vanilla options?

The call is worth $23.96, and the put is worth $2.75, for a combined value of $26.71. The chooser is worth $23.96 if the choice must be made in one day, more or less immediately. If the choice can be deferred for 149.99 days, more or less until expiration, the chooser is worth $26.71.

If the choice can be deferred to expiration, the chooser is worth the same as a portfolio of the call and the put. The call plus put portfolio is a straddle, so a chooser with a choice date at expiration is equivalent to a straddle. If the choice must be made immediately, the chooser is worth the same as the more valuable of the two options. In our example, the call is more valuable, and the call and chooser are both worth $26.71 in this situation of an immediate choice for the chooser.

64. Consider the following situation. A stock trades for $100 per share and has a standard deviation of 0.4. The risk-free rate is 0.07, and the stock pays no dividend. All of the options considered in this problem expire in 182.5 days and have an exercise price of $90. Price an up-and-in call and an up-and-out call on this stock with a barrier price of $120. Repeat for a barrier price of $110. Price a plain vanilla European call on this stock. What does a study of these various option prices reflect?

The plain vanilla European call is worth $18.31. For a barrier price of $120, the up-and-in call is worth $16.61 and the up-and-out call is worth $1.70. For a barrier price of $110, the up-and-in call is worth $17.95 and the up-and-out call is worth $.36. The combined value of the up-and-in and up-and-out call is $18.31 for both barrier prices. This is the same as the price of a plain vanilla European call. This is as it must be, because the portfolio of two barrier options will have the same payoff as the single plain vanilla European call.

Consider a call on the best of two risky assets and cash. The cash amount is $100. The two assets (stocks) both trade for $100. The option expires in one year, and the risk-free rate is 0.1. The correlation between the two stocks is 0.5. Complete the following table for various standard deviations, which are assumed to be identical for the two stocks. Why does the value of the option decline as the standard deviation declines? For the given stock prices, fixed cash amount, time to expiration, and risk-free rate, what could drive the price lower? What is the lower bound on the price? Why?

After completing the table, consider the same situation with a standard deviation of 0.001. If the fixed cash amount were changed from $100 to $50, what would be the effect on the price of this option? If the fixed cash amount were changed from $100 to $150, what would be the effect on the price of this option? Compute the prices under these two conditions. Explain the results.

Consider the situation as originally described, but now specifying a standard deviation for both stocks of 0.001 and a correlation between the stocks of 0.999. Find the price of this option for cash amounts of $100 and $110. Explain the relationship between these results. What is the future value of $100 at expiration of the option using continuous compounding? What if the cash amount is now $110.50? Does the option value change? Why or why not?

Common Standard Deviation for Both Stocks	Price of a Call on the Best of Two Assets and Cash
0.8	$146.32
0.5	127.54
0.3	115.37
0.1	104.23
0.01	100.40
0.001	100.04

As the standard deviation declines, the chance of a big stock increase falls. The price could be driven lower by a lower standard deviation or a higher correlation of returns between the two shares. The lower bound for the option price is $100.00. With a zero standard deviation and perfect correlation between the returns on the two shares, the option is essentially pricing one share of the stock (either one, because they are identical with a perfect correlation and the same standard deviation). The option is worth the present value of the now certain value of the stock in one year; this is equal to the current price of the stock.

If the cash amount were changed to $50, there would be no change in the price of the option, because the option is pricing a share of stock. Reducing the cash payoff, therefore, does not affect the price of the option. If the cash payoff is increased to $150, this amount is far in excess of any possible stock price in one year, given a standard deviation of 0.001. Therefore, the price of the option is just the present value of the future $150 payment, $135.73.

If the standard deviation of both stocks is 0.001 and the correlation of returns between the two stocks is 0.999, the following option prices will be observed: for a fixed cash amount of $100, the option price will be $100.001784; for $110, the option price will be $100.001784; for $110.5171, the option price will be $100.040874. For a risk-free asset currently worth $100, the future value in one year will be $110.5171, given continuous compounding. If the standard deviation of the stocks were zero and the correlation between the returns on the shares were perfect, the price of the option would not increase for any increase in the cash payoff up to $110.5171. For any higher cash amount, the option would just be worth the present value of the cash payoff. With our data (standard deviations of 0.001 and a correlation of 0.999), there is a very small effect on the price of the option starting somewhere between $110 and $110.5171.

66. Use the U.S. yield curve data from Table 22.10 (see Chapter 22) for this problem. Consider a bond with an embedded option that has a 10-year maturity, a coupon rate of 0.06, and a yield-to-maturity of 0.095. The equivalent T-bond (the one having the same maturity) also has a coupon rate of 0.06. Both bonds have annual coupon payments. Find the price of the bond with the embedded option, the price of the T-bond, the yield-to-maturity on the T-bond, and the option-adjusted spread between the two bonds.

The bond with the embedded option is worth 78.024207. The T-bond yields 0.082188 and is worth 85.257762. The OAS is 128.784180 basis points.

67. Use the U.S. yield curve data from text problem 8 in Chapter 22 for this problem. Price a plain vanilla interest rate swap with a tenor of five years (10 payments) in this yield curve environment. Consider a forward swap to begin in three years and to have a tenor of five years. Will the fixed rate on the forward swap be greater or less than that on the original plain vanilla swap? Why? Calculate the fixed rate on the forward swap. Consider now an interest rate swap with a tenor of five years, but with a notional principal that is twice as large for the last five periods as it is for the first five periods. Without calculating, will the fixed rate for this swap with a varying notional principal be greater or less than the fixed rate on the plain vanilla swap? Explain. Calculate the fixed rate on this swap.

The fixed rate on the plain vanilla swap is 0.060649, while the fixed rate on the forward swap is 0.068354. Because the yield curve is upward sloping, the fixed rate on the forward swap must necessarily be higher. The swap with a varying notional principal will have a higher fixed rate, because the notional principal amounts are higher in later periods when the implied forward rates are higher. The swap fixed rate is 0.061644. (To calculate this fixed rate, create a notional principal file that has any arbitrary notional principal amount for the first five periods, and a notional principal twice as large for the last five periods. Use the module "Interest Rate Swaps—Varying Notional Principal" with the created notional principal file to price the swap.)

68. Use the U.S. term structure data from text problem 8 in Chapter 22 to solve this problem. For an interest rate swap with 10 periods and a notional principal of $100,000,000, find the up-front cash flow necessary to enter the receive-fixed side of the swap with a fixed rate of 0.07.

For a plain vanilla swap with a tenor of five years (10 periods), the fixed rate would be 0.060649. To receive 7 percent instead would require an up-front payment that equals the present value of the difference between 7 percent and the equilibrium SFR. This is $3,998,421.10, which must be paid by the receive-fixed party who will receive the 7 percent.

69. Use the U.S. and Japanese term structures from text problem 12 of Chapter 21 to solve this problem. For a four-year plain vanilla foreign currency swap, what is the fixed rate for a U.S. dollar and a Japanese yen payer? Intuitively, would these be the same fixed rates for a fixed-for-fixed currency annuity swap of the same tenor? Explain.

For the U.S. dollar payer, the SFR = 0.071988. For the Japanese yen payer, the SFR = 0.053157. In general, these will not be the same rates for a fixed-for-fixed currency annuity swap, because there are no principal payments on the currency annuity swap.

70. Use the U.S. and Japanese term structures from text problem 12 in Chapter 21 to solve this problem. Consider a floating-for-floating currency annuity swap with a tenor of four years. The U.S. interest rates are higher for this period. Intuitively, will the U.S. payer have to pay a spread or receive a spread?

Alternatively, will the U.S. payer make or receive an up-front cash payment? Assume the notional principal amount is $1,000,000 = ¥121,000,000. Price the swap.

The payer in the term structure environment with higher interest rates will receive a spread or will receive an up-front cash payment. Assuming the U.S. payer is the domestic payer, the Japanese payer will have to pay a spread of 159.46 basis points. Alternatively, the Japanese payer could pay ¥6,895,098.21, from which the dollar payer would receive $56,984.28.

71. Use the U.S. and Japanese term structures from text problem 12 in Chapter 21 to solve this problem. Consider a fixed-for-floating currency annuity swap with a tenor of four years, in which the dollar payer pays fixed. First, what is the plain vanilla *SFR* for the dollar payer in a swap with this tenor? Assume a notional principal of $1,000,000 = ¥121,000,000. If the fixed rate is 0.08, what up-front cash flow will be exchanged? What if the dollar payer's fixed rate is 0.071988? What is special about this fixed rate? Why is a payment necessary for this last swap?

The plain vanilla *SFR* for the dollar payer is 0.071988. In the fixed-for-floating currency annuity swap, if the dollar fixed rate is 8 percent, the dollar payer will receive $84,468.83 and the yen payer will pay ¥10,220,728.07. If the dollar fixed rate is 0.071988, this is the same as the dollar *SFR* on a plain vanilla currency swap. However, the up-front cash flow is for the dollar payer to receive $56,984.09 and the yen payer to pay ¥6,895,075.14. An up-front payment is still necessary because of the absence of any principal being exchanged at the outset of the swap and re-exchanged at the termination of the swap. Without this re-exchange, the fixed-rate of 0.071988 will not generate payment streams of equivalent present value.

72. Use the U.S. and Japanese term structures from text problem 12 in Chapter 21 to solve this problem. Consider a fixed-for-fixed currency swap with a tenor of four years and a notional principal of $1,000,000 = ¥121,000,000. The dollar fixed rate is 0.071988, and the yen fixed rate is 0.053157. What relationship do these fixed rates bear to the fixed rates that each party would pay on a plain vanilla currency swap structure? Would an up-front payment of any type be necessary? If so, what is the payment, and why must it be made?

These are the same rates as the fixed rates on a plain vanilla swap for the two parties. A payment will still be necessary, because there is no exchange of principal as in the plain vanilla swap. The dollar payer will receive $56,984.73, and the yen payer will pay ¥6,895,152.30. Notice that this is the same amount (except for a very slight rounding error) as in the previous problem. This makes sense, because in the previous problem the yen payer was paying floating, and in this problem the yen payer is paying a fixed rate that has the same prospective present value as the yen LIBOR rate flat.

73. Use the U.S. and Japanese term structures from text problem 12 in Chapter 21 to solve this problem. Consider a diff swap with a tenor of four years to be paid in U.S. dollars, which we treat as the domestic currency. Without calculation, what spread will the payer basing payments on U.S. interest rates pay? Calculate the spread that the payer basing payments on yen interest rates will pay. Explain why the current exchange rate and notional principal are not necessary inputs to this pricing solution.

Because the payment currency is dollars, the dollar payer pays U.S. LIBOR flat in dollars by convention. The spread is on the side of the payer basing payments on the nonpayment currency, which is yen in this case. The payer paying based on yen interest rates will pay yen LIBOR plus 94.53 basis points. The exchange rate and notional principal are irrelevant. The exchange rate is not needed because all payments are in one currency, even though the payment amounts are based on interest rates for two different currencies. The notional principal amount is not needed, because both parties pay based on the same notional principal amount.

74. Use the term structure data from Table 22.13 (see Chapter 22) for this problem. Consider a loan with a 10-year (20-payment) maturity and a principal amount of $100,000,000. Price a 7.6–8.5 percent collar on this loan, assuming that all relevant forward LIBOR rates have a standard deviation of 0.3. What are the costs of the constituents of the collar? What is the *SFR* for a swap covering this period? What is the cost of capping the loan at 8.03 percent? What is the value of accepting a floor rate of 8.03 percent? What is the cost of an 8.03–8.03 percent collar?

The collar would cost $1,652,870.41. The cap portion of the collar would cost $12,191,257.96, which is off-set by the value of the floor, which is $10,538,387.55. The *SFR* is 0.0803.

Capping the loan at 0.0803 costs $13,210,271.62. Accepting a floor rate of 0.0803 is worth $13,210,284.17. These values are identical (within rounding error). So the 8.03–8.03 percent collar is a zero-cost collar. A zero-cost collar is possible when the floor and cap rates are equal to the *SFR* on a plain vanilla interest rate swap.

75. Use the term structure data from Table 22.13 (see Chapter 22) for this problem. Consider a forward swap to begin in five years (10 periods) and to have a tenor of five years (10 periods). What is the *SFR* for the forward swap? Consider now a swaption on this same forward swap, with a strike rate of 0.07 and a notional principal of $100,000,000. Assume that the standard deviation of the *SFR* is 0.37. What is the value of the receiver and payer swaption in this case? Which is likely to have the greater value, given the *SFR* for the forward swap? Would a swaption in this situation have any value if the strike rate on the swaption were equal to the *SFR* for the forward swap? If a swaption might have value in this situation, what relationship would the values of a receiver and payer swaption have? What are those actual values?

The fixed rate for the forward swap is 0.092150. The receiver swaption would be worth $4,509,335.08, or 450.93 basis points. The payer swaption would be worth $10,646,592.56, or 1,064.66 basis points. The payer swaption has greater value, because it gives the holder the right to pay at a rate below the *SFR* for the forward rate, while the receiver swaption only gives the right to receive at a rate below the *SFR* for the forward rate.

A swaption with a strike rate equal to the *SFR* for the forward swap would have value whether we consider a receiver or payer swaption. At present, one can costlessly enter the forward swap at the prevailing *SFR*. The payer and receiver swaptions, with a strike rate equal to the *SFR* on the forward swap, each give a choice about whether to enter the swap when the swap is scheduled to begin in five years. This ability to wait and see whether the swap is attractive has real value. Both the payer and receiver swaptions will be worth $8,193,254 (ignoring rounding error). The two have the same value because the strike rate equals the *SFR* for the forward swap.

76. Consider a call option on LIBOR with a notional principal of $1,000,000 and an expiration in three years. The yield curve is flat at 8 percent, and the strike rate on the option is 0.07. The underlying maturity for the hypothetical instrument is a half year. Assume that the standard deviation of the relevant forward LIBOR rate is 0.3. Using the continuous time model, price this call on LIBOR. Now create a term structure file with a yield curve that is flat at 8 percent. In this term structure environment, price a cap at 7 percent on a loan with a maturity of five years (10 semiannual payments) and a loan principal amount of $1,000,000. Having priced the cap, observe the price of the caplet that pays off at period 7. The computed price of this caplet and the previously calculated price of the call on LIBOR are (presumably) too similar to have arisen by chance, yet are not identical. Explain why the price of the call on LIBOR and the caplet are close, but not identical.

The price of the call on LIBOR is $7,885.40. The price of the caplet is $7,928.53, which is a difference of about one-half percent. A cap on a loan consists of a portfolio of calls on LIBOR. The seventh caplet in the cap covers a period from year 3 to 3.5, with the payment occurring at the end of period 7 (3.5 years from now). The caplet has a notional principal amount that is the same as the call on LIBOR and assumes the same standard deviation for forward LIBOR. The pricing of the call on LIBOR uses continuous compounding, while the pricing of the caplet uses the zero-coupon discount factor from the term structure. The discount factor for continuous compounding in this case is:

$$e^{-0.08 \times 3.5} = 0.786628$$

For the discrete case, the discount factor is:

$$\frac{1}{Z_{0,8}} = \frac{1}{1.04^7} = 0.759918$$

The implied amount subjected to discounting in the continuous case is:

$$\frac{\$7,885.40}{0.755784} = \$10,433.41$$

In the discrete case, the amount subjected to discounting is:

$$\frac{\$7,928.53}{0.759918} = \$10,433.40$$

These values, before discounting, are close enough to count as identical. Therefore, the entire difference in the price of the call on LIBOR and the caplet is due to the difference between discrete and continuous discounting.